THE EU'S HUMAN RIGHTS RESPONSIBILITY GAP

Can the EU be held legally responsible for its contributions to human rights harms in its Integrated Border Management policy? Or do systemic legal design flaws in the EU's human rights responsibility regime give rise to a significant responsibility gap?

This book addresses these pressing questions, offering a transversal analysis of applicable legal frameworks under international and EU law. Following the introduction, the book first analyses the international and EU human rights responsibility frameworks, revealing both 'normative incongruence' as well as 'liability incongruence' (Part II). The EU's human rights responsibility regime is subsequently applied to specific illustrations within the four tiers of the EU's Integrated Border Management, exposing the critical points where responsibility falters (Part III). Building on these findings and drawing from shared responsibility and relationality theories, the fourth and final part of the book briefly introduces 'Relational Human Rights Responsibility' as an alternative method to establishing human rights responsibility of the EU specifically, and of international organisations more generally (Part IV).

The EU's Human Rights Responsibility Gap

Deconstructing Human Rights Impunity of International Organisations

Joyce De Coninck

•HART•
OXFORD • LONDON • NEW YORK • NEW DELHI • SYDNEY

HART PUBLISHING

Bloomsbury Publishing Plc

Kemp House, Chawley Park, Cumnor Hill, Oxford, OX2 9PH, UK

1385 Broadway, New York, NY 10018, USA

29 Earlsfort Terrace, Dublin 2, Ireland

HART PUBLISHING, the Hart/Stag logo, BLOOMSBURY and the Diana logo are trademarks of Bloomsbury Publishing Plc

First published in Great Britain 2024

A catalogue record for this book is available from the British Library.

A catalogue record for this book is available from the Library of Congress.

Library of Congress Control Number: 2024941275

ISBN: HB: 978-1-50997-735-2
ePDF: 978-1-50997-737-6
ePub: 978-1-50997-736-9

Typeset by Compuscript Ltd, Shannon

Foreword

THIS BOOK ADDRESSES whether an individual can hold the European Union legally responsible before a court of law for its contributions to human rights harms that the individual has been subjected to. Answering this question demands looking at not just the EU's responsibility rules which answer how the EU can be held legally responsible under EU law. In an attempt to be exhaustive, this question also requires looking at the international rules on responsibility of international organisations and whether the EU can be held legally responsible thereunder.

In addition, answering this question requires insight as to whether and to what degree the EU is even bound by human rights norms and ensuing human rights obligations, in a manner that can be relied upon by individuals in pursuit of a remedy before a court of law. This latter question can also only be exhaustively answered by looking at both international and EU human rights law.

In a nutshell, answering the question of EU human rights responsibility demands an analysis of the relevant responsibility rules under EU and international law, as well as an analysis of the human rights regime that applies to the EU under EU and international law. Answering this question thus becomes a technical affair that inevitably means navigating multiple legal domains but also adopting a functional lens and looking beyond the terminological and conceptual differences and idiosyncrasies that characterise international human rights law and EU human rights law. And for that reason, this book has been an arduous endeavour.

The perceived academic compulsion towards expertise in a particular domain (of law), has functioned as both a driver for this book and its nemesis. When addressing the question of EU responsibility for contributions to human rights harms, accounts typically focus on addressing whether the EU can be held responsible according to the relevant rules under international law or, conversely, under the relevant rules of EU law. In that sense, many accounts on EU responsibility remain within the strict confines of their academic lanes and are lauded on account thereof. Entire books have been written about single procedures or single conditions to establish EU human rights responsibility or that of international organisations, under their respective legal regimes. But such sanitised and severed inquiries into EU (human rights) responsibility reveal only partial insights into whether the EU can meet its human rights commitments, and flowing from that, whether individuals can effectively enforce their human rights claims against the EU. Accounts of EU responsibility (understandably) do not necessarily feature the cross-fertilisation that implicitly and explicitly occurs between international and EU law and intimately links these two fields together. More than that, severed analyses of EU responsibility cannot fully reveal the scope and legal implications of the legal design flaws that taint the EU's human rights responsibility regime, much less how this impacts individual attempts at holding the EU responsible for inflicted human rights harms. Some will repond by insisting that international law applies exclusively to States and that international organisations – special as they may be – simply cannot be considered as duty-bearers of international law. Such objections, however, do not account for the breadth of scholarship and practice that has been devoted to the question of international (human rights) responsibility of international organisations.

By looking at both regimes under which the EU could theoretically incur human rights responsibility, and applying these regimes to a domain of EU conduct which has been rife with accusations of human rights harms contributed to by the EU, the book seeks to overcome this divide. The book tries to provide a transversal (though not exhaustive) analysis of the effectiveness of human rights responsibility claims by individuals directed at the EU, regardless of whether such claims are founded in international law, EU law or both.

Throughout this endeavour it was pointed out to me that I am asking the wrong questions. It was pointed out to me that the question should not be the technical one of how an individual can challenge EU complicity in human rights harms in a court of law, or what obstacles there are for an individual to seek redress for such EU contributions, or what this suggests about the effectiveness of the EU's human rights responsibility regime more generally. Instead, should one be concerned about the technicalities of the EU's human rights regime and EU responsibility, when the human rights regime at large is flawed? It struck me as a meaningful and existential objection to my work, which at times destabilised my dedication to this project.

Within this vein, one of the questions that has repeatedly resurfaced in refining this manuscript concerns the legitimacy of the critiques levelled against human rights, notably, the TWAIL and neo-colonial critiques of international human rights law. Indeed, as I developed this book, I was continuously struck by whether I have been misguided about human rights all along and whether human rights truly are no more than another form of 'Othering' lacking any actual universalist considerations of justice, especially as applied in the EU's borders, asylum and migration policies. Do human rights truly apply differently depending on your skin colour? I can hear the screams loud and clear: 'Yes of course they do! How can you be so obtuse?!' And precisely this consensus has consistently reoriented me to the question of whether it is better to disavow the human rights regime altogether, or instead try to salvage the underlying tenets of humanity intended to apply across ethnicities, gender, regions and nationalities. While recognizing the flaws of the human rights regime, César Rodriguez-Garavito makes a compelling point regarding the 'end of endism of human rights'. He convincingly reasons that political, practical and academic objections and critiques notwithstanding, human rights remain a normative and legal bedrock against which public power is tested, even in the face of mass disavowal of international law that the world is currently witnessing. In my humble opinion, this is evinced by individual accounts such as that provided by Nadia Murad, who in the face of the Yazidi Genocide, has arisen as a champion for human rights. To put it bluntly, even in the face of the most egregious atrocities, human rights provide a normative and resilient anchor to revert back to in reimaging the way forward for a world on fire.

This brings me to an altogether different question that has been plaguing me from the onset of my research stays at NYU's School of Law. What is the relevance of this book in light of Earth System Governance studies and the current developing research on Planetary Governance? What does it matter whether the EU's human rights responsibility regime is effective or not, if human history has truly run its course in light of natural history? Are the goals pursued by planetary governance and human rights truly antithetical? I do not yet have an answer to this, except for my continued hope that should mankind in its ingenuity, find a way to re-align its existence (or a variation thereof) sustainably within the boundaries of our planet, human rights regimes will have developed in such a manner that they are effective – not just for the select few.

Bearing this in mind, the attempt of this book is to contribute – however small – to unveiling some of the inadequacies of the human rights regime as it applies to the EU and international organisations generally, and provide insights on how to re-align the application of the EU's human rights regime with one of the core objectives of the international and EU human rights regime: to ensure that human rights remain protected by the rule of law, both in theory and in practice. If exhuming and deconstructing the EU's human rights responsibility regime to assess, critique and improve its transversal effectiveness from the perspective of the individual regardless of their passport, is subsequently considered 'scholactivist', I will eagerly accept that critique.

Table of Contents

PART III
EU HUMAN RIGHTS RESPONSIBILITY IN PRACTICE

PART IV
RELATIONAL HUMAN RIGHTS RESPONSIBILITY

List of Abbreviations

AFSJ	Area of Freedom, Security and Justice
ARIO	ILC Articles on the Responsibility of International Organizations
ARSIWA	ILC Articles on the Responsibility of States
BAM	Borders, Asylum and Migration
CAT	Convention against Torture
CEAS	Common European Asylum System
CFI	Court of First Instance
CFR	Charter of Fundamental Rights of the European Union
CJEU	Court of Justice of the European Union
CSDP	Common Security and Defence Policy
EBCG	European Border and Coastguard
ECHR	European Court of Human Rights
ECtHR	European Court of Human Rights
EU	European Union
GAM(M)	Global Approach to Migration
IBM	Integrated Border Management
ICC Communication	Communication to the Office of the Prosecutor of the International Criminal Court – EU Migration Policies in the Central Mediterranean and Libya
ICCPR	International Covenant on Civil and Political Rights
ICESCR	International Covenant on Economic, Social and Cultural Rights
ICJ	International Court of Justice
ILC	International Law Commission
IOs	International Organizations

ITLOS	International Tribunal for the Law of the Sea
LTV	Limited Territorial Visa
MEAs	Multilateral Environmental Agreements
MPF	Migration Partnership Framework
OPLAN	Operational Plan
PCIJ	Permanent Court of International Justice
RABIT	Rapid Border Intervention Operations
SAR	Search and Rescue Missions/Operations
STC	Safe Third Country/Safe Third Countries
TCN	Third country national(s)/third country national protection-seeker
UDHR	Universal Declaration of Human Rights
VCLT	Vienna Convention on the Law of Treaties
VCLTIO	Vienna Convention on the Law of Treaties Between States and International Organizations

Part I

Introduction

CONSIDER THE FOLLOWING: you are on a ramshackle boat without propulsion capacity, somewhere in the Mediterranean, inching towards European Union territory at a snail's pace. You notice a small drone hovering above, and what seems like an eternity later, you notice an incoming vessel approaching. Ever so briefly, you consider yourself and your companions rescued. Mere minutes later, it dawns on you that the vessel you see approaching will not be disembarking you in Europe. Instead, you are brought back to Libya, where your fate is unknown.

Consider now, that rather than being disembarked in Libya, you did reach European Union shores, where you are detained upon arrival, in what is referred to as a reception centre, but bears all the features of what you would consider as detention. You are confused – why are you being detained? Almost instantaneously – contrary to many of your peers who are subject to ongoing and seemingly endless processing – you are told you are not eligible for international protection in the European Union and are told you will be expelled. When boarding the 'return flight', you are physically separated from your children, who call out to you in tears. Again, your fate upon arrival in the third country you are flown to is unknown.

Consider a third scenario: you arrive on European Union territory, and somehow manage to escape processing and the reception centres. You are now roaming between EU Member States, without identification papers, without access to employment, without access to the housing market, and facing an uphill battle to find schooling for your children. If you request asylum, you risk being expelled to the country in which you arrived, or to a third country altogether. If you do not, you have no means of legitimizing your presence, and thus no effective means of accessing basic amenities for you and your family.

What may seem like abstractions are in fact ongoing and real struggles faced by third country nationals (TCNs) trying to reach European territory irregularly. These exact fact patterns have formed the factual background for a number of cases lodged before the Court of Justice of the European Union, the European Court of Human Rights and domestic EU Member State courts. All three fact patterns have in common that the fate of the individuals concerned is the result of concerted – joint – action involving EU Member States, EU entities, private actors and third countries. All of these actors are bound to the commitment to respect human rights under international and/or EU law to varying degrees. All three examples give rise to a number of experienced human rights harms ranging from potential violations of the *non-refoulement* principle, the prohibition of torture, the right to life, to a wide range of socio-economic human rights, such as the right to move, to housing, and education. These outcomes are referred to here as human rights *harms*, as opposed to *violations*, as they have not yet legally been qualified as such by a court of law. The question then becomes, why – if bound by human rights commitments – these actors are not being held legally responsible for their respective contributions to human rights harms?

1

IOs, the EU and Human Rights Responsibility

THIS BOOK EXAMINES whether an individual can hold the European Union (EU) – a *sui generis* international organisation – legally responsible before a court of law, for its contribution to human rights harms stemming from EU Integrated Border Management (IBM). To date, practice suggests that this is not possible in an effective manner, despite the EU's commitment to human rights protection, and notwithstanding the existing procedural framework to institute legal proceedings against the EU. This question demands an analysis of the EU's *human rights* regime on the one hand, and its applicable *responsibility regime* on the other hand. By investigating these two regimes together, this book thus investigates the EU's 'human rights responsibility regime' specifically, but additionally offers insights into the human rights responsibility regime of international organisations (IOs) more generally. This is because the question of the EU's human rights responsibility is governed simultaneously by two bodies of law: international law and EU law. In turn, these two bodies of law govern two dimensions of the responsibility question: what are the human rights norms by which the EU is bound, and what are the responsibility rules that govern conduct by the EU? Within the realm of international law, the EU is guided by customary international human rights law (*human rights norms*) and by the Articles on the Responsibility of International Organizations (*responsibility rules*) which the EU actively contributed to. Within the realm of EU law, the EU is bound by the Charter of Fundamental Rights and general principles of EU law (*human rights norms*) and the rules governing the action for damages (*responsibility rules*). By scrutinizing the EU's human rights responsibility regime simultaneously through the lens of international law and EU law, this study explores whether the right to an effective remedy of individuals can be respected when IOs such as the EU are implicated in human rights harms. The right to an effective remedy points to an international customary norm, which applies to individuals irrespective of their status, and holds that individuals have 'accessible and effective remedies to vindicate those rights' and that 'Such remedies should be appropriately adapted so as to take account of the special vulnerability of certain categories of person'.[1]

[1] Article 8 Universal Declaration of Human Rights; William A Schabas, *The Customary International Law of Human Rights* (Oxford, Oxford University Press, 2021) 273.

The premise of this book is that the inquiry into the EU's human rights responsibility regime, unveils significant though (potentially) unintended, legal design flaws: so-called *incongruencies*, preventing access to an effective and accessible procedural remedy. Incongruence in this context refers to the disharmony between the objective of the EU's human rights responsibility regime on the one hand – namely to ensure human rights protection – and the human rights norms and responsibility rules that exist to meet this objective on the other hand. These incongruencies detrimentally affect the ability of aggrieved individuals to hold IOs responsible for their contributions to unlawful human rights conduct, impacting their access to an accessible and effective (procedural) remedy at large and generating an EU human rights responsibility gap. Put plainly, these incongruencies give rise to a responsibility gap on two related but distinct levels. First, the responsibility gap arises in the relation between the aggrieved individual and the EU. The individual will encounter a debilitating number of legal obstacles in holding the EU responsible for its contribution to unlawful human rights conduct (*independent responsibility*). Second, the incongruencies inherent to the EU's human rights responsibility regime, may also detrimentally impact the ability of individuals to hold other State and non-state actors (NSAs) responsible for their respective contributions in cases of *shared* unlawful human rights conduct between the EU and other actors (*shared responsibility*). The incongruencies giving rise to this two-dimensional responsibility gap require us to think differently about *how* human responsibility may be established and allocated in situations involving the EU (and IOs more generally), to safeguard the right to an effective remedy.

Rethinking human rights in this manner demands that we meaningfully move beyond the mere recognition that (international) human rights law applies to non-state actors (NSAs). Instead, we must articulate *how* such normative commitments to human rights may be enforced in practice. Additionally, it demands (re-)calibrating the human rights responsibility regime of IOs in such a manner that it meaningfully aligns with the human rights responsibility regime of States,[2] to prevent an additional responsibility gap from arising when both types of actors are implicated in a single human rights harm. Finally, the recalibration of the human rights responsibility regime at large, demands a certain degree of flexibility, mindful of continuously evolving, changeable and differentiated governance structures that characterise IOs from an internal perspective, and in their relations with States and NSAs externally.[3] Not only is the public/private divide non-static, reminiscent of a 'battleground, with ideological forces wishing to shift the frontline in order to consolidate their own gains',[4] governance structures involving States and IOs similarly show significant variations of power dynamics.[5]

[2] For a tailored analysis of how the distinct human rights responsibility regime of States, international organisations, and transnational corporations may be misaligned, see: Joyce De Coninck, 'Relational Human Rights Responsibility' (2023) 45 *University of Pennsylvania Journal of International Law* 109.

[3] Benedict Kingsbury, Nico Krisch, and Richard B Stewart, 'The Emergence of Global Administrative Law' (2005) 68 *Law and Contemporary Problems* 3/4, 15–61.

[4] Andrew Clapham, *Human Rights Obligations of Non-State Actors* (Oxford, Oxford University Press, 2006).

[5] Fernando Lusa Bordin, *The Analogy between States and International Organizations* (Cambridge, Cambridge University Press, 2008) 107–146; Mark Konstantinidis, 'Demystifying Autonomy: Tracing

1. EMBEDDING THE EU HUMAN RIGHTS RESPONSIBILITY QUESTION IN LARGER HUMAN RIGHTS DEBATES

Scrutinizing and reconsidering the EU's human rights responsibility regime demands its contextualisation in larger human rights debates.

The first and traditional source of reticence against the EU's human rights responsibility is founded in the idea that international (human rights) law is reserved solely for states. Accordingly, focusing on the responsibility of IOs may detract from the continued role played by and responsibility of States in their obligation to respect, protect and fulfil human rights. This objection is overstated, however, as the responsibilities of IOs and States are not mutual exclusives. Both in theory and practice, the continued human rights responsibility of States is uncontested. Instead – inspired by Andrew Clapham's project on NSAs[6] – the inquiry of this book pursues complementarity and alignment between State responsibility and IO responsibility for single human rights harms to which both actors have indissociably contributed. This pursuit is achieved by taking the EU and its collaboration with its Member States as an illustration, to dissect the EU's human rights responsibility regime in its current form. This exhumation of the EU's human rights responsibility regime as it applies to the EU, allows the identification of its incongruencies, including in scenarios when the EU works indissociably together with the Member States. The analysis is then complemented with a number of suggestions on how to remedy these perceived incongruencies, mindful of its relation to State responsibility for unlawful human rights conduct.

A second and more substantive debate which calls into question the relevance of the EU's human rights responsibility regime, concerns the absence of meaningful engagement with critical scholarship on 'planetary justice'[7] or the 'more than human' (MOTH) project.[8] These strands of research call into question the very nature of the rights- and human-centric approach of the human rights regime at large, and thus indirectly, the redundancy of improving the EU's human rights responsibility regime.

Indeed, there are compelling critiques directed at the rights-centric approach of human rights law, its colonial and exclusionary undertones, its human-centricity[9] and its tendency towards temporal discounting.[10]

the International Law Origins of the EU Principle of Autonomy' (2024) *German Law Journal* 1; Sarah Nouwen, 'Organizing International Organizations' (*EJIL:Talk*, 4 December 2023). www.ejiltalk.org/ejil-the-podcast-episode-22-organizing-international-organizations/.

[6] Clapham, n 4 at 56–57.

[7] Benedict Kingsbury and Nahuel Maisley, 'Glimmers of Political Community in Planetary Governance? International Law's Animations' forthcoming; Frank Biermann, Elizabeth Dirth and Agni Kalfagianni, 'Planetary Justice as a Challenge for Earth System Governance: Editorial' (2020) 6 *Earth System Governance* 100085.

[8] César Rodríguez-Garavito, 'More Than Human Rights: What Can We Learn from Trees, Animals, and Fungi?' (*OpenGlobalRights*, 28 October 2023). www.openglobalrights.org/more-than-human-rights-trees-animals-fungi/.

[9] See for example: John S. Dryzek and Jonathan Pickering, *The Politics of the Anthropocene* (Oxford, Oxford University Press, 2019); Frank Biermann, Dirth, Kalfagianni n 7.

[10] See for example: Katharina Hunfeld, 'The Coloniality of Time in the Global Justice Debate: De-Centring Western Linear Temporality' (2022) 18 *Journal of Global Ethics* 1,100–117.

However, the pursuit of complementarity also manifests itself here. The human rights regime is considered by some, as antithetical to planetary justice and MOTH considerations of justice and by more, as ill-equipped to pursue (distributive) justice,[11] warranting its disavowal. Yet the 'end of endism' thesis[12] and 'institutional inertia' thesis[13] demand that so long governance structures involving IOs remain in place, and human rights – flawed as they may be – remain the normative bedrock against which power is tested, the accrued power of IOs demands an enforceable and reconceptualised understanding of human rights responsibility. To neglect this, runs the risk of further facilitating and exacerbating the ineffectiveness of human rights vis-à-vis IOs. This is an altogether different endeavour from substantively rethinking the human rights project mindful of planetary and MOTH considerations, but not decidedly incompatible therewith: the former addresses questions of enforcement, whereas the latter addresses the *subject* of enforcement and *underlying objective* of justice. The question of how human centricity and exclusionary effects of the human rights regime can and should give way to a planetary-centric and non-exclusionary understanding of justice, must go hand in hand with a rethinking of how such pursuits may be enforced in practice – amounting to complementary questions.

A third objection to the inquiry into the EU's human rights responsibility regime concerns the contested presumption of human rights universalism and human rights typologies. In line with the foregoing objection, this book does not depart from the premise of universality or a monolithic or one-dimensional understanding of human rights at large. In fact, this book does not directly engage with a substantive appraisal of the state of human rights internationally. Instead, the focus is on the compatibility and relationship of the human rights regime on the one hand, with the responsibility regimes of IOs and the EU on the other hand – a matter of enforcement rather than normative appraisal. While this inevitably entails engaging with EU fundamental rights norms in illustrating the workings of the EU's human rights responsibility regime, reference to these norms pursues no immediate normative agenda. Adopting the language of international law scholars and experts, this means investigating how *secondary* rules of responsibility of IOs (Articles on the Responsibility of International Organisations) interact with *primary* human rights norms (customary international human rights norms). In the language of EU scholarship and practice, this means investigating how the EU's fundamental rights norms (Charter of Fundamental Rights and EU general principles) may be enforced through legal procedures before the Court of Justice of the European Union (CJEU) against the EU's institutions, bodies, offices and agencies (action for damages).

[11] For a synthesis of many such critiques, see: Gráinne de Búrca, *Reframing Human Rights in a Turbulent Era* (Oxford, Oxford University Press, 2021) 4–7, 9–17.

[12] César Rodríguez-Garavito, 'Human Rights at 75: The End of Endism' (*OpenGlobalRights*, 1 December 2023). www.openglobalrights.org/human-rights-75-end-of-endism/.

[13] De Búrca n 11 at 42.

2. A FUNCTIONAL APPRAISAL OF THE EU'S HUMAN RIGHTS RESPONSIBILITY REGIME

The foregoing considerations bring to the fore one of the hallmarks and distinguishing features of this book: the effectiveness of the human rights responsibility regime of IOs and the EU specifically, is investigated functionally. This means that the analysis investigates the EU's human rights responsibility regime's *function* in holding the EU legally responsible for its contributions to human rights harms and to ensure access to an effective remedy for TCNs that fall victim to human rights harms contributed to by the EU's border management policy.[14] In other words, this analysis inquires whether the EU's human rights responsibility regime can fulfil its function to provide remedy against contributions to human rights harms by the EU and provide individuals with a remedy for human rights harms that arise from EU conduct. As the EU's human rights responsibility regime has developed as an aggregate of international (human rights) law and EU law (based also on the common constitutional traditions of the EU Member States), this also means that the adopted lens for the inquiry does not restrict itself exclusively to international law, nor does it restrict itself exclusively to EU law. Both bodies of law inform the EU's human rights responsibility regime. The investigation takes into account *both* bodies of (developing) law and their role in contributing to the right to an effective remedy. While a functional lens brings certain risks,[15] it is justified for three distinct reasons, related to the EU's status in the international legal order as a *sui generis* international organisation.[16]

Normative Parallelism. First, in assessing the human rights responsibility of the EU, the normative baseline is analogous for IOs generally. This means that the human rights commitments binding on the EU, which are found in international human

[14] Though functionalism in international (organisations) law has not been defined in a singular manner, the definition referred to in the present work draws from the work by Jan Klabbers, who holds that functionalism in this domain 'brings together authors as varied as Paul Reinsch and Frank Sayre, Henry Schermers and Chittharanjan Amerasinghe, Ignaz Seidl-Hohenveldern and Michel Virally. These may have held different opinions on many issues, and may have had diverging political sympathies, but all have adhered to the basic insight that international organisations are functional entities, set up to perform specific tasks for the greater good of mankind and, as such, in need of legal protection'. Jan Klabbers, 'The EJIL Foreword: The Transformation of International Organizations Law' (2015) 26 *European Journal of International Law* 1, 9–82. To trace the development of functionalism in international organisations law, see: Jan Klabbers, 'The Emergence of Functionalism in International Institutional Law: Colonial Inspirations' (2014) 25 *European Journal of International Law* 3, 645–675. See also on functionalism: Mark Tushnet, 'The Possibilities of Comparative Constitutional Law' (1999) 108 *The Yale Law Journal* 6, 1228.

[15] One of the risks that arises from applying international law to the question of EU responsibility, flows from the observation that IOs are not homogenous, making it difficult to develop any rules that are transversally applicable to IOs. On this point Bordin holds that the functional speciality of IOs may militate against any broad-stroke comparisons and analyses. While he recognises that the speciality principle holds value in distinguishing the types of IOs that exist, he argues that it 'fails to generate prescriptions'. This suggests that overstating the distinction that applies between different IOs – and by extension the general regime that applies to IOs and the EU's specific regime – does not reveal anything prescriptive on how to move forward in ascribing accountability and responsibility to IOs for their contributions to (human rights) law violations. Bordin n 5 at 238–242.

[16] Jed Odermatt, *International Law and the European Union* (Cambridge, Cambridge University Press, 2021) 9–32.

rights law, as well as in EU law (based on the common constitutional traditions of EU Member States),[17] are sufficiently comparable to permit an inquiry into how international law, as well as EU law, treat the question of human rights responsibility of IOs. This is of course, an overstatement, precisely because EU human rights law is inspired by both by international law, as well as the common constitutional traditions of the EU Member States.[18] The common constitutional traditions in turn, will to certain degrees *reflect* international human rights law, at other times *inform* international human rights law and at other times still, live in '*discordant parity*' with international human rights law.[19] But as indicated, the book does not provide a substantive appraisal of the state of human rights globally, nor a substantive appraisal of human rights between different international, regional, and domestic regimes. Instead, it recognises and uses as a starting point the compelling normative parallelism between the international human rights law and EU human rights law, which is made explicit in part through Article 52(3) of the EU's Charter of Fundamental Rights (CFR), as well as Article 6 and Article 21 of the Treaty on European Union. The fact that the EU and IOs generally, are not *a priori* excluded from the scope of application of international and EU human rights law (contrary to constitutional regimes), warrants their contemporaneous investigation on the question of human rights responsibility all the more.[20]

Rights, Politics and Legitimacy. The investigation of the EU's responsibility under international and EU law is furthermore justified by the continuous cross-referencing and cross-fertilisation of both domains of (human rights) law on substance[21]

[17] Mindful of the different sources that inspired the EU's human rights *acquis*, Moreno-Lax advances the 'aggregate standards' method to identify the content of EU fundamental rights, which in turn allows for an integrated form of human rights protection, going beyond a singular and severed understanding of those rights in their respective regimes. Violeta Moreno-Lax, *Accessing Asylum in Europe: Extraterritorial Border Controls and Refugee Rights under EU Law* (Oxford, Oxford University Press, 2017) 245.

[18] Article 6 Treaty on European Union.

[19] The human rights agenda pursued by the EU and IOs (to varying degrees) is not set solely by reference to international human rights sources, and the latter are not the product of static, universal rigidity, or monolithic understandings of human rights. Instead, human rights law broadly speaking, is the product – among others – of the on-going tension between constitutional and international law: Eyal Benvenisti and Alon Harel, 'Embracing the Tension Between National and International Human Rights Law: The Case for Discordant Parity' (2017) 1 *International Journal of Constitutional Law* 35–59. For a specific example of how human rights law may be iterated differently between constitutional regimes and international human rights law, see in turn: Michaela Hailbronner, *Traditions and Transformations: The Rise of German Constitutionalism* (Oxford, Oxford University Press, 2015) 41–66; Bundesverfassungsgericht [BverfG] [Federal Constitutional Court], Judgment of the First Senate of 19 May 2020–1 BvR 2835/17 -, paras. 1–332 (*on extra-territorial fundamental rights jurisdiction in the German Basic Law concerning surveillance*); Bundesverfassungsgericht [BverfG] [Federal Constitutional Court], Mar. 24, 2021, Case No. BvR 2656/18/1, BvR 78/20/1, BvR 96/20/1, BvR 288/20 (*on extra-territorial fundamental rights jurisdiction in the German Basic Law concerning climate change*); Bundesverfassungsgericht [BverfG] [Federal Constitutional Court], Order of the Second Chamber of the Second Senate of 18 November 2020–2 BvR 477/17 -, Rn. 1–37 (*on extra-territorial fundamental rights jurisdiction in the German Basic Law concerning airstrikes and the right to life*).

[20] Where differences arise in the understanding of the *non-refoulement* principle as the human right under scrutiny and applied throughout the different illustrations in this book, these differences will be highlighted.

[21] On the relationship concerning substantive human rights appraisals between the ECtHR and the CJEU, see, eg: Allan Rosas, 'The Court of Justice of the European Union: A Human Rights Institution?' (2022) 14 *Journal of Human Rights Practice* 204; Koen Lenaerts, 'The ECHR and the CJEU: Creating Synergies in the Field of Fundamental Rights Protection' (*Council of Europe*, 26 January 2018) www.echr.coe.int/

and procedure.[22] Both in theory and in practice, the EU's human rights regime makes note of and indirectly binds itself to international human rights standards. Similarly, the international human rights regime encompasses, recognises, facilitates and draws inspiration from regional human rights regimes. The recurring cross-fertilisation that occurs, contributes (though not flawlessly) to the coherent and continuous development of the human rights *acquis*,[23] and serves as a compelling force against the fickleness of politics in appraising the continued and substantive relevance of the human rights regime at large.[24] In other words, there is an understandable reticence on behalf of both regimes to fully cut the proverbial umbilical cord which binds them, warranting an investigation of how both regimes impact the ability to hold IOs generally, and the EU specifically, responsible for (complicity in) unlawful human rights conduct.

The *Lex Generalis* and *Lex Specialis* Dichotomy. In that same vein, the responsibility framework developed for IOs internationally, recognises – adopting the *lex generalis* and *lex specialis* dichotomy – that the general (soft law) rules on IO responsibility under international law, do not preclude or prejudice more specific rules on responsibility developed by individual and specific international organisations.[25] Indeed, while EU scholars will point out the EU's *sui generis* and ultimately, *lex specialis* nature, international scholars will point to the (customary) relevance of the Articles on the Responsibility of International Organizations (ARIO) (despite not being formally binding), as the *lex generalis*. Since the ARIO is the *lex generalis* to the EU's *lex specialis* on international legal responsibility – as acknowledged by the European Commission during the negotiations of the ARIO – no analysis of the EU's legal responsibility regime could be considered fully exhaustive without engaging with the ARIO's *lex generalis* regime.

documents/d/echr/Speech_20180126_Lenaerts_JY_ENG. See also (and sources cited therein): Federico Fabbrini and Joris Larik, 'The Past, Present and Future of the Relation Between the European Court of Justice and the European Court of Human Rights' (2016) 35 *Yearbook of European Law* 145; Thomas Streinz, 'Fraternal Twins: The European Union and the Council of Europe' in Henri de Waele and Jan-Jaap Kuipers (eds), *The European Union's Emerging International Identity* (Leiden, Brill, 2013) 123–126. On the EU and international dispute settlement more generally: Jed Odermatt, 'The Court of Justice of the European Union and International Dispute Settlement: Conflict, Cooperation and Coexistence' (2022) 24 *Cambridge Yearbook of European Legal Studies* 95–97. Antônio Augusto Cançado Trindade, 'The Continuity of Jurisprudential Cross-Fertilization in the Case-Law of International Tribunals in their Common Mission of Realization of Justice' in Giuliana Ziccardi Capaldo (ed), *The Global Community Yearbook of International Law and Jurisprudence 2018* (Oxford, Oxford University Press, 2019).

[22] On the status of the EU within the ARIO as negotiated in the ILC's preparatory works: ILC, 'Responsibility of International Organizations: Comments and Observations Received from International Organizations' (UN Doc. A/CN.4/637) 14 and 17 February 2011, p. 167. On the status of the EU in the recommenced ILC proceedings on the 'Responsibility of international organizations': Simona Popan, 'EU Statement – UN General Assembly 6th Committee: Responsibility of International Organizations' (*European External Action Service*, 18 October 2023). www.eeas.europa.eu/delegations/un-new-york/eu-statement-%E2%80%93-un-general-assembly-6th-committee-responsibility-international-organizations_en.

[23] Trindade n 21.

[24] Koskenniemi depicts the dynamic between human rights and politics as the 'management of the tension between human rights and sovereignty, or the search for autonomy and community': Martti Koskenniemi, *The Politics of International Law* (Oxford, Hart, 2011) 153–164.

[25] Article 64 ARIO.

3. A TRANSVERSAL AND APPLIED APPRAISAL OF THE EU'S HUMAN RIGHTS RESPONSIBILITY REGIME

The book differentiates itself from other works on responsibility of IOs because it moves beyond the level of theoretical abstraction,[26] but also steers away from a deep and granular study of a case-specific study of IO responsibility,[27] or a specific aspect of legal responsibility.[28] Instead, it combines theory and practice by applying its theoretical findings on the human rights responsibility regime of IOs to four different concretised illustrations of EU IBM, in both the EU's internal and external relations. In both domains, the question of responsibility for human rights harms is considered by scrutinizing both (quasi-)legislative instruments on the one hand, and operational conduct on the other hand. These findings serve as an illustration from which inferences can be drawn that may be extrapolated to other domains of EU law where similar dynamics of cooperation between the EU and its Member States emerge, as well as to other (less-integrated) IOs. IOs – as legal constructs enacted by States and other actors – inevitably involve some form of cooperation between the IO and States and will, to varying degrees, be bound by international human rights law through custom, international legal instruments or their own constituent treaties. Accordingly, the conclusions drawn from the EU's ability to be held responsible for complicity in human rights harms – given the EU's extensive and unparalleled constitutional commitment to human rights adherence – will inevitably (though not comprehensively) inform the ability to hold IOs responsible for human rights harms under this same regime that have a much less developed constitutional agenda binding them to human rights. With this in mind, the book is first and foremost a diagnostic

[26] Scholarship on theoretical approaches to international (human rights) responsibility of international organisations: André Nollkaemper, Jean d'Aspremont, Christiane Ahlborn, Berenice Boutin, Nataša Nedeski and Ilias Plakokefalos, 'Guiding Principles on Shared Responsibility in International Law' (2020) 31 *European Journal of International Law* 15–72; Magdalena Pacholska, *Complicity and the Law of International Organizations: Responsibility for Human Rights and Humanitarian Law Violations in UN Peace Operations* (Edward Elgar Publishing Limited 2020); Stian Øby Johansen, *The Human Rights Accountability Mechanisms of International Organizations* (Cambridge, Cambridge University Press, 2020); André Nollkaemper and Ilias Plakokefalos (eds.), *The Practice of Shared Responsibility* (Cambridge, Cambridge University Press, 2017); Vladyslav Lanovoy, *Complicity and Its Limits in the Law of International Responsibility* (Oxford, Hart Publishing 2016); James Crawford, Alain Pellet, Simon Olleson, Kate Parlett (eds), *The Law of International Responsibility* (Oxford, Oxford University Press, 2015); Miles Jackson, *Complicity in International Law* (Oxford, Oxford University Press, 2015); Jan Wouters and Eva Brems (eds), *Accountability for Human Rights Violations by International Organizations* (Cambridge, Intersentia, 2010); Moshe Hirsch, *The Responsibility of International Organizations Toward Third Parties: Some Basic Principles* (Leiden, Martinus Nijhoff Publishers, 1995).

[27] Scholarship on specific EU case studies concerning international (human rights) responsibility: Melanie Fink, *Frontex and Human Rights: Responsibility in 'Multi-Actor Situations' under the ECHR and EU Public Liability Law* (Oxford, Oxford University Press, 2018); Andrés Delgado Casteleiro, *The International Responsibility of the European Union – From Competence to Normative Control* (Cambridge, Cambridge University Press, 2016); Roberta, *Frontex and Non-refoulement. The International Responsibility of the EU* (Cambridge, Cambridge University Press, 2017); Moreno-Lax n 17; Malcolm Evans and Panos (eds), *The International Responsibility of the European Union: European and International Perspectives* (Oxford, Hart, 2013).

[28] Nedeski observes for example, that scholarship overwhelmingly considers international responsibility of international organisations by focusing on the concept of attribution, at the expense of an analysis of the role of international obligations in determinations of shared responsibility. Nataša Nedeski, 'Shared Obligations and the Responsibility of an International Organization and Its Member States: The Case of EU Mixed Agreements' (2021) 18 *International Organizations Law Review* 139.

appraisal of the EU's human rights responsibility regime: while there are prescriptive suggestions provided based on this diagnosis, these prescriptions are not the main objective of the book.

4. URGENCY OF THE INQUIRY: TRANSNATIONAL COOPERATIVE GOVERNANCE AND TECHNOLOGY

Two distinct but interrelated developments underscore the relevance and urgency of this book. The first relates to the increased recourse to 'transnational cooperative governance'. The second relates to the rise of techno-borders or meta-borders in relation to transnational cooperative governance and how this challenges conceptualisations of the territorial border and jurisdiction, which have traditionally played an important role in the determination of human rights responsibility.

a. Transnational Cooperative Governance

Transnational cooperative governance points to the scenario in which States and NSAs work indissociably together in addressing transnational areas of concern, inevitably blurring the line between public and private powers, while communally wielding significant power over individual and collective human rights.[29] The human rights implications associated to the rise of NSAs in a wide range of regulatory domains is not a new topic, particularly as concerns powerful transnational corporations.[30] Similarly, there is continued awareness and consensus on the need for a human rights responsibility regime that applies to IOs. What is under-scrutinised, however, is the more fine-grained development where both types of NSAs (IOs; private actors) collaborate indissociably with States in a transnational manner, in addressing issues of transnational concern. This is an altogether different question from whether NSAs have any regulatory power *tout court* and what responsibilities come with such power. Instead, the question tries to understand what happens when NSAs with significant regulatory powers interact with States through indissociable, entangled modes of cooperation.[31]

Despite the (laudable) developments on human rights responsibility of States (1), IOs (2), as well as Businesses (3), these three separate sets of rules on human rights responsibility have developed in large part, independently of each other. That is not to say that the approach to IO responsibility for example, is not inspired by the

[29] De Coninck n 2.

[30] See among others: Philip Alston (ed), *Non-State Actors and Human Rights* (Oxford, Oxford University Press, 2005); Clapham, n 4; César Rodríguez-Garavito (ed), *Business and Human Rights: Beyond the End of the Beginning* (Cambridge, Cambridge University Press, 2017); Manfred Nowak and Karolina Miriam Januszewski, 'Non-State Actors and Human Rights' in Math Noortman, August Reinisch and Cedric Ryngaert (eds), *Non-State Actors in International Law* (Oxford, Hart, 2015). See also: Kingsbury, Krisch, and Stewart n 3; Sabino Cassese (ed), *Research Handbook on Global Administrative Law* (Oxford, Oxford University Press, 2016). Jan Wouters, Eva Brems, Stefaan Smis and Pierre Schmitt (eds), *Accountability for Human Rights Violations by International Organisations* (Intersentia, 2010).

[31] Nedeski n 28.

rules underpinning state responsibility – as this is very much the case.[32] Instead, the point is rather that the crux of the rules of IO responsibility focus on scenarios where the IO conducts itself independently from other (complicit) State actors and NSAs under international (human rights) law. Conversely, there is only ancillary focus on the allocation of responsibility in cases of *shared* conduct between the IO and States. In fact, there is no focus on how these actor-specific rules interact, when the actors are engaged in shared conduct and the implications of such interaction on the right to an effective remedy.[33] For example, the rules of shared responsibility embedded in the IO responsibility regime, focus exclusively on the responsibility of the IO, without considering whether the application of its rules (mis-)align with rules on state responsibility and/or responsibility of businesses. Put differently, the ARIO spell out the rules on how to hold an IO responsible for aid and assistance, or direction and control exercised over the conduct of its Member States. For aid or assistance or direction and control to be established, however, high thresholds have to be met, entailing that it is entirely plausible that such high – and to date, opaque – thresholds, will simply not be met. In theory, an aggrieved individual would then still retain the possibility of holding the implicated State responsible. Yet, here the problem may very well arise that the complicit state may successfully argue that it had neither effective nor ultimate normative control over the unlawful conduct (due to the involvement of the IO, which is not considered by ARSIWA) under the rules of State responsibility, as a result of which the conduct will not be attributable to the state either. The application of these distinct rules on responsibility may thus generate a situation where neither actor can be held responsible, on account of the fact that these rules appear misaligned.

Similarly, the EU's rules on responsibility of the EU institutions, bodies, offices and agencies, address exclusively the responsibility of these EU entities in a singular, siloed manner, without considering how determinations on the basis of these rules impact the right to an effective remedy in cases of shared conduct with EU Member States and/or other entities such as transnational businesses. In fact, when the EU Courts are called upon to consider questions of human rights responsibility of its Member States or EU entities, the outcome of such procedures may impact and guide analogous proceedings addressing the same question but from the angle of state

[32] Pierre Klein, 'Responsibility' in Jacob Katz Cogan, Ian Hurd and Ian Johnstone (eds), *The Oxford Handbook of International Organizations* (Oxford, Oxford University Press, 2016) 1027; Alain Pellet, 'International Organizations Are Definitely Not States. Cursory Remarks on the ILC Articles on the Responsibility of International Organizations' in Maurizio Ragazzi (ed), *Responsibility of International Organizations – Essays in Memory of Sir Ian Brownlie* (Leiden, Martinus Nijhoff Publishers, 2013) 41–54.

[33] There has been extensive scholarship in the domain of global governance, which considers the myriad of interactions between different types of public and private actors. However, the focus of this book is different in that it does not focus on the idiosyncrasies and typologies of global governance conduct. Instead, it considers the different iterations of governance stemming from EU cooperation with its Member States, and the impact of such interaction on the ability to ensure the right to an effective remedy under the legal human rights framework. This latter question, together with the broader question of human rights responsibility of NSAs, remains a topic of controversy and ambiguity. See: Axel Marx, Kari Otteburn, Diana Lica, Geert Van Calster and Jan Wouters, 'Introduction to the Research Handbook on Global Governance, Business and Human Rights' in Axel Marx, Geert Van Calster, Jan Wouters, Kari Otteburn and Diana Lica (eds), *Research Handbook on Global Governance, Business and Human Rights* (Cheltenham, Edward Elgar, 2022) 19–20.

responsibility before different courts.[34] In essence, what one is left with is three sets of rules on responsibility (States, IOs, Businesses) which – due to the absence of a holistic, integrated and importantly, a relational approach, that prioritises the right to an effective remedy – may generate misalignment. This means that in cases of shared conduct between two or more of these actors, a plausible outcome may very well be, that an individual applicant is left without access to an effective remedy.

While recognizing the (at times compelling) critiques directed at the human rights regime, proponents of such critiques do not appear to convincingly champion an all-encompassing ban on directly enforceable human rights.[35] As held by de Búrca, 'even to the extent that they are well-targeted, the blitz of intellectual criticisms do not signal the death or decay of the human rights movement, or the desirability of the death or decay of that movement, any more than well-targeted criticisms of democratic systems and their dysfunctions today in themselves signal the end of democracy or desirability of the end of democracy'.[36] Hence, where such rights do exist, evolving iterations and permutable power dynamics between States and NSAs should not have the effect of either obscuring or obstructing direct enforceability of such rights. Yet, when analysing these three sets of rules on human rights responsibility (of States, the EU/IOs, and Businesses), it becomes clear that there are significant incongruencies giving rise to misalignments between these sets of rules, which in turn, may very well impede access to an effective remedy in cases of shared conduct between two or more of these actors. The incongruencies which taint these sets of rules, resulting in their misalignment, make it attractive for different actors to collaborate, as increased and diversified forms of collaboration may in effect, minimise the risk of any one of these actors being held responsible under (international) human rights law for contributions to human rights harms. In other words, by engaging in modes of cooperation involving 'many hands',[37] these three types of actors increase the chances of circumventing the human rights restraints upon their power. Transnational cooperative governance has as a result that the unlawful human rights conduct giving rise to a single human rights harm, is an aggregate of a number of smaller contributions divided across a greater number of actors. This disaggregation of actors and contributions – much like a crumbled cookie – makes it near-impossible to identify the 'correct' and 'responsible' author and the main cause for the single human rights harm stemming from their cooperation: a development not foreseen by the traditional rules governing state responsibility, IO responsibility and responsibility of businesses. It is precisely transnational cooperative governance and its actor-contribution disaggregation effect that exposes these incongruencies and underscores the need to consider the misalignment consequences stemming therefrom.

[34] See for example: [On short-term visas to lodge an international protection request] CJEU (Grand Chamber) Judgment of 7 March 2017, *X and X v Belgium*, C-638/16 PPU, ECLI:EU:C:2017:173 and ECtHR (Grand Chamber) Judgment of 5 March 2020, *M.N. and others v Belgium*, App no 3599/18.

[35] For a summary overview of contemporary critiques directed at human rights, see: de Búrca n 11 at 2–4, 9–10.

[36] ibid at 4.

[37] Mariana Gkliati and Jane Kilpatrick, 'Crying Wolf Too Many Times: The Impact of the Emergency Narrative on Transparency in FRONTEX Joint Operations' (2021) 17 *Utrecht Law Review* 57–72. Mark Bovens, *The Quest for Responsibility – Accountability and Citizenship in Complex Organizations* (CUP, 1998).

One may question whether it is even desirable to identify the 'correct' author of a line of conduct or contributions for the purpose of human rights responsibility in cases of transnational cooperative governance. The outcome of the analysis in this book may very well be that the more appropriate way forward is a new collective approach to human rights responsibility altogether, eschewing the attempt to distinguish between different actors and their individual contributions for the purpose of human rights responsibility. Be that as it may, for now, the obfuscation that remains in scenarios of transnational cooperative governance, runs counter to the finding by the European Court of Human Rights (ECtHR) in the seminal *Bosphorus* judgment. Here, the ECtHR recalled that although transfers of sovereign power by Signatory States are not problematic on the basis of the Convention, such transfers do not ipso facto absolve the transferring State from its responsibilities under the European Convention of Human Rights (ECHR).[38] At first glance, the three sets of rules on human rights responsibility of States, IOs (e.g., the EU) and businesses, suggest that all complicit actors may be held accountable for unlawful human rights conduct. And sure enough, establishing responsibility is a reasonable pursuit when the actors are conducting themselves in a manner that is sufficiently independent from each other. However, as soon as the actors interact and conduct themselves indissociably with each other, through reciprocated and indissociable transfers of (enforcement) powers, the responsibility rules appear to contribute to the absence of responsibility for all complicit actors, rather than safeguarding access to an effective remedy.

This book takes a first stab at untangling these misalignments, by uncovering the incongruencies that lie at the heart of the rules on IO and EU human rights responsibility as exposed and operationalised by transnational cooperative governance.

b. Transnational Cooperative Governance and Technology

The relevance and urgency of this project is furthermore underscored by how transnational cooperative governance is impacted by the continued trend of datafication[39] in the public sphere, and the concomitant use of evolving technologies. The use of data and (new) technologies are symptomatically governed by a (continuously developing) panoply of legal regimes regarding their development and manufacturing, their use and operation and at times, dependent on the actors that make use of them.[40]

[38] ECtHR (Grand Chamber) Judgment of 30 June 2005, *Bosphorus Hava Yollari Turizm Ve Ticaret Anonim Sirketi v Ireland*, App no 45036/98 §152–153.

[39] Datafication is understood as 'the contemporary phenomenon which refers to the quantification of human life through digital information, very often for economic value' for the purpose of categorisation, and quantifiable representational forms. See for a comprehensive definition of datafication and its development: Ulises A Mejias and Nick Couldry, 'Datafication' (2019) 8 *Internet Policy Review* 1–10.

[40] EU Data protection rules apply differently for example, to private entities, law enforcement entities and the EU institutions and bodies: Regulation (EU) 2016/679 of the European Parliament and of the Council of 27 April 2016 on the protection of natural persons with regard to the processing of personal data and on the free movement of such data, and repealing Directive 95/46/EC (General Data Protection Regulation) (GDPR); Directive (EU) 2016/680 of the European Parliament and of the Council of 27 April 2016 on the protection of natural persons with regard to the processing of personal data by competent

Crucially, datafication and the use of new technologies share the commonality that they can have a profound (and erosive) impact on the protection of human rights, as abstraction is made of the human experience, reaching far beyond questions of data protection, into the domain of qualified and absolute civil and political rights. The borderless flow of data that ensues and the objectives pursued by new technologies giving rise to data flows, raise serious unresolved governance questions that transcend the territorial State. Through the introduction of new technologies in border management for example, an attempt is made to deal with structural enforcement and expediency issues of EU IBM. The use of drones arguably help locate TCNs in the Mediterranean faster than would a Frontex vessel at sea. At the same time, locating individuals in the Mediterranean with drones, severs the physical nexus with the individuals concerned, thereby 'datafying' them by reducing them to mere location data points to be transmitted to the Libyan Coast Guard.[41] By 'datafying' TCNs in the Mediterranean and transmitting their location data to the Libyan Coast Guard, which subsequently engages in pullback operations, abstraction is made of the lived experiences of the individuals onboard, at risk of violating fundamental rights such as the prohibition of *non-refoulement*, the right to life, the right to an effective remedy and the prohibition of collective expulsion. By 'datafying' the individuals, in other words, the individuals are prevented from asking for asylum and deprived of the opportunity of demonstrating their eligibility for international protection.

Datafication and the use of new technologies also brings to the fore the territorial constraints of establishing human rights responsibility.[42] This is not a novel consideration,[43] and captured perfectly by Giulia Raimondo who holds that 'the ubiquitous nature of border controls, performed remotely through an arsenal of new technologies and cooperative tactics, challenges the traditional notion of human rights jurisdiction linked to physical control over a territory or a person'.[44]

authorities for the purposes of the prevention, investigation, detection or prosecution of criminal offences or the execution of criminal penalties, and on the free movement of such data, and repealing Council Framework Decision 2008/977/JHA (Data protection by law enforcement entities); Regulation (EU) 2018/1725 of the European Parliament and of the Council of 23 October 2018 on the protection of natural persons with regard to the processing of personal data by the Union institutions, bodies, offices and agencies and on the free movement of such data, and repealing Regulation (EC) No 45/2001 and Decision No 1247/2002/EC (Data protection by EU entities).

[41] For a general analysis on unequal control over data, as a form of data inequality, and the harms this may give rise to, see: Angelina Fisher and Thomas Streinz, 'Confronting Data Inequality' (2022) Columbia Journal of Transnational Law 829–956. See for an application specific to the EU's IBM: Violeta Moreno-Lax, 'Meta-Borders and the Rule of Law: From Externalisation to 'Responsibilisation' in Systems of Contactless Control' (2024) *Netherlands International Law Review*, (Special Issue on the externalisation of borders – *forthcoming*) ssrn.com/abstract=4710194.

[42] ECtHR (Grand Chamber) Judgment of 12 December 2001, *Banković and others v Belgium*, App no 52207/99, §61–66.

[43] Chris Jones, Romain Lanneau, Yasha Maccanico, 'Europe's Techno Borders' (*Euromed Rights and Statewatch*, July 2023) www.statewatch.org/media/3964/europe-techno-borders-sw-emr-7-23.pdf. See also: Dimitri Van Den Meerssche, 'Virtual Borders: International Law and the Elusive Inequalities of Algorithmic Association' (2022) 33 European Journal of International Law 171.

[44] Giulia Raimondo, *The European Integrated Border Management: Frontex, Human Rights, and International Responsibility* (Oxford, Hart, 2024) 5.

The exceptional circumstances that trigger extra-territorial applicability of human rights obligations (spatial effective control, state-agent control and the 'special features' doctrine) currently do not effectively accommodate the extra-territorial dimensions of the use of such new technologies (see infra). At the same time, the use of technology in borders, asylum, and migration – through Multipurpose Aerial Surveillance (MAS) for example – frequently have real-time effects on the civil and political rights of TCNs. The EU's IBM relies increasingly on aerial surveillance and datafication measures with profound impacts on the human rights of TCNs *outside* of EU territory (on high seas), but without any concomitant enforceable human rights obligations. In brief, EU aerial surveillance is used to locate individuals on the high seas and their location coordinates are subsequently transferred to third country national border and coast guards, which then execute a pullback operation. By using (new) technologies beyond the territorial remit of the EU, an adjudicatory 'jurisdictional black hole' is created, where individuals are stripped of any meaningful human rights safeguards.[45]

The legal ambiguity surrounding the extra-territorial use and effects of technology, as well as the unwillingness or inability of States to assume human rights responsibilities concerning the digital sphere and/or new technologies outside of EU territory, does not mean that they exert no influence at all. Quite the contrary – the turn to transnational cooperative governance through the EU's institutional framework, has resulted in the instrumentalisation of technology to the detriment of human rights safeguards. Real-time surveillance data is obtained by the (unmanned) 'aircraft, provided by contractors and analysed in real time by Frontex officials, who direct the aerial assets and process the collected data before passing it on to Member States and other EU Agencies for various purposes'.[46] In other words, the administration, use, and application of border-transcending technology becomes disaggregated across Member States, EU entities and private contractors. And as no single Member State, contractor or EU entity exercises individualised and discernible regulatory power over the conduct, applying any of the respective human rights responsibility rules over the administration, use and application of the technology will be unlikely to yield definitive determinations of responsibility in situations where the technology facilitates human rights violations.[47] This jurisdictional blackhole could arguably be partially remedied insofar the datafication and use of the technology by the different actors was matched with access to information. However, such

[45] Jurisdictional blackholes are also referred to as 'legal black holes'. Anna Liguori, *Migration Law and the Externalization of Border Controls: European State Responsibility* (Abingdon, Routledge, 2019). Technology in this context appears to fulfil a dual use, namely, to prevent human trafficking and smuggling and search and rescue on the one hand (humanitarian objective), and the deterrence of irregular migration on the other hand (securitisation objective). On the use and dangers of dual use technology generally, see: Margaret E Kosal (ed), *Proliferation of Weapons and Dual-use Technologies: Diplomatic, Information, Military and Economic Approaches* (New York, Springer, 2021).

[46] Consultative Forum, 'Tenth Annual Report: Frontex Consultative Forum on Fundamental Rights' (*Frontex*, 2023) 72–73 www.frontex.europa.eu/media-centre/news/news-release/frontex-consultative-forum-publishes-tenth-annual-report-OogSMw.

[47] Molnar discusses this issue in relation to the increased use of AI in migration management specifically: Petra Molnar, 'AI and Migration Management' in Markus D. Dubber, Frank Pasquale and Sunit Das (eds), *The Oxford Handbook of Ethics of AI* (Oxford, Oxford University Press, 2020) 770–771, 785–786.

requests are typically successfully denied by Frontex under the paradigmatic 'public security exception'.[48] In short, the indissociable involvement of these three different types of actors, their indissociable use of the surveillance data and new technologies, and the ensuing lack of transparency, appears to amplify the existing risk of a human rights responsibility gap stemming from transnational cooperative governance in the field of borders, asylum and migration.

Consider for example, the use of drones through an EU naval military operation, to locate TCNs in the Mediterranean, which are subsequently returned to unsafe third countries in violation of the EU's human rights commitments.[49] The use of drones for such operations does not fall within the regulatory power of any given Member State, as its deployment, use and consequences stemming therefrom flow from the EU's military operation. In turn, the EU's military operation is an example of transnational cooperative governance, whereby the actor responsible for the unlawful returns is composed of a disaggregated number of entities (Member States, EU entities and external contractors) working indissociably together, and the conduct giving rise to the harm, is composed of a disaggregated number of contributions. The use of drones in this scenario contribute to both the disaggregation of actors, as well as the conduct, as it adds another number of questions to consider for the purpose of establishing human rights responsibility: who exerts effective control over the drone? Which entity is operating the drone? Who makes use of the data-transfers made available by the drone? Who decides when and to who the data provided by the drone is made available? Are data-transfers that have potentially unlawful consequences as a result, violations of human rights? And if so, on what basis and what is the relevant burden, standard and method of proof to establish a violation of this sort, particularly where the use of borderless technology makes it even harder to identify the entity with effective control over its use? Even if the CJEU in *Naass and Sea Watch v Frontex* imposes an obligation of transparency on Frontex to disclose information on the administration, use and transfer of data, this would only answer questions surrounding data protection.[50] It remains to be seen, whether this would have any bearing on which entity would be held responsible for contestable returns of TCNs to unsafe third countries in violation of the *non-refoulement* principle (Article 19 CFR) and the right to asylum (Article 18 CFR).[51]

As can be deduced from the foregoing, questions are complicated further when the mode of transnational cooperative governance involves not just EU entities and EU Member States, but also involves transnational businesses engaged in provision of data services or sale of their technology, while located outside of the EU. HawkEye 360 is a US-based satellite company engaged in commercialised satellite-imaging in real-time, which was contracted by Frontex to provide satellite-imaging

[48] CJEU (General Court) Judgment of 27 November 2019, *Izuzquiza and Semsrott v Frontex*, T-31/18, ECLI:EU:T:2019:815.

[49] For a discussion, see: Ágoston Mohay, 'Attribution and Responsibility Regarding CFSP Acts in Light of the Renegotiation of the EU's Accession to the ECHR' (2023) 19 *Croatian Yearbook of European Law and Policy* 281; Joyce De Coninck, 'Effective Remedies for Human Rights Violations in EU CSDP Military Missions: Smoke and Mirrors in Human Rights Adjudication?' (2023) 24 *German Law Journal* 342.

[50] ibid.

[51] Consultative Forum, n 46 at 73–74.

of the Mediterranean for the duration of their contract.[52] The precise terms of this contract – particularly concerning its potential human rights implications – were not publicly available, complicating questions of who may be considered complicit should the use of this satellite imaging in the Mediterranean run afoul of EU and its Member States' human rights obligations. As will be developed in the following chapters, decision-making by Frontex, necessarily constitutes a form of transnational cooperative governance involving the EU Member States, EU entities and third states. By contracting a US-based company for the daily provision of satellite-imaging, the company becomes part of the aforementioned actor-disaggregation, and its provision of satellite-imaging data helps further disaggregate the conduct potentially giving rise to unlawful conduct in the Mediterranean. The commercial use of satellites and satellite-imaging moves the entire operation of data-transfers outside the territorial jurisdiction of the EU and its Member States and does not fall within the categories commonly accepted to establish extra-territorial jurisdiction. And it is precisely jurisdiction which functions as a first condition to be able to trigger and establish human rights responsibility.

The finesse of these examples will be developed in greater detail in the following chapters. Suffice it to say for now, that the use of new technologies, exacerbates the disaggregation trend that stem from transnational cooperative governance. New technologies challenge the manner in which human rights responsibility is typically triggered (under international human rights law) and contribute to further actor-disaggregation and conduct-disaggregation, all the while making abstraction of the individual the human rights regime sought to protect. The on-going AI revolution and the regulatory race in this space, will likely contribute to the complexification of these questions.[53] Though regulatory initiatives are abundant, a common critique to these initiatives is that they fail to acknowledge the multitude of actors involved in the manufacture, design and operation of AI systems: the so-called AI black box.[54] For the purpose of this book and the question under scrutiny this means: more actors and more contributions, including by non-humans, which may all contribute to a single human rights harm. And so, the cookie continues to crumble.

Actor-disaggregation and conduct-disaggregation, the erosion of the human through datafication, the fading of the territorial border as a trigger for human rights jurisdiction, and the incongruencies in the approaches to state, IO and business responsibility for human rights, all suggest that the human rights responsibility regime is no longer the appropriate regime to pursue human rights protection. Bearing in mind the – at times – compelling critiques raised against human rights, this leaves one wondering whether the human rights project remains a venture worth pursuing. With a flawed system, the question will always be whether it is preferrable to disavow the system altogether, or instead, to seek ways to improve this system building on its foundational structures. This book decidedly and passionately pursues the latter.

[52] For a discussion, see: De Coninck n 2.
[53] Molnar, n 47 at 770.
[54] ibid, 771.

5. SEQUENTIAL QUESTIONING AND STRUCTURING

The question of human rights responsibility of IOs and the EU specifically, gives rise to three distinct but sequential questions that are normative, procedural and pragmatic in that same order. Firstly, should, and if so, to what extent should the EU and IOs be bound by normative human rights commitments? If the answer to this first question is yes, the next question probes the (procedural) rules that should and will ensure effective respect for these normative commitments. Finally, if established that IOs and the EU specifically are bound by normative commitments (1) and procedural rules have been established to ensure the effective enforcement of these normative commitments (2), how do these commitments and procedural rules translate into effective protection in practice (3)?

It is now uncontested that IOs and the EU in particular, are bound by normative human rights commitments (1) and that both soft and binding (procedural) rules have been developed internationally and within the EU's legal framework to safeguard the effective protection of these normative commitments before a court of law (2). Yet, copious sources continuously and increasingly attest to the purported non-compliance of the EU with its human rights commitments, particularly in the field of IBM without this giving rise to successful legal review and despite the normative commitments and procedural rules that exist to ensure their enforcement.

Three immediate reasons surface which may explain why – despite the existence of normative human rights commitments and the procedural rules to ensure their enforcement – the practical application thereof does not give rise to successful actions.[55] Firstly, it may very well be the case that the EU's conduct simply does not meet the established standards and thresholds to be held legally responsible for complicity in human rights harms. This may be because of competing theories of justice that underly the human rights responsibility question, which in effect would generate different outcomes.[56] Secondly, it may also be the case that the normative commitments and/or the procedural rules to ensure the enforcement of these commitments are inappropriate or ill-developed to effectively give rise to human rights responsibility. Finally, the absence of successfully lodged claims against the EU by aggrieved individuals may simply be a question of legal mobilisation,[57] whereby these questions of responsibility – for a large number of reasons – may simply not reach adjudicatory mechanisms. This may be because

[55] The reasons provided do not purport to be exhaustive and are indicative instead.

[56] While the EU legal framework may pursue a form of *procedural* justice in the development of its human rights responsibility regime, whereby less focus goes to the outcome of particular EU conduct, and instead justice is safeguarded by EU entities adopting correct procedures in the implementation of EU policies, this may not align with the pursued or sought-after objectives of the individuals invoking human rights against the EU. This latter category may instead be pursuing alternative cosmopolitan, global or distributive forms of justice in holding the EU to account. While it may be argued that these different conceptualisations of justice are not ipso facto irreconcilable, the present study suggests that the conceptualisations of justice underpinning the EU's human rights framework as applied to IBM reveal under-scrutinised tension. See for example: Ernst-Ulrich Petersmann, 'Theories of Justice, Human Rights, and the Constitution of Internal Markets' (2003) 37 *Loyola of Los Angeles Law Review* 2, 407.

[57] Virginia Passalacqua, 'Legal Mobilization via Preliminary Reference: Insights from the Case of Migrant Rights' (2021) 58 *Common Market Law Review* 3, 751.

individual litigants may (still) be more inclined to pursue human rights responsibility of states rather than that of IOs. It may be because other avenues of accountability exist for IOs that are preferable to the route of human rights responsibility of IOs before a court of law. Or it may simply be because individuals fear legal recourse due to unresolved legal status.[58]

The absence of successful litigation against the EU for human rights complicity may also be a joint product of all of the above. However, this book is concerned with the second question – namely whether the normative commitments and the responsibility rules in place, are sufficiently developed and designed to accommodate the question of EU responsibility. The focus of this book is partly informed by the numerous actions that have been lodged before the CJEU to hold EU entities responsible for unlawful human rights conduct and complicity, with limited success.[59]

In developing this question, the book introduces EU IBM as an area of EU transnational cooperative governance, infamous for alleged EU complicity in human rights harms.[60] This governance domain and the widespread allegations of human rights abuses at the behest of the EU, provides a sombre but salient illustration to test the EU's and the IO human rights responsibility regime, while introducing the notion of transnational cooperative governance and the associated effect of datafication and the use of technology.

Part II scrutinises the responsibility regime according to which the EU can (theoretically) incur human rights responsibility under both international and EU law (the **EU's human rights responsibility regime**). In doing so, it investigates two incongruence clusters that contribute to the EU's perceived human rights responsibility gap: *normative* incongruence, and *liability* incongruence.

In investigating 'normative incongruence', this section focuses on the (international and EU) human rights commitments which bind the EU to varying degrees, and identifies the international, EU and domestic sources of these norms (the so-called *primary norms*). In other words, this section addresses the human rights commitments by which the EU is bound under international and EU law in theory, pointing out how and when difficulties arise in trying to enforce the obligations stemming from these normative commitments.

Next, the analysis turns to 'liability incongruence' in the EU's human rights responsibility regime. In doing so, this section investigates the so-called *secondary* rules, which determine under what conditions international organisations generally

[58] Clare Fox-Ruhs and Martin Ruhs, 'The Fundamental Rights of Irregular Migrant Workers in the EU' (2022) Study for the European Parliament LIBE Committee, 7.

[59] See generally on EU BAM policy: CJEU (Grand Chamber) 2017, *X and X v Belgium*, n 34; CJEU (First Chamber) Order of 12 September 2018, *NF, NG and NM v European Council*, Joined Cases C-208/17 P – 210/17 P, ECLI:EU:C:2018:705. See concerning Frontex specifically: [Action for Annulment] CJEU (General Court) 2019 *Izuzquiza and Semsrott* n 48; CJEU (General Court) Order of 15 December 2022, *Leonardo SpA v Frontex*, T-675/20, ECLI:EU:T:2022:870; CJEU (General Court) Judgment of 26 January 2022, *Leonardo SpA v Frontex*, T-849/19, ECLI:EU:T:2022:28; CJEU (General Court) Action of 7 February 2022 (pending), *Naass and Sea Watch v Frontex*, T-205/22; [Action for failure to act] CJEU (General Court) Order of 7 April 2022, *SS and ST v Frontex*, T-282/21, ECLI:EU:T:2022:235; CJEU (General Court) Order of 28 November 2023, *ST v Frontex*, T-600/22, (not yet published); [Action for damages] CJEU (General Court) Judgment of 6 September 2023, *WS and Others v Frontex*, T-600/21, ECLI:EU:T:2023:492; CJEU (General Court) Order of 13 December 2023, *Hamoudi v Frontex*, T-136/22, ECLI:EU:T:2023:821.

[60] See for a recent account: Raimondo n 44.

and the EU specifically, may incur responsibility for unlawful human rights conduct. These international and EU conditions are divided into two categories, covering independent responsibility and shared responsibility in that order:

> the ***traditional conditions*** for independent responsibility (attribution and causation, wrongful conduct)
>
> the ***relational conditions*** for shared responsibility of the various implicated parties (knowing intent, opposability, relational causality)

This section identifies and explains the theoretical and practical obstacles that arise when applying the *traditional conditions* and *relational conditions* to the EU's indissociable cooperation with its Member States. By dissecting the traditional, and relational conditions for IO and EU responsibility, inferences are drawn about the theoretical effectiveness of the EU's human rights responsibility regime and whether liability incongruencies in these rules prevent individuals from obtaining reparations in practice, for EU contributions to unlawful human rights conduct.

Part III applies the EU's human rights responsibility regime to EU conduct in IBM and tests the aforementioned inferences to the four tiers of IBM. To concretise this, the study relies on the *non-refoulement* principle as an illustration of a human right to which the EU is normatively committed, in light of its practical significance in IBM and in light of its widespread recognition as a norm of customary international law.[61] Following an analysis of the human rights obligations (negative, positive, procedural and substantive) that flow from the *non-refoulement* principle and observations regarding adjudicatory jurisdiction, for each of the four tiers of IBM, a case study was selected based on widespread (state and non-state) consensus that EU conduct disregards the *non-refoulement* principle from the perspective of the victim, albeit without this translating into succesful justiciable action before a court of law. The case studies were furthermore selected to ensure sufficient diversification, so that both *operational* and *legislative* measures are scrutinised, with *territorial* and *extra-territorial* effects. The focus on the *non-refoulement* principle *in casu*, does not entail that the findings of the analysis are exclusive to the *non-refoulement* principle. The issues that arise in determining the concrete (positive and negative, procedural, and substantive) obligations stemming from the normative commitment to respect *non-refoulement*, also reappear with other non-absolute, derogable, and qualified human rights.

After elaborating on how these findings may be extrapolated to other domains of EU conduct, and IOs more generally, as well as beyond the sphere of *non-refoulement*, the book concludes in **Part IV** with recommendations on how to reconcile and remedy the deficiencies of the EU's responsibility regime, with the values embedded in Article 2 TEU (rule of law and effectiveness of human rights protection). In doing so, an alternative approach to apportion human rights responsibility is offered, identified as *relational human rights responsibility* (based on relational

[61] Part I of the monograph discusses *non-refoulement* within the broader framework of international human rights norms applicable to international organisations generally and the EU specifically. Part II of the monograph relies on the *non-refoulement* principle as an illustration of a primary human rights norm by which the EU is bound both in theory and in practice.

complicity of the implicated actors). This approach may inspire responsibility models for IOs more generally and seeks to accommodate the power dynamics more adequately at play in hybrid forms of transnational cooperative governance. The idea of 'relational human rights responsibility' ensures that responsibility is not unduly placed on certain actors to the exclusion of others, but more importantly, safeguards and prioritises the right to an effective (legal) remedy for individual rights-holders. In other words, it ensures that cooperation and diffused conduct between the EU and other State and NSAs, does not prevent access to an effective remedy for the victims of human rights violations stemming therefrom. In doing so, the book reconciles the functional speciality of the EU (militating *against* full responsibility of the EU for unlawful human rights conduct), while safeguarding the individual right to an effective remedy.

2

EU Integrated Border Management and the Right to an Effective Remedy

The legal foundations for the EU's border management, asylum and migration policy are embedded in the EU's constituent treaties (the Treaty on European Union, Treaty on the Functioning of the European Union and the Charter of Fundamental Rights), namely Chapter 2 of Title V TFEU, which addresses in turn, the need for a Union-developed policy on border controls (Article 77 TFEU), the adoption of a common EU policy on asylum (Article 78 TFEU), the adoption of a common EU policy on immigration (Article 79 TFEU) and reaffirms that such common policies must be adopted and 'governed by the principle of solidarity and fair sharing of responsibility'.[62] Title V TFEU, governing the EU area of freedom, security and justice (AFSJ), requires more generally that the policies that fall within its ambit, be adopted with 'respect for fundamental rights and the different legal systems and traditions of the Member States' (Article 67 TFEU).

These provisions signal the EU's treaty-entrenched normative commitment to human rights in the implementation of the AFSJ and border management, and legally connect the implementation of the EU's AFSJ to the Charter of Fundamental Rights and the EU's human rights regime more generally. This does not explain however, the consequences that flow from this normative commitment, and more importantly, which entities bear the responsibility of safeguarding and enforcing this normative commitment. Answering the latter demands some insight into the historical development of IBM within the EU's approach to borders, asylum and migration, particularly as concerns its competence divisions between the EU and its Member States.

[62] Article 80 TFEU: 'The policies of the Union set out in this Chapter and their implementation shall be governed by the principle of solidarity and fair sharing of responsibility, including its financial implications, between the Member States. Whenever necessary, the Union acts adopted pursuant to this Chapter shall contain appropriate measures to give effect to this principle'. The full text of Article 80 TFEU, which includes the reference to shared responsibility concerning financial implications in the realm of borders, asylum and migration, following a textual interpretation, suggests that the solidarity and burden sharing envisaged thereby is not limited to the volumes of admitted TCNs. Rather, the terminology of Article 80 TFEU suggests a broader interpretation of burden sharing, which underpins the EU's asylum and migration policy generally. The relevance of this observation lies in the fact that this may have implications for the determinations of responsibility more generally, following unlawful human rights conduct stemming from EU immigration and asylum policy.

1. COMPETENCE DIVISION AND INTEGRATED BORDER MANAGEMENT

EU competence in the AFSJ is defined and elaborated on in Part 3, Title V of the TFEU and requires compliance with fundamental rights and respect for the legal pluralism of the Member States (Chapter 1). Under Chapter 2 specifically, Article 77 TFEU establishes EU competence with respect to border management, Article 78 TFEU addresses competence within the realm of asylum and international protection more generally and Article 79 TFEU addresses (im-)migration. Article 80 TFEU functions as an overarching guiding principle, and requires solidarity to govern the policies on borders, asylum and immigration (BAM).

The underlying objective of Article 77 TFEU is to ensure an 'effective' and 'efficient' monitoring system of the EU's external border,[63] in line with its earlier competences in this domain.[64] In ensuring this, Article 77(1) TFEU first requires a common policy to be adopted for the abolition of internal border controls.[65] Next, a policy concerning the carrying out of checks on persons and the monitoring of the external border,[66] followed by the requirement to incrementally introduce IBM.[67]

The terminology used in Article 77(1) TFEU, indicates that this provision does not result in judicially enforceable obligations of *result* against which action (or inaction) by the EU can tested.[68] Instead, the objectives of Article 77(1) TFEU impose instead, an obligation of means. In turn, this leaves the exact scope and delimitation of the shared competences to be further developed in secondary legislation.[69] While EU action will be limited by the principle of subsidiarity and proportionality, the open-textured and dynamic nature of the competences, may affect the responsibility question, as the concretisation of competence division in this domain plays a significant role in attribution of (unlawful) conduct to either the EU, implicated Member States and/or both (see below).

Article 77(2) TFEU sets out a number of measures to achieve an efficient border management regime:

[63] Article 77(1)(b) TFEU. Hailbronner and Thym point out that depending on which language version is consulted, the terminology shifts from 'efficient' to 'effective', as demonstrated by the German reference to '*wirksame*'. This textual distinction could bear some relevance, as it may entail a different type of obligation, namely an obligation of means or an obligation of results, which could impact the responsibility question. Regardless of the terminology, however, the objectives remain open-ended and require further concretization in order to define the contours of the division of competences between the EU and its member states. Kay Hailbronner and Daniel Thym, *EU Immigration and Asylum Law – A Commentary* (Munich, Verlag C.H. Beck, 2016) 35–36.

[64] For a comparative analysis, see: Bernd Martenczuk, 'Migration Policy and EU External Relations' in Loïc Azoulai and Karin de Vries (eds), *EU Migration Law: Legal Complexities and Political Rationales* (Oxford, Oxford University Press, 2014) 75.

[65] Article 77(1)(a) TFEU.

[66] Article 77(1)(b) TFEU.

[67] Article 77(1)(c) TFEU.

[68] Hailbronner and Thym n 63, 36.

[69] See for example, the reference to 'common policies on visas' and the discussion concerning common and uniform policies under the CEAS provided for by Article 78 TFEU. The semantic distinction is demonstrative of a lesser or higher degree of harmonization.

Article 77 TFEU

2. For the purposes of paragraph 1, the European Parliament and the Council, acting in accordance with the ordinary legislative procedure, shall adopt measures concerning:

(a) the common policy on visas and other short-stay residence permits;
(b) the checks to which persons crossing external borders are subject;
(c) the conditions under which nationals of third countries shall have the freedom to travel within the Union for a short period;
(d) any measure necessary for the gradual establishment of an integrated management system for external borders;
(e) the absence of any controls on persons, whatever their nationality, when crossing internal borders.

While these measures narrow the scope of EU competences in this domain to a certain degree, this perceived clarification should not be exaggerated, as exemplified by the requirement to *incrementally* introduce IBM in line with Article 77(2)(d) TFEU. IBM is characterised by the 'four-tier access control model', encompassing measures in third countries (1); cooperation with neighbouring countries (2), control measures at the EU border (3) and measures within EU territory including measures concerning return (4).[70] Within this four-tier access control model however, it remains possible for Member States and the EU *together* but also, *independently of each other*, to conclude parallel arrangements of 'consensual containment'[71] with third countries to dissuade departures of TCNs towards the EU (tier 1 of IBM) or to conclude arrangements on return with third countries (tier 4 of IBM). The aggregate of such formal or informal measures may diffuse responsibility for potential human rights harms across a number of different actors.[72] Such diffusion of conduct can be exemplified by the bilateral Memorandum of Understanding between Libya and Italy, and the parallel cooperation between the EU and Libya through (former)

[70] Integrated Border Management is defined in recital 11 (and Article 3) of Regulation (EU) 2019/1896 of the European Parliament and of the Council of 13 November 2019 on the European Border and Coast Guard and repealing Regulations (EU) No 1052/2013 and (EU) 2016/1624 (EBCG Regulation 2019) [2019] OJ L295/1 (see also consideration 3 of the repealed 2016 Frontex Regulation): 'European integrated border management, based on the four-tier access control model, comprises measures in third countries, such as under the common visa policy, measures with neighbouring third countries, border control measures at the external borders, risk analysis and measures within the Schengen area and return'. IBM may be construed more broadly, as underscored also by Moreno-Lax, who identifies three variations through which to understand IBM: the constitutional conceptualization of IBM, which focuses on its practical importance of IBM in safeguarding an internal space without borders particularly within the context of accession procedures; the security conceptualization of IBM, which focuses on a preventative (surveillance) function of IBM post-9/11 and not limited to the (safe-)guarding of the territorial border; and finally the harmonization conceptualization of IBM, which focuses on the development of common rules and practices applied in a coordinated manner. Moreno-Lax n 17 at 27–28. See also: Council of the European Union, 'Council Conclusions on Integrated Border Management – 2768th Justice and Home Affairs Council meeting' (*Council of the European Union*, 4–5 December 2006) ec.europa.eu/commission/presscorner/detail/en/PRES_06_341.

[71] See generally on 'consensual containment' policy: Mariagiulia Giuffré and Violeta Moreno-Lax, 'The Rise of Consensual Containment: From 'Contactless Control' to 'Contactless Responsibility' for Forced Migration Flows' in Satvinder Singh Juss (ed), *Research Handbook on International Refugee Law* (Cheltenham, Edward Elgar Publishing, 2019).

[72] 'Memorandum d'intesa sulla cooperazione nel campo dello viluppo, del contrasto all'immigrazione illegal, al traffic di esseri umani, al contrabbando e sul rafforzamento della sicurezza delle frontier tra

operation EUNAVFOR MED Sophia and its successor operation EUNAVFOR MED Irini. The combined effect of such Member State and EU measures, geared towards the realisation of IBM, have as a direct result that individual TCNs may be pushed and pulled back into Libya, albeit without clarity as to the author of the actual conduct resulting in the push- or pullback at the time of its execution. As will be developed, not being able to definitely identify the responsible author for a given line of conduct, complexifies any attempt at trying to establish responsibility under the EU's contemporary human rights responsibility regime.

The reasons for the nebulous nature of competence division in border management in practice, are not surprising. On the one hand this is arguably the result of the constant balancing between supranational and intergovernmental regulation of the area of freedom, security and justice (AFSJ).[73] By ensuring dynamic and malleable competence division in practice, transnational cooperation in border management is achieved, while the Member States continue to retain certain powers to adopt own border control measures and assert their sovereignty. On the other hand, this opaqueness is also a direct consequence of the constitutional architecture of the EU. While the EU legislator 'concentrates on legislative harmonization and administrative support measures', the Member State authorities remain responsible for the decisions made vis-à-vis individual persons, and the implementation of these legislatively harmonised measures.[74] Depending on the intensity of the harmonisation measures, the Member States will enjoy differing degrees of discretion in the implementation of such measures to concrete cases. The immediate consequence for human rights responsibility is that conduct will be diffused across different actors working indissociably together. To then be able to identify the responsible author(s) of a given line of conduct, a case-by-case assessment will be necessary. This diffusion of competence, conduct, and authorship is not problematic as such and flows from the very nature of shared competences in the EU's legal framework. The diffusion becomes potentially obstructive however, when applied in the EU's human rights responsibility framework.

2. THE TRANSFORMATIONS OF INTEGRATED BORDER MANAGEMENT

a. Changing Priorities in Integrated Border Management

The initial references to the regulation of Borders, Asylum and Migration (BAM) as 'common interests' of the European Union pursuant to the Treaty of Maastricht,

lo Stato della Libia e la Repubblica Italiana' http://itra.esteri.it/vwPdf/wfrmRenderPdf.aspx?ID=50975. See for a discussion: Anja Palm and Sarah Cole, 'The Italy-Libya Memorandum of Understanding: The Baseline of a Policy Approach Aimed at Closing All Doors to Europe' (*EU Migration Law Blog*, 2 October 2017) eumigrationlawblog.eu/the-italy-libya-memorandum-of-understanding-the-baseline-of-a-policy-approach-aimed-at-closing-all-doors-to-europe/.

[73] Steve Peers, *EU Justice and Home Affairs Law: Volume I: EU Immigration and Asylum Law* (Oxford, Oxford University Press, 2016) 3–4, 5–6; Hailbronner and Thym n 63 at 2; Vincent Chetail, 'The Common European Asylum System: Bric-à-brac or System?' in Vincent Chetail, Philippe De Bruycker and Francesco Maiani (eds), *Reforming the Common European Asylum System – The New European Refugee Law* (Leiden, Brill, 2016) 8–9.

[74] Hailbronner and Thym n 63 at 36.

and the incremental supranationalisation of these policies following the Treaty of Amsterdam, were initially intended to facilitate the abolition of internal borders so as to create an internal space in which market freedoms reigned. With the Treaty of Amsterdam, the AFSJ was formally introduced, of which BAM policies constituted a crucial component. In addition to EU legislation spelling out the contours of this EU competence, the delineation and demarcation of this domain of EU law, is furthermore guided by multi-annual political programming.[75] These political programmes, although not legally binding, identified the policy priorities to be pursued by the EU and were frequently tailored to current events that helped shape the AFSJ at the time.[76] As these political programmes were not legally binding, these could not be enforced as judicial parameters against which the validity of EU measures could be tested. Nevertheless, to varying degrees these programmes served as the necessary impetus to further develop and clarify the scope of BAM legislation.[77] This is evidenced by the Tampere European Council in 1999, which set forth the four priorities of BAM, of which one was the development of the first phase of the Common European Asylum System (CEAS).[78] In the 2004 Hague Programme, political focus shifted towards securitisation of the EU's external border in the wake of a number of terrorist attacks globally, making a priority of cross-border cooperation concerning terrorism and organised crime.[79] Following the Tampere and the Hague political programming, the Stockholm Programme of 2010 did away with the security-centric approach and focused instead on making fundamental rights adherence and EU citizenship a political priority, while maintaining security in the European Union.[80] Following the Stockholm Programme, the Ypres Guidelines of 2014[81] had limited value and additionally lost much of its value pursuant to the Treaty of Lisbon innovations, which partially clarified the scope and content of BAM measures.[82]

With the Treaty of Lisbon, the AFSJ was no longer perceived as a 'means to an end' in ensuring internal market freedoms, and instead fulfilled the role of a self-standing objective for integration, of which the abolition of internal borders was only one component. Rather than merely focusing on the abolition of the internal borders, BAM measures pursued a number of differing, albeit sometimes somewhat

[75] Cian C. Murphy and Diego Acosta Arcarazo, 'Rethinking Europe's Freedom, Security and Justice' in Diego Acosta Arcarazo and Cian C. Murphy (eds.), *EU Security and Justice Law After Lisbon and Stockholm* (Oxford, Hart, 2014) 5.

[76] Hailbronner and Thym n 63, 5–6.

[77] ibid.

[78] European Council, 'Presidency Conclusions of the Meeting on 15/16 October 1999 in Tampere' (*European Parliament*, 15–16 October 1999) §10–27.

[79] The European Council Hague Programme: Strengthening Freedom, Security and Justice in the European Union (2005) *Official Journal of the European Union* C 53/1, 1, 7–11. See for a general discussion: Murphy and Acosta Arcarazo n 75 at 5–6; Sergio Carrera, 'The Impact of the Treaty of Lisbon over EU Policies on Migration, Asylum and Borders: The Struggles over the Ownership of the Stockholm Programme' in Elspeth Guild and Paul Minderhoud (eds), *The First Decade of EU Migration and Asylum Law* (Leiden, Martinus Nijhoff Publishers, 2011) 235–236.

[80] The European Council Stockholm Programme – An Open and Secure Europe Serving and Protecting Citizens (2010) *Official Journal of the European Union* C 115/1, 4. For a general discussion, see: Carrera n 79 at 237–239.

[81] European Council, 'European Council of 26 and 27 June 2014 – Draft Conclusions' (*Council of the European Union*, 25 June 2014).

[82] Hailbronner and Thym n 63, 5–6.

contradictory, objectives.[83] Specifically, BAM policy increasingly focused on the combatting of irregular migration. Depending on how this policy priority is presented, it may prove to difficult to reconcile with the constitutionalised requirement of respect for the *non-refoulement* principle, which encompasses obligations that go beyond the mere 'restraint from sending back individuals' to countries where they risk ill-treatment upon return. Similarly, depending on how these objectives are presented, it may prove problematic to reconcile 'efficient migration management' with ensuring fair treatment of TCNs. In that same vein, it may also prove problematic to reconcile the informalisation of readmission agreements with the right to an effective remedy for TCNs subjected to such return procedures. Finally, the objective of developing effective visa regimes to facilitate regular migration without any specific provisions directed at applicants for international protection, may jeopardise the objective of fair treatment of TCNs, the right to an effective remedy of TCNs and the overall pursued objective of ensuring *non-refoulement* and access to international protection proceedings for TCNs.

These potentially counter-intuitive objectives and political priorities characterised the European Commission 2015 Agenda on Migration and Asylum,[84] as well as the recent 2020 European Commission New Pact on Migration and Asylum.[85] While legislative instruments concerning BAM increasingly incorporate references to fundamental rights adherence both in terms of compliance to the CFR, as well as in terms of international human rights law generally, the 2020 European Commission New Pact on Migration and Asylum and its predecessor, the 2015 Agenda on Migration and Asylum consistently stress the (political) need for the externalisation, securitisation and militarisation of border control and migration management.[86] These political priorities are not ipso facto irreconcilable with fundamental rights. In fact, outsourcing and externalisation of migration management is neither novel,

[83] Fahey, 'Hyper-legalisation and de-legalisation in the AFSJ: on contradictions in EU external migration law' in Sergio Carrera, Juan Santos Vara and Tineke Strik (eds.), *Constitutionalising the External Dimensions of EU Migration Policies in Times in Crisis – Legality, Rule of Law and Fundamental Rights Reconsidered* (Cheltenham, Edward Elgar Publishing 2019).

[84] European Commission, 'Communication from the Commission to the European Parliament, the Council, the European Economic and Social Committee and the Committee of the Regions – A European Agenda on Migration – COM(2015)240' (*European Commission*, 13 May 2015) ec.europa.eu/home-affairs/sites/homeaffairs/files/what-we-do/policies/european-agenda-migration/background-information/docs/communication_on_the_european_agenda_on_migration_en.pdf (*hereafter* 2015 Agenda on Migration).

[85] The negotiations at the time of completing this book are ongoing and are expected to come to a conclusion in the Spring of 2024. European Commission, 'Communication from the Commission to the European Parliament, the Council, the European Economic and Social Committee and the Committee of the Regions on a New Pact on Migration and Asylum – COM/2020/609 final' (*European Commission*, 23 September 2020) eur-lex.europa.eu/legal-content/EN/TXT/?qid=1601287338054&uri=COM%3A2020%3A609%3AFIN (2020 New Pact on Migration and Asylum).

[86] See concerning the 2015 Agenda on Migration, enhanced focus on resettlement (p. 4–5), on cooperation with third countries and operations deployed in those countries (p. 5), and on consensual containment (p. 7–9). See concerning the 2020 New Pact on Migration and Asylum, enhanced focus on return sponsorship (§2.2), on a common system for returns (§2.5), on enhancing integrated border management (Section 4) and on working with international partners (Section 6). In both instruments, the focus is overwhelmingly on returning individuals and reducing incentives for TCNs to reach the EU's external border. See for a discussion on the 2020 New Pact on Migration and Asylum: Daniel Thym, 'Special Collection on the 'New' Migration and Asylum Pact' (*EU Immigration and Asylum Law and Policy*, 28 September 2020) http://eumigrationlawblog.eu/series-on-the-migration-pact-published-under-the-supervision-of-daniel-thym/.

nor limited to the EU.[87] However, textual references to human rights standards in the legislative instruments notwithstanding, these provisions have failed to meaningfully safeguard human rights.[88]

b. Traits and Transformations of Integrated Border Management[89]

The legislative reforms and concomitant policy priorities of IBM are significant in that they demonstrate that the manner of implementation of IBM is highly context- and time-driven, mindful of global, international, regional and national politics. These developments bring to the fore some key features that distinguish EU border management from border management by a single Member State.

Firstly, Member States are not susceptible to the same dualistic logic which undergirds EU IBM.[90] The dualistic logic of IBM prioritises internal mobility among Member States, while in parallel endeavouring to prioritise external border security. Put differently, to build and safeguard an AFSJ, IBM seeks heightened external border security to maintain fluid internal movement of goods, capital, services, and persons on a much larger scale than any single Member State.

Another key distinction concerns the dualistic and dichotomous legislative framing of TCNs in the EU's legislation governing IBM. The law incorporates textual references to the need to safeguard fundamental rights of TCNs. Yet, in equal measure, it also designates TCNs as potential security threats, by emphasising the need to detect and manage irregular migrants, underscoring the need to cooperate for the purpose of cross-border crimes and '*to prevent any threat to the Member States' internal security, public policy, public health and international relations*'.[91] Simultaneously designating TCNs as rights-holders but also as security liabilities, allows for the erosion of the human rights safeguards to which they are entitled, given that such security exceptions are typically relied upon to justify the curtailing of rights-based safeguards. Again the distinction with border management of a single Member State is one of scale: whereas a single Member State remains bound by (international) human rights standards concerning the treatment of TCNs, the degree to which this will be counterbalanced with security concerns operates differently on an EU level. Unlike Member States, when the EU adopts a course of action

[87] Thomas Gammeltoft-Hansen, *Access to Asylum – International Refugee Law and the Globalisation of Migration Control* (Cambridge, Cambridge University Press, 2011) 3; Thomas Gammeltoft-Hansen, 'The Externalisation of European Migration Control and the Reach of International Refugee Law' in Elspeth Guild and Paul Minderhoud (eds), *The First Decade of EU Migration and Asylum Law* (Leiden, Martinus Nijhoff Publishers, 2011) 273–298.

[88] For a preliminary, albeit extensive analysis on the (human rights) issues associated to the European Commission 2020 New Pact on Migration and Asylum, see: Thym n 86.

[89] Joyce De Coninck and Giulia Raimondo, 'Understanding European Border Management: A Tale of Transformation and Orchestrated Impunity' (*Verfassungsblog*, 27 February 2024) verfassungsblog.de/understanding-european-border-management/.

[90] Raimondo n 44.

[91] Recital 4, Proposal for a Regulation of the European Parliament and of the Council introducing a screening of third country nationals at the external borders and amending Regulations (EC) No 767/2008, (EU) 2017/2226, (EU) 2018/1240 and (EU) 2019/817 (Screening Regulation).

that militates more in the direction of securitisation, at the expense of a rights-based approach to border management this sets a standard for Member States to follow – thus legitimizing a security-centric approach adopted by single Member States more broadly. This broader form of legitimisation which occurs through the obligations borne through the EU's legal framework and the duty of sincere cooperation, provides individual Member States with the impetus and justification to minimise human rights protections in the interest of complying with their duties under EU law, and fosters a defence for minimizing or discarding their individual human rights obligations.

Finally, the EU's IBM distinguishes itself from Member State border management through its governance, which has transitioned from intergovernmental cooperation to a supranational structure. Whereas traditionally, the EU relies on its Member States for the execution of its policies, increasingly the tasks of implementation are entrusted (at least partially) to the EU's own agencies and officials. This means that the supranational structure within which IBM is embedded, increasingly relies on different actors and technologies at different governance levels to be executed, rather than relying predominantly on Member States for its implementation.

These distinctions give rise to two notable features of the EU's IBM: the involvement of numerous actors at various (domestic, national, regional and international) governance levels and the coordination complexities this generates on a horizontal axis between various Member States, as well as vertically, between the EU, its Member States, and transnational non-state actors. These features are exacerbated by the ongoing transformations of IBM. IBM finds its origin in flanking measures intended to *facilitate* internal freedoms. It has since incrementally transformed from mere *border* management, with a focus on monitoring, into a tool of *migration* management, with a view to minimizing inbound TCNs. This mode of migration management flows from a strict application of the 'in/out' dichotomy, which relies on methods of externalisation, informalisation, securitisation including militarisation, digitalisation, and agencification.

The latest EU Pact on Migration and Asylum, which has been under negotiation since 2020, continues this trend of migration and border management. Externalisation refers to the process whereby the EU's physical territorial border is transformed into an intangible and imperceptible border, which moves border management far beyond actual EU territory.[92] Contemporary externalisation techniques are visa restrictions[93] and carrier sanctions regulations,[94] pullback

[92] Giulia Raimondo, 'Beyond Progress: Interrogating the Limits of Jurisdiction and Migrant Rights through Negative Dialectics' (2024) forthcoming; Chris Jones, Romain Lanneau and Yasha Maccanico, 'Access Denied: Secrecy and the Externalisation of EU Migration Control' (Statewatch, December 2022) www.statewatch.org/media/3781/secrecy-and-externalisation-of-migration-control.pdf.

[93] See among others: Lena Laube, 'The Relational Dimension of Externalizing Border Control: Selective Visa Policies in Migration and Border Diplomacy' (2019) 7 *Comparative Migration Studies* 29. Liguori n 45.

[94] Council Directive 2001/51/EC of 28 June 2001 supplementing the provisions of Article 26 of the Convention implementing the Schengen Agreement of 14 June 1985 (Carrier Sanctions Directive). Theodore Baird, 'Carrier Sanctions in Europe: A Comparison of Trends in 10 Countries' (2017) 19 *European Journal of Migration* 307–334.

operations and safe third country designations by and of third countries,[95] as well as the deployment of migration management teams in third countries.[96] The turn to informalised border and migration management refers to the reliance on informal arrangements[97] with third countries to prevent departure of TCNs to EU territory, thus constraining the individuals' right to leave.[98] The securitisation and increased militarisation of the EU's external border is demonstrated by the deployment of EUNAVFOR MED Operation Sophia and its successor Operation Irini, which, under the EU's Common Foreign and Security Policy, have been deployed to combat human smuggling and trafficking.[99] These operations have simultaneously been used to obtain location data of TCNs making passage through the Mediterranean, and are subsequently communicated to the Libyan Coast Guard which have effectuated pullback operations as a result thereof.[100] Through the method of digitalisation and datafication, IBM has given rise to virtual borders.[101] These virtual borders are the result of interoperable IT systems which allow for data transfers that may impact the likelihood of success of an international protection claim. Virtual borders are also created through the use of drones and satellite imaging to monitor, track, and prevent TCNs from approaching the EU territorial border and from leaving the third state altogether. In so doing, the EU's IBM severs the physical nexus between EU border officials and TCNs through recourse to technologies. In turn this obscures if human rights law can be triggered and applied to the affected TCNs. Finally, agencification refers to the increased reliance on EU agencies for the purpose of implementing the EU's border management. The reliance on Frontex and its executive powers serves as the most prominent and salient example of the transformation of IBM.

[95] See contributions by Fink and Idriz, Pijnenburg, Dicle Ergin, and Roman: Eva Kassoti and Narin Idriz (eds), *The Informalization of the EU's External Action in the Field of Migration and Asylum* (New York, Springer, 2022).

[96] Protocol between the Government of the Italian Republic and the Council of Ministers of the Albanian Republic (*Odysseus Network*, translation by Giovanni Meledandri) odysseus-network.eu/wp-content/uploads/2023/11/Protocol-between-the-Government-of-the-Italian-Republic-and-the-Council-of-Minister-of-the-Albanian-Republic-1-1.pdf (Italy-Albania Agreement); Memorandum of Understanding on a strategic and global partnership between the European Union and Tunisia (European Commission, 16 July 2023) ec.europa.eu/commission/presscorner/detail/en/ip_23_3887 (EU-Tunisia Agreement).

[97] Kassoti and Idriz n 95; Paul James Cardwell and Rachel Dickson, 'Formal Informality in EU External Migration Governance: The Case of Mobility Partnerships' (2023) 49 *Journal of Ethnic and Migration Studies* 12, 3121–3139; Violeta Moreno-Lax, 'The Informalisation of the External Dimension of EU Asylum Policy: The Hard Implications of Soft Law' in Evangelia Tsourdi and Philippe De Bruycker (eds), *Research Handbook on EU Migration and Asylum Law*, (Leiden, Edward Elgar Publishing Limited, 2022) 282; Catherine Briddick, 'When Treaties are Forbidden' (*Verfassungsblog*, 29 February 2024) verfassungsblog.de/when-treaties-are-forbidden/.

[98] Nora Markard, 'The Right to Leave by Sea: Legal Limits on EU Migration Control by Third Countries' (2016) 27 *European Journal of International Law* 3.

[99] Statewatch et al., 'Telling the Story of EU Border Militarization' (*Statewatch*, August 2023) www.statewatch.org/media/4000/eu-border-militarisation-narrative-guide.pdf.

[100] De Coninck, n 49 at 342–363.

[101] Chris Jones, Romain Lanneau, Yasha Maccanico, 'Frontex and Interoperable Databases – Knowledge as Power?' (Statewatch, February 2023) www.statewatch.org/frontex-and-interoperable-databases-knowledge-as-power/; Jones, Lanneau, Maccanico, n 43; Dimitri Van Den Meerssche, 'Virtual Borders: International Law and the Elusive Inequalities of Algorithmic Association' (2022) 33 *European Journal of International Law* 1, 171–204.

3. TRACING THE HUMAN RIGHTS CONSEQUENCES OF IBM TRANSFORMATIONS

Through externalisation and informalisation, the implementation of IBM implicates new actors (third states) in the execution of particular measures. Securitisation and militarisation contribute to the framing of TCNs as security threats and militarisation under the EU's legal framework largely shields conduct adopted within these operations from judicial review by both the EU Courts and the Member State courts. Digitalisation and datafication of border management and TCNs respectively, reduce and thwart access for TCNs to procedures to request international protection (e.g. asylum, subsidiary protection) which prevent TCNs from conveying their lived experiences to demonstrate refugee status or eligibility for subsidiary protection. Finally, the increased powers of EU agencies in the implementation of EU IBM brings to the fore the thorny question of (the degree of) conferred competences of EU agencies in IBM operations and concomitant questions of accountability, including legal responsibility.

While in and of themselves, these transformations are not irreconcilable with human rights, practice intimates that their current application fall severely short of the safeguards embodied in the Charter of Fundamental Rights and the human rights regime governing the EU more generally. TCNs are routinely reported as being subjected to illegal push- and pullbacks in Mediterranean and Aegean waters to unsafe third countries (eg., push- and pullbacks to Libya, Tunisia, and Turkey with concomitant risks of direct and indirect refoulement) where they are subsequently subjected to a wide array of ill-treatment through contributory EU conduct, as well as contributory conduct by Member States. Such reporting is compounded by reports of individuals starving at the EU's external territorial border following illegal collective expulsions and refused access to international protection proceedings (eg., at the Polish-Belarusian, Spanish and the Greek border). Additional evidence attests to deplorable detention conditions for and ill-treatment of TCNs in EU Member States, in addition to automatic individual and collective expulsions (eg., in Greece, Italy). The informal and covert nature of many of the techniques of IBM complexify access to legal recourse before domestic courts and before the EU courts (eg., Operation Sophia and Irini). The transformations of the EU's IBM, which have given rise to the increased involvement of different actors at various governance levels, exacerbate the opaqueness that characterises Member State and EU IBM. From the perspective of the individual, the transformations of EU IBM have thus failed to render border management more humane, as the effect of IBM measures results in the subjugation of TCNs seeking refuge in Europe, to (the real risk of) significant ill-treatment. TCNs are subjected to among others, externalisation, delocalisation, militarisation, digitalisation with little to no regard for the human rights implications of these measures. EU IBM has additionally complexified access to legal recourse through the expansion of complicit actors, their (more granular and indissociable) respective contributions, and the implementation of IBM across different legal spatial regimes (eg., at the border, within territorial waters, within high seas, above high seas and within the territory of third states). Even without advancing a claim of (near-) universal jurisdiction whereby the EU and its Member States would be bound by human rights commitments in their implementation of IBM, it is clear that conduct mandated through EU IBM, entails the exercise of a (diluted) form of power to the exclusion of other public authorities. When the EU Member States and EU entities transmit location-coordinates of TCNs on high seas to the Libyan Coast Guard for example, this is conduct that is the exclusive result of these European actors. And if the exercise of such (quasi-) exclusive powers comes at the expense of human rights of TCNs, can such EU conduct be reconciled with the human rights obligations borne by EU entities and EU Member States? Can and should the EU be held responsible for the operationalisation of continuously transforming border management that contributes to the subjugation of TCNs to human rights harms? Should afflicted individuals be provided a form of legal recourse against the EU, given their de facto stateless nature and the unavailability of other forms of legal recourse and legal forums to safeguard their human rights?

The EU differentiates itself from other IOs in this regard, by the fact that it is both bound to adhere to the constitutionally embedded set of fundamental rights in the Charter of Fundamental Rights and has a legal regime in place that – at least in theory – allows for the enforcement of these obligations. The EU's functions are thus not normatively neutral and must be interpreted and implemented with due respect for the Charter of Fundamental Rights,[102] including with the right to an effective remedy. For the functions of the EU to subsequently be executed according to its mandate and in line with the EU's human rights regime, the (procedural) right to a remedy demands that such a remedy be both effective and accessible. And that is precisely the question that undergirds the current analysis: can the EU be held legally responsible for disregarding its human rights commitments under the Charter of Fundamental Rights and human rights law more generally, and can the right to an effective remedy for individuals be effectively safeguarded?

In answering the question whether the EU can – in theory and in practice – be held legally responsible for violations of (international) human rights law it contributes to in the implementation of IBM, and whether the right to an effective remedy can be safeguarded, an in-depth understanding is required of the EU's Human Rights Responsibility Regime.

[102] Klabbers notes that when analysing IOs, a functionalist lens does not provide much insight on how responsibility of IOs must be considered. With the Charter of Fundamental Rights, however, and Article 51 CFR specifically, the EU's functions must be understood as having to comply with fundamental rights at risk of incurring responsibility under the EU's liability regime. This reading suggests that the objection raised by Klabbers is less prominent in the case of the EU than IOs more generally. See n 14.

Part II

The EU's Human Rights Responsibility Regime

TWO LEGAL DOMAINS govern the EU's Human Rights Responsibility Regime, covering two sets of rules each. International law and EU law each have developed rules on responsibility, which govern how an IO and the EU specifically can incur responsibility. Additionally, international and EU law have developed human rights law which dictates whether and how public actors are bound by human rights commitments and when these public actors may be considered to have violated these commitments. Investigating the extent to which the EU can be held legally responsible by an individual, warrants engaging with and exhuming these four sets of rules in an integrated manner, given the extensive cross-fertilisation and reciprocated engagement with each other.

Figure 1 The EU's Human Rights Responsibility Regime (J. De Coninck)

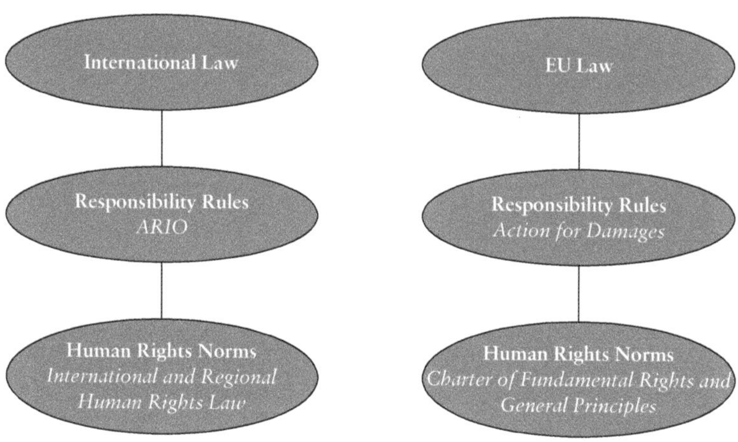

The international legal regime is embedded in the Articles on the Responsibility of International Organisations (ARIO) which applies to IOs generally, providing both general rules (the *lex generalis*) on how to determine responsibility, while acknowledging that individual IOs may develop their own, specific responsibility regime (the *lex specialis*) that may supplement or replace these general rules. Following eight reports drafted by Special Rapporteur Giorgio Gaja over the course of nine years, the ILC adopted the ARIO in 2011, which largely mirror and follow the structure of the

Articles on the Responsibility of States for Internationally Wrongful Acts (ARSIWA). Although the ARIO are largely considered non-binding and many critiques have been leveled at the methodology adopted in drafting the ARIO, its two-fold approach – *lex generalis* and *lex specialis* – provides a compelling analytical framework through which to consider the EU's responsibility. The ARIO provide for responsibility rules and presuppose that for responsibility to be established the IO is bound by international legal obligations. To address the EU's human rights responsibility *under international law*, these legal obligations are found in international human rights law, comprised of *jus cogens*, customary international law, treaty law and general principles.

To invoke EU responsibility under EU law and before the CJEU, a number of procedures are theoretically available. Protection against EU conduct may result in an action for annulment (Article 263 TFEU), an action for failure to act on behalf of the Union (Article 258 TFEU), a preliminary ruling on the validity and interpretation of EU law (Article 267 TFEU), or an action for damages (Article 268 TFEU *in juncto* Article 340 TFEU *in juncto* Article 41(3) CFR). Article 268 TFEU recalls that the (exclusive) competence to rule on EU responsibility is a prerogative of the CJEU. Mindful of the procedure-specific conditions and difficulties that arise for TCNs wishing to invoke EU responsibility for human rights violations, the most appropriate avenue to obtain redress – the so-called *lex specialis* governing the *conditions* for responsibility – is the action for damages embedded in Article 268 *in juncto* Article 340 TFEU. In addition to the (stringent) procedure-specific conditions inherent to the alternative direct actions and indirect action before the Court, the obligation to provide reparations for caused damages, will not be met by declaratory orders annulling or interpreting particular provisions or acts of EU law, as this would not place the individual in a position where the wrongs done would be at least partially remedied.[103] Consequently, the focus here will be on the EU-specific procedure that is functionally most analogous to international human rights procedures and most likely to yield the sought after reparations in case of human rights violations. Similarly to the international rules on responsibility of IOs embedded in the ARIO, these procedural rules under EU law must be complemented by EU human rights law to hold the EU legally responsible for its contributions to human rights harms.

Although these two regimes under international and EU law, adopt marginally different terminology, are binding (on the EU) to different degrees, and have developed differently, this does not detract from the fact that both regimes pursue the responsibility of the EU when considered simultaneously with the EU's human rights obligations under international *and* EU law. As human rights law purports to endow individuals with actionable rights vis-à-vis public actors, this integrated and four-tier analytical framework will be adopted in assessing the effectiveness of the EU's Human Rights Responsibility Regime in contesting harms contributed to in IBM in what follows.

[103] Angela Ward, 'Remedies under the EU Charter of Fundamental Rights' in Sionaidh Douglas-Scott and Nicholas Hatzis (eds), *Research Handbook on EU Law and Human Rights* (Cheltenham, Edward Elgar Publishing, 2017) 183–184.

Human rights responsibility can only be established under both international and EU law, insofar the EU (as a *sui generis* IO) is bound by certain human rights *obligations* (Chapter 3), which – through attributable conduct – it has violated, causing damage (Chapter 4). This section argues that the EU's Human Rights Responsibility Regime is riddled with incongruencies regarding its human rights obligations, as well as its responsibility rules, foiling access to an effective remedy for individuals afflicted by harmful EU human rights conduct in IBM.

3

Normative Incongruence: Human Rights Obligations of International Organisations and the EU

TO ANSWER THE question whether and how the EU can be held legally responsible for its contributions to human rights harms in IBM, it is indispensable to first determine the extent to which the EU is effectively bound by human rights *obligations*. From the very onset, it is crucial to underscore the difference between human rights *commitments* and the legally actionable human rights *obligations* that stem from such commitments. All too often this nuance is overlooked, and reference is made to human rights without making this distinction. For the purpose of this book, human rights 'commitments' refer to the norms embedded in human rights instruments, as well as customary international law, such as the commitment to the right to life, or the right to an effective remedy. Conversely, human rights 'obligations' refer to the actionable negative, positive, procedural and substantive legally enforceable obligations that flow from these (theoretical) commitments to ensure that those human rights may be respected, protected and fulfilled.[104]

This section argues that – unlike for Member States – there is 'normative incongruence' between the EU's human rights commitments on the one hand, and the EU's (positive, negative, procedural and substantive) human rights obligations on the other hand. Although the EU's human rights commitments are now well-established and stem from a variety of sources in international human rights law, as well as from its own constituent instruments, these human rights commitments have not yet been meaningfully translated into concrete human rights obligations. The absence of binding, concretised human rights obligations significantly complexifies any legal recourse by individuals seeking to assert a human rights violation against the EU, as developed below.

1. THE SOURCES OF EU HUMAN RIGHTS LAW

In theory, various international legal sources impose human rights commitments on the EU. However, the contemporary international human rights regime pays no

[104] Vladislava Stoyanova, *Positive Obligations under the European Convention on Human Rights – Within and Beyond Boundaries* (Oxford, Oxford University Press, 2023).

heed to the explicitly recognised functional and constitutional differences between States and international organisations. This is problematic as the contemporary human rights framework and ensuing articulation of concretised obligations, have traditionally developed to identify when *States* have failed to comply with negative, positive, procedural and substantive human rights obligations stemming from their respective human rights commitments. As States and IOs are entirely different subjects of international law by their very nature, it is hard to contend that these same concretized obligations can simply be transposed to and imposed on IOs *en masse*.[105] It is commonly accepted that human rights bind IOs to a certain degree,[106] and, at a minimum, that these rights include a negative obligation on the IO to abstain from actions that could compromise the fulfilment and effective enjoyment of those rights.[107] However, this does not clarify the legal obligations or implications of contributory negligence, or whether positive obligations would have to be adopted by the IO in respecting, fulfilling and protecting these human rights. This opaqueness affects TCNs seeking to enforce their human rights against the EU for its design and implementation of IBM. Mere recognition that the EU is bound by human rights norms (to varying degrees)[108] does not reveal much about its enforceability in a court or tribunal.

To determine to what extent the EU is bound by human rights generally, and the precise scope of the obligations emanating from such (binding) human rights commitments, the various *sources* of human rights law, must first be identified. IOs may be bound directly or indirectly by human rights norms due to the pre-existing obligations of its Members, due to general applicable international human rights law, and directly, through its own commitments to uphold international human rights law. Specifically, these obligations may be found in *jus cogens*, international human rights treaties to which an international organisation is party,[109] the pre-existing obligations

[105] This is also hinted at by Jan Klabbers, who holds that 'the discipline still lacks adequate theory concerning the basis of obligation for international organizations'. Jan Klabbers, *An Introduction to International Institutional Law* (Cambridge, Cambridge University Press, 2009) 284. See more generally: Jan Klabbers, 'International Organisations and the Quest for Accountability' in Malcolm Evans and Panos Koutrakos (eds), *The International Responsibility of the European Union: European and International Perspectives* (Oxford, Hart, 2013) 77.

[106] For an extensive discussion on the different sources of and degree to which international human rights law are binding on the EU and IOs generally, see: Joyce De Coninck, *Catch-22 in the Law of Responsibility of International Organizations : Systemic Deficiencies in the EU Responsibility Paradigm for Unlawful Human Rights Conduct in Integrated Border Management* (Ghent University, 2021) 62–86 biblio.ugent.be/publication/8721431.

[107] De Schutter appeared to be in favour of transposing only negative obligations under international human rights law. However, in the present work and in light of the highly integrated nature of the EU legal order, the argument is made that merely transposing the negative human rights obligations to the EU, is not sufficient in ensuring that the rights concerned are practical and effective rather than theoretical and illusory. Olivier De Schutter, 'Human Rights and the Rise of International Organizations: The Logic of Sliding Scales in Law of International Responsibility' in Jan Wouters and Eva Brems (eds), *Accountability for Human Rights Violations by International Organizations* (Cambridge, Intersentia, 2010) 128.

[108] De Schutter explains that a distinction must be made between whether an IO is effectively bound by human rights standards generally, and the precise *content* of those rights and standards. De Schutter n 107 at 54.

[109] International organizations may also conclude 'mixed agreements' – as does the European Union – for matters falling in part within the competence of the organization and in part within the competences of the State parties. However, the study of mixed agreements falls beyond the remit of the present research

that are binding upon the States, customary international law and/or general principles of international law.[110] In addition, the IO may be bound by human rights obligations through their own constituent instruments.

A *jus cogens* norm is defined as '*a norm accepted and recognized by the international community of states as a whole as a norm from which no derogation is permitted and which can be modified only by a subsequent norm of international law having the same character*'.[111] A limited number of norms have been defined as having attained the status of *jus cogens*, including the prohibition of genocide and slavery.[112] In addition, the argument has been advanced that the principle of *non-refoulement* has likewise attained the status of *jus cogens*,[113] which bears relevance in the present study as the *non-refoulement* principle is the human rights norm against which conduct of the EU is analysed.

States may not avoid adherence to *jus cogens* norms by hiding behind the veil of an IO and obligations stemming therefrom. However, this does not clarify the types of obligations flowing from *jus cogens* norms. The argument here is thus, that by virtue of the potential *jus cogens* nature of the *non-refoulement* principle, states and the EU as a subject of international law, are legally bound to respect it, and may not invoke international law to avoid compliance therewith. Yet, a distinction must be made here between *non-refoulement* as a human rights commitment that may not be violated, and the concrete negative and positive obligations, both procedural and substantive, that operationalise *jus cogens* norms. While the commitment to the *non-refoulement* principle may indeed be regarded as *jus cogens* (ie, an individual cannot be returned to the required threshold of ill-treatment), the concrete negative and positive obligations stemming from *non-refoulement* as such have not attained the status of *jus cogens*.[114]

and will not be discussed. See for a brief and general discussion: Moshe Hirsch, *The Responsibility of International Organizations Toward Third Parties: Some Basic Principles* (Martinus Nijhoff Publishers 1995) 19–26; Joni Heliskosi, 'Mixed Agreements: the EU Law Fundamentals' in Robert Schütze and Takis Tridimas (eds.) *Oxford Principles of European Union Law – Volume I: The European Union Legal Order* (Oxford University Press 2018) 1174–1207.

[110] Moshe Hirsch, The Responsibility of International Organizations Toward Third Parties: Some Basic Principles (Martinus Nijhoff Publishers 1995) 18, 31, 37.

[111] Article 53 VCLT.

[112] Christian J. Tams and Alessandra Asteriti, 'Erga Omnes, Jus Cogens and Their Impact on the Law of Responsibility' in Malcom Evans and Panos Koutrakos (eds.) *The International Responsibility of the European Union – European and International Perspectives* (Hart Publishing 2013) 163–164.

[113] ECtHR Concurring Opinion Judge Pinto De Albuquerque of 23 February 2012, *Hirsi Jamaa and others v Italy*, App no. 27765/09, §64 (and sources cited therein). See for a doctrinal discussion: Cathryn Costello and Michelle Foster, 'Non-refoulement as Custom and Jus Cogens? Putting the Prohibition to the Test' in Maarten den Heijer and Harmen van der Wilt (eds.) *Netherlands Yearbook of International Law 2015 – Jus Cogens: Quo Vadis?* (Springer 2016) 273–324; Roberta Mungianu, *Frontex and Non-refoulement – The International Responsibility of the EU* (Cambridge University Press 2016) 103.

[114] It may be interesting to note that if indeed, '2. *in certain cases, the practice of international organizations also contributes to the formation, or expression of rules of customary international law*', surely opposing practice by international organisations could detract from the customary status and *mutadis mutandis* from the *jus cogens* nature of rules of international law? See on the topic: Conclusion 4(2) – International Law Commission, 'Draft Conclusions on identification of customary international law with commentaries' (*ILC*, 2018) < https://legal.un.org/ilc/guide/1_13.shtml#fout > 130. See more generally on the development of *jus cogens* and customary international law in relation to international organizations: Fernando Lusa Bordin, *The Analogy between States and International Organizations* (Cambridge University Press 2018) 118–126.

Additionally, IOs including the EU, may be directly or indirectly bound through treaty law. Although accession by the EU to the ECHR is envisaged by Article 6 TEU[115] and Protocol 8 TFEU[116] and negotiations on the matter have recently restarted,[117] accession has not yet been achieved.[118] The EU is thus currently not party to international human rights treaties of a *generalist* nature concerning civil and political rights.[119] Additionally, while international human rights treaties theoretically offer ample sources to interpret human rights within the EU and may indirectly affect how the EU is bound by them, directly enforcing these norms to establish EU responsibility is more difficult. Indeed, there are a number of ways by which an IO may inherit international human rights obligations stemming from treaties to which Member States are signatories.[120] However, the means of inheriting such obligations does not necessarily have an immediate bearing on the self-executing nature of such norms, nor does it necessarily clarify the exact scope and concrete international human rights obligations that may be binding upon international organisations and the EU specifically. Accordingly, we run into the same issue as we did with respect to *jus cogens* norms: there is a discrepancy between being directly and indirectly bound by human rights treaty law, and how such commitments translate into concretised obligations of the EU that are justiciable in a court of law.

[115] '2. *The Union shall accede to the European Convention for the Protection of Human Rights and Fundamental Freedoms. Such accession shall not affect the Union's competences as defined in the Treaties.*' Article 6 TEU.

[116] This protocol sets out the additional conditions for EU accession to the ECHR. Protocol (No. 8) relating to Article 6(2) of the Treaty on European Union on the accession of the Union to the European Convention on the Protection of Human Rights and Fundamental Freedoms TFEU.

[117] Council of Europe, '6th Meeting of the CDDH Ad Hoc Negotiation Group ("47+1") on the Accession of the European Union to the European Convention on Human Rights' (*Council of Europe – Human Rights Intergovernmental Cooperation*, 22 October 2020) <https://www.coe.int/en/web/human-rights-intergovernmental-cooperation/accession-of-the-european-union-to-the-european-convention-on-human-rights>.

[118] In light of the infamous Opinion 2/13 it is uncertain when and if accession will effectively occur.

[119] The EU is currently bound by the Convention on the Rights of Persons with Disabilities, which it ratified on 23 December 2010. However, this convention is not of a general scope, and is instead limited *ratione materiae*. Interestingly, this specific human rights instrument (contrary to human rights treaties of a more general nature), includes a provision on the accession of 'regional integration organizations'. This provision limits the obligations for regional integration organisations under the Convention, to those matters falling within its competence. Article 44 United Nations, *Convention on the Rights of Persons with Disabilities*, [24 January 2007] A/RES/61/106 (*hereafter* UN Disabilities Convention). See also: Allan Rosas, 'Exclusive, Shared and National Competence in the Context of EU External Relations: Do Such Distinctions Matter?' in Inge Govaere, Erwan Lannon, Peter Van Elsuwege and Stanislas Adam (eds.) *The European Union in the World – Essays in Honour of Marc Maresceau* (Martinus Nijhoff Publishers 2014) 30.

[120] See among others: Moshe Hirsch, *The Responsibility of International Organizations Toward Third Parties: Some Basic Principles* (Martinus Nijhoff Publishers 1995) p 49; Frederik Naert, 'Binding International Organizations to Member State Treaties or Responsibility of Member States for their Own Actions in the Framework of International Organizations' in Jan Wouters and Eva Brems (eds.) *Accountability for Human Rights Violations by International Organizations* (Intersentia 2010) p 132; Olivier De Schutter, 'Human Rights and the Rise of International Organizations: The Logic of Sliding Scales in Law of International Responsibility' in Jan Wouters and Eva Brems (eds.) *Accountability for Human Rights Violations by International Organizations* (Intersentia 2010) 63; Henry G. Schermers, 'The European Communities Bound by Fundamental Human Rights' (1990) 27 Common Market Law Review, 249.

The general absence of treaty-based obligations does not relieve the EU from international human rights obligations altogether. The ICJ held in its *WHO Agreement* advisory opinion, that IOs may also be bound general rules of international law, including customary international human rights law, which may or may not have been codified in the abovementioned treaties.[121] This is likewise confirmed under EU law by the CJEU in the *Racke* case.[122] An international (human rights) norm will have attained the status of custom insofar as identifiable state practice has been established, which must be demonstrative of '*a belief that this practice is rendered obligatory by the existence of a rule of law requiring it*'[123] (*opinio juris*).[124] Within the particular context of human rights as customary international law, arguments have been advanced – which De Schutter references as the 'modern view of custom' – to adapt the traditional test of custom, to accord greater weight to authoritative instruments, such as for example resolutions of the UN General Assembly, official declarations, or participation in international human rights instruments as evidencing state practice or *opinio juris*.[125] Similarly, Special Rapporteur Sir Michael Wood noted in the preparations for the Draft Conclusions on the Identification of Customary International Law,[126] that regard should be had for the possibility of variations of the traditional conditions to establish custom.[127] Within a European human rights context, it has indeed been argued that there is a 'human rights method' to determining whether a norm has attained the status of customary international law, which implies that more emphasis is placed on the requirement of *opinio juris*, as opposed to state practice.[128]

[121] ICJ Advisory Opinion of 20 December 1980, *Interpretation of the Agreement of 25 March 1951 Between the WHO and Egypt*, §37. See also (and sources cited therein): Moshe Hirsch, *The Responsibility of International Organizations Toward Third Parties: Some Basic Principles* (Martinus Nijhoff Publishers 1995) 31.

[122] CJEU Judgment of 16 June 1998, *Racke v Hauptzollamt Mainz*, C-162/96, ECLI:EU:C:1998:293, §51.

[123] ICJ Judgment of 20 February 1969, *North Sea Continental Shelf Case (Federal Republic of Germany v Netherlands)* §77.

[124] ibid. See also: ILC, 'First Report on Formation and Evidence of Customary International Law by Mr. Sir Michael Wood, Special Rapporteur' (UN Doc. A/CN.4/663) 17–25 July 2013; ILC, 'Second Report on Identification of Customary International Law by Mr. Sir Michael Wood, Special Rapporteur' (UN Doc. A/CN.4/672) 11–18 July 2014.

[125] Olivier De Schutter, 'Human Rights and the Rise of International Organizations: The Logic of Sliding Scales in Law of International Responsibility' in Jan Wouters and Eva Brems (eds.) *Accountability for Human Rights Violations by International Organizations* (Intersentia 2010) 68–70.

[126] International Law Commission, 'Draft Conclusions on identification of customary international law with commentaries' (*ILC*, 2018) < https://legal.un.org/ilc/guide/1_13.shtml#fout >.

[127] ILC, 'First Report on Formation and Evidence of Customary International Law by Mr. Sir Michael Wood, Special Rapporteur' (UN Doc. A/CN.4/663) 17–25 July 2013, §19. However, this was not adopted in the final 'Draft conclusions on identification of customary international law'. See comment 4 to conclusion 2, International Law Commission, 'Draft Conclusions on identification of customary international law with commentaries' (*ILC*, 2018) < https://legal.un.org/ilc/guide/1_13.shtml#fout >. The draft conclusions do elaborate however, in conclusion 10 and 12, on what type of evidence may be consulted to determine whether the requirements of the (maintained) traditional test have been met.

[128] The lack of state practice, which is evidenced *inter alia* by (purported) violations of fundamental rights, is not necessarily indicative of whether a human rights norm has or has not acquired the status of custom. Anne van Aaken, Iulia Motoc and Johann Justus Vasel, 'The European Convention on Human Rights and General International Law' in Anne van Aaken and Iulia Motoc (eds.) *The European Convention on Human Rights and General International Law* (Oxford University Press 2018) 6–7; Ineta Ziemele, 'European Consensus and International Law' in Anne van Aaken and Iulia Motoc (eds.) *The European Convention on Human Rights and General International Law* (Oxford University Press 2018) p. 23–40.

Regardless of the approach adopted in determining whether a human rights norm has acquired the status of custom, it is generally accepted that the predominant rights relevant to IBM, such as the right to life, the prohibition of *refoulement*, the right to liberty and the right to an effective remedy, have attained the status of custom.[129]

However, as was the case with the rights and obligations derived from treaties, the mere acknowledgment that a human right constitutes custom and thus *binds* the IO does not necessarily reveal much about the scope and concrete obligations that may be imposed on the organisation for it to comply with the norm. In addition, similarly to treaty-based human rights obligations, the binding nature of the norm does not necessarily mean that it can be directly invoked by individual applicants in a court of law. Rosas[130] and Moreno-Lax point out that the criteria to establish direct effect of a customary norm have been interpreted more stringently by the CJEU, due to the fact that '*a principle of customary international law does not have the same degree of precision as a provision of an international agreement*' as a result of which '*judicial review must necessarily be limited to the question whether, in adopting the act in question, the institutions of the European Union made manifest errors of assessment concerning the conditions for applying those principles*'.[131] Consequently, the path of customary international law, does not – besides acknowledging the binding nature of such international human rights on the EU – help identify what concrete obligations flow from such binding norms.

General principles also constitute a key (constitutive, albeit secondary) source of international human rights obligations in the EU legal order.[132] These principles are distilled from '*common rules drawn from the major legal systems of the world, which are appropriate for application in the international community*'.[133] In addition to the foregoing sources of international human rights obligations, general principles of international and European law are frequently invoked as a means to ensure the protection of fundamental rights. This is evidenced by the ICJ's use thereof in its case law, such as the *Tehran Hostages* case, where it recalled that the provisions of the UDHR constitute '*fundamental principles*'.[134]

[129] See generally: Bruno Simma and Philip Alston, 'The Sources of Human Rights Law: Custom, Jus Cogens, and General Principles' (1992) 12 The Australian Yearbook of International Law, 82–108.

[130] Allan Rosas, 'International Responsibility of the EU and the ECJ' in Malcom Evans and Panos Koutrakos (eds.) *The International Responsibility of the European Union – European and International Perspectives* (Hart Publishing 2013) 158.

[131] CJEU Judgment of 21 December 2011, *ATAA and others v Secretary of State for Energy and Climate*, C-366/10, ECLI:EU:C:2011:864, §110; CJEU Judgment 3 June 2008, *The Queen, on the application of International Association of Independent Tanker Owners (Intertanko) and Others v Secretary of State for Transport*, C-308/06, ECLI:EU:C:2008:312, §51; CJEU Judgment of 16 June 1998, *A. Racke GmbH & Co. v Hauptzollamt Mainz*, C-162/96, ECLI:EU:C: 1998:293, §45–46; CJEU Judgment of 24 November 1992, *Anklagemyndigheden v Peter Michael Poulsen and Diva Navigation Corp*, C-286/90, ECLI:EU:C:1992:453; §9–10. See also: Violeta Moreno-Lax, *Accessing Asylum in Europe: Extraterritorial Border Controls and Refugee Rights under EU Law* (Oxford University Press 2017) 212.

[132] Article 6(3) TEU.

[133] Moshe Hirsch, *The Responsibility of International Organizations Toward Third Parties: Some Basic Principles* (Martinus Nijhoff Publishers 1995) 37.

[134] ICJ Judgment of 24 May 1980, *Case Concerning United States Diplomatic and Consular Staff in (United States of America v. Iran)* §92. See also (and the cases cited therein): Olivier De Schutter, 'Human Rights and the Rise of International Organizations: The Logic of Sliding Scales in Law of International Responsibility' in Jan Wouters and Eva Brems (eds.) *Accountability for Human Rights Violations by International Organizations* (Intersentia 2010) 71–73.

Akin to these developments under international law, the CJEU developed the doctrine of general principles of EU law, in an attempt to integrate fundamental rights into the EU legal order. This judge-developed conceptualisation of fundamental rights initially sought to appease (German) constitutional concerns with respect to the supremacy of the EU legal order. It has also been regarded as a means to legitimise EU action, as opposed to being an independent objective of the Union.[135] In addition, these principles operated and continue to operate as a means of '*negative integration*', whereby they are seen as a means of constitutional constraint on behalf of the EU, limiting its actions and preventing a '*competence creep*'.[136] Eventually, the CJEU's case law on the matter was constitutionalised by the incorporation of general principles of EU law as a source of human rights obligations in Article F Treaty of Maastricht, and Article 6(3) TEU, which holds that '*Fundamental rights as guaranteed by the ECHR and as they result from the constitutional traditions common to the Member States, shall constitute general principles of the Union's law*'.[137] In view of the now legally binding Charter of Fundamental Rights, the question has been posed whether these general principles have lost their value in the EU legal order. Douglas-Scott argues that this is not the case in light of the fact that reference to general principles as a source of international human rights law allows for reference to be made to conceptualisations and interpretations of human rights that do not necessarily fall within the ambit of the ECHR and/or the CFR.[138] Despite the well-developed body of case law on both an international and European Union level, concerning human rights as a general principles, the extent to which these norms impose concrete obligations upon international organisations, again, remains unclear.

Although the EU's human rights commitments are inspired and informed by international human rights law and the common constitutional traditions of the EU Member States, these sources predominantly establish the EU's human rights *commitments*. Conversely, these sources do not establish the negative, positive, procedural and substantive obligations that make those commitments actionable in

[135] Takis Tridimas, 'Competence, Human Rights, and Asylum: What Price Mutual Recognition', in Sacha Garben and Inge Govaere (eds.) *The Division of Competences Between the EU and the Member States – Reflections on the Past, the Present and the Future* (Hart Publishing 2017) 152; Sionaidh Douglas-Scott, 'The European Union and Fundamental Rights' in Robert Schütze and Takis Tridimas (eds.) *Oxford Principles of European Union Law – Volume I: The European Union Legal Order* (OUP 2018) 384. Douglas-Scott rightfully points out however, that the legitimisation of Union action was not the sole objective pursued by the integration of human rights as general principles of EU law. The economic integration project, and the pursued peace across the region as a direct response to the atrocities of World War II could not be achieved without acknowledging the need for individual rights protection.

[136] Takis Tridimas, 'Competence, Human Rights, and Asylum: What Price Mutual Recognition', in Sacha Garben and Inge Govaere (eds.) *The Division of Competences Between the EU and the Member States – Reflections on the Past, the Present and the Future* (Hart Publishing 2017) 152.

[137] Sionaidh Douglas-Scott, 'The European Union and Fundamental Rights' in Robert Schütze and Takis Tridimas (eds.) *Oxford Principles of European Union Law – Volume I: The European Union Legal Order* (OUP 2018) 407.

[138] Arguably the effect of this would be limited in view of the extensiveness of the CFR. Sionaidh Douglas-Scott, 'The European Union and Fundamental Rights' in Robert Schütze and Takis Tridimas (eds.) *Oxford Principles of European Union Law – Volume I: The European Union Legal Order* (OUP 2018) 390, 413.

a court of law. Normative incongruence thus arises because of the schism between the normative commitment on the one hand and the absence of rules that can operationalise these commitments on the other hand. With the advent of the EU's own catalogue of human rights, some considered that this opaqueness would be remedied.[139]

2. THE EU'S CHARTER OF FUNDAMENTAL RIGHTS

As recalled by Advocate General Sharpston in *Ruiz Zambrano* before the CJEU, the Court 'is not, as such, a "human rights court"'.[140] Similarly, the EU was not (originally) a human rights actor.[141] The EU was initially understood to facilitate economic integration and focused on the creation of a common market, as a response to and to prevent the atrocities that preceded it.[142] Protection of human rights was largely absent in this first phase of integration, unlike the Council of Europe and its ECHR which developed in parallel, and where human rights protection was the sole 'core' objective.[143] The integration of human rights protection in the EU legal order was an incremental and quirky process,[144] resulting in respect for human rights as a foundational value since the Treaty of Maastricht.[145] Its incremental inclusion stems from – among others – the need to legitimise EU action politically and to appease (e.g., German[146]) constitutional concerns with respect to the supremacy of EU law,[147]

[139] Joseph H H Weiler, 'A Constitution for Europe? Some Hard Choices' (2002) 40 *Journal of Common Market Studies* 4, 563–580.

[140] Opinion of Advocate General Sharpston of 30 September 2010, *Gerardo Ruiz Zambrano v Office national de l'emploi*, C-34/09, ECLI:EU:C:2010:560, §155.

[141] Gráinne de Búrca, 'The Road Not Taken: The EU as a Global Human Rights Actor' (2017) 105 *American Journal of International Law* 4, 649–693.

[142] Sybe A de Vries, 'The Charter of Fundamental Rights and the EU's "Creeping" Competences: Does the Charter have a Centrifugal Effect for Fundamental Rights in the EU?' in Sionaidh Douglas-Scott and Nicholas Hatzis (eds), *Research Handbook on EU Law and Human Rights* (Cheltenham, Edward Elgar Publishing Limited, 2019) 59.

[143] Opinion Sharpston 2010, *Zambrano* n 140 at §153–154; Paul Craig and Gráinne de Búrca, *EU Law: Texts, Cases and Materials (7th edition)* (Oxford, Oxford University Press, 2020) 416. See earlier work concerning human rights in the EU: Pierre Pescatore, 'The Context and Significance of Fundamental Rights in the Law of the European Communities' (1981) 2 *Human Rights Law Journal*, 295–308; Pierre Pescatore, 'Fundamental Rights and Freedoms in the System of the European Communities' (1970) 18 *American Journal of Comparative Law*, 343–351.

[144] Bill Davies, '*Internationale Handelsgesellschaft* and the Miscalculation at the Inception of the ECJ's Human Rights Jurisprudence' in Fernanda Nicola and Bill Davies (eds), *EU Law Stories* (Cambridge, Cambridge University Press, 2017) 157–177.

[145] Article F(2) Treaty of Maastricht held specifically that, 'The Union shall respect fundamental rights, as guaranteed by the European Convention for the Protection of Human Rights and Fundamental Freedoms … as they result from the constitutional traditions common to the Member States, as general principles of Community law'. See also: Christoph Grabenwarter and Katharina Pabel, 'Article 6: Fundamental Rights – The Charter and the ECHR' in Hermann-Josef Blanke and Stelio Mangiameli (eds), *The Treaty on European Union (TEU) – A Commentary* (New York, Springer, 2013) 289.

[146] CJEU Judgment of 17 December 1970, *Internationale Handelsgesellschaft mbH v Einfuhr- und Vorratsstelle für Getreide und Futtermittel*, C- 11/70, ECLI:EU:C:1970:114.

[147] Davies n 144.

when EU norms were considered to be in tension with Member State constitutional provisions.[148]

Another significant milestone in human rights integration in the EU-*acquis* was prompted by the entry into force of the Treaty of Lisbon on 1 December 2009, following which Article 6 TEU accorded the same legal status to the CFR as the EU's Treaties and following which the European Union became the first IO to provide human rights protection against its own conduct.[149] By virtue of Article 51 CFR, the CFR is binding not only on the Member States, but also – unlike other IOs – upon the EU. This is notable as human rights treaties are typically addressed to states and do not typically identify IOs as their addressees, nor do they foresee in accession thereto by IOs. Hence, the fact that the Charter explicitly notes that its provisions are binding on the EU, as well as the 'institutions, bodies, offices and agencies of the Union' is rather unique and novel.[150] Its unique nature is underscored all the more by Article 41(3) CFR which holds that 'Every person has the right to have the Community make good any damage caused by its institutions or by its servants in the performance of their duties, in accordance with the general principles common to the laws of the Member States'. Unlike other IOs, the CFR thus not only imposes binding human rights commitments on the EU's institutions, bodies, offices and agencies, but explicitly holds the EU to make good any damage it gives rise to in the implementation of its powers.[151]

a. Charter Idiosyncrasies

The Charter functions explicitly as a binding source of EU human rights law, against which (legislative) EU conduct and Member State conduct may be tested.[152]

[148] Georges Vallindas, 'The Role of the Court of Justice in the Legitimation of the EU's Action: The Transparency Principle Example' in Sacha Garben, Inge Govaere and Paul Nemitz (eds), *Critical Reflections on Constitutional Democracy in the European Union* (Oxford, Hart, 2019) 225; Takis Tridimas, 'Competence, Human Rights and Asylum: What Price Mutual Recognition' in Sacha Garben and Inge Govaere (eds), *The Division of Competences Between the EU and the Member States – Reflections on the Past, the Present and the Future* (Oxford, Hart, 2017) 152; Moreno-Lax n 17 at 207; Grabenwarter and Pabel n 145 at 290; Giacomo Di Federico, 'Fundamental Rights in the EU: Legal Pluralism and Multi-Level Protection After the Lisbon Treaty' in Giacomo Di Federico (ed), *The EU Charter of Fundamental Rights – From Declaration to Binding Instrument* (New York, Springer, 2011) 19; Ola Zetterquist, 'The Charter of Fundamental Rights and the European *Res Publica*' in Giacomo Di Federico (ed), *The EU Charter of Fundamental Rights – From Declaration to Binding Instrument* (New York, Springer, 2011) 5.

[149] Koen Lenaerts, 'Exploring the Limits of the EU Charter of Fundamental Rights' (2012) 8 *European Constitutional Law Review* 376; Zetterquist, n 148 at 7; Grabenwarter and Pabel n 145 at 289.

[150] Article 51 CFR.

[151] The Explanations to the Charter indicate that Article 41(3) CFR sought to replicate the provisions on the EU's action for damages. Paul Craig, 'Article 41' in Steve Peers, Tamara Hervey, Jeff Kenner, Angela Ward (eds), *The EU Charter of Fundamental Rights: A Commentary* (London, Bloomsbury, 2021) 1130–1131. See also: Melanie Fink, Clara Rauchegger and Joyce De Coninck, 'The Action for Damages as a Fundamental Rights Remedy' in Melanie Fink (ed), *Redressing Fundamental Rights Violations by the EU: The Promise of the 'Complete System of Remedies'* (Cambridge, Cambridge University Press, 2024) *forthcoming*.

[152] Grabenwarter and Pabel n 145 at 300–301.

In enforcing the CFR, a distinction is made between rights (also referred to as freedoms) and principles.[153] The distinction is relevant as it indicates whether further implementing measures should be taken by the Member States.[154] Whereas the Charter rights – which are of a civil, political and social nature – must be respected,[155] the principles enshrined in the CFR 'do not however give rise to direct claims for positive action by the Union's institutions or Member State authorities',[156] rendering legal review of compliance with Charter-specific principles somewhat more difficult.[157] In addition, the Charter is characterised by a number of idiosyncrasies, differentiating it from other – more traditional and 'state-centric'-human rights instruments.

i. Competence-Constrained Charter Rights

Unlike most international human rights instruments, the Charter aggregates and protects a whole range of rights of a civil, political, social, collective and even digital nature.[158] This expansive and inclusive approach to human rights provisions in the Charter may generate the idea that the EU thus has wide regulatory powers in fulfilling these human rights commitments. However, the principle of conferral entails that the EU is only authorised to act if it has been granted the powers and authorisation by the Member States to do so.[159] As far as the Charter is concerned, it has been repeatedly confirmed and emphasised that the entry into force of the Charter and its provisions do not extend the powers that the EU has received from the EU Member States through its constituent treaties.[160] This means that the Charter does not confer new regulatory powers on the EU to act, nor does it provide with a general power to pursue human rights protection.[161] The explicit and consistent reaffirmation of the need to respect the conferred competences as enshrined in

[153] ibid 305.

[154] Comment 8 to Article 52, Explanations to the Charter.

[155] Zetterquist, n 148 at 73.

[156] Comment 8 to Article 52, Explanations to the Charter.

[157] Grabenwarter and Pabel n 145 at 305. In the current analysis, the normative base against which EU action is tested, is the *non-refoulement* principle (textually, yet wrongfully identified as a 'principle' for the purpose of the categorisation in the CFR), which does give rise to such positive action.

[158] Zetterquist n 148 at 12–13. Notably, the American Convention on Human Rights protects different categories of human rights.

[159] Article 4(1) TEU: 'competences not conferred upon the Union in the Treaties remain with the Member States'. Article 5 TEU: '1. The limits of Union competences are governed by the principle of conferral. The use of Union competences is governed by the principles of subsidiarity and proportionality. 2. Under the principle of conferral, the Union shall act only within the limits of the competences conferred upon it by the Member States in the Treaties to attain the objectives set out therein. Competences not conferred upon the Union in the Treaties remain with the Member States'.

[160] Various references to this limitation include: Article 6(1)(2) TEU; Article 51(2) CFR; Declaration No.1 concerning the CFR. See also: Lenaerts n 149 at 377; Angela Ward, 'Art. 51' in Steve Peers, Tamara Hervey, Jeff Kenner, Angela Ward (eds), *The EU Charter of Fundamental Rights: A Commentary* (London, Bloomsbury, 2014) 1413.

[161] Article 51(2) CFR. See also: CJEU Opinion of 28 March 1996, *Accession by the Community to the European Convention for the Protection of Human Rights and Fundamental Freedoms*, Opinion 2/94, ECLI:EU:C:1996:140, §27; Fink, Rauchegger and De Coninck n 151.

Article 5(2) TEU,[162] underscores Member States' concern that the Charter may trigger and perpetuate a competence creep by the EU.[163] While De Vries argues that this competence creep has already occurred and continues to occur, Advocate General Sharpston argues that the potential for a competence creep is extremely limited as firstly, the Charter regulates the relationships between the EU and Member States vis-à-vis individuals, and not the relationship between the EU and its Member States.[164] Furthermore, the Charter regulates and *constrains* conduct, but does not provide a legal basis to act, nor does it create any new rights.[165] The latter view is shared by Tridimas, who argues that the human rights embedded in the Charter set limits to the EU legislators' ability to act, rather than provide a legal basis to adopt new measures.[166] The discussion on whether a competence creep has occurred in violation of the principle of conferral, however, bears little relevance *in casu*. In the discussion on whether the EU as an IO can be held responsible for internationally wrongful acts, it is irrelevant whether the acts occurred in conformity with the rules of the organisation or, rather, whether the acts constituted *ultra vires* actions. In other words, even if an EU representative, institution or agency had acted outside the bounds of the conferred competence, the act would theoretically remain reviewable.[167]

As a necessary corollary to the foregoing, the provisions embedded in the Charter are not self-standing.[168] In other words, a Charter provision cannot be invoked independently of (other provisions of) EU law,[169] and unlike (traditional) international human rights instruments, the Charter will only be triggered insofar EU law is called into question. The means that the protection offered by the Charter does not operate in a legal vacuum and can only be invoked in tandem with other provisions of EU law.[170]

[162] Lenaerts n 149 at 377.

[163] De Vries n 142 at 60, 59–60, 73–74; Grabenwarter and Pabel n 145 at 307; Lenaerts n 149 at 376.

[164] Grabenwarter and Pabel n 145 at 303.

[165] How this limitation in the Charter is interpreted is of crucial relevance in the development of a positive obligations doctrine for the provisions the Charter protects. The CJEU has incrementally and in a limited manner, permitted a departure from a textual interpretation of Article 51 CFR in *Max Planck* and *Bauer*, by affirming horizontal direct effect for certain Charter provisions, despite the CFR being addressed (textually) to the EU and its Member States. The argument is made here, that despite the absence of clearly identifiable positive obligations in the Charter provisions directed at the EU, its bodies, offices, institutions and agencies, such obligations are inherent to its provisions and as such, *without extending the conferred competences by the Member States*.

[166] Tridimas n 148 at 153. Precisely here lies the tension though: the CFR does not authorize to act and merely constrains but does it prohibit to act sectorally where the EU has acquired competences? If the CFR truly prohibited taking positive action, it would bar the EU legislator in adopting human rights provisions within the sphere of its competence and thus form an impediment thereupon. It would additionaly make it implausible that more extensive protection in line with Art. 52(3) CFR would ever granted.

[167] Article 7 ARIO. Ultra vires conduct may give rise to other direct actions such as the action for annulment. Such proceedings may subsequently impact actions for damages, but in and of themselves do not necessarily give rise to reparations.

[168] CJEU (Grand Chamber) Judgment of 26 February 2013, *Åkerberg Fransson*, C-617/10, ECLI:EU:C:2013:105, §20–21. See also: Craig and de Búrca n 143 at 441; Ward n 160 at 1425–1426.

[169] De Vries n 142 at 65–71, 82–83.

[170] ibid.

ii. Functions of the Charter

The Charter as a 'multi-layered canvas of fundamental rights protection'[171] fulfils three functions.[172] It provides initial insights on how human rights must be interpreted and applied in the EU legal order.[173] Secondly, it functions as a source of authority for the identification and acknowledgement of general principles of EU law, drawing inspiration from a multitude of national and international sources.[174] Finally, and most importantly, the Charter facilitates legal review of EU (legislative) conduct, as well as Member State conduct within the realm of EU law, against the standards in the Charter.[175] This constitutional-like shift was noticeable in case law from the onset, as in the same month of the entry into force of the Charter, the CJEU already referred in its case law solely to the CFR as a source of human rights law.[176] In the *Kücükdeveci* judgment in 2010, the CJEU furthermore explicitly reaffirmed the legal status of the CFR, following which, two strands of case law concerning human rights by the CJEU can be discerned.[177] First, there is the case law concerning human rights compliance by Member States implementing EU law (including implementation of substantive EU provisions, measures derogating from EU law and measures that fall within the scope of EU law).[178] Second, there is the strand of case law concerning the validity of EU secondary legislation, which arguably confirms the (high) standard followed by the CJEU in invalidating secondary legislation on account of not complying with the safeguards enshrined in the CFR.[179] Concerning the latter, the Charter functions as a tool of 'constitutional constraint' by setting limits to what the EU (legislator) can do.[180]

iii. Interpreting the Charter

In interpreting the scope of application of the rights and principles incorporated in the Charter, the horizontal provisions enshrined in Articles 51–54 must

[171] Tridimas n 148 at 153.
[172] Lenaerts n 149 at 375.
[173] ibid.
[174] De Vries n 142 at 75.
[175] The Explanations to the Charter and the CJEU explain that the fundamental rights protection offered by the CFR functions as a constraint on EU and EU Member State conduct, albeit subject to the caveat that such protection cannot come at the expense of the primacy, unity, and effectiveness of EU law or the autonomy of EU law. See CJEU Opinion of 18 December 2014, *Opinion 2/13*, ECLI:EU:C: 2014:2454, §188. See also: Article 52(3) and Article 53 Explanations to the CFR.
[176] The reference concerned the rights of the child as protected by Article 24 CFR. CJEU Judgment of 23 December 2009, *Easna Detiček v Maurizio Sgueglia*, C-403/09 PPU, ECLI:EU:C:2009:810, §6, 53. Zetterquist n 148 at 7.
[177] CJEU Judgment of 19 January 2010, *Seda Kücükdeveci v Swedex GmbH & Co. KG*, C-555/07, ECLI:EU:C:2010:21 §22; Grabenwarter and Pabel n 145 at 292–294.
[178] See inter alia: CJEU Judgment of 5 October 2010, *J. McB. V L.E.*, C-400/10 PPU, ECLI:EU:C:2010:582, §45; Grabenwarter and Pabel n 145 at 292–294.
[179] For case law by the CJEU concerning compliance of EU secondary legislation with Charter provisions, see inter alia: CJEU (Grand Chamber) Judgment of 9 November 2010, *Volker and Markus Schecke and Eifert*, Joined Cases C-92/09 and C-93/09, ECLI:EU:C:2010:662.
[180] Tridimas n 148 at 153.

be considered. These provisions identify which entities are bound by the Charter, namely Member States when implementing EU law, as well as EU institutions, bodies, offices and agencies.[181] In addition, Article 52(1) CFR provides the legal standard that must be respected for a limitation or derogation of a Charter provision to be justified and permissible.[182] Article 52 CFR furthermore briefly delineates the dynamic between the Charter and national and international human rights provisions. Article 53 CFR elaborates upon the latter by holding that nothing in the Charter 'shall be interpreted as restricting or adversely affecting human rights and fundamental freedoms as recognised, in their respective fields of application, by Union law, international law, by international agreements to which the Union or all the Member States are party, including the European Convention for the Protection of Human Rights and Fundamental Freedoms, and by the Member States' constitutions. Finally, Article 54 CFR contains an anti-abuse clause and holds that nothing in the Charter shall be understood as permitting an interpretation or application of the Charter aimed at circumventing its rights and principles.

In addition to these normative guidelines, Article 6(1) TEU sets forth that 'the rights, freedoms and principles in the Charter shall be interpreted … with due regard to the explanations referred to in the Charter, that set out the sources of those provisions'. This is furthermore echoed and repeated in Article 52(7) CFR and in a number of cases before the CJEU.[183] Although the Explanations are considered as an inventory of the pluralist sources that inform the Charter,[184] as well as an authoritative guide for the interpretation and application of the Charter, it has been repeatedly underscored that they are not legal by nature and thus not enforceable in a strict sense.[185] Arguably, however, the principle of legal certainty justifies *consistent* due regard for the interpretative guidelines in the Explanations, which is furthermore amplified by the fact that the Praesidium of the Convention – the drafters of the CFR – drafted the interpretative Explanations.[186]

[181] Article 51 CFR. In a select number of cases, horizontal direct effect of Charter provisions has been recognised by the CJEU (see above).

[182] See for a discussion: Steve Peers and Sacha Prechal, 'Art. 52 – Scope of Guaranteed Rights' in Steve Peers, Tamara Hervey, Jeff Kenner, Angela Ward (eds.) *The EU Charter of Fundamental Rights: A Commentary* (London, Bloomsbury, 2014) 1461–1486.

[183] See, inter alia: CJEU Judgment of 15 February 2016, *JN v Staatssecretaris van Veiligheid en Justitie*, C-601/15 PPU, ECLI:EU:C:2016:84 §21; CJEU (Grand Chamber) 2013, *Åkerberg Fransson* n 138 at §20; CJEU (Grand Chamber) Judgment of 21 December 2011, *NS v Secretary of State for the Home Department and ME and Others v Refugee Applications Commissioner and Minister for Justice, Equality and Law Reform*, C-411/10 and C-493/10, ECLI:EU:C:2011:865, §119.

[184] See for an extensive discussion: Jean-Paul Jacqué 'The Explanations Relating to the Charter of Fundamental Rights of the European Union' in Steve Peers, Tamara Hervey, Jeff Kenner and Angela Ward (eds), *The EU Charter of Fundamental Rights: A Commentary* (London, Bloomsbury, 2014) 1715–1724.

[185] See Preamble, Explanations to the Charter: 'Although they do not as such have the status of law, they are a valuable tool of interpretation intended to clarify the provisions of the Charter'.

[186] Jacqué n 184 at 1715–1718; Grabenwarter and Pabel n 145 at 308.

b. The Idiosyncratic Relationship of the EU with the ECHR

A unique aspect of human rights protection in the European Union, concerns the dynamic between the EU system of human rights protection and that of the Council of Europe. In the aftermath of World War II, the Council of Europe adopted its European Convention of Human Rights, codifying a number of civil and political rights and freedoms and considered to be an enforceable translation of the Universal Declaration of Human Rights. In parallel, the first steps towards European economic integration were being taken. Initially, the European Coal and Steel Community and the European Economic Community had the development of a common market through economic integration as a core objective.[187] Hence, no references concerning the respect for human rights were to be found in the respective treaties, nor in the case law resulting therefrom.[188] In fact, Smismans argues that the retroactive and *post-factum* assertion that human rights were always inherent to the economic integration project, is flawed and unsubstantiated at best.[189] Rather, Member States initially rejected the idea of embedding human rights in its constituent documents, and the CJEU demonstrated apathy, if not opposition towards the protection of fundamental rights in the case of *Stork* and the case *Sgarlata and others*.[190] Others argue that human rights have always been inherently connected to the economic integration project, and that the CJEU itself was responsible for the early recognition of fundamental rights in the EU legal order,[191] in addition to certain treaty provisions and legislative acts that were considered to have a human rights dimension, particularly in the realm of equal opportunities and employment law.[192] Nevertheless, it is clear that human rights protections developed in parallel under both regimes from the very early days. Member States of the European Community were bound by the EU's general principles concerning human rights, as clarified by the CJEU, while at the same time being bound by the ECHR and the ensuing interpretations by the ECtHR. It was clear from the onset that the substantive parallelism or correspondence between the rights embedded in the ECHR and the rights protected through the then European Community framework, could give rise to potential norm conflicts, as the

[187] Craig and de Búrca n 143 at 416–417; Annabel Egan and Laurent Pech, 'Respect for Human Rights as a General Objective of the EU's External Action' in Sionaidh Douglas-Scott and Nicholas Hatzis (eds), *Research Handbook on EU Law and Human Rights* (Cheltenham, Edward Elgar Publishing Limited, 2019) 243. See also: de Búrca n 11.

[188] Craig and de Búrca n 143 at 424; de Búrca n 141 at 649–650.

[189] Stijn Smismans, 'Fundamental Rights as a Political Myth of the EU: Can the Myth Survive?' in Sionaidh Douglas-Scott and Nicholas Hatzis (eds), *Research Handbook on EU Law and Human Rights* (Cheltenham, Edward Elgar Publishing Limited, 2019) 18. CJEU Judgment of 1 April 1965, *Marcello Sgarlata and others v Commission of the EEC*, C-40/64, 227; CJEU Judgment of 4 February 1959, *Friedrich Stork & Cie v High Authority of the European Coal and Steel Community*, C-1/58, ECLI:EU:C:1959:4, 28.

[190] Craig and de Búrca n 143 at 417, Smismans n 189 at 18.

[191] Opinion Sharpston 2010, *Zambrano* n 140 at §153–154. See more generally on the role of the CJEU in the integration of fundamental rights in the EU legal order: Antonio Tizzano, 'The Role of the ECJ in the Protection of Fundamental Rights' in Anthony Arnull, Piet Eeckhout and Takis Tridimas (eds), *Continuity and Change in EU Law: Essays in Honour of Francis Jacobs* (Oxford, Oxford University Press, 2008); Francis Jacobs, 'Human Rights in the European Union: The Role of the Court of Justice' (2001) 26 *European Law Review*; Davies n 144 at 157.

[192] Craig and de Búrca n 143 at 416; De Vries n 142 at 64.

CJEU would inevitably be tasked with balancing the objective European (economic) integration with the protection of human rights, in a manner that exceeds what the ECtHR is tasked to balance.

From the onset, it was also clear that the concurrent applicability of the Charter and the ECHR to the same Member States, would require special attention.[193] This is particularly so because Member States remain bound by the ECHR and ensuing case law, notwithstanding the executive federalist structure of the Union[194] and the inability to directly review conduct by the EU, bodies, agencies and offices, as well as its representatives before an external human rights court such as the ECtHR.[195] Elaborating in full on this relationship, goes beyond the ambit of this project. In what follows, the most crucial points of this relationship are discussed, focusing particularly on the jurisprudential relationship between the ECtHR and the CJEU, as well as the willingness of the Strasbourg Court as an external human rights adjudicator, to review EU conduct. Generally, the relationship between the EU and the ECHR and their respective courts, has been described as being one of 'coherence and comity', whereby the necessity to ensure consistency between human rights protection in the realm of the Council of Europe and human rights protection in the realm of the EU (in line with Article 52(3) CFR) is underscored.[196] Furthermore, in line with a more general practice, the Strasbourg Court has generally refrained from ruling, or dismissed actions that were (in-)directly directed at international organisations generally and the EU specifically (see *infra*).[197] This relationship was arguably affected by two pivotal events, of which the effects are still felt today. On the one hand there was the aforementioned Lisbon Treaty, which brought with it the entry into force of the much-heralded Charter (see above) and on the other hand there was the highly controversial Opinion 2/13 concerning the accession of the European Union to the ECHR, delivered by the CJEU on 18 December 2014, as briefly discussed below.

i. An Emerging Relationship

There is a notable number of shifts in the (jurisprudential) relationship between the EU's CJEU and the ECtHR prior to and following the entry into force of the Treaty of Lisbon.[198] Prior to its entry into force, the relationship between both Courts underwent a number of different phases whereby at times the Courts cooperated – albeit not always directly – and at other times the Courts appeared to take a rather

[193] Tobias Lock, 'The EU Before the European Court of Human Rights After Accession' in Sionaidh Douglas-Scott and Nicholas Hatzis (eds), *Research Handbook on EU Law and Human Rights* (Cheltenham, Edward Elgar Publishing Limited, 2019) 226.

[194] ibid 229.

[195] Fink n 27 at 87; Sionaidh Douglas-Scott, 'The Relationship Between the EU and the ECHR Five Years on from the Treaty of Lisbon' in Sybe de Vries, Ulf Bernitz and Stephen Weatherill (eds), *The EU Charter of Fundamental Rights as a Binding Instrument: Five Years Old and Growing* (Oxford, Hart, 2015) 22.

[196] Moreno-Lax n 17 at 228.

[197] ECtHR Judgment of 9 December 2008, *Connolly v 15 Member States of the European Union*, App no 73724/01, §38; Fink n 27 at 88.

[198] Craig and de Búrca n 143 at 454–455.

non-cooperative stance vis-à-vis each other.[199] Bearing in mind the objectives pursued by the Council of Europe in the enactment of the ECHR and the very different constitutional objectives that were at the heart of the establishment of the European Union, which by its very nature was not (exclusively) human rights oriented,[200] it need not surprise that the relationship between both Courts was tumultuous. While at times, the jurisprudential relationship between the CJEU and the ECtHR could be seen as rather weak, at other times the case law of the respective Courts appeared to be in tension with each other.[201]

A notable illustration of this tension is evident in Opinion 2/94, where the CJEU explicitly stated that for the Union to accede to the ECHR, treaty amendments would be necessary.[202] The ECtHR replied in turn with the *Cantoni*[203] case as well as the *Matthews*[204] case, in which it engaged in a limited review (contrary to the first phase) of the applicable EU (primary) law in EU Member States.[205] In *Matthews* specifically, the Strasbourg Court held that 'acts of the EC as such cannot be challenged before the Court because the EC is not a Contracting Party. The Convention does not exclude the transfer of competences to international organisations provided that Convention rights continue to be "secured". Member States' responsibility therefore continues even after such a transfer'.[206] However, the review in both cases was not directed at the validity of Union measures in light of the ECHR, but rather the manner in which the Member States respected the ECHR while complying with EU (primary) law.[207]

In 2005, the ECtHR further clarified its relationship with the union with the precedent-setting *Bosphorus* judgment, which established the foundations of the 'equivalent protection' doctrine. With this case, The Strasbourg Court emphasised that Member States remain responsible for human rights violations stemming from domestic or international law. Any attempt to broadly absolve responsibility due to a transfer of competences to an international organisation would contradict the very essence of the ECHR.[208] However, to reconcile the potentially competing objectives of respect for human rights on the one hand and compliance with Union legislation by EU Member States on the other hand, the Strasbourg Court introduced the

[199] Fabbrini and Larik n 21 at 171–172.

[200] Dean Spielmann, 'The Judicial Dialogue between the European Court of Justice and the European Court of Human Rights – Or How to Remain Good Neighbours After Opinion 2/13' (*Frame*, 27 March 2017) http://www.fp7-frame.eu/wp-content/uploads/2017/03/ECHRCJUEdialog.BRUSSELS.final_.pdf; Craig and de Búrca n 143 at 454.

[201] Fabbrini and Larik n 21 at 149, 151–155.

[202] CJEU Opinion of 28 March 1996, *Accession by the Community to the European Convention for the Protection of Human Rights and Fundamental Freedoms*, Opinion 2/94, ECLI:EU:C:1996:140, §35.

[203] ECtHR (Grand Chamber) Judgment of 15 November 1996, *Cantoni v France*, App no 17862/91.

[204] ECtHR (Grand Chamber) Judgment of 18 February 1999, *Matthews v the United Kingdom*, App no 24833/94.

[205] Fabbrini and Larik n 21 at 151–155.

[206] ECtHR (Grand Chamber) Judgment of 18 February 1999, *Matthews v the United Kingdom*, App no 24833/94, §32.

[207] Craig and de Búrca n 143 at 458–460; Laurens Lavrysen, 'European Asylum Law and the ECHR: An Uneasy Coexistence' (2012) 4 *Goettingen Journal of International Law* 1, 226–227.

[208] ECtHR 2005, *Bosphorus* n 38 at §152–153.

equivalent protection doctrine.[209] Accordingly, full human rights review of conduct by Member States will be limited when such conduct (acts or omissions) derive from EU law, under the presumption that the Member States complied with the ECHR safeguards.[210] This line of reasoning was developed because the EU as an international organisation, has integrated both *procedural* and *substantive* human rights safeguards in its constitutional architecture that are *equivalent* (not identical) to the safeguards provided by the ECtHR. The equivalent protection doctrine holds, more concretely, that insofar an IO provides protection that is equivalent to the protection offered by the Strasbourg Court, it will not engage in a full and rigourous review of human rights compliance by a Member State implementing acts stemming from that IO.[211] Equivalence is not to be equated to identical protection, but requires rather comparable protection, which operates at two levels.[212]

Firstly, there must be *procedural* equivalence, as evinced *in casu* by direct and indirect access to the CJEU for potential human rights violations by the Member States and/or the EU.[213] This legal review access must be effective and available for the equivalent protection doctrine to be triggered.[214] Bearing this in mind, the Strasbourg Court clarified that the theoretical availability to submit individual applications for damages in a functionally equivalent system of rights protection is not necessarily sufficient for the equivalent protection doctrine to be triggered. In *Michaud*[215] and *Avotinš*[216] the Strasbourg Court clarified that equivalence remains a presumption, which may be rebutted. In *Michaud*, the denied access to the preliminary reference proceeding before the CJEU was considered as evidence that equivalent protection wasn't established in the circumstances of that particular case.[217] On the other hand, in *Avotinš*, the Strasbourg Court held that the decision not to refer a question to the CJEU was not decisive, as the Applicant *in casu* did not advance

[209] ibid §154–155. In earlier case law, the CJEU had already implied that the level of human rights protection offered within the EU legal order is functionally analogous to that of the Member States holding that, 'In fact, respect for fundamental rights forms an integral part of the general principles of law protected by the Court of Justice. The protection of such rights, whilst inspired by the constitutional traditions common to the Member States, must be ensured within the framework of the structure and objectives of the Community'. CJEU 1970, *Handelsgesellschaft* n 146 at §4. The German Constitutional Court was subsequently assured that a 'presumption of compatibility' in fundamental rights protection could be established between its own domestic protection of fundamental rights and the level of protection offered by the Community legal order following *Solange I* (BverfGE 37, 271 (280)) and *Solange II* (BverfGE 73, 339 (379), concerning the primacy of EU (fundamental rights) law. De Schutter notes in this regard, that *Bosphorus* was inspired by *Solange I* and *Solange II*. See De Schutter n 107 at 80–81.

[210] ECtHR 2005, *Bosphorus* n 38 at §156.

[211] ibid.

[212] ibid §155; ECtHR Judgment of 6 December 2012, *Michaud v France*, App no 12323/11, §103; ECtHR (Grand Chamber) Judgment of 23 May 2016, *Avotinš v Latvia*, App no 17502/07, §101. See also: De Schutter n 107 at 89.

[213] ECtHR 2005, *Bosphorus* n 38 at §159–165.

[214] ibid §155, 160.

[215] ECtHR 2012, *Michaud* n 212 at §115. Although the Strasbourg Court held generally that the supervisory mechanisms of the European Union are generally equivalent and trigger the presumption of equivalent protection, *in casu* the choice not to refer the question at stake to the preliminary reference proceeding before the CJEU, resulted in the disapplication of this presumption. In turn the ECtHR was thus obliged to engage in full review of compliance with Article 8 ECHR.

[216] ECtHR 2016, *Avotinš* n 212 at §11.

[217] ECtHR 2012, *Michaud* n 212 at §115.

arguments to substantiate why a preliminary reference concerning human rights compliance was warranted.[218]

Secondly, guarantees and rights must also be *substantively* equivalent. On an EU level such substantive equivalence has theoretically been attained on account of Article 6 TEU, the role that national courts play in the preliminary rulings procedure, the possiblity for individual applications for damages, the legal status of the Charter and the equivalence that is pursued by virtue of Article 52(3) CFR for corresponding rights in the Charter and the ECHR.[219]

The equivalent protection doctrine solely applies when a Member State is *implementing* a (legislative) act or measure founded in the EU-*acquis* and does not have discernable discretion in the matter.[220] If the Member States retain a significant amount of discretion, the Strasbourg Court will engage in a full review of compliance with the ECHR.[221] In applying this discretionary test, the Strasbourg Court distinguishes between cases where the Member States are strictly implementing Union law and there is an 'absence of any margin of manoeuvre on the part of the domestic authorities …',[222] and cases where sufficient discretion was retained and the Member States were not bound to strictly implement Union law. In *Bosphorus*,[223] *Povse*[224] and *Avotinš*,[225] the Strasbourg Court held that there had been strict implementation, as there was not only secondary legislation but this secondary legislation had been clarified by means of a preliminary procedure, ultimately leaving no discretion to the Member States for the purpose of implementation. Consequently, the equivalent protection doctrine was deemed triggered. In the cases of *Michaud*[226] and *MSS*[227] on the other hand, the Strasbourg Court determined that sufficient discretion was

[218] ECtHR 2016, *Avotinš* n 212 at §111. The clarification by the ECtHR that whilst generally the supervisory mechanism available by virtue of the CJEU may generally trigger the *Bosphorus* presumption, the particular circumstanes of a case may lead to the conclusion that the presumption cannot be deemed triggered, is particularly relevant for Union-mandated CFSP measures. For such measures the CJEU has highly limited jurisdiction (see above, Chapter 7), arguably leading to the conclusion that the equivalent protection doctrine would not be applicable in such cases. This would have as an immediate ramification that the burden of human rights compliance rests overwhelmingly upon the Member States in matters concerning CFSP, despite involvement of EU bodies and institutions.

[219] ECtHR 2005, *Bosphorus* n 38 at §159–165; Fink n 27 at 94–95.

[220] ECtHR 2012, *Michaud* n 212 at §103; ECtHR 2016, *Avotinš* n 212 at §105; See De Schutter n 107 at 80–8180. Where no implementing act by the Member State(s) is concerned, the ECtHR has held that it has no jurisdiction to rule and thus indirectly review EU action. ECtHR 2008, *Connolly* n 197.

[221] ECtHR 2012, *Michaud* n 212 at §103; ECtHR (Grand Chamber) Judgment of 23 May 2016, ECtHR 2016, *Avotinš* n 212 at §105.

[222] ECtHR 2016, *Avotinš* n 212 at §105. Arguably the only situation in which Member States have no discretion whatsoever, is the situation where a preliminary ruling has indicated how a Member State is to implement a given EU measure. As a result, the presumption of equal protection would be deemed applicable, unless manifest deficiencies are established. However, as the CJEU is constrained in its preliminary references to refrain from applying its interpretation to the specific facts giving rise to the domestic dispute, this scenario appears unlikely. See for a discussion: Fink n 27 at 94.

[223] ECtHR 2005, *Bosphorus* n 38 at §165–166.

[224] ECtHR Judgment of 18 June 2013, *Sofia and Doris Povse v Austria*, App no 3890/11, §82–83.

[225] ECtHR 2016, *Avotinš* n 212 at §112.

[226] ECtHR 2012, *Michaud* n 212 at §115.

[227] ECtHR (Grand Chamber) Judgment of 21 January 2011, *MSS v Belgium and Greece*, App no 30696/09, §340.

retained by the Member States involved, holding that the Member States remained responsible and subject to full human rights review. The foregoing means that Member States will remain responsible for conduct that may run counter to the ECHR, albeit that the level of scrutiny will differ depending on whether the Member States do or do not retain discretion and whether the presumption is or isn't triggered.[228] De Schutter argues that 'the equivalent protection doctrine' may be problematic for two reasons. Firstly, the presumption obscures the added value of an external supervisory mechanism bound by protection of the rights of the individuals vis-à-vis the EU and its Member States. It is hard to ensure, according to De Schutter, substantive equivalence, where the standard against which acts are reviewed by the CJEU are predominantly and increasingly internal, whereas the ECHR standard is by its very nature, external as it is not bound by other considerations, other than that of the rights of the individual.[229] In addition, De Schutter recalls that the presumption of equivalent protection facilitates a situation where Member States that have transferred powers to the Union, may escape responsibility. In view of the fact that the ECtHR does not (yet) have jurisdiction to hold the Union responsible as a subject of international law, this may create a responsibility gap.[230] Bringing this back to the question of responsibility of the EU, such (state) responsibility gaps function to the detriment of the TCN as the joint conduct diffuses responsibility across various actors and even relinquishes the need for a full legal review of conduct vis-à-vis certain actors. This could be remedied by ensuring that the EU as an additional actor, and the author of EU-mandated conduct, could additionally be held responsible for any human rights violations stemming from such acts, particularly where Member States retain hardly any discretion in the implementation thereof.

Furthermore, the doctrine holds that the presumption of equivalent protection will be rebutted, where indications arise that there are manifest deficiencies in the protection of human rights by the international organisation.[231] In such cases 'the interest of international cooperation would be outweighed by observance of the Convention as a "constitutional instrument of European public order" in the field of human rights'.[232] In *Avotinš* the Strasbourg Court recalled that such manifest deficiencies are to be determined on a case-by-case basis, thus preventing a fully automated application of the equivalent protection doctrine where 'a serious and substantiated complaint is raised … to the effect that the protection of Convention right has been manifestly deficient and that this situation cannot be remedied by European Union law'.[233]

In summary, the ECtHR has adopted an approach concerning Member State interaction with the EU, that where an act is *solely* attributable to the international organisation (*in casu* the EU), it will be deemed inadmissible. Where an act is in part attributable to the Member States, a determination will have to be made of

[228] De Schutter n 107 at 82.
[229] ibid 83.
[230] ibid 84.
[231] ECtHR 2012, *Michaud* n 212 at §103; ECtHR 2016, *Avotinš* n 212 at §112.
[232] *Ibid*.
[233] *Ibid* §113, 116; Fink n 27 at 95–96.

the level of discretion retained by the State on a case-by-case basis. Where there is no discernable discretion, the presumption of equivalent protection will be triggered, with the exception of situations of manifest deficiencies. Where conduct is (in part) attributable to Member States, and the Member States retain discretion in implementing such acts, full scrutiny will be applied by the ECtHR vis-à-vis the Member States.

Bearing in mind the foregoing, and with the exception of an odd outlier in terms of case law, both Courts appeared to refrain from engaging in direct confrontation with each other via the means of their respective rulings.[234] This cooperative approach however stands in contrast to the subsequent approach taken by the CJEU in (the infamous) Opinion 2/13 delivered several years later.

ii. (Post-)Opinion 2/13

Opinion 2/13 has sparked considerable debate, and this contribution refrains from delving into yet another analysis thereof.[235] However, a common thread throughout these discussions is that the Opinion is viewed as a departure from the previously discussed conciliatory approach taken by the EU in strengthening relations between the ECtHR and CJEU pursuant to the Treaty of Lisbon.[236] This new schism in the relationship of the Courts, reverberated – and continues to do so – clearly in the case law by the CJEU (see *infra*).[237]

The CJEU held that the Draft Accession Agreement concerning the accession of the EU to the ECHR was incompatible with Article 6(2) TEU and Protocol No. 8 due to four general contentions.[238] Firstly, it held that the Draft Accession Agreement was

[234] See for a brief discussion on the current relationship: Craig and de Búrca n 143 at 460–461.

[235] For detailed discussions, see amongst others: Piet Eeckhout, 'Opinion 2/13 on EU Accession to the ECHR and Judicial Dialogue: Autonomy or Autarky' (2015) 38 *Fordham International Law Journal* 955; Daniel Halberstam, 'It's the Autonomy, Stupid: A Modest Defense of Opinion 2/13 on EU Accession to the ECHR, and the Way Forward' (2015) 16 *German Law Journal* 105–146; Eleanor Spaventa, 'A Very Fearful Court? The Protection of Fundamental Rights in the European Union after Opinion 2/13' (2015) 22 *Maastricht Journal of European and Comparative Law* 35–56; Jed Odermatt, 'A Giant Step Backwards – Opinion 2/13 on the EU's Accession to the European Convention on Human Rights' (2015) 47 *Journal of International Law and Politics* 783–798; Adam Lazowski and Ramses A Wessel, 'When Caveats Turn into Locks: Opinion 2/13 on Accession of the European Union to the ECHR' (2015) 16 *German Law Journal* 179–212; Christoph Krenn, 'Autonomy and Effectiveness as Common Concerns: A Path to ECHR Accession after Opinion 2/13' (2015) 16 *German Law Journal* 147–168; Paul Gragl, 'EU Accession to the ECHR' in Steve Peers, Tamara Hervey, Jeff Kenner, Angela Ward (eds), *The EU Charter of Fundamental Rights: A Commentary* (London, Bloomsbury, 2014) 1734.

[236] See (and sources cited therein): Craig and de Búrca n 143 at 454–457; Bruno de Witte and Sejla Imamovic, 'Opinion 2/13 on the Accession to the ECHR: Defending the EU Legal Order Against a Foreign Human Rights Court' (2015) 40 *European Law Review* 683–705; Spaventa n 235 at 35–56.

[237] See generally on this topic: Jasper Krommendijk, 'Opinion 2/13 as a Game Changer in the Dialogue Between the European Courts?' in Emmanuelle Bribosia and Isabelle Rorive (eds), *Human Rights Tectonics – Global Dynamics of Integration and Fragmentation* (Cambridge, Intersentia, 2018) 243–303. Krommendijk provides a five-pronged typology of how the CJEU positions itself vis-à-vis the ECHR in its case law, ranging from extensive reliance upon the ECHR, to making no references to the ECHR at all.

[238] CJEU Opinion 2014, *Opinion 2/13* n 175 at §258; Protocol (No. 8) relating to Article 6(2) of the Treaty on European Union on the accession of the Union to the European Convention on the Protection of Human Rights and Fundamental Freedoms TFEU.

incompatible with the specific characteristics of the autonomous EU legal order, as it allowed EU Member States to provide for more extensive human rights protection in fields of EU law that were already subject to full EU harmonisation.[239] In other words, the fact that the Member States would be permitted via the Draft Accession Agreement to provide for more extensive human rights protection, could – according to the CJEU – upset the autonomy of the EU legal order alongside the primacy, effectiveness and unity of EU law.[240] Secondly, the incompatibility was alleged on account of the fact that it did not explicitly exclude the possibility for the ECtHR to rule on disputes of EU law between Member States, violative of the CJEU's prerogative as provided for by Article 344 TFEU.[241] This is yet again a clear assertion that the CJEU would thus not tolerate any form of external control concerning interstate disputes that fall within the scope of EU (Fundamental Rights) law. Thirdly, the CJEU held that the perceived co-respondent mechanism whereby a procedure could be started before the ECtHR with both Member States and the EU as parties, similarly would permit the ECtHR to rule on EU law – a prerogative reserved exclusively for the CJEU by the Treaties.[242] Finally, concerning the provisions of the Union's Common Foreign and Security Policy in which the CJEU has only limited jurisdiction, the CJEU recalls 'that jurisdiction to carry out a judicial review of acts, actions or omissions on the part of the EU, including in the light of fundamental rights, cannot be conferred exclusively on an international court which is outside the institutional and judicial framework of the EU'.[243]

The stance adopted by the CJEU in Opinion 2/13 did not go unnoticed by the ECtHR, which up until that point – in line with the *Bosphorus* ruling – had generally shied away from engaging in indirect review of acts by States stemming from EU measures.[244] However, post-Opinion 2/13 saw several judgments by the ECtHR which reaffirmed the *Bosphorus* 'equivalent protection' doctrine, albeit to a much lesser degree.[245] In fact, Dean Spielmann – former president of the ECtHR and current judge in the General Court of the EU – contends that the *Avotiņš* judgment by the ECtHR[246] indicates that the latter Court is no longer steadfast in applying the *Bosphorus* presumption in an automated manner and that this should no longer be taken for granted.[247] Rather, he holds that the ECtHR, following Opinion 2/13,

[239] CJEU Opinion 2014, *Opinion 2/13* n 175 at §179–200; Steve Peers, 'The CJEU and the EU's Accession to the ECHR: A Clear and Present Danger to Human Rights Protection' (*EU Law Analysis*, 18 December 2014) http://eulawanalysis.blogspot.com/2014/12/the-cjeu-and-eus-accession-to-echr.html.

[240] CJEU Opinion 2014, *Opinion 2/13* n 175 at §179–200.

[241] ibid §201–214; Peers n 209.

[242] CJEU Opinion 2014, *Opinion 2/13* n 175 at §215–235.

[243] ibid §256.

[244] Spielmann n 200.

[245] ibid.

[246] ECtHR 2016, *Avotinš* n 212.

[247] Spielmann n 200. See in particular: ECtHR 2016, *Avotinš* n 212 at §116: 'In this spirit, where the courts of a State which is both a Contracting Party to the Convention and a member State of the European Union are called upon to apply a mutual-recognition mechanism established by EU law, they must give full effect to that mechanism where the protection of Convention rights cannot be considered manifestly deficient. However, if a serious and substantiated complaint is raised before them to the effect that the protection of

seems more inclined to strictly scrutinise acts by States stemming from EU measures, as opposed to the cooperative stance it had previously adopted.[248]

iii. Status Quo of the Dynamic Interplay between the EU and the ECHR

The foregoing reveal two trends. On the one hand, it appears the Union legislator pursues a relationship of cooperation and coherence with the ECtHR, as attested to by Article 52(3) CFR, which explicitly identifies the ECHR as the absolute minimum standard that must be respected for corresponding rights in the Charter.[249] Moreover, it holds that more extensive human rights protection may be provided than envisaged by the ECtHR in matters pertaining to EU law, insofar this does not upset the autonomy of the EU legal order, along with the primacy, effectiveness and unity of EU law.[250] Accordingly, the ECHR appears to be the absolute point of reference for corresponding rights, and the reference to autonomy is solely of relevance in cases where more extensive protection would be provided than envisaged by the ECHR.[251]

Yet on the other hand, the CJEU adopts a more nuanced approach to the ECHR (and international law more generally), as it is tasked with safeguarding the autonomy of the EU legal order, while maintaining a dynamic of symbiosis with international and constitutional law, to ensure external acceptance, of the EU autonomous legal order.[252] As pointed out by Govaere, a number of (non-)exhaustive conditions have been which identified by the CJEU, to be met to safeguard the autonomy of the EU legal order, including the fact that external dispute settlement such as by the ECtHR, should not be binding upon the EU insofar it concerns the application and/or interpretation of EU law.[253] Moreover, neither the role of the CJEU should be affected or undermined in safeguarding the uniform interpretation of EU law, nor should the delineation of competences between the EU, its institutions and the Member States be affected by external adjudicatory mechanisms.[254] This more nuanced approach to the absorption of human rights law in the EU legal order, including the prospect of external adjudicatory powers of the ECtHR vis-à-vis the EU is evidenced in the infamous Opinion 2/13.

a Convention right has been manifestly deficient and that this situation cannot be remedied by European Union law, they cannot refrain from examining that complaint on the sole ground that they are applying EU law'.

[248] Spielmann n 200.

[249] Peers and Prechal n 182 at 1498–1503.

[250] ibid.

[251] ibid. While this observation flows from a textual interpretation of the Charter, case law by the CJEU appears to adopt a slightly more lenient reading of this rule: CJEU (Grand Chamber) Judgment of 26 February 2013, *Stefano Melloni v Minsterio Fiscal*, C-399/11, ECLI:EU:C:2013:107.

[252] See Article 3(5) TEU which holds that the EU shall contribute to 'the protection human rights, in particular the rights of the child, as well as to the strict observance and the development of international law' and CJEU Opinion 2014, *Opinion 2/13* n 175 at §165–177.

[253] Inge Govaere, 'Interconnecting Legal Systems and the Autonomous Legal Order: A Balloon Dynamic' in Inge Govaere and Sascha Garben (eds), *The Interface Between EU and International Law – Contemporary Reflections* (Oxford, Hart, 2019) 28.

[254] ibid.

In keeping with the balloon dynamic discussed by Govaere, which illustrates the delicate balance to be struck between the safeguarding of the EU autonomous legal order and the avoiding of open conflict with the international and domestic legal orders,[255] the CJEU appears to continuously walk a tightrope, unsurprisingly leading to rejection of the previous Draft Accession Agreement.

What remains remarkably absent in the discussions concerning Opinion 2/13, however, is the novelty of the EU and (highly integrated) IOs generally, as duty-bearers of human rights obligations – an issue which transcends the question of how the CJEU approaches potential accession of the EU to the ECHR, transcends the question of autonomy and transcends the sought-after acceptance of such autonomy by the international and domestic legal orders. If anything, a clear conceptualisation of the concrete positive and negative human rights obligations borne by the EU, could serve to help dispel many of the issues that surfaced in Opinion 2/13. Moreover, a clear identification of the positive and negative human rights obligations borne by the EU, would be in keeping with human rights instruments under EU law and international law, as 'living instruments' which should be 'practical and effective' in their application, instead of 'theoretical and illusory'. If nothing else, this would be entirely in line with the obligation under Article 3(5) TEU by which the EU is to contribute to the 'development of international law'.[256]

3. INTERIM CONCLUSIONS

The incorporation of human rights into the EU legal order has been an incremental but laudable development. Despite not initially being constructed as a means to safeguard human rights, it became apparent early on that to achieve the sought-after objectives of economic integration, safeguarding of (individual) rights would be instrumental. In protecting human rights, the CJEU proved to be a driving force, recognizing fundamental rights first as legally enforceable general principles of EU law. The Charter of Fundamental Rights embedded human rights more firmly and explicitly in the EU-*acquis*, by equating its legal value to that of the constituent Treaties. Despite these laudable advancements, human rights protection in the EU cannot be considered entirely self-sufficient, much less self-contained, as the rights and freedoms enshrined therein, cannot be invoked independently of EU measures and must be read in tandem with other international human rights and constitutional law provisions. While the extent of analogy and correspondence between the Charter provisions and provisions of international and constitutional (human) rights may be debated, the CJEU's case law suggests inconsistency in referencing other international and domestic law provisions. As argued by Moreno-Lax, it is be counterintuitive, if not illegal, for the CJEU to be exclusively self-referential in cases involving corresponding

[255] ibid 21.
[256] Jan Wouters and Michal Ovádek, *The European Union and Human Rights, Analysis, Cases and Materials* (Oxford, Oxford University Press, 2021) 212–312.

human rights provisions.[257] Arguing in particular that the rights embedded in the CFR should be read consistently with the corresponding provisions under international (and national) law, she continues that the pre-eminence of the Charter in EU fundamental rights law should not entail that abstraction be made of international human rights standards.[258] Again, while the CJEU does mention international human rights standards, it does so – particularly in BAM policy – somewhat haphazardly manner: At times, the CJEU extensively cites international and domestic human rights standards and sometimes relies exclusively on the CFR as the source of authority.[259]

The degree to which the CJEU – as the sole interpreter of EU law – relies on international and constitutional human rights law to inform its own understanding of human rights law within the internal EU legal order, is relevant for and complicates the question of the EU's responsibility on three levels:

Self-Referentialism and Misalignment. Firstly, the degree of self-reference in determining human rights obligations will impact the alignment or misalignment of the EU's human rights obligations with human rights obligations of the Member States under EU law and international law. Situations giving rise to human rights harms on account of EU conduct, that do not provide the Member States with any implementation discretion for example, may absolve Member States human rights responsibility under the ECHR (through the *equivalent protection* doctrine), as well as under the EU's legal framework (to preserve the autonomy, effectiveness, unity and primacy of EU law). Insofar the responsibility of the EU's complicity in such human rights harm is subsequently determined in an entirely self-referential manner that does not heed its implications with respect to state responsibility under international, EU and constitutional law, a risk arises that the EU will also be absolved of responsibility. This implies that the CJEU's self-referential path-dependency might create a situation where the outcome of a particular course of conduct which has given rise to a human rights harm flowing from indissociable EU and Member State conduct, results in both types of actors being absolved of responsibility across different adjudicatory mechanisms and legal fora, at the expense of individual rights. And where state responsibility under human rights law was originally intended to prevent and remedy such harms, the EU's idiosyncrasies and the CJEU's self-referential approach could complicate and even prevent the allocation of responsibility in such instances, giving rise to a significant responsibility gap.

Self-Referentialism and Deliberative Human Rights Discourse. Secondly, the degree of self-referentialism adopted by the CJEU may erode the democratic undercurrent of the Charter. The manner in which positive, negative, procedural and substantive obligations flowing from international, regional and domestic human rights commitments as developed for States are understood, are the result of a

[257] Moreno-Lax n 17 at 243.

[258] ibid.

[259] This section is inspired by Joyce De Coninck, 'The Impact of ECtHR and CJEU Judgments on the Rights of Asylum Seekers in the European Union: Adversaries or Allies in Asylum' in Wolfgang Benedek, Philip Czech, Lisa Heschl, Karin Lukas and Manfred Nowak (eds), *European Yearbook on Human Rights* (Cambridge, Intersentia, 2018) 343–374.

dynamic, and experimentalist form of consensus building.[260] In other words, these concretised obligations are the result of a granular, continuous process of consensus building, whereby their understanding and development has been advocated for and discussed in court proceedings, through legislative processes and the topic of much deliberative debate. The democratic, consensus-driven and experimentalist developments that drove the development of human rights obligations for States is largely missing for human rights obligations as they apply to the EU. Where the CJEU retains quasi-exclusive power to determine the scope of concretised human rights obligations, which cannot be presumed to be identical to those of Member States, a two-fold risk arises. Firstly, the lack of deliberative discourse in the determination of such concretised EU obligations, which is exacerbated by the difficult access to the CJEU could mean that the EU's human rights obligations may not reflect the underlying conceptualisations of justice pursued by the EU legal framework or polity, much less reflect consensus on the degree to which the EU as a *sui generis* organization should be bound by human rights obligations. Secondly, there is the risk that the CJEU may be reluctant in articulating the EU's human rights obligations in the absence of ex ante determined human rights obligations by the EU legislator.

Self-Referentialism and Access to an Effective Remedy. Finally, without clarification on how positive, negative, procedural and substantive obligations of States modulate and apply to the EU in meeting its human rights commitments under the Charter, the right to an effective remedy becomes a guessing game for individual applicants. This is not reconcilable with the requirement that access to an effective remedy entails that it must be accessible and not unreasonably difficult.[261] This risk

[260] De Búrca n 11; Benvenisti and Harel n 19 at 35–59.

[261] The right to an effective remedy as understood in the relation between a State and the individual, is required to be 'prompt, accessible and capable of offering a reasonable prospect of success'. The Explanations to the CFR note that Article 47 CFR concerning the right to an effective remedy provides more extensive protection than the analogous right under Article 13 ECHR, as it extends to all freedoms and rights under EU law and is not limited ratione materiae to the CFR. Neither the CFR nor the ECHR provide a definition of the right to an effective remedy and require instead that for it to be considered effective, a number of factors affecting must be considered. See for example '290. In order to be effective, the remedy required by Article 13 must be **available in practice as well as in law**, in particular in the sense that its exercise **must not be unjustifiably hindered by the acts or omissions of the authorities** of the respondent State. 291. Article 13 requires the provision of a domestic remedy allowing the competent national authority both to deal with the **substance of the relevant Convention complaint** and to **grant appropriate relief**, although Contracting States are afforded some discretion as to the manner in which they conform to their obligations under this provision. 292. Particular attention should be paid to the **speediness** of the remedial action itself, it not being excluded that the adequate nature of the remedy can be undermined by its excessive duration. 293. Lastly, in view of the importance which the Court attaches to Article 3 of the Convention and the **irreversible nature of the damage which may result if the risk of torture or ill-treatment materialises**, the effectiveness of a remedy within the meaning of Article 13 imperatively **requires close scrutiny by a national authority**, independent and rigorous scrutiny of any claim that there exist substantial grounds for fearing a real risk of treatment contrary to Article 3 (see Jabari, cited above, § 50), as well as a **particularly prompt response** (see *Batı and Others v Turkey*, nos. 33097/96 and 57834/00, § 136, ECHR 2004-IV); it also requires that the person concerned should have access to a **remedy with automatic suspensive effect** (see *Čonka v Belgium*, no. 51564/99, §§ 81–83, ECHR 2002-I, and *Gebremedhin [Gaberamadhien]*, cited above, § 66); ECtHR Judgment of 21 January 2011, *M.S.S. v Belgium*, App no. 30696/09 § 290–293. See also: Carla Ferstman, *International Organizations and the Fight for Accountability: the Remedies and Reparations Gap* (Oxford University Press 2017) p 75–76. For an extensive discussion on the need for remedies against unlawful (human rights) conduct of international organizations, see: Karel Wellens, *Remedies against International Organizations* (Cambridge University Press 2009).

is furthermore exacerbated and, as aforementioned could give rise to a responsibility gap in situations where the equivalent protection doctrine and similar judicial techniques, shield implicated Member States from responsibility, for their cooperation with EU entities.

In sum, the absence of deliberative discourse on how human rights commitments (stemming from *jus cogens*, customary international law, treaty law and general principles of law) should translate into justiciable human rights obligations, due to immunities and considerations of autonomy, complicate holding the EU (and IOs generally) legally responsible for contributions to human rights harms. Despite the laudable aspirations of the Charter, this obscurity has not been meaningfully remedied. Even if the CJEU reverts to international law and the common constitutional traditions of the EU Member States, these sources are plagued by the same shortcomings as they have not given rise to modulated articulations of human rights obligations of IOs generally and the EU specifically. Additionally, there is the looming potential self-referentialism and insularity in how EU human rights obligations are developed, interpreted, and applied by the CJEU. Such self-referentialism may very well serve to shield EU entities from human rights responsibility by not articulating human rights obligations where the EU legislator has also neglected to meaningfully do this through EU legislative acts. The ongoing negotiations of EU accession to the ECHR do not appear to address this gap.

Normative incongruence thus taints the EU's human rights responsibility regime, as despite the multiple sources of EU human rights commitments, these commitments have largely not (yet) been translated in actionable, democratically substantiated and consensus-driven obligations by either the EU legislator or the CJEU. Proving the EU's contribution to human rights harms becomes extremely tenuous in the absence of even an elemental understanding of its actual obligations.

4

Liability Incongruence: Establishing Responsibility of IOs and the EU

We have now established the degree to which the EU as a *sui generis* IO is bound by international and EU human rights law, coming to the conclusion that although the EU is bound to respect human rights commitments under international and EU law in theory, the manner in which these commitments can be invoked and enforced against the EU remains largely opaque. This opaqueness exists because the EU's commitment to human rights has not yet been meaningfully transposed to concrete and actionable human rights obligations. There is thus normative incongruence between the EU's human rights commitments on the one hand, and the manner in which these commitments can be enforced and made judicially actionable on the other hand.

Is this normative incongruence the sole reason behind the difficulties experience by an individual in seeking redress against unlawful human rights conduct by the EU and IOs more generally? Chapter 4 argues that this is not the case and that the difficulties encountered in understanding how human rights obligations apply to the EU and IOs generally, are exacerbated by the liability (responsibility) rules that apply to the EU and IOs generally. This next chapter elaborates on 'liability incongruence' and how the rules of international law and EU law which govern how to establish and enforce human rights responsibility in practice against the EU (the so-called liability rules) are also designed in a manner that prevents EU (and IO) human rights responsibility in practice. In other words, the argument is advanced that there is 'liability incongruence' between the objectives of the liability rules in theory as established under international and EU law on the one hand, and how these liability rules operate in practice on the other hand.

Under international law, the liability rules are called 'secondary rules' and are found in the ARIO.[262] Under EU law these rules are found in EU procedural law, and

[262] General Commentary 3 ARIO. It must be observed that the dichotomy between primary and secondary rules as understood under international law should not be overstated, as arguably the rules concerning indirect or joint responsibility are considered as constituting 'meta-primary' rules and the rules in ARIO concerning the content and consequences of internationally wrongful acts are arguably of a primary nature. See on the topic of the indirect responsibility: Nikolaos Voulgaris, *Allocating International Responsibility Between Member States and International Organizations* (Oxford, Hart, 2020) 98; Lanovoy n 26 at 11. See on the topic of certain provisions concerning the consequences of international responsibility: Mirka Möldner, 'Responsibility of International Organizations – Introducing the ILC's DARIO' in Armin von Bogdandy and Rüdiger Wolfrum (eds), *Max Planck Yearbook of United Nations Law* (Leiden, Brill, 2012) 308.

more specifically in the rules governing the 'action for damages' against the EU.[263] Although the EU is relied on to illustrate liability incongruence, the ensuing analysis will follow the frame of reference provided by the ARIO, which is currently the sole generalist international framework to establish legal responsibility for IOs.[264] While the choice to rely on the ARIO to guide the following analysis may be counterintuitive for many, especially given its contested nature,[265] the reason for this methodological choice is simple.[266] The ARIO spell out the general rules (*lex generalis*[267]) that exist to hold IOs responsible as informed by international law on state responsibility, existing and emerging custom and progressive development of international law,[268]

[263] Ward n 103 at 183–184.

[264] Klein n 32 at 1027–1029. In addition to the ARIO, the Guiding Principles on Shared Responsibility in International Law were developed as a result of research conducted under the supervision of André Nollkaemper. Building on, elaborating and clarifying lacunae in the regulation of shared responsibility in ARIO, the Guiding Principles were developed with the objective of providing 'guidance to judges, practitioners and researchers when confronted with legal questions of shared responsibility of states and international organizations for their contribution to an indivisible injury of third parties'. See on the topic: Nollkaemper, d'Aspremont, Ahlborn, Boutin, Nedeski and Plakokefalos n 26 at 15–72.

[265] Pellet n 32 at 53.

[266] An additional reason in favour of the ARIO concerns the need to avoid legal impunity of IOs. The recourse to the ARIO prevents increased fragmentation in the law of responsibility for IOs, which could otherwise facilitate system-shopping by IOs, to circumvent responsibility. Additionally, while certain treaties may regulate scenarios of joint responsibility, many treaties simply do not recognize international organizations as duty-bearers of international law. In such cases, the ARIO provide a normative framework to fill this lacuna and ensure that complicit IOs may also be held responsible for the commission or complicity in unlawful acts. Filling this lacunae is of paramount importance in light of one of the functions of international responsibility, which is to ensure access to effective remedies for aggrieved victims of unlawful conduct. Already in 1927, the Permanent Court of International Justice recalled that, 'It is a principle of international law, and even a general conception of law, that any breach of an engagement involves an obligation to make reparation … Consequently, the essential principle contained in the actual notion of an illegal act is that reparation must, as far as possible, wipe out all the consequences of the illegal act'. Permanent Court of International Justice Judgment of 8 February 1928, *Factory at Chorzów*, Series A No. 17, 27, 47. At the same time, acknowledging the importance of having an overarching set of (soft) rules for IO responsibility, does not mean that these rules in their current understanding are shielded from criticism, which is precisely one of the conclusions of the following chapter. On the topic of the relevance and necessity of the ARIO, see: Möldner n 262 at 323; Lanovoy n 26 at 6. See on the topic of human rights instruments not being applicable to international organizations and the need to address this legal lacuna: Øby Johansen n 26; Pierre Schmitt, *Access to Justice and International Organizations – The Case of Individual Victims of Human Rights Violations* (Cheltenham, Edward Elgar Publishing, 2017); Antônio Augusto Cançado Trindade, *The Access of Individuals to International Justice* (Oxford, Oxford University Press, 2011); Eric Debrabandere, 'Non-State Actors, State-Centrism and Human Rights Obligations' (2009) 22 *Leiden Journal of International Law* 191–209; Alston n 30. On the topic of the role of international responsibility more generally, see: Ilias Plakokefalos, 'Causation in the Law of State Responsibility and the Problem of Overdetermination: In Search of Clarity' (2015) 26 *European Journal of International Law* 475.

[267] Despite the overwhelming heterogeneity of international organizations, the ILC adopted a unitary view on the responsibility framework vis-à-vis international organizations, which serves as a set of general rules insofar no special rules (*lex specialis*) have been adopted by the international organization. Klein n 32 at 1027–1028; Niels Blokker, 'Member State Responsibility for Wrongdoings of International Organizations: Beacon of Hope or Delusion?' in Ana Sofia Barros, Cedric Ryngaert and Jan Wouters (eds), *International Organizations and Member State Responsibility* (Leiden, Brill, 2016) 38. Delgado Casteleiro n 27 at 58; Pieter-Jan Kuijper and Esa Paasivirta, 'EU International Responsibility and Its Attribution: From the Inside Looking Out' in Malcolm Evans and Panos Koutrakos (eds), *The International Responsibility of the European Union – European and International Perspectives* (Oxford, Hart, 2013) 35–36.

[268] On provisions of the ARIO having attained the status of customary international law, see: Kuijper and Paasivirta n 267 at 67.

while simultaneously acknowledging the importance of IO-specific rules on responsibility. The recognition of IO-specific rules on responsibility is found in Article 64 ARIO (*lex specialis*). This provision holds that insofar other rules of international law exist regulating the responsibility regime of a particular international organisation[269] and/or where an IO has its own (internal) rules regulating responsibility, these rules *may* prevail (although not necessarily)[270] over, or supplement, the general default regime encompassed in the ARIO.[271] Considering the EU's involvement in the development of the rules in the ARIO and its decisive role in the inclusion and development of Article 64 ARIO, an examination of the EU's responsibility regime would arguably be fractional without taking into account the liability rules under both international and EU law.[272]

The ARIO identify the constitutive conditions required to establish the responsibility of IOs, both when an IO has acted independently – that is to say, on its own – as well as when an IO has cooperated with other IOs or States.[273] For *independent* responsibility to arise under the ARIO, the IO must have committed a breach of an

[269] There are different and complementary liability rules that exist across different domains of international law. Where this is of relevance to the EU, this will be highlighted.

[270] Comment 9 to Article 10 ARIO recalls that although special rules may exist concerning the determination of a violation of an international obligation, such special rules 'do not necessarily prevail over principles set out in the present draft articles'. Hence, although the ARIO acknowledge the functional speciality inherent to international organizations, special rules as a result thereof do not *automatically* displace the more general, default regime.

[271] Comment 1 to Article 64 ARIO; Klein n 32 at 1027.

[272] The European Commission advocated for an additional clause for the EU specifically or concerning regional economic integration organizations (REIOs) more generally. The European Commission underlined the unique and special features of the EU, arguing in particular that the *lex specialis* referenced in Article 64 ARIO in its draft version did not adequately reflect the peculiarities and functional speciality of REIOs and the EU. Accordingly, the European Commission advocated for an additional clause concerning the REIO's and the EU specifically, to attribute Member State conduct *exclusively* to the EU, when adopting acts in the implementation of an EU act without any margin of discretion: 'The EU member States and their authorities are obliged to carry out binding decisions and policies adopted by the EU according to the EU's internal rules. This requires special rules of attribution and responsibility in cases where EU member States are in fact only implementing a binding rule of the international organization. In other words, the EU exercises normative control of the member States who then act as Union agents rather than on their own account when implementing Union law'. The European Commission underlined the need to emphasize that any reference to the *lex specialis* should be drafted to 'explicitly allow for the hypothesis that not all of its provisions [of ARIO] can be applied to regional (economic) integration organizations'. See on European Commission involvement in the negotiations of the ARIO: ILC, 'Seventh Report on the Responsibility of International Organizations by Mr Giorgio Gaja, Special Rapporteur' (UN Doc. A /CN.4/610) 27 March 2009, 95 §121–124; ILC, 'Responsibility of International Organizations: Comments and Observations Received from International Organizations' (UN Doc. A/ CN.4/637) 14 and 17 February 2011, 147, 167–168; Simone Vezzani, 'The International Responsibility of the European Union and of Its Member States for Breaches of Obligations Arising from Investment Agreements: Lex Specialis or European Exceptionalism?' in Mads Adenas, Luca Pantaleo, Matthew Happold and Cristina Contartese (eds), *EU External Action in International Economic Law – Recent Trends and Developments* (The Hague, Asser Press/Springer, 2020) 281, 288; Jean d'Aspremont, 'A European Law of International Responsibility? The Articles on the Responsibility of International Organizations and the European Union' in Vasiliki Kosta, Nikos Skoutaris and Vassilis Tzevelekos (eds), *The EU Accession to the ECHR* (Oxford, Hart, 2014) 75. See more generally: Eileen Denza, 'Responsibility of the EU in the Context of Investment' in Malcolm Evans and Panos Koutrakos (eds), *The International Responsibility of the European Union – European and International Perspectives* (Oxford, Hart, 2013) 224–225; Möldner n 262 at 323–325; Stefan Talmon, 'Responsibility of international organizations: Does the european Community Require special Treatment?' in maurizio Ragazzi (ed), *International Responsibility Today: Essays in Memory of Oscar Schachter* (Leiden, Martinus Nijhoff publishers, 2005) 406–407.

[273] Articles 6–13 and 14–19 ARIO.

international obligation, which can be attributed to the IO. For *shared* responsibility to arise, there must have been 'knowing intent' on behalf of the IO, when contributing to the unlawful conduct, which must be unlawful for both complicit actors (the so-called 'opposability' condition). Highly analogous though slightly more detailed rules on responsibility exist under EU law. For (human rights) responsibility to arise under the EU's liability scheme, there must have been a sufficiently serious breach of EU law, that can be causally connected to an EU entity, and which must have given rise to identifiable damage. While *shared* or *joint* responsibility is not explicitly ruled out under EU law, the conditions to establish shared or joint responsibility remain obscure to date. These conditions will be dealt with critically and mindful of the differences that exist between the relevant rules of international law and EU law in what follows.

1. TRADITIONAL CONDITIONS FOR RESPONSIBILITY

Under both international and EU law, independent responsibility – that is to say, EU responsibility that stems for conduct exclusively committed by the EU – presupposes that there is conduct that is attributable to the EU, which caused the harm and that this conduct constitutes a violation of a (human rights) obligation by which the EU is bound. Of course, the terminology varies slightly across these two regimes: under the ARIO, responsibility arises from a violation of an international obligation, whereas under EU law responsibility arises from a breach of an EU obligation.[274] More specifically, the relevant norms under international law are defined as 'human rights', whereas the relevant norms under EU law are typically referred to as 'fundamental rights'. Their function remains analogous, however and the normative incongruence these norms give rise to, has been discussed in the previous chapter. Conversely, while attribution features prominently under the ARIO with little to no focus on the element of causation, the inverse is true for the assessment of responsibility under EU law. In light of these terminological and conceptual nuances, the rules on independent responsibility will be discussed sequentially to highlight their similarities and differences and critically appraise their potential in ensuring the EU's responsibility for contributions to human rights harms.

a. Attribution and Causation

Before delving into the various modes of attribution foreseen by the ARIO, it is necessary to clarify the meaning of the concept of attribution, in relation to the concept of causation. Attribution and causation operate at different ends of the responsibility question. While attribution connects an actor to a particular line of

[274] While the terminology may vary between the international and EU frameworks, when viewed through a functional perspective, it becomes evident that human rights under international law and fundamental rights under EU law, each reflecting international and EU obligations respectively, serve the common purpose of protecting the rights of individuals rooted in international, regional, and domestic human rights legislation.

(unlawful) conduct, causation connects the conduct to the damage. These concepts thus govern two different but sequential segments of the responsibility question and must thus be analyzed separately. Notably, the test of causality is not explicitly defined in the letter of the law under either (international or EU). Attribution, however, features explicitly and prominently the ARIO but is addressed implicitly and inconsistently within the EU's responsibility framework under the action for damages.

i. The Lex Generalis *Rules*

Under the ARIO, for responsibility to be established, conduct must first be attributed to the IO. Attribution of conduct to an IO generally (and the EU specifically) may be established on a number of grounds. Firstly, conduct will be attributed to the IO to the extent that the conduct was performed by an agent or organ of the organisation (Article 6 ARIO). Secondly, conduct will be attributed to an organisation insofar the individual/entity responsible for the conduct was placed 'at the disposal of the organization' (Article 7 ARIO). Thirdly, conduct will be attributed to the organisation 'if the organ or agent acts in an official capacity and within the overall functions of that organization, even if the conduct exceeds the authority of that organ or agent or contravenes instructions' (Article 8 ARIO). Finally, conduct will be attributed to the organisation, insofar the conduct is acknowledged by the IO as being its own (Article 9 ARIO). Yet, the rules to attribute conduct according to these scenarios are tainted by such indeterminacy which frustrate determinations of when conduct is to be attributed to an IO, and ultimately access to a remedy for individual claimants.

– Article 6 ARIO – Conduct by an Organ or Agent

Article 2 ARIO identifies organs as 'any person or entity which has that status in accordance with the rules of the organization'[275] and agents as 'an official or other person or entity, other than an organ, who is charged by the organization with carrying out, or helping to carry out, one of its functions, and thus through whom the organization acts'.[276] This latter category points to entities that have been entrusted by the IO to carry out some of its functions, thereby establishing a functional link between the entity concerned and the IO.[277]

The Commentaries to the ARIO clarify that although Article 6 ARIO holds that organs are (generally) identified by the internal rules of the organisation, this criterion alone is not sufficient to exclusively and exhaustively make such determinations,[278]

[275] Article 2(c) ARIO. In the *travaux préparatoires* it is confirmed that the reference to the 'rules of the organization', is to be interpreted broadly, allowing it to 'give considerable weight to practice'. ILC, 'Second Report on the Responsibility of International Organizations by Mr Giorgio Gaja, Special Rapporteur' (UN Doc. A /CN.4/541) 2 April 2004, 8–9.

[276] Article 2(d) ARIO.

[277] ILC Second Report n 275 at 7–8. As will be discussed below, the degree of this functional link and the required degree of authority and control exercised by the international organization over the entity, remains obscure.

[278] Ramses A Wessel and Leonhard den Hertog, 'EU Foreign, Security and Defence Policy: A Competence-Responsibility Gap?' in Malcolm Evans and Panos Koutrakos (eds), *The International Responsibility of the European Union – European and International Perspectives* (Oxford, Hart, 2013) 348.

as 'attribution can hardly depend on the use of a particular terminology in the internal law …'.[279] The Commentaries do not explicitly address how an organ of an IO is to be alternatively identified, hinting only at a functional criterion, whereby due consideration is given to the entrusted tasks and functions of the entity concerned.[280]

Agents are liberally identified as entities entrusted by organs of the organisation to carry out the functions of the organisations.[281] The Commentaries again underscore the need for due consideration to be given to the functions with which an entity is entrusted (as opposed to the status of the individual according to the internal rules of the organisation) indicating that for a determination of attribution to be established based on this provision, a case-by-case assessment would be required, taking into account both the internal rules of the organisation and its functions.

Finally, Article 6 ARIO conversely does not intend to cover conduct by organs or agents that 'clearly exceed[s] the authority of the organs or agents, or when it obviously contravene[s] the instructions of the organization'.[282] Such scenarios fall within the ambit of Article 8 ARIO.

Although the flexibility inherent to Article 6 ARIO provides sufficient leeway to cover a wide array of constitutional arrangements across a variety of different IOs, this leniency also paves the path for ambiguity and legal inconsistencies,[283] particularly in scenarios where IOs work indissociably together with other public and private actors. This is demonstrated in part by scholarship on the topic, which has identified two – arguably three[284] – distinct models of attribution on the basis of Article 6 ARIO. Firstly, there is the (exculpating or exonerating)[285] normative control model

[279] Comment 1 to Article 6 ARIO.

[280] Comment 7 and Comment 9 to Article 6 ARIO. The latter comment clarifies that 'by not making the rules of the organization the only criterion, the wording of paragraph 2 [of Article 6 ARIO] is intended to leave the possibility open that, in exceptional circumstances, functions may be considered as given to an organ or agent even if this could not be said to be based on the rules of the organization'.

[281] Comment 2–4 to Article 6 ARIO.

[282] ILC Seventh Report n 272 at 81 §34.

[283] Delgado Casteleiro n 27 at 68–71; Klein n 32 at 1030–1031. The argument has been made that while Member States implementing binding EU acts cannot be considered as organs of the Union, they could be considered as agents, 'charged by the organization with carrying out, or helping to carry out, one of its functions, and thus through whom the organization acts'. However, this only further demonstrates the division in scholarship and does not alter the conclusion that ambiguity permeates the normative control model for attribution. Philipp Theodor Stegmann, *Responsibility of the EU and the Member States under EU International Investment Protection Agreements – Between Traditional Rules, Proceduralisation and Federalisation* (New York, Springer, 2019) 86–88. This furthermore affirms the finding of Talmon in 2005, where it was held that the 'general rule on attribution of conduct to an international organization seems wide enough to cover the relationship between the EC and the authorities of its member States. The latter may be regarded as agents of the EC'. Stefan Talmon, 'Responsibility of International Organizations: Does the European Community Require Special Treatment?' in Maurizio Ragazzi (ed), *International Responsibility Today: Essays in Memory of Oscar Schachter* (Leiden, Martinus Nijhoff Publishers, 2005) 412.

[284] Kuijper and Paasivirta explain that the 'consensus model' constitutes a third model of attribution, albeit that this concerns joint responsibility, which will be dealt with separately. Kuijper and Paasivirta n 267 at 63.

[285] The addition of 'exculpating or exonerating' to the doctrinal conceptualisation of normative control, is to indicate – according to Vezzani – that attribution based on this model prevents attribution for the same conduct to Member States, ensuring that they shall not bear international responsibility for conduct under the normative control of the international organization, *in casu* the EU. However, practice and doctrine are

and on the other hand the competence model.[286] The third model – the 'consensus' model – will be discussed within the context of shared responsibility.

The Normative Control Model

The **normative (organic/institutional) control model**[287] holds that conduct is attributed to the IO, when that conduct is the result of its organs and/or agents.[288] This embodies the 'self-evident proposition that the organization acts through its organs with the consequence that the latter's acts are attributable to the former'.[289] Conduct is accordingly attributed to the IO, on account of the normative control that is exercised by the international organisation over its organs and agents. However, this leaves open the required degree of normative control, for an entity to be considered as an organ or agent of an IO, and importantly, whether such normative control exonerates other complicit parties (e.g., the Member State(s)) from ultimate responsibility. Vezzani correctly observes that the degree of normative control exercised by IOs differs significantly across IOs, but may also vary significantly within one single IO, depending on the substantive issue(s) at stake.[290] A clear example can be found in the difference of normative control exercised by the EU in the exercise of exclusive competences as opposed to non-exclusive (shared or coordinating) competences. Whereas Member States may have less discretionary margin to act when implementing EU acts within the EU's exclusive competences, and thus function more as an organ, this arguably would not be the case in areas where the EU shares competence with the Member States and the latter retain more discretionary powers.

The ambiguity surrounding the required standard of normative control for an entity to be considered as an organ or agent of the IO, has given rise to an additional divide in the normative control model for attribution. While on the one hand there is the *strict normative control model*,[291] which identifies organs and agents as

extremely divided on the matter as discussed extensively below. Generally, it can be held that those in favour of the non-exonerating or non-exculpatory normative control model, similarly acknowledge that joint responsibility is effectively possible, even when the Member States and the EU commit the same unlawful conduct. Conversely, joint responsibility would only be possible under an exculpatory approach to normative control, insofar the complicit parties committed different wrongs resulting in one single harm. Vezzani n 272 at 288. Alhborn appears to suggest that practice is in favour of the exonerating normative control model, by stating that 'while international organizations and their member States may often incur shared responsibility as a result of the concurrent exercise of competences, this responsibility will generally be implemented separately, possibly in different legal orders, because the internal division of competences is not opposable to third parties without their consent'. Christiane Ahlborn, 'The Rules of International Organizations and the Law of International Responsibility' (2011) 8 *International Organizations Law Review* 481.

[286] Vezzani n 272 at 288–291.

[287] These terms are used interchangeably in doctrine. See on the topic: Christiane Ahlborn, 'To Share or Not to Share? The Allocation of Responsibility Between International Organizations and their Member States' (2013) 88 *Die Friedens-Warte* 49.

[288] Kuijper and Paasivirta n 267 at 49, 54; Vezzani n 272 at 288; Delgado Casteleiro n 27 at 68–69.

[289] Frank Hoffmeister, 'Litigating Against the European Union and Its Member States – Who Responds under the ILC's Draft Articles on International Responsibility of International Organizations?' (2010) 21 European Journal of International Law 3, 723.

[290] Vezzani n 272 at 288–289.

[291] The 'strict normative control model' may also be referred to as the 'purely organic model'. Kuijper and Paasivirta n 267 at 54.

only those entities that have been formally integrated into the architectural structure of the organisation,[292] *the broad normative control model* holds that Member States may be considered as de facto organs or agents[293] of the EU to the extent that they are implementing EU acts.[294] This latter argument flows from the regulatory powers that have been transferred by Member States to the EU, the implementation of which – by the Member States – remains subject to legal review at an EU level. Accordingly, as the implementation remains under EU normative and judicial control to varying degrees, the Member States could be considered as de facto organs or agents.[295] This is of relevance for the question of EU responsibility, as by and large the EU Member States constitute the executing arm of EU policies. A method of attribution that does not capture this particular dynamic, may have as a result that conduct may only be attributed to the EU in a highly limited number of scenarios.

Special Rapporteur Gaja appears to support the former strict approach to the normative control test for attribution, based upon international practice that supported this model at the time of the drafting of the ARIO.[296] Building on the *Bosphorus* case[297] before the ECtHR and the *Kadi and Al Barakaat International Foundation v Council and Commission* case[298] before the CJEU, the Special Rapporteur held that these cases – which concerned the implementation of acts without any discretionary margin by Member States – 'did not lend support to the proposal of considering that conduct implementing an act of an international organization should be attributed to that organization'.[299] Mere implementation of

[292] Delgado Casteleiro n 27 at 69.

[293] Hoffmeister n 289 at 734. Particularly in the jurisprudence under the *chapeau* of the WTO it has been held that – insofar the EU enjoys exclusive competences in a given area – it will incur responsibility for the implementation of EU acts by Member States. See for example: Panel Report of 11 December 2006, *European Communities – Selected Customs Matters*, WT/DS315/R, §2.2, 2.14, 2.23; Appellate Body Report of 11 December 2006, *European Communities – Selected Customs Matters*, WT/DS315//AB/R, §152-154, 210, 218-227; Panel Report, *European Communities – Geographic Indications*, WT/DS174/R, §7.725.

[294] Delgado Casteleiro n 27 at 68–69. Certain authors such as Talmon and Stegmann clarify that authorities of Member States could not be considered as 'organs' for the purpose of Article 6 ARIO. However, the conceptualization of 'agent' under the ARIO is sufficiently broad to encompass the dynamic between the EU and its Member States (see above). Stegmann n 283 at 88; Talmon n 283 at 412–413.

[295] Stegmann n 283 at 85–86. See also on the topic of the broader normative control model for attribution: Hoffmeister n 289 at 741–743; d'Aspremont n 272 at 76–77; José Manuel Cortés Martín, 'Exceptionalism in International Law? The European Union and the System of International Responsibility' in Maurizio Ragazzi (ed), *Responsibility of International Organizations: Essays in Memory of Sir Ian Brownlie* (Leiden, Martinus Nijhoff Publishers, 2013) 194–199.

[296] ILC Seventh Report n 272 at 80 §33; Giorgio Gaja, 'The Relations Between the European Union and Its Member States from the Perspective of the ILC Articles on Responsibility of International Organizations' (*SHARES*, 11 April 2013) www.sharesproject.nl/publication/the-relations-between-the-european-union-and-its-member-states-from-the-perspective-of-the-ilc-articles-on-responsibility-of-international-organizations/ 3; Stegmann n 283 at 87.

[297] ECtHR 2005, *Bosphorus* n 38 at §153.

[298] CJEU (Grand Chamber) Judgment of 3 September 2008, *Yassin Abdullah Kadi and Al Barakaat International Foundation v Council of the European Union and Commission of the European Communities*, C-402/05P and C-415/05P, ECLI:EU:C:2008:461, §314.

[299] ILC Seventh Report n 272 at 80 §33; Giorgio Gaja, 'The Relations Between the European Union and Its Member States from the Perspective of the ILC Articles on Responsibility of International Organizations' (*SHARES*, 11 April 2013) www.sharesproject.nl/publication/the-relations-between-the-

acts for which Member States lacked any discretion, was not sufficient to attribute the conduct to the IO. Following this line of reasoning, the Member States could not be seen as organs or agents of the EU, and this model would consistently result in attribution of conduct to the Member States instead of the EU, even when they are merely implementing EU acts without any regulatory discretion. Notably, the Special Rapporteur has also acknowledged that in cases where entities and persons are implementing conduct at the behest of the organisation, a factual link may result in attribution to the organisation.[300]

Scholarship spearheaded by Kuijper and Paasivirta contests the approach advanced by the Special Rapporteur inasmuch as it concerns the strict implementation of EU acts by Member States and the constitutional set-up of the Union.[301] The underlying premise here is tailored around the executive federalist structure of the EU, whereby the Member States are considered independent administrations and not formally integrated in the EU architectural administrative machinery, but nevertheless remain obligated to implement EU law in accordance with Article 291 TFEU.[302] In other words, they are considered decentralised functional European entities as a result of which the Member States exercise a dual role (*dédoublement fonctionnel*). On the one hand, the Member States are charged with the implementation of own legislation and on the other hand, they act as de facto organs or agents of the EU, when implementing EU-mandated acts. This is echoed by Hoffmeister, who holds that 'the Member States are under a duty not to overstep certain boundaries set by Union law' concluding that when EU law governs the substantive legality of an EU act, as well as judicial review over the act, the Member States are under de facto normative control of the EU.[303]

This argument is buttressed by the observation that the Special Rapporteur's narrow approach, 'closes the door for the establishment of the responsibility of the EU on the basis of the normative control by virtue of Article 6 ARIO', which in turn would leave the Member States with the consistent burden of responsibility, even when left with no discretionary implementation powers.[304] Notably, the European Commission echoes this line of reasoning and argued against Special Rapporteur Gaja's stricter reading of the normative control model in its observations

european-union-and-its-member-states-from-the-perspective-of-the-ilc-articles-on-responsibility-of-international-organizations/ 3; Stegmann n 283 at 87.

[300] Giorgio Gaja, 'Articles on the Responsibility of International Organizations' (*Audiovisual Library of International Law*, 9 December 2011) legal.un.org/avl/ha/ario/ario.html 5.

[301] Kuijper and Paasivirta n 267 at 70; Delgado Casteleiro n 27 at 42–43. See also: Stegmann n 283 at 84–91.

[302] Article 291 TFEU: '1. Member States shall adopt all measures of national law necessary to implement legally binding Union acts. 2. Where uniform conditions for implementing legally binding Union acts are needed, those acts shall confer implementing powers on the Commission, or, in duly justified specific cases and in the cases provided for in Articles 24 and 26 of the Treaty on European Union, on the Council. 3. For the purposes of paragraph 2, the European Parliament and the Council, acting by means of regulations in accordance with the ordinary legislative procedure, shall lay down in advance the rules and general principles concerning mechanisms for control by Member States of the Commission's exercise of implementing powers. 4. The word "implementing" shall be inserted in the title of implementing acts'.

[303] Hoffmeister n 289 at 741–742. This was then recalled by Wessel and den Hertog. See: Wessel and den Hertog n 278 at 349.

[304] Delgado Casteleiro n 27 at 70.

made to the ARIO. The European Commission held that 'the EU exercises normative control of the member States who then act as Union agents rather than on their own account when implementing Union law'.[305] However, this appears to conflict with the earlier stance taken by the CJEU in the *Kadi* judgment of 2008.[306] This suggests a degree of inter-institutional inconsistency and/or uncertainty on the application of the normative control model, depending on the area of EU law that is at stake.[307]

An additional argument against the strict approach to the normative model proposed by Special Rapporteur Gaja, concerns the institutional set-up of the EU. While on the surface there would be no issues attributing conduct to the EU emanating from the institutions, bodies, offices and agencies without separate and independent legal personality,[308] the question of attribution becomes slightly more difficult depending on the area of EU law that is at stake. Particularly in cases of joint *military* action, where competences are shared between the Member States and the EU, and the EU military missions are dependent upon Member State military contingents, the question of normative control becomes more complex.[309] In this latter case, the *strict* normative control test would arguably not result in EU responsibility, as the Member States make use of their military contingents, albeit in missions that to a certain extent, enjoy a status and operate independent from the Member States under the control of EU institutions.[310]

With these considerations in mind, it may be argued that applying a strict interpretation of the normative control model problematizes the very objective of the rules of attribution in ARIO – as correctly noted by the European Commission in its aforementioned observations – namely to ensure that IOs do not 'escape accountability for international wrongs'.[311]

Alternatively, some scholars posit that a systematic and comprehensive reading of the ARIO lends support to the strict approach advocated by the Special Rapporteur, whereby (implementing) conduct by states cannot be attributed (under the normative control model) to the IO, even when such conduct falls within the exclusive competences of the organisation.[312] This line of reasoning argues that situations where Member States implement binding acts of the IO, instead fall within the purview

[305] ILC, 'Responsibility of International Organizations: Comments and Observations Received from International Organizations' (UN Doc. A/CN.4/637) 14 and 17 February 2011, 167.

[306] CJEU (Grand Chamber) 2008, *Kadi and Al Barakaat* n 298.

[307] See also on this point, concerning international investment protection agreements and how the practice of the EU concerning WTO (and fundamental rights) cannot necessarily be transposed to this field of EU action: Stegmann n 283 at 88, 98.

[308] The normative control model under the ARIO, similarly, does not provide any guidance on how conduct should be attributed with respect to EU agencies, which enjoy their own independent legal personality. On the one hand, such agencies are institutionally embedded in the architecture of the European Union. On the other hand, they enjoy separate legal personality, as a result of which it is unclear, who *effectively* exercises normative control over its conduct, particularly *in theatre*. Wessel and den Hertog n 247 at 348.

[309] Kuijper and Paasivirta n 267 at 51–54.

[310] ibid 53.

[311] ILC, 'Responsibility of International Organizations: Comments and Observations Received from International Organizations' (UN Doc. A/CN.4/637) 14 and 17 February 2011, 149 §3.

[312] See (and sources cited therein) Vezzani n 272 at 285.

of Chapter IV ARIO, which governs joint action and joint responsibility as opposed to independent responsibility (see below). Following this line of reasoning, Member States when they are implementing EU acts for example, would not be considered as organs or agents, and would remain primarily responsible for their conduct. Where Member States are implementing binding acts emanating from the IO without regulatory discretion, they would accordingly be considered as acting under the IOs 'direction and control' in line with Article 15 ARIO.[313] A systematic and purposive interpretation of the ARIO lends support to this assertion,[314] but its consequences are significant. This would have as an immediate ramification that the responsibility of the IO for generating binding acts that are subsequently implemented by Member States, would not only be 'secondary' to the *fait générateur* (the unlawful conduct by the State) but would also be subject to a whole new array of conditions that are conceptually distinct from attribution.[315] In the understanding that such situations would indeed be (exclusively) caught by Article 15 ARIO instead of Article 6 ARIO, the responsibility of an IO would solely arise insofar the conditions of opposability, knowing intent and causality are demonstrated for the IO. However, these conditions in and of themselves are replete with ambiguities and further frustrate attempts at effectively holding an IO such as the EU responsible.[316]

In any event, the normative control model is only one of two – arguably three – models of attribution for independent responsibility. As the application of the normative control model is tainted by uncertainty and inconsistency, the focus shifts to the competence model as an alternative model for the determination of attribution.

The Competence Model

In addition to the normative control model on attribution as developed under the ARIO, scholarship and practice have identified a related, albeit slightly different model of attribution. This variation referred to as the 'competence model', holds that conduct must be attributed to the entity that has the legal competence to act.[317] Recalling that the principle of conferral holds that the EU can only act insofar it has been conferred the power through primary EU law to do so, this model of attribution

[313] Following this reasoning international responsibility for direction and control would only be established insofar the conditions of opposability, knowing intent and causality are met. However, the threshold to meet the conditions of Article 15 ARIO, is quite high and similarly, fraught with inconsistencies and ambiguity. However, this supposition departs from the assumption that attribution under Article 6 and responsibility arising from the meta-primary norm in Article 15 ARIO, are mutually exclusive. Talmon argues in conformity with the Commentary to ARIO, thereby weakening the line of reasoning by Vezzani. Comment 2 to Article 5 ARIO; Talmon n 283 at 413.

[314] Odile Ammann, *Domestic Courts and the Interpretation of International Law* (Leiden, Brill, 2020) 203, 209.

[315] Comment 2 to Article 5 ARIO. Already in 2005 Talmon argued that the conditionality for joint responsibility would be difficult if not impossible to meet in order to effectively hold the EU responsible. The current study builds on this reasoning and consolidates these findings. Talmon n 283 at 410.

[316] ibid.

[317] Vezzani n 272 at 289. See also: Joni Heliskoski, 'EU Declarations of Competence and International Responsibility' in Malcolm Evans and Panos Koutrakos (eds), *The International Responsibility of the European Union – European and International Perspectives* (Oxford, Hart, 2013) 193; Kuijper and Paasivirta n 267 at 54–55; Frederik Naert, 'Responsibility of the EU Regarding Its CSDP Operations' in

was conceptualized to accommodate some of the peculiarities of specific organisations, and the executive federalist structure of the EU in particular.[318] Analogously to the (exonerating) normative model of attribution (see above), the competence model knows two variations: the '*purely competence-based model*' and a more *moderate version of the competence model*.[319] While the first version of the competence model entails that conduct would be attributed to the actor that has competence according to the letter of the law, the second variation requires that for conduct to be attributed, the actor must have effectively exercised its competence.

This model broadens the scope for conduct to be attributed to the EU and thus for EU responsibility to arise in light of the EU's exclusive competences as well as its shared competences in light of the pre-emption principle.[320] Moreover, this model accommodates the idiosyncrasies of the EU executive federalist structure, where Member States are under an obligation not to disregard EU acts and where only the EU's institutions can remedy (via restitution) unlawful conduct as a result of EU conduct.[321]

One of the most straightforward applications of the competence model can be found in EU mixed agreements, which are oftentimes accompanied with declarations of competence identifying whether the EU as an entity, the Member States or both are competent to act within the scope of an international agreement.[322] Among these mixed agreements, UNCLOS is a prominent example whereby use is made of the competence model for the purpose of attribution.[323] Article 5 of Annex IX of UNCLOS requires that an IO acceding to UNCLOS must make a declaration of competence and provides State Parties the possibility of requesting clarifications of competence in any given matter.[324] While this model on attribution differs somewhat from the (exonerating) normative control model on attribution, these differences should not be exaggerated either. As Member States implement EU acts, the EU inevitably exercises some degree of control over the implementation of those acts, as a result of which there may be overlap with the aforementioned model of normative control.[325] And similar to the normative control model, a number of issues have arisen that render it difficult to distil a consistent and tenable rule of attribution from the competence model.

Malcolm Evans and Panos Koutrakos (eds), *The International Responsibility of the European Union – European and International Perspectives* (Oxford, Hart, 2013) 335–336.

[318] Kuijper and Paasivirta n 267 at 54.

[319] Vezzani n 272 at 289–290; Kuijper and Paasivirta n 267 at 54–63.

[320] Kuijper and Paasivirta n 267 at 54; Vezzani n 272 at 289.

[321] Vezzani n 272 at 289. Kuijper and Paasivirta n 267 at 55–57.

[322] Cristina Contartese, 'Competence-Based Approach, Normative Control, and the International Responsibility of the EU and Its Member States – What Does Recent Practice Add to the Debate?' (2020) 17 *International Organizations Law Review* 422; Kuijper and Paasivirta n 267 at 55. See more generally on the topic of mixed agreements: Joni Heliskoski, *Mixed Agreements as a Technique for Organizing the External Relations of the European Community and Its Member States* (Alphen aan den Rijn, Kluwer, 2001).

[323] Vezzani n 272 at 289–290.

[324] Failure to provide such clarification within a reasonable amount of time, results in the application of joint liability, as a result of which conduct may be attributed to both the Member States, as well as the EU. Vezzani n 272 at 290.

[325] Kuijper and Paasivirta n 267 at 56.

A first drawback of this second model on attribution,[326] is that it does not account for situations in which EU entities act beyond the competences they have been accorded – it does not account for ultra vires conduct. Conversely, the normative control model embedded in Article 6 ARIO, is complemented by Article 8 ARIO, which is focused in its entirety on the attribution of ultra vires conduct.[327] Secondly, having the competence to act or legislate, does not always perfectly align with the competence to *enforce* or *implement* a legally binding obligation.[328] Finally, notwithstanding the conceptual and terminological variations[329] that plague the competence model on attribution,[330] the general premise behind the competence model on attribution suggests that competence is of a static nature, whereas EU competence division is, in effect, often more dynamic.[331] The EU may only act insofar it has been accorded the power to do so by its Member States. Competence division thus refers to the degree of power transferred and afforded to the EU by its Member States, circumscribing the EU's regulatory power. While there may be no conceptual difficulties in attributing conduct to the EU insofar it has exclusive competence in a given matter, the use of the competence model becomes significantly more difficult in the context of shared competences.[332] When the EU conducts which itself within the realm of its shared competences (that is to say-powers it shares with EU Member State), the principle of pre-emption may be triggered, entailing that where Member States previously retained regulatory powers, they no longer do.[333] Similarly in cases concerning international agreements, the AETR/ERTA principle may be triggered, as a result of which the dynamic of the competence division may change from what had initially been established in a declaration of competence.[334]

While this dynamism is by no means an unsurmountable obstacle to establishing attribution, it does require a case-by-case assessment of competence division both according to the letter of the law, as well as in practice to ascertain to what actor conduct should be attributed.[335] The difficulties inherent to the competence model on attribution, have led Heliskoski to conclude that no matter how meticulously competence declarations are drafted, they cannot provide sufficiently nuanced accounts of the actual division of competence, following which 'the incidence of competence should not be conceived of as providing an appropriate criterion for

[326] Contartese n 322 at 421.
[327] Vezzani n 272 at 289.
[328] Vezzani n 272 at 289–290.
[329] Contartese n 322 at 422–423.
[330] Stegmann n 283 at 113–122.
[331] Kuijper and Paasivirta n 267 at 57.
[332] Allan Rosas, 'Exclusive, Shared and National Competence in the Context of EU External Relations: Do Such Distinctions Matter?' in Inge Govaere, Erwan Lannon, Peter Van Elsuwege and Stanislas Adam (eds), *The European Union in the World – Essays in Honour of Marc Maresceau* (Leiden, Martinus Nijhoff Publishers, 2014) 23; Kuijper and Paasivirta n 267 at 59.
[333] Robert Schütze, 'EU Competences: Existence and Exercise' in Damian Chalmers and Anthony Arnull (eds), *The Oxford Handbook of European Union Law*, Oxford Handbooks (Oxford, Oxford University Press, 2015) 86.
[334] Rosas n 332 at 23; Kuijper and Paasivirta n 267 at 59.
[335] For the sake of thoroughness, Annex IX UNCLOS does not discuss attribution of conduct, but rather, attribution of *responsibility*. For a discussion on the matter: 'Second Report on the Responsibility of International Organizations by Mr. Giorgio Gaja, Special Rapporteur' (UN Doc. A /CN.4/541) 2 April 2004, 6.

determining the incidence of responsibility'.[336] While competence division may thus be a component in determining who holds normative control, the competence model would arguably not be sufficient to elicit an overarching rule on attribution.[337]

The competence model has also given rise to diverging practice concerning the responsibility of the EU by (international) adjudicatory bodies, as well as the CJEU (see *infra*),[338] which has not been subject of any significant clarifications since the adoption of the ARIO by the UN General Assembly in 2011.[339] Contartese notes that the inconsistencies that arise in the case law of the CJEU, particularly where mixed agreements are at stake, are in part dependent on the nature and the terminology of the mixed agreement.[340] While the CJEU famously declared in the *Parliament v Council* ruling of 1994, that where no express derogations have been adopted, the Member States and the EU are 'jointly liable … for the fulfilment of every obligation arising from the commitments undertaken …', this finding was based upon the bilateral nature of the agreement at stake as a result of which the EU and its Member States acted as one indivisible party.[341] However, Advocate General Mischo questioned the suitability of this suggested general rule of joint responsibility (and attribution) in *Parliament v Council*, particularly in cases where the EU and its Member States are distinct and separate parties to a mixed agreement.[342] Advocate General Mischo notes that 'the very fact that the Community and its Member States had recourse to the formula of a mixed agreement announces to non-member countries that that agreement does not fall wholly within the competence of the Community and that, consequently, the Community is, a priori, only assuming responsibility for those parts falling within its competence',[343] which appears to underscore the dynamic nature of EU competence division. Taken in conjunction with the varying terminology used in mixed agreements, the CJEU case law suggests that the division of competence (and attribution according to this model) is consequently a matter to be assessed on a case-by-case basis, bearing in mind the particularities of each individual mixed agreement as well as the nature of the competence enjoyed by the EU.[344] In sum, the normative control test in fact consists of a strict and broad variation, as well as another variation altogether known as the competence test. While the existence

[336] Heliskoski n 317 at 192. This echoes the findings of Talmon in the preparatory phases of the ARIO where he held that 'these declarations are often formulated in such general and nebulous terms that it may be difficult for other treaty parties to determine whether a certain obligation is incumbent upon the organization or upon its member States'. Talmon n 283 at 419.

[337] Heliskoski n 317 at 192.

[338] Contartese notes that following the *Parliament v Council* ruling of 1994, where the CJEU famously held that where no express derogations have been stipulated, the Member States and the EU are 'jointly liable … for the fulfilment of every obligation arising from the commitments undertaken …' (§29).

[339] Contartese n 322 at 420.

[340] Contartese n 322 at 424–425.

[341] CJEU Judgment of 2 March 1994, *Parliament v Council*, C-316/91, ECLI:EU:C:1994:76, §29; Kuijper and Paasivirta n 267 at 64.

[342] Contartese n 322 at 425.

[343] Opinion of Advocate General Mischo of 27 November 2001, *Commission v Ireland*, C-13/00, ECLI:EU:C:2001:643, §30.

[344] Contartese concludes that the CJEU case law suggests that the terminology used in mixed agreements prevails over the internal rules of the EU in terms of competence division. Contartese n 322 at 426. Here it is held that what is relevant in the current study, is that multiple elements have bearing on how the competence division is established in fact for the determination of attribution – both the wording of international (mixed) agreements, as well as the internal rules of the organization have relevance.

of these attribution tests may appear to benefit those seeking to attribute conduct to the EU, practice suggests that these tests are applied haphazardly by (different) adjudicatory bodies and on a case-by-case basis.

– Article 7 ARIO – Conduct by an Entity at the Disposal of the Organisation

The ARIO hold that in scenarios where Member State entities do not qualify as organs or agents of the organisation but are placed at the disposal of the organisation, conduct by those Member State entities may also be attributed to the IO.[345] In other words, scenarios in which Member State entities are *partially* seconded to an organisation,[346] while Member States retain a (limited) level of (for example, criminal or disciplinary) control over the entities concerned, fall under Article 7 ARIO.[347] This provision was specifically developed to address situations of peace-keeping operations and peace enforcement operations, including situations where military contingents are placed at the disposal of IOs.[348] For conduct emanating from such entities to be attributed to the IO, Article 7 ARIO mandates that the IO must exert 'effective control' over these entities.[349] This form of control is to be distinguished from the normative control model on attribution under Article 6 ARIO, as the latter requires *full secondment*, implying a higher threshold of control than 'effective control' required under Article 7 ARIO.[350]

[345] Article 7 ARIO does not mention the term 'agents' specifically, but agents are nevertheless caught by the provision. Comment 2 to Article 7 ARIO; ILC Second Report n 275 at 114 §49.

[346] In the case of *full* secondment to an organization, the entity concerned will – according to the interpretation advanced by the Special Rapporteur in the ARIO – be considered as an organ or agent architecturally embedded in the international organization, thus falling in the ambit of the previously discussed Article 6 ARIO. Mindful of this, the argument could be made – following a systematic interpretation and based on the reference to 'full secondment' in the Commentaries to Article 7 ARIO – that the grounds for attribution in Articles 4–9 ARIO are to be interpreted strictly, and act as 'exonerating' or 'exculpating' models of attribution. Even in the case where states have no level of discretion in the implementation of certain acts stemming from the international organization, they can never be considered as being 'fully' seconded to the organization. This would entail that in a case of joint action, a finding of attribution based on Articles 4–9 ARIO, prevents dual or multiple attribution, *unless* joint responsibility is pursued on the basis of Articles 14–17 ARIO. This appears to be supported by Vezzani. On the other hand, the Special Rapporteur does not seem to exclude the possibility of dual or multiple attribution, entailing that the grounds for attribution under Articles 4–9 ARIO are not exculpatory in nature, which additionally appears to be implicitly supported by doctrine in and case law. See for potentially opposing views on the matter: ILC Second Report n 275 at 14 §48; Kjetil Mujezinović Larzen, 'Attribution of Conduct in Peace Operations: The 'Ultimate Authority and Control' Test' (2008) 19 *European Journal of International Law* 516–517; Vezzani n 272 at 286; Ahlborn n 287 at 46, 51–52.

[347] Comment 1 to Article 7 ARIO. On this point the Special Rapporteur notes in the *travaux préparatoires* that the retention of criminal and disciplinary powers by the contributing State may influence the question of attribution. This was the case in the *Attorney General v Nissan* case, where the United Kingdom was ultimately required to provide compensation for conduct by the British forces part of UNFICYP. Notably, this ruling was ultimately reversed on appeal and the British troops were subsequently considered as acting on behalf of the UN. This case is demonstrative of a larger trend whereby (inter-)national courts struggle in concrete cases with the question of the degree of effective control and the retention of certain powers by contributing states in determining to which party conduct is to be attributed. ILC Second Report n 275 at 11–12 §34–41.

[348] Comment 3 to Article 7 ARIO; Second Report n 243 at 11; ILC Seventh Report n 272 at 78–80. See also: Delgado Casteleiro n 27 at 72–75.

[349] 'The conduct of an organ of a State or an organ or agent of an international organization that is placed at the disposal of another international organization shall be considered under international law an act of the latter organization if the organization exercises effective control over that conduct' – Article 7 ARIO.

[350] Comment 1 to Article 7 ARIO.

Despite the apparent simplicity of the provision, its actual application again proves much more challenging. The application of Article 7 ARIO necessarily hinges on how the concept of 'effective control' is interpreted. The scope of this concept prompted a number of interventions during the preparatory drafting phases of the ARIO. Doctrine generally advocates for a factual and operational approach to determining which entity has effective control over a specific line of conduct, mindful of the context and circumstances of the conduct at stake.[351] Practice however, paints a different picture and evidences significantly more divergence in the interpretation of what constitutes 'effective control' and whether this should even be the prevailing ground for attribution in cases where Member State entities are placed at the disposal of an IO.[352] Not inconceivably, and as held by the UN Secretary General at the time of the drafting, the question boils down to the required *degree* of effective control for an act to be attributed to an IO.[353]

On this point, Larzen – focusing on the parallels between ARIO and ARSIWA – advances the argument that the cross-references in the *travaux préparatoires* on Article 7 ARIO to Article 6 ARSIWA, suggests an analogous understanding of what constitutes 'effective control'. Article 6 ARSIWA concerns conduct of an organ placed at the disposal of a state. For conduct by a state to be attributed to an IO, a certain level of control must be maintained by the organisation, which the Special Rapporteur links with the notion 'exclusive direction and control' used in the Commentary to Article 6 ARSIWA.[354] This reference to 'direction and control', however, is also reminiscent of Article 8 ARSIWA concerning attribution of conduct directed or controlled by a (receiving) State, which holds that conduct of person(s) will be considered emanating from the state, if the former was under instruction or direction and control of the latter. Larzen argues that the notion of effective control under Article 7 bears more resemblance to the latter, as opposed to the 'effective control' under Article 6 ARSIWA, holding that Article 7 ARIO was thus inspired by Article 8 ARSIWA.[355] Mindful of these explicit and implicit references to Article 6 and 8 ARSIWA respectively, Larzen argues that to determine whether an IO had effective control over a given line of conduct in line with Article 7 ARIO, two elements would have to be considered: factual control 'assessed with regard to specific conduct in question' resembling Article 8 ARSIWA (1) and 'overall control over an operation' resembling Article 6 ARSIWA (2).[356] However, factual/operational control and overall control are not necessarily within the hands of the same entity in (operational) scenarios involving both Member States and the EU.

Practice supports this divide between 'effective factual and operational control', and 'overall authority and control' in determining attribution. Within a UN setting, standard practice has been for the UN to acknowledge conduct stemming from its peacekeeping operations as its own. This is based on the consideration that

[351] Comment 4 to Article 7 ARIO; Second Report n 275 at 10–14; ILC Seventh Report n 272 at 80 §30; Mujezinović Larzen n 346 at 513. See also: Øby Johansen n 26 at 42; Tom Ruys, 'Mukeshimana-Ngulinzira and others v. Belgium and others' (2020) 114 *American Journal of International Law* 272–274.

[352] ILC Second Report n 275 at 10–14.

[353] Comment 9 to Article 7 ARIO.

[354] ILC Second Report n 275 at 14 §48.

[355] Mujezinović Larzen n 346 at 514.

[356] Mujezinović Larzen n 346 at 516.

peacekeeping operations function as subsidiary organs of the UN.[357] However, the UN Secretary General has underlined that peacekeeping operations are to be distinguished from other forms of joint action adopted within the UN framework. In the latter scenario, (operational command and) control is determined according to arrangements made between the implicated Member States and the UN,[358] and, in the absence of such arrangements, based on the degree of effective (operational and factual) control retained by the parties.[359] Building on this, the argument was advanced that this factual approach to effective control should also be applied to UN peacekeeping operations, giving rise to some divergence on the effective control test of attribution within a UN setting.[360] By adopting and advocating this factual approach to the effective control test, the UN (with the exception of its practice concerning peacekeeping operations) appears to being placing less weight on the abstract, normative 'overall control' assessment to determine attribution of conduct by entities placed at its disposal, in favour of a case-by-case assessment of effective control.

The ECtHR in its case law, initially adopted an approach that did not appear reconcilable with the concept of 'effective control' proposed by the Special Rapporteur, as demonstrated by the *Behrami and Saramati* ruling.[361] Though making note of attribution as referenced in ARIO, the ECtHR in *Behrami and Saramati*, held that KFOR 'was exercising lawfully delegated Chapter VII powers of the UNSC so that the impugned action was, in principle, "attributable" to the UN' which had – crucial in its reasoning – retained ultimate authority and control.[362] In other words, the ECtHR – unlike the general test for attribution adopted within a UN setting – considered that not *effective operational* control, which had been retained by NATO, was relevant in the determination of attribution, but rather, the retained *ultimate authority and control* was relevant for the purpose of attribution. Rather than relying on the effective factual control criterion, the determining factor here was a normative 'overall control' criterion.[363] The ECtHR followed this line of reasoning in

[357] This would entail that peacekeeping operations under the responsibility of the UN would result in attribution of conduct to the latter, albeit under Article 6 ARIO. Alternatively, the argument could be advanced that this could also bring the matter under Article 9 ARIO concerning the acknowledgment of attribution by the international organization (see below). ILC Second Report n 275 at 11 §35.

[358] Such arrangements do not, however, 'affect the question of attribution of conduct under general international law'. ILC Second Report n 275 at 13 §43.

[359] Comment 9 to Article 7 ARIO; ILC Second Report n 275 at 12 §41.

[360] Comment 9 to Article 7 ARIO.

[361] ECtHR (Grand Chamber) Admissibility Decision of 2 May 2007, *Agim Behrami and Bekir Behrami v France, and Ruzhdi Saramati v France, Germany and Norway*, App no 71412/01 and App no 78166/01. The *Behrami and Saramati* case has been extensively analysed in doctrine and an additional analysis thereof *in casu* would be redundant and not conducive to the research conducted. ILC Seventh Report n 272 at 79–80 §26-30. For discussions on the matter, see: Marko Milanović and Tatjana Papić, 'As Bad as It Gets: The European Court of Human Rights's Behrami and Saramati Decision and General International Law' (2009) 58 *International & Comparative Law Quarterly* 267–296; Alexander Breitegger, 'Sacrificing the Effectiveness of the European Convention on Human Rights on the Altar of the Effective Functioning of Peace Support Operations: A Critique of *Behrami & Saramati* and *Al Jedda*' (2009) 11 *International Community Law Review* 155–183; Mujezinović Larzen n 346 at 514.

[362] ECtHR (Grand Chamber) Admissibility Decision of 2 May 2007, *Agim Behrami and Bekir Behrami v France, and Ruzhdi Saramati v France, Germany and Norway*, App no 71412/01 and App no 78166/01 §140.

[363] The approach taken by the ECtHR in *Behrami and Saramati* arguably sits uneasy with its earlier stance in *Bosphorus*. Though the facts are not comparable, in the latter case the ECtHR was adamant that (Member) States remain bound by and responsible for violations of the ECHR, irrespective of any transfer of power to an international organization. ECtHR 2005, *Bosphorus* n 38 at §153. This approach is

a number of ensuing cases,[364] until the equally infamous *Al Jedda* case, where it held that the UNSC had 'neither effective control, nor ultimate authority and control over the acts and omissions of troops', entailing that the detention at stake in that case, could not be attributed to the UN.[365] Arguably, this last case suggested the willingness of the ECtHR to entertain the idea that effective factual and operational control was also an available test for attribution.[366]

This same ambiguity as to the degree of (effective) control required in order to establish attribution, is evident in the decisions of the District Court of the Hague on the responsibility of the Dutch contingent for conduct concerning the massacre in Srebrenica.[367] Whereas the initial ruling attributed the conduct at stake to the UNPROFOR as a matter of principle, the appeal judgment applied the effective (factual) criterion to determine attribution, ultimately holding the Netherlands responsible for the conduct of the Dutch contingent.[368]

Conversely, in the case of *Mukeshimana-Ngulinzira and others v Belgium and others*, the Brussels Court of First Instance in an interim judgment, ruled that the withdrawal of the *Groupe Sud* Belgian contingent of UNAMIR from the *École Technique Officielle Don Bosco*, where an approximated two thousand Rwandan refugees had sought refuge resulting in their murder, was an act attributable to the Belgian State.[369] This ruling was however, overturned by the Brussels Court of Appeal, which held that the decision to withdraw the Belgian continent from the *École Technique Officielle Don Bosco* was exclusively attributable to the UN, which had retained exclusive

indicative of the ECtHR following more factual approach to the notion of attribution, thereby disregarding the potentially highly limited margin of discretion of signatory states and the normative authority exercised by the organization vis-à-vis signatory States. Instead, the Strasbourg Court focuses on the fact that the Member States remain responsible for the manner in which they implement measures stemming from the EU legal order, regardless of the limited margin of discretion they retain. In the *Behrami and Saramati* case, the ECtHR appears to shift gears, and focuses instead on the normative control component and the ultimate authority retained by the international organization. Though a number of reasons may lay at the basis for this apparent divergence, which go beyond the scope of the present research, what remains important *in casu* is the divergence in and of itself.

[364] ECtHR Admissibility Decision of 16 October 2007, *Dušan Berić and Others v Bosnia and Herzegovina*, Application nos. 36357/04, 36360/04, 38346/04, 41705/04, 45190/04, 45578/04, 45579/04, 45580/04, 91/05, 97/05, 100/05, 101/05, 1121/05, 1123/05, 1125/05, 1129/05, 1132/05, 1133/05, 1169/05, 1172/05, 1175/05, 1177/05, 1180/05, 1185/05, 20793/05 and 25496/05, §27; ECtHR Admissibility Decisions of 28 August 2007, *Slavisa Gajic v Germany*, App no 31446/02, 5–6 (concerning purported limitations of the right to property due to the use of the Applicant's apartment by German contingent of KFOR); ECtHR Admissibility Decision of 5 July 2007, *Ilaz Kasumaj v Greece*, App no 6974/05 3 (concerning a continuing violation of Article 1 Protocol No. 1 ECHR, Article 6 ECHR and Article 13 ECHR due to occupation of lands owned by the Applicant by Greek KFOR soldiers).

[365] ECtHR (Grand Chamber) Judgment of 7 July 2011, *Al Jedda v the United Kingdom*, App no 27021/08, §84. This ruling is to be distinguished from the earlier ruling in *Al Jedda v the United Kingdom* before the House of Lords, which concluded that there was no effective command and control of the UN vis-à-vis the UK forces upon detaining the applicant, as a result of which the acts were attributed to the contributing State. See for a discussion on the topic: Comment 12 to Article 7 ARIO.

[366] For the recent cases on extra-territorial jurisdiction based on 'special features', see Chapter 5.

[367] Comment 14 to Article 7 ARIO. See on the topic: Tom Dannenbaum, 'A Disappointing End of the Road for the Mothers of Srebrenica Litigation in the Netherlands' (*EJILTalk*, 23 July 2019) www.ejiltalk.org/a-disappointing-end-of-the-road-for-the-mothers-of-srebrenica-litigation-in-the-netherlands/.

[368] Appeal Court of the Hague Judgment of 27 June 2017, *Mothers of Srebrenica Ass'n v Netherlands*, ECLI:NL:GHDHA:2017:3376; Supreme Court Judgment of 19 July 2019, *Mothers of Srebrenica Ass'n v Netherlands*, ECLI:NL:HR:2019:1284.

[369] Brussels Court of First Instance Judgment of 8 December 2010, *Mukeshimana-Ngulinzira and others v Belgium and others*, RG No 04/4807/A and 07/15547/A.

control over the operation and the conduct at stake.[370] Though the latter case and its appeal went relatively unnoticed, when taken together with the *Mothers of Srebrenica* line of cases in the Netherlands, it is clear that on a domestic level, within national judiciaries, ambiguity persists as to the standard which is to be applied in scenarios involving State contingents placed at the disposal of IOs. Depending of course, on whether an exculpatory approach (that is to say, attribution to one entails that conduct can no longer be attributed to another) is adopted in the application of attribution based upon the provisions in the ARIO, this could result in the implicated organisation being relieved of any responsibility for its involvement in the unlawful conduct.

Within an EU setting, it is again unclear whether any EU-specific rules on attribution have emerged in cases of partial secondment. As aforementioned, Article 7 ARIO envisages in particular, the (operational) action taken by contingents that have been placed at the disposal of an IO, and thus act at the behest of this organisation. The *travaux préparatoires* indicate that this provision is intended to cover peacekeeping and peace enforcement measures, bringing the matter squarely into the CFSP/CSDP-arena of EU competences.[371] Much like the divergence in scholarly and adjudicatory approaches to attribution for seconded staff to an IO under Article 7 ARIO, a similar trend of divergence appears to have manifested under EU law.

Article 42 and 43 TEU, lay out the basic framework within which civil and military assets are provided to the EU for the purpose of missions for 'peacekeeping, conflict prevention and strengthening international security in accordance with the principles of the United Nations Charter'. Article 43 TEU notes that these missions may consist of 'joint disarmament operations, humanitarian and rescue tasks, military advice and assistance tasks, conflict prevention and peacekeeping tasks, tasks of combat forces in crises management, including peace-making and post-conflict stabilisation'. Such operations involve a number of actors, and the EU is reliant upon Member State (military) contributions for the implementation of its operations.[372] Article 42 and 43 TEU remain silent, however, on matters of attribution and more generally on the apportionment of responsibility for (unlawful) conduct as a result of such operations. Within the context of military operations under the CFSP/CSDP specifically, the absence of standing EU military headquarters and the reliance

[370] Brussels Court of Appeal Judgment of 8 June 2018, *Mukeshimana-Ngulinzira and Others v Belgium and Others*, 2011/AR/292 and 2011/AR/294, §40. For a discussion on the topic, see: Ruys n 351.

[371] Comment 3 to Article 7 ARIO; Second Report n 275 at 11; ILC Seventh Report n 272 at 79. Casteleiro raises the question whether Article 7 ARIO was exclusively intended to address scenarios of military and peacekeeping operations, signalling that this is what Special Rapporteur Gaja intended and that scholars predominantly follow this line of reasoning. In the particular case of the EU, some have argued that the fact that Member States are bound by the judicial control exercised by the CJEU, entails that they too are 'placed at the disposal' of the international organization. Generally, the control exerted by the EU via its legal framework and legal review is not sufficiently effective to consider the Member States as being placed at the disposal of the EU. However, Casteleiro correctly acknowledges that Article 7 ARIO 'is drafted in a broad way, opening the possibility not only for its application to new fields where a similar degree of effective control may develop' but that its broad scope may be 'opening the door to a complete misreading of the rationale underpinning the provision'. Delgado Casteleiro n 27 at 71–75. See also: Øby Johansen n 26 at 42. On the notion of normative control by the organization where the Member States have no discretion, as opposed to the factual or operational control at the basis of Article 7 ARIO, see: Hirsch n 26 at 87.

[372] Frederik Naert, 'European Union Common Security and Defence Policy Operations' in André Nollkaemper and Ilias Plakokefalos (eds) *The Practice of Shared Responsibility* (Cambridge, Cambridge University Press, 2017) 674.

upon Member State contributions, entail that a newly agreed-upon and distinct military chain of command is required for each distinct operation.[373] Although similarities may be discernible in chains of command across various civil and military operations,[374] to make any definitive pronouncements on attribution in a given case, the various chains of command would have to be verified on a case-by-case basis to determine the concrete arrangements for every operation.

The ambiguity within the EU concerning the appropriate rule for attribution, resurfaces in the 2013 Draft Accession Agreement. Article 1(3) of the Draft Accession Agreement holds that the EU (following accession) would only be responsible for conduct committed or omitted by its institutions, bodies, offices, agencies or, alternatively, persons acting on its behalf. Conversely, Article 1(4) of the Draft Accession Agreement holds that 'an act, measure or omission of organs of a member State of the European Union or of persons acting on its behalf shall be attributed to that State, even if such act, measure or omission occurs when the State implements the law of the European Union, including decisions taken under the Treaty on European Union and under the Treaty on the Functioning of the European Union'. These two provisions appear to indicate, that first and foremost, Member States are to bear the burden of responsibility for unlawful conduct, even when implemented in pursuance of EU-mandated acts, including in the field of CFSP/CSDP. The final sentence of Article 1(4) clarifies, however, that attribution to a State does not 'preclude the European Union from being responsible as a co-respondent'. Following a literal and conjunctive interpretation of these two provisions, the EU may thus bear responsibility, albeit solely as a co-respondent. Arguably, the latter means that the EU would only be responsible on a subsidiary level, even when the Member States have done no more than merely implement EU law. The explanatory report to the Draft Accession Agreement confirms this, making any determination of attribution reliant upon who the entity is acting on behalf of.[375]

Dismayingly, neither the Draft Accession Agreement nor the explanatory report explain the standard to determine when an entity is 'acting on behalf' of the EU or the sending State. In other words, the ambiguity on which test is most appropriate to determine attribution under Article 7 ARIO, also permeates within the EU setting. NAERT argues that it would be difficult to maintain that persons implicated in an EU-mandated (military) mission are acting on behalf of a Member State, given the (operational) chain of military command. Conversely, it may be argued that

[373] ibid.

[374] For EU missions on the *territory* of a third country, the EU has developed model Status of Forces Agreement (SOFA) and a model Status of Mission Agreement (SOMA), which regulate the status and functions of an EU mission in the host state. These agreements typically include provisions concerning inter alia the use of arms, exercise of criminal jurisdiction, immunities and dispute settlement. Here too, similarities may arise across various EU missions. The relevance of SOFA's and SOMA's remains minimal in the present study however, as the study does not concern military operations *on the territory* of third states. Instead, the one case study concerning a military EU mission, is enacted on high seas. Naert n 358 at 672–673. See on the topic of SOFA's and SOMA's: Aurel Sari, 'Status of Forces and Status of Mission Agreements under the ESDP: The EU's Evolving Practice' (2008) 19 *European Journal of International Law* 67–100.

[375] CDDH Ad Hoc Negotiation Group and the European Commission, 'Final Report to the CDDH' (*Council of Europe*, 3–5 April 2013) www.echr.coe.int/documents/d/echr/UE_Report_CDDH_ENG 19, §23 (*hereafter* Explanatory Report Draft Accession Agreement).

attribution is entirely dependent upon the test that is used to determine who an entity is acting on behalf of. If the notion of 'acting on behalf of' is construed in line with the 'ultimate (overall) authority' test, then indeed, the point made by NAERT holds true. Under the 'ultimate (overall) authority' test as applied in *Behrami and Saramati*, conduct occurring in the implementation of an EU-mandated operation would in (all likelihood) be attributed to the EU. This because ultimately, EU-mandated operations are the result of a Council Decision which lays the groundwork for such operations. The Council Decisions that lay at the basis of these such operations, delegate degrees of command and control to entities under its supervision and responsibility. The CJEU appears to apply this test of attribution haphazardly. In *H. v Council* concerning a staff dispute (though the question of attribution was not necessarily at stake) the CJEU recalled that the Political and Security Committee, as well as the Civilian Operation Commander of the European Union Police Mission in Bosnia, were tasked ultimately with the obligation to implement the Council Decisions, 'under the responsibility of the Council'.[376] Accordingly, the CJEU held that *in casu* 'the contested decisions are imputable to the Council'.[377] Interestingly, in the recent *Bank Refah Kargaran* ruling, Advocate General Hogan appears to follow the 'ultimate (overall) authority' test for attribution, based upon Article 29 TEU[378] of Title V concerning the general provisions on the Union's external action. This provision requires Member States to adapt national policies and align these with the Union positions. On the basis of this provision, Advocate General Hogan holds that when acting on the basis of a Council Decision in the field of EU external (CFSP/CSDP) action, 'by virtue of the second sentence of Article 29 TEU, Member States are obliged to enforce any decisions adopted by virtue of that provision. On any view of the Francovich doctrine, individual Member States cannot be held liable for damage caused by a national measure in order to comply with such a decision, since any possible illegality, cannot be imputed to them'.[379]

However, if 'acting on behalf of' is understood according to the more 'traditional' effective factual and operational control test, then it may very well be possible to attribute acts to the Member States. Adopting this test of attribution would require a case-by-case assessment of facts to identify what entity had effective factual and operational control over a given line of conduct, as opposed to overall authority. Recalling the textual and conjunctive reading of the provisions in the Draft Accession Agreement, arguably, the EU appeared more inclined at the time of the Draft Accession Agreement, to adopt a more factual and operational test for attribution, given its apparent reluctance to open up the possibility for attribution to and responsibility of the EU for human rights violations.

[376] CJEU Judgment of 19 July 2016, *H. v Council and Commission*, C-455/14P, ECLI:EU:C:2016:569, §67–68.

[377] ibid.

[378] Article 29 TEU 'The Council shall adopt decisions which shall define the approach of the Union to a particular matter of a geographical or thematic nature. Member States shall ensure that their national policies conform to the Union positions'.

[379] Opinion of Advocate General Hogan of 28 May 2020, *Bank Refah v Council*, C-134/19P, ECLI:EU:C:2020:396, §64.

Practice concerning attribution of conduct to the Member States and/or the EU in CFSP/CSDP measures, similarly, does not resolve the conundrum. Within the context of EUNAVFOR Med Atalanta, both in first instance proceedings and on appeal, German courts held that the conduct at stake was attributable to the German authorities, leaving open the question of (dual) attribution and (joint) responsibility of the EU for its naval mission.[380] Similarly, in the preparatory phases for the Draft Accession Agreement, NAERT points out that there were 'significant divergent views' on the topic of attribution of conduct in CFSP/CSDP operations, which the CJEU neglected to address.[381]

The manner in which attribution is addressed in an EU setting, mindful of the foregoing, is inconsistent at best, even in the same domains of EU law. Naturally this prompts the question whether it is even necessary to identify a test for attribution, and whether it would be more beneficial to instead determine attribution on a case-to-case basis. Better yet, the question could be raised whether a system of joint and several liability would be preferable, as it would arguably do away with the need to definitively attribute conduct to the complicit actors.[382] Not needing to apply a test for attribution in these cases would undoubtedly provide the advantage of flexibility and would certainly work in favour of the individual.[383]

Mindful of the foregoing, under the current circumstances the determination of attribution and ultimately legal responsibility under these international rules, is entirely reliant on the analysis by the presiding judges on a case-by-case basis at various adjudicatory levels. In practice this could mean that a Member State is brought before a domestic judge that applies the effective factual and operational control test for attribution, whereas for the same operation in a different Member State, the choice could be made for the overall authority test, and different still, the test applied by EU judges in the EU Courts may very well be an altogether different test. The application by different courts of different tests of attribution, for different actors but for one single line of concerted conduct may have significant ramifications on the availability of recourse and remedies for individual claimants. Consider for example that before a national court the 'overall authority' test is applied, and unlawful conduct therefor cannot be attributed to the Member States but should instead be attributed to the EU which cannot be adjudicated by domestic judges.[384] Consider also, that for this same line of conduct the EU Courts adopt the 'effective control' test instead. The simultaneous application of two different tests of attribution by two different

[380] Oberverwaltungsgericht Nordrhein-Westfalen Judgment of 18 September 2014, 4 A 2948/11 openjur.de/u/731026.html; Joni Heliskoski, 'Responsibility and Liability for CSDP Operations' in Steven Blockmans and Panos Koutrakos (eds), *Research Handbook on the EU's Common Foreign and Security Policy* (Cheltenham, Edward Elgar Publishing, 2018) 149–150; Naert n 372 at 697–698.

[381] Naert n 372 at 697.

[382] See for example: CJEU (Grand Chamber) Judgment of 5 March 2024, *Marián Kočner v European Union Agency for Law Enforcement Cooperation*, Case C-755/21P, ECLI:EU:C:2024:202.

[383] ibid. Opinion of Advocate General Rantos of 15 June 2023, *Marián Kočner v European Union Agency for Law Enforcement Cooperation*, C-755/21P, ECLI:EU:C:2023:481, §43. See also: Joyce De Coninck, 'Europol's Joint and Several Liability Regime: Revolutionizing EU Fundamental Rights Responsibility?' (*EU Law Analysis*, 1 November 2023) eulawanalysis.blogspot.com/2023/11/europols-joint-and-several-liability.html.

[384] Absent any authorization by the CJEU, the EU enjoys immunity from measures of constraint. Article 1, Protocol (No. 7) on the privileges and immunities of the European Union [2012] OJ C 326/1.

courts for one specific line of conduct, may very well result in the conduct not being attributed to a single actor. For the aggrieved individual this means that the condition of attribution would not be met, rendering access to an effective remedy extremely precarious. While procedural justice in each of these separate procedures may have been achieved, such an approach sits uneasy with the idea of retributive or remedial justice.[385] Hence, the ambiguity on how to ascertain attribution on an EU level, could be inimical to the principles of legal certainty, legitimate expectations, the principle of legality, effectiveness of fundamental rights protection generally and the right to an effective remedy, presupposing of course that the objective of the right to an effective remedy is to ensure restorative or remedial justice.

– Article 8 ARIO – Ultra Vires Conduct

'International organizations are generally responsible for acts of their organs, provided that the latter act in their official capacity'.[386] The aforementioned grounds for attribution, operate under the assumption that the entities concerned are conducting themselves in line with their accorded powers.[387] Article 8 ARIO departs from the scenario where an organ or agent of the IO, conducts itself either beyond what is permitted according to its powers, or as an entity of the organisation,[388] as a result of which it either violates international law directly, or places Member States in a position requiring unlawful conduct.[389] Generally, IOs act in accordance with the powers that have been conferred upon it, and organs and agents, in accordance with the instructions received in the exercise of such conferred powers.[390] Article 8 ARIO addresses situations where organs or agents conduct themselves beyond the instructions they have received and/or beyond the competences that have been conferred upon the IOs.[391]

[385] On the EU and theories of justice, see: João Labareda, *Towards a Just Europe: A Theory of Distributive Justice for the European Union* (Manchester, Manchester, Manchester University Press, 2021); Floris De Witte, *Justice in the EU – The Emergence of Transnational Solidarity* (Oxford, Oxford University Press 2015); Dimitry Kochenov, Gráinne de Búrca and Andrew Williams (eds), *Europe's Justice Deficit?* (Oxford, Hart, 2015); Julie Dickson and Pavlos Eleftheriadis (eds), *Philosophical Foundations of European Union Law* (Oxford, Oxford University Press, 2012).

[386] Hirsch n 26 at 88.

[387] For a doctrinal analysis of the notion of ultra vires conduct, in light of the theory of functionalism concerning international organizations, see: Jan Klabbers, 'Contending Approaches to International Organizations' in Jan Klabbers and Âsa Wallendahl (eds), *Research Handbook on the Law of International Organizations* (Cheltenham, Edward Elgar Publishing, 2011) 10–11.

[388] Second Report n 275 at 14 §52.

[389] Article 8 ARIO – 'The conduct of an organ or agent of an international organization shall be considered an act of that organization under international law if the organ or agent acts in an official capacity and within the overall functions of that organization, **even if the conduct exceeds the authority of that organ or agent or contravenes instructions**'.

[390] ICJ Advisory Opinion of 8 July 1996, *Legality of the Threat or Use of Nuclear Weapons*, 78 §25; Second Report n 243 at p. 14 §51; Enzo Cannizzaro and Paolo Palchetti, 'Ultra Vires Acts of International Organizations' in Jan Klabbers and Âsa Wallendahl (eds), *Research Handbook on the Law of International Organizations* (Cheltenham, Edward Elgar Publishing, 2011) 365.

[391] Second Report n 275 at 14 §51; Delgado Casteleiro n 27 at 71; Pierre Klein, 'The Attribution of Acts of International Organizations' in James Crawford, Alain Pellet, Simon Olleson and Kate Parlett (eds), *The Law of International Responsibility* (Oxford, Oxford University Press, 2015) 304–306.

The explicit reference to the 'organ and agent' of the organisation in Article 8 ARIO, reveals its connection with Article 6 ARIO[392] meaning it must be read in tandem therewith.[393] This provision was drafted to prevent a responsibility gap where organs or agents acting beyond the remits of the received instructions and powers of the organisation, would otherwise not be covered by the scope of Article 6 ARIO.[394] The intertwined nature of these two provisions entails that the ambiguities concerning the definition of 'organs' or 'agents' of IOs, will be of equal relevance in determinations on attribution under Article 8 ARIO.

Ultra vires conduct is understood broadly, and refers to both conduct 'exceeding the powers of a specific'[395] organ or agent but within the competences of the IO, as well as conduct that simply surpasses the competences of the IO altogether.[396] The inverse is not necessarily true, however – when conduct is beyond the conferred competences of the IO as a whole, this does not mean that the conduct will never be attributable to the organisation.[397] Typically, the rules of the organisation will determine the (limits of the) powers accorded to an organ or agent, as well as the competences that have been conferred upon the IO.[398] However, the impact of these rules of the organisation will only be relevant for determinations of attribution, insofar the instructions and allotted powers were binding upon the organ or agent.[399]

In the preparatory works on Article 8 ARIO, it was furthermore underscored that when conduct of an organ or agent manifestly exceeds the competence of the organisation, 'the proposed rule [on ultra vires attribution] becomes less persuasive'.[400] To attribute ultra vires conduct of an organ or agent to the IO, a close link must be established between the conduct at stake and the actual functions or powers of the organ or agent. In other words, the organ or agent would have to be acting within the official capacity and within the overall functions of the organisation, for an act to be attributed to the latter.[401] The terminology on the matter refers interchangeably to situations where organs or agents act under 'apparent authority of the organization', 'under the general scope of authority', 'under the cover of authority' or 'in close connection with the exercise of the official function'.[402] However, these terminological discrepancies have no legal bearing on the matter.[403]

The underlying *rationale* for this provision is that third parties should not be deprived of access to remedies simply because an organ or agent conducted themselves

[392] Special Rapporteur Gaja indicated in this respect, that analogous to term 'agent' under Article 6 ARIO, the term in Article 8 ARIO should be broadly construed to include persons irrespective of their official capacity. Second Report n 275 at 15 §54.

[393] Comment 1 and Comment 2 to Article 8 ARIO.

[394] Delgado Casteleiro n 27 at 71.

[395] Second Report n 275 at 14 §51.

[396] Comment 1 to Article 8 ARIO.

[397] Second Report n 275 at 14 §51.

[398] Comment 2 to Article 8 ARIO.

[399] Comment 2 to Article 8 ARIO.

[400] ILC Seventh Report n 272 at 81 §36.

[401] Comment 4 to Article 8 ARIO.

[402] The difference in terminology has no legal relevance. Klein n 391 at 305; Hirsch n 26 at 89; Jean Salmon, 'Quelques réflexions sur l'immunité de juridiction des fonctionnaires internationaux pour les actes accomplis en qualité officielle' [1969] 4 *Cahiers de droit européen,* 456–457.

[403] ibid.

beyond the bounds of what is permissible according to the rules of the organisation, especially when acting within the overall functions of the organisation.[404] The ICJ summarises this point concisely in the advisory opinion concerning *Certain Expenses of the United Nations*:

> If is agreed that the action in question is within the scope of the functions of the Organization but it is alleged that it has been initiated or carried out in a manner not in conformity with the division of functions among the several organs which the Charter prescribes, one moves to the internal plane, to the internal structure of the Organization. If the action was taken by the wrong organ, it was irregular as a matter of that internal structure, but this would not necessarily mean that the expense incurred was not an expense of the Organization. Both national and international law contemplate cases which the body corporate or politic may be bound, as to third parties, by an ultra vires act of an agent.[405]

While an act may thus be declared invalid under the rules of the organisation on account of it being ultra vires, this should not detrimentally affect the availability of legal review and responsibility towards a third party. This echoes the general principle of international law according to which the internal rules of the organisation cannot be enforced vis-à-vis third parties to their detriment.[406] Internal (in-)validity of an act according to the rules of the organisation, thus has limited relevance on whether an act should be attributed to the organisation under international law.[407] Klein argues that attribution to the IO in such cases is warranted by virtue of 'the organization's shortcomings in relation to the obligation of vigilance which requires it to ensure that the means or powers that it has made available to its agents and organs for the accomplishment of their mission are utilised exclusively for that purpose and are not abused'.[408] Conversely, acts by organs or agents of an IO conducted within their private spheres or capacities, would not be caught by this provision, and accordingly would not trigger attribution to the organisation.[409]

Mindful of the foregoing, the nature of this provision inevitably requires that attribution of ultra vires conduct is assessed on a case-by-case basis.[410]

In earlier scholarship on the topic of ultra vires conduct and its attributability to the IO the question was raised whether knowledge on behalf of the third party (of the ultra vires nature of the conduct) should be considered.[411] In other words, if a third party invoking the responsibility of the IO, was aware that the organ or agent was engaging in ultra vires conduct, should this affect the attribution of the unlawful conduct to the IO? Hirsch reasoned that there should be a test of awareness on behalf of the third party, based upon an objective criterion.[412] This would disincentivise third parties from engaging with organs or agents that are manifestly

[404] Comment 5 to Article 8 ARIO; Second Report n 275 at 14 §53; Hirsch n 26 at 88–90.
[405] ICJ Advisory Opinion of 20 July 1962, *Certain Expenses of the United Nations*, 168.
[406] Article 32 ARIO; Klein n 360 at 305.
[407] Delgado Casteleiro n 27 at 72.
[408] Klein n 391 at 305.
[409] Klein n 391 at 306.
[410] Comment 9 to Article 8 ARIO.
[411] Hirsch n 26 at 93.
[412] ibid.

acting beyond the scope of their allotted powers, or beyond the powers of the organisation.[413] Interestingly, this subjectivity test was neither incorporated into the ARIO, nor raised in its Commentaries.[414] In any event, a test of awareness would be relevant only in disputes concerning states and the organisation – not in disputes concerning individuals and the IO. The question *in casu* concerns whether the EU and/or its organs and agents, may be considered as responsible for ultra vires conduct that results in unlawful human rights conduct vis-à-vis individuals (as opposed to signatory or third states).

Bearing the aforementioned nuance in mind – a number of conceptual difficulties arise when attempting to attribute unlawful human rights conduct that occurred ultra vires to the EU. First and foremost, the question of what entities constitute organs and agents, which plagued the question of attribution under Article 6 ARIO, remains equally tenuous under Article 8 ARIO. Naturally, EU entities can be considered as organs or agents of the EU. What remains unclear however, is whether and when Member States can be considered organs or agents of the EU. Under a broad approach in defining organs and/or agents, Member States could be considered as such, as a result of which, ultra vires conduct could still be attributed to the EU. As already elaborated upon, however, there is no consensus on whether Member States can or cannot be considered as organs or agents of the EU and much of this is determined by the substantive area of EU law at stake (see above). In situations where the EU has in fact substituted the Member States in their obligations vis-à-vis third parties, the argument can be made, that indeed, ultra vires conduct could be attributed to the EU. Yet, this seems unlikely for the purpose of ultra vires human rights conduct, where the EU appears to take the stance that such conduct remains the responsibility of the Member States (see above).

A second issue that arises, relates again to the dynamic nature of competence division. To know whether an organ or agent of the EU has acted beyond the permitted bounds of the conferred competence, it is necessary to ascertain what those bounds are. However, as aforementioned, competence division within the EU is by no means immutable or static. Instead, competence conferral can be explicit or implicit and vary depending on the area of substantive EU law at stake. In this respect, Cannizzaro and Palchetti underline that the various (differing) criteria used to delimitate the scope of conferred competences, may ultimately affect whether conduct is considered as ultra vires conduct.[415] The authors conclude that the lack of precision and unity on when conduct can be considered as ultra vires, prevents a comprehensive, all-encompassing rule:[416]

> Since the scope of the competence of the various international organizations varies according to the criteria around which the competence is determined, the conditions which

[413] ibid.

[414] The point was only fleetingly referenced by Special Rapporteur Gaja in the preparatory works. Second Report n 275 at 14 §53.

[415] See for a number of differing tests concerning potential ultra vires conduct by the CJEU alone: Paul Craig, 'The ECJ and Ultra Vires Action: A Conceptual Analysis' (2011) 48 *Common Market Law Review* 397.

[416] Cannizzaro and Palchetti n 390 at 366, 389.

> indicate that a certain act is ultra vires also vary accordingly. If the international organization is assigned competence in a certain substantive field, the notion of an ultra vires act refers to a substantive criterion. If the competence is of functional character, a functional analysis must be undertaken, and so on.[417]

In this respect the authors emphasise that focusing on these separate factors, may lead to wrongful conclusions about the actual scope of conferred competences of an IO, and ultimately lead to an enlargement of their competences.[418] Without clarity on what factor(s) determine the scope of competence and thus ultra vires conduct, an IO may interchangeably make use of various factors for competence determinations to suit its purpose.[419] This ambiguity in combination with the requirement that a sufficiently close link exists between the ultra vires conduct and the exercise of the functions entrusted to it, allows haphazard determinations on when an entity has or has not acted within the framework of the organisation and ultimately, whether ultra vires conduct is to be attributed to the EU.

At the same time, the danger of haphazard determinations of attribution should also not be exaggerated. Within the context of certain substantive areas of EU law, particularly where the EU enjoys exclusive competences (see above), determinations of ultra vires conduct and subsequent attribution will be straightforward. Yet, in the realm of human rights protection, it appears that the *point de départ* is consistently that Member States bear the primary responsibility burden, separate from the EU, entailing that they will not be considered as agents or organs for the purpose of Article 8 ARIO. This last observation appears to be in line with the implicit point made on ultra vires conduct in *Sayag v Leduc*, where the Court held that the Community would only be responsible for acts of its servants, 'which, by virtue of an internal and direct relationship, are the necessary extension of the tasks entrusted to the institutions'.[420] As human rights protection is not 'task entrusted to the institutions' in and of itself but functions rather as a parameter against which EU and Member State conduct is to be assessed, it will be difficult to successfully construe an argument of ultra vires unlawful conduct to be attributed to the EU across domains of EU law for the purpose of attributing unlawful human rights conduct.

Finally, Article 8 ARIO does not reveal much with respect to consequences that flow from ultra vires conduct and the ramifications this may have on individuals seeking redress for unlawful human rights conduct. Whereas ultra vires conduct may lead to the invalidity of an act internally, such invalidity is not automatic. Moreover, the invalidity of the ultra vires conduct does not reveal much in terms of the effect this has on the individual who was affected by the invalid conduct. Whereas the invalidity of a measure may pave a path to additional legal actions for the purpose of obtaining damages, this is also not automatic, and the invalidity has no bearing on whether the breach would be considered sufficiently serious and thus give rise to a remedy under the EU's action for damages (see below).

[417] ibid 367.
[418] ibid 368.
[419] ibid 369.
[420] CJEU Judgment of 11 July 1968, *Claude Moïse and S.A. Zurch v Jean-Pierre Leduc*, C-5/68, ECLI:EU:C:1968:42.

In sum, notwithstanding the laudable attempt to limit responsibility gaps as a result of the conceptual and scope-related restrictions to determine attribution under Articles 6 and 7 ARIO, the provision of ultra vires conduct is analogously tainted by conceptual and practical deficiencies in the quest for redress. In addition to the definitional ambiguity surrounding organs and agents, the application of Article 8 ARIO is obscured by mutable competence conferral. Although Article 8 ARIO thus provides an additional ground for attribution vis-à-vis the EU, its added value appears limited and yet again, subject to an ad hoc and ex post adjudicatory appraisal.

– Article 9 ARIO – Conduct Acknowledged by the Organisation as Own Conduct

Finally, in accordance with Article 9 ARIO, conduct can be attributed to the IO insofar the conduct is acknowledged by the organisation as being its own. This ground of attribution was drafted analogously to its twin provision in ARSIWA[421] and establishes attribution based upon the adopted attitude of the IO in relation to a particular conduct.[422] Within the context of this ground for attribution, use is interchangeably made of terms such as 'acknowledgement', 'adoption', 'recognition', 'approval' and 'ratification'[423] – all of which signify the attitude of the IO in assuming conduct as its own. Such assumption of conduct may occur when the conduct at stake would otherwise be attributed to the implicated States according to aforementioned grounds of attribution in the ARIO,[424] or alternatively, when conduct could not otherwise (according to those same rules) be attributed to any given entity.[425] In addition, Article 9 ARIO allows for IO to acknowledge and adopt the unlawful conduct as being its own only partially.[426] However, notwithstanding the examples cited in the Commentaries to the ARIO, such forms of attribution and acknowledgment of conduct, do not occur frequently.[427]

Article 9 ARIO does not appear to be a particularly controversial ground for attribution, but is of course wholly dependent upon the willingness of the organisation to acknowledge potentially unlawful conduct. Practice is limited in this respect[428] and the question may be raised whether in those particular examples, the question is not one of attribution of conduct, but rather assumption of responsibility in its entirety?[429] When the UN for example, acknowledges the conduct of peacekeeping operations as its own, it appears rather that it is assuming responsibility, as opposed to attribution, for the conduct that has taken place.[430] Similarly,

[421] This provision on attribution appears to be the least controversial ground for attribution, as evidenced by the concise analysis thereof in the *travaux préparatoires*, the Commentary to the ARIO, as well as the limited analysis thereof in scholarship. Comment 2 to Article 9 ARIO; Second Report n 275 at 16 §60, 63.

[422] Comment 1 to Article 9 ARIO.

[423] Second Report n 275 at 16 §62.

[424] Comment 1 to Article 9 ARIO.

[425] Comment 2 to Article 9 ARIO.

[426] Comment 1 to Article 9 ARIO.

[427] ILC Seventh Report n 272 at 81 §37.

[428] ILC Second Report n 275 at 16 §61.

[429] Comment 3 to Article 9 ARIO.

[430] ILC Second Report n 275 at 11 §35.

within an EU-setting, it appears more as though the EU in WTO-cases, has assumed responsibility, as opposed to merely the attribution of (unlawful) conduct. This last point is demonstrated by the statements made by the then European Community in the *European Communities – Customs Classification of Certain Competence Equipment* case, holding specifically that it was 'ready to assume the entire international responsibility for all measures in the area of tariff concessions, whether the measure complained about has been taken at the EC level or at the level of Member States'.[431] Again, much appears to depend on the substantive area of EU law that is at stake. In WTO-related matters, where the EU has effectively substituted the Member States, it need not surprise that the EU would be more willing to assume attribution (and responsibility). However, recalling the absence of general EU regulatory powers in human rights, where human rights function first and foremost as a judicial yardstick to assess the legality of conduct implemented in a shared manner between Member States and the EU, it appears unlikely that the EU will simply assume responsibility for unlawful human rights conduct. Practice has not disproven this thus far, at least as concerns IBM.

On a final note, Special Rapporteur Gaja saw no evidence of a special rule of international law governing the matter of acknowledgment by an international organisation of conduct as being its own, but nevertheless underlined that the rules of the organisation will be remain relevant here, particularly to identify the entities that are competent to make such declarations of acknowledgment.[432]

ii. The Lex Specialis *Rules*

– Introductory Remarks

The reference to the *lex specialis* in Article 64 ARIO functions as a conflict-solution rule[433] and prescribes that the more general rules embodied in the ARIO 'do not apply where and to the extent that the conditions for the existence of an internationally wrongful act or the content or implementation of the international responsibility of an international organisation, or a State in connection with the conduct of an international organisation, are governed by special rules of international law'. In line with the Commentary, this means that the special rules of the organisation concerning its international responsibility, may either *supplement* or *replace* the more general framework embodied in the ARIO.[434] Indeed, following a textual interpretation of the ARIO, an all-encompassing system of internal rules of the determination of international responsibility is by no means necessary and single rules regulating only specific aspects of international responsibility can and will be sufficient to be

[431] The document concerned is not published but mentioned in the commentaries to Article 9 ARIO. See Comment 3 to Article 9 ARIO. ILC Second Report n 275 at 16 §61. Vezzani n 272 at 293–294.
[432] Comment 5 to Article 9 ARIO.
[433] Dorota Marianna Banaszewska, '*Lex Specialis*' in Rüdiger Wolfrum (ed.) *Max Planck Encyclopaedia in Public International Law* (Oxford, Oxford University Press, 2015) §14–15.
[434] Commentary 1 to Article 64 ARIO.

considered a *lex specialis* for the purpose of Article 64 ARIO.[435] Accordingly, IOs may have special rules governing the ***conditions** for the existence of an internationally wrongful act* (1),[436] *the **content** of international responsibility including the consequences stemming from the responsibility and associated reparations* (2),[437] and *the **implementation** of the responsibility* (3).[438] Crucially, to replace the general framework on responsibility, it is presumed that the *lex specialis* provision(s) are not identical to the *lex generalis* regime, which is being contracted out of[439] as long as the provisions cover the same subject matter.[440]

The focus of the next section will be limited to determining whether a *lex specialis* exists concerning the *conditions* for the existence of (human rights) responsibility, as this is the focus of the analysis.

Applied to the particular case of the EU, some authors have compellingly argued that a *lex specialis* regime governing (international) responsibility of the EU has emerged, whereas others have argued that the divergence in practice prevents any conclusive determinations of a *lex specialis* regime.[441] *In casu*, it is argued that an overarching *lex specialis* regime has partially emerged concerning the *conditions* for the existence of responsibility.[442] Crucially, however, it will be demonstrated that

[435] This assertion is furthermore corroborated by the language used in the Commentary to Article 64 ARIO, which uses words such as 'or' to indicate the non-exhaustive nature of the rules of the organization referenced in Article 64 ARIO. See also Commentary 7 to Article 64 ARIO, which explains the raison d'être of the provision, which was to prevent a situation where every single provision of the ARIO would be supplemented by the proviso that its contents would be without prejudice to the special rules of the organization on the matter: Article 64 ARIO 'is designed to make it unnecessary to add to many of the preceding articles a proviso such as "subject to special rules"'. Similarly, Commentary 8 to Article 64 ARIO holds that 'the rules of the organization may, expressly or implicitly, govern various aspects of the issues dealt with in Parts Two to Five'.

[436] Rules on the ***conditions for the existence of an internationally wrongful act*** refer to the constituent conditions (according to secondary rules) that would give rise to international responsibility, thus referring broadly to the conditions of attribution and internationally unlawful conduct, as well as the conditions for the preclusion of wrongfulness of the unlawful conduct.

[437] Rules on ***the content of international responsibility including the consequences stemming from the responsibility and associated reparations*** refer to the rules of the organization that concern the consequences stemming from the unlawful conduct, including the measures to remedy the unlawful conduct and the potential requirements regarding reparations and the apportionment thereof.

[438] Rules on ***the implementation of the responsibility*** of the international organization, refer to rules that dictate how responsibility may be invoked, by what parties, and the (procedural) requirements in this respect for the claim to be deemed admissible or when parties are considered to have lost their rights to invoke claims of unlawful conduct.

[439] Ahlborn n 287 at 437–438.

[440] ibid 437.

[441] See Comment 2 to Article 64 ARIO. In literature, the approach on responsibility adopted by the WTO vis-à-vis the EU, is often juxtaposed with the approach taken within the framework of human rights protection by the ECtHR, the approach taken by ITLOS within the framework of law of the sea, as well as the approach taken within the context of investment disputes. See on the topic: Hoffmeister n 289 at 723. Kuijper en Paasivirta suggest that the competence model on attribution, functions as a *lex specialis*, albeit in the realm of exclusive competences. Kuijper and Paasivirta n 267 at 69–71. See also Martin, who argues in favour of an emerging *lex specialis* (on attribution): José Manuel Cortés Martin, 'European Exceptionalism in International Law? The European Union and the System of International Responsibility' in Maurizio Ragazzi (ed), *Responsibility of International Organizations – Essays in Memory of Sir Ian Brownlie* (Leiden, Martinus Nijhoff Publishers, 2013) 199.

[442] It may also be argued that an EU-specific *lex specialis* has partially emerged concerning the *content* and *consequences* stemming from an internationally wrongful act. Finally, a regime as such, has also (partially) emerged concerning the *implementation* of the international responsibility. However, analysing all of these components goes beyond the remit of what the intended research attempts to answer. On the (partial) emergence of a *lex specialis*, see Hoffmeister n 289 at 740.

these specific *lex specialis* rules are by no means a self-contained regime, sufficiently comprehensive or effective to replace the more general rules embodied in the ARIO. Echoing Klabbers, it will be illustrated that these rules are also fraught with ambiguity, resulting in their ultimate ineffectiveness and inability to meet their function.[443]

Although the EU's constituent treaties do not explicitly address the international responsibility of the EU in general terms,[444] international responsibility is generally understood as implying a duty to repair.[445] Indeed, in *Riva Fire*, the CJEU recalled that 'a breach must be sanctioned in an action for damages … since such an action constitutes an effective remedy'.[446] The obligation to provide reparations for damage following unlawful EU conduct is considered to be a principle of EU law and a manifestation of the principle of effective judicial protection,[447] and militates in favour of an underlying objective of restorative or remedial justice. To invoke the responsibility of the EU or one of its institutions according to the rules of the organisation for human rights violations before the CJEU, a number of procedures may be relied upon.[448] This includes the indirect action known as the preliminary ruling on the validity and interpretation of EU law (Article 267 TFEU), as well as the direct actions: action for annulment (Article 263 TFEU), an action for failure to act (Article 258 TFEU), an action for damages (Article 268 TFEU *in juncto* Article 340 TFEU *in juncto* Article 41(3) CFR).[449] Within these procedures the exclusive prerogative to rule on the responsibility of the EU remains with the CJEU.[450] Mindful of the functions of these different indirect and direct EU actions, the *lex specialis* concerning the *conditions* for responsibility is the action for damages[451] as the obligation to provide reparations cannot be met with mere declaratory orders annulling or rulings interpreting specific provisions or acts of EU law.[452]

[443] On whether (a) mechanism(s) exists to prevent and remedy unlawful conduct by international organizations, Klabbers noted that such unlawful conduct 'raises the obvious question: does international institutional law lack any form of mechanism to prevent them from doing such things? The answer is both yes and no: yes, such mechanisms exist; no, they are not terribly effective'. Klabbers n 387 at 5.

[444] Arguably the international responsibility of the EU can be considered implicitly covered by Article 51 CFR. Esa Paasivirta, 'The Responsibility of Member States of International Organizations – A Special Case for the European Union' (2015) 12 *International Organizations Law Review* 454.

[445] Ahlborn n 287 at 55–56.

[446] CJEU Judgment of 21 September 2017, *Riva Fire SpA en liquidation v European Commission*, C-89/15P, ECLI:EU:C:2017:713, §54.

[447] Opinion of Advocate General Geelhoed of 3 July 2003, *Mediator v Lamberts*, C-234/02P, ECLI:EU:C:2004:174, §82–86; Fink n 27 at 183.

[448] See generally: Koen Lenaerts, Ignace Maselis, Kathleen Gutman and Janek Tomasz Nowak (eds) *EU Procedural Law* (Oxford, Oxford University Press, 2014). See also on the basic conditions for responsibility: Fink n 27 at 15.

[449] The 'objection of illegality' shall not be discussed in the present matter as it does not constitute an independent plea of law which may be invoked by the Applicants. Additionally, the CJEU opinions on the compatibility of international agreements with EU law shall, shall likewise, not be discussed in the present analysis as it is not applicable.

[450] Article 268 TFEU holds that: 'The Court of Justice of the European Union shall have jurisdiction in disputes relating to compensation for damage provided for in the second and third paragraphs of Article 340'. This is reconcilable with the approach taken in the preparation of the Draft Accession Agreement and Opinion 2/13, where it was underlined that although joint responsibility between Member States and the EU is possible in theory, the nature and implications resulting therefrom would not be ruled upon by an external court. Fink n 27 at 184.

[451] Ward n 103 at 184.

[452] ibid 183–184.

The action for damages "*seeks to address the situation where an EU institution has caused loss through the exercise of its legislative, administrative or executive functions*".[453] The action for damages constitutes an independent action that may be invoked in tandem with the action for annulment or the action for failure to act.[454] However, this is by no means required, nor does it necessarily have any bearing on the (successful) outcome of the action for damages.[455] The indirect and direct proceedings before the CJEU all pursue differing objectives, and following this, differing procedural admissibility conditions.[456] It is entirely plausible that an action for annulment be declared inadmissible, and yet still obtain a successful claim for damages on the same matter.[457]

– Identifying the Conditions to Establish EU Responsibility

While the Treaties do foresee in a legal basis for the purpose of establishing non-contractual liability of the EU in Article 340(2) and 340(3) TFEU, these provisions are not elaborated upon to clarify what the conditions are for such responsibility to arise. Rather, this was intended to be developed by the CJEU 'in accordance with the general principles common to the laws of the Member States …'.[458] The CJEU-driven clarification(s) of the responsibility framework result in the judicial architecture of the *lex specialis* concerning EU (international) responsibility being an intricate composition of factors and clarifications scattered across various cases, in various substantive domains of EU law. However, the seminal cases to date in the determination of non-contractual liability of the Union, remain the *Schöppenstedt*[459] judgment and the *Bergaderm*[460] judgment, with the latter remaining largely applicable today,[461] albeit with slight alterations.[462]

[453] Andrea Biondi and Martin Farley, 'Damages in EU Law' in Robert Schütze and Takis Tridimas (eds), *Oxford Principles of European Union Law – Volume I: The European Legal Order* (Oxford, Oxford University Press, 2018) 1053.

[454] Lenaerts, Maselis, Gutman and Nowak n 448 at §11.09.

[455] ibid; CJEU (CFI) Judgment of 26 January 2006, *Medici Grimm KG v Council of the European Union*, T-364/03, ECLI:EU:T:2006:28, §61–62 (concerning an annulment action that is not sufficient to establish a sufficiently serious breach required for the purpose of a successful action for damages). See similarly: CJEU (General Court) Judgment of 23 November 2011, *Sison v Council*, T-341/07, ECLI:EU:T:2011:687, §31 holding in particular: 'it must be recalled that, according to settled case-law, a finding of the unlawfulness of a legal measure – like the measures challenged in the present case and found to be unlawful in the light of Article 2(3) of Council Regulation No 2580/2001 of 27 December 2001 (OJ 2001 L 344, p. 70), and of Article 1(4) of Council Common Position 2001/931/CFSP of 27 December 2001 on the application of specific measures to combat terrorism (OJ 2001 L 344, p. 93) – is not enough, however regrettable that unlawfulness may be, for it to be held that the condition for the incurring of the Community's non-contractual liability relating to the unlawfulness of the institutions' alleged conduct has been satisfied (see, to this effect, Case C-282/05 P *Holcim (Deutschland) v Commission* [2007] ECR I-2941, paragraph 47; Case T-56/00 *Dole Fresh Fruit International v Council and Commission* [2003] ECR II-577, paragraphs 72 to 75; and Case T-212/03 *MyTravel v Commission* [2008] ECR II-1967, paragraphs 43 and 85)'.

[456] Lenaerts, Maselis, Gutman and Nowak n 448 at §11.09.

[457] ibid.

[458] Article 340(2) TFEU.

[459] CJEU Judgment of 2 December 1971, *Aktien-Zuckerfabrik Schöppenstedt v Council of the European Communities*, C-5/71, ECLI:EU:C:1971:116.

[460] CJEU Judgment of 4 July 2000, *Bergaderm and Goupil v Commission*, C-352/98 P, ECLI:EU:C:2000:361.

[461] Fink n 27 at 189; Lenaerts, Maselis, Gutman and Nowak n 448 at §11.45.

[462] Fink n 27 at 185.

Bergaderm elaborated upon the conditions that must be met for EU responsibility to arise, holding in particular that the 'Court has held that Community law confers a right to reparation where three conditions are met: the rule of law infringed must be intended to confer rights on individuals; the breach must be sufficiently serious; and there must be a direct causal link between the breach of the obligation and the damage sustained by the injured parties'.[463] In other words, there must be damage caused by the Union (implicitly encompassing the notion commonly referred to as attribution) (1); unlawful conduct (2); and the rule of law at stake must have been intended to confer rights on the individual invoking the provision (3).[464] Failure to meet one of these cumulative conditions results in the inadmissibility of the application, without the other criteria being examined.[465]

Finally, as is the case under international law and the ARIO specifically, EU law and the CJEU have recognised the possibility of both independent responsibility vis-à-vis the Union, as well as shared responsibility between the Union and the Member States (see below).

– Attribution

Whereas the ARIO explicitly identify attribution as one of the two cumulative conditions for international responsibility to arise, the EU *lex specialis* on responsibility remains (textually) vague on the matter. Lenaerts and others hold, however, that attribution is inherent to causality, clarifying that attribution follows implicitly from the aforementioned direct causality requirement.[466] Occasionally, the CJEU has referred to attribution as a fourth condition for a successful claim for damages,[467] albeit inconsistently and at times has conflated the concepts of attribution and causation.[468] These two concepts (attribution and causation) should not be conflated, however, as they are conceptually distinct and operate at different junctures of the

[463] CJEU Judgment of 4 July 2000, *Bergaderm and Goupil v Commission*, C-352/98 P, ECLI:EU:C:2000:361, §42. Lenaerts, Maselis, Gutman and Nowak n 448 at §11.38; Fink n 27 at 186.

[464] With the exception of the third and last condition, the conditions to establish responsibility under EU law, largely correspond to the constituent elements to establish (international) responsibility under the ARIO (see above), where it is held in Article ARIO that the elements of an internationally wrongful act require conduct (act or omission) to be attributable to the international organization (1), and that said conduct constitutes a breach of an international obligation owed by that international organization (2). This is relevant as the ARIO hold that for a *lex specialis* to be capable of supplementing or replacing the *lex generalis*, the rules must concern the same subject area. *In casu*, this consequently does not pose a problem.

[465] CJEU (General Court) Judgment of 15 January 2015, *Ziegler SA and Ziegler Relocation SA v European Commission*, T-539/12 and T-150/13, ECLI:EU:T:2015:15, §59–60; Biondi and Farley n 439 at 1053.

[466] Lenaerts, Maselis, Gutman and Nowak n 448 at §11.18–11.19, 11.81–11.84.

[467] 'According to settled case-law, in order for the European Union to incur non-contractual liability, a number of conditions must be satisfied, namely (i) the conduct alleged must be attributable to an EU institution or body, (ii) that conduct must be unlawful, (iii) there must be damage and (iv) there must be a direct causal link between the conduct and the alleged damage. If any one of those conditions is not satisfied, the action must be dismissed in its entirety and there is no need to consider whether the other conditions are met (see the judgment of 10 July 2012 in Case T-587/10 *Interspeed v Commission*, not published in the ECR, paragraph 38 and the case-law cited)': CJEU (General Court) Judgment of 18 September 2014, *Holcim (Romania) v Commission*, T-317/12, ECLI:EU:T:2014:782, §86.

[468] CJEU (General Court) 2023, *WS and others v Frontex* n 59; Joyce De Coninck, 'Shielding Frontex: On the General Court's "WS and Others v Frontex"' (*Verfassungsblog*, 9 September 2023); Fink, Rauchegger and De Coninck n 151. Conversely, this confusion is avoided in other domains of EU law. See for example

responsibility question. Whereas causation connects the incurred damage with the (sufficiently serious unlawful) conduct, attribution connects the unlawful conduct to an implicated actor.[469] The connection of these elements in the responsibility questions, operate under different tests – a test of causality,[470] as opposed to a test of attribution.[471]

Bergaderm neither explicitly addresses the notion of attribution, nor the tests of attribution that may arise under EU law. Based moreover, upon the variety of approaches to attribution adopted under substantive areas of EU law, it is not clear whether there is even an overarching *lex specialis* of attribution to speak of. Despite the absence of an explicit reference to attribution in Article 340 TFEU and despite the absence of various tests for attribution (as is the case under the ARIO), however, the test of attribution constitutes a *sine qua non* for a successful action for damages to arise.[472] This was confirmed, in *Delice and Delice v Erlangen and Commission* where it was held that:

> 18. En ce qui concerne le chef de conclusions relatif à la réparation des dommages matériel et moral prétendument subis par les requérants, il convient de rappeler tout d'abord la compétence limitée du Tribunal (voir point 12 ci-dessus). En application des dispositions des articles 235 CE et 288 CE, et plus particulièrement de l'article 288, deuxième alinéa, CE, le Tribunal est uniquement compétent pour connaître des recours en indemnité introduits à l'encontre des institutions et des organes communautaires, créés par les traités ou par des actes pris pour leur application.
>
> 19. Dans la mesure où ce chef de conclusions **a pour objet d'obtenir une indemnisation de la part de la Commission, le recours est manifestement irrecevable. Les requérants n'ont avancé aucun argument permettant d'identifier un acte ou un comportement attribuable en ce sens à cette institution**[473] (emphasis added).

Under the EU-*acquis*, attribution appears to be in part determined by the decision-making powers in a given area.[474] In turn, decision-making powers are determined by the division of competences, which gave rise to the 'competence-model' on attribution as developed by Kuijper and Paasivirta.[475] The CJEU has clarified that when Member States lack competence in a given area, acts taken within that context may be attributable to the EU.[476] However, insofar Member States retain 'genuine discretion' in the adoption of acts that stem from an underlying EU act (without being bound by

on joint and several liability: CJEU (Grand Chamber) Judgment of 5 March 2024, *Marián Kočner v European Union Agency for Law Enforcement Cooperation*, Case C-755/21P, ECLI:EU:C:2024:202.

[469] ibid; see also: Gábor Kajtár, Basak Çali, and Marko Milanovic (eds), *Secondary Rules of Primary Importance in International Law* (Oxford, Oxford University Press, 2023); Fink n 27 at 233; Ahlborn n 287 at 57–58.

[470] This may be the *sine qua non* test or the test of immediate causality as adopted by the CJEU.

[471] This may encompass the normative control model for attribution or the competence model for attribution, both which encompass either a stringent or broad approach.

[472] Lenaerts, Maselis, Gutman and Nowak n 434 at §11.81.

[473] CJEU Judgement (CFI) of 19 May 2009, *Baki Delice et Seval Delice v Stadt Erlangen et Commission des Communautés eropéenes*, T-528/08, ECLI:EU:T:2009:162; §18–19.

[474] Lenaerts, Maselis, Gutman and Nowak n 448 at §11.25.

[475] Kuijper and Paasivirta n 267 at 54.

[476] CJEU Judgment of 19 May 1992, *Mulder and Others v Council and Commission*, C-104/89 and C-37/90, ECLI:EU:C:1992:217, §9. See also: Lenaerts, Maselis, Gutman and Nowak n 448 at §11.25; Kuijper and Paasivirta n 267 at 59.

specific instructions by the EU) the contested act will be attributable to the implicated Member State and not the EU.[477]

However, more generally, the EU's approach to attribution seemingly combines the normative and competence models of attribution as elaborated upon under the ARIO (see above). While the pitfalls of these models have been elaborated upon, the practice under the EU-*acquis* complicates the matter of attribution even more, in light of the fact that different approaches to attribution are adopted under differing areas of substantive EU law. While this is an understandable choice in light of the differing competences of the EU in substantive areas of EU law, this makes it more difficult to determine whether an overarching *lex specialis* indeed exists concerning attribution, and more generally, concerning the conditions for independent responsibility. Vezzani argues that the approach adopted by the EU in determinations of attribution and ensuing responsibility, do not appear to follow a set standard and are applied haphazardly, as a result of which it is hard to contend a that *lex specialis* currently exists, capable of replacing the *lex generalis* regime on attribution.[478]

– Causation

Article 340(2) TFEU holds that 'In the case of non-contractual liability, the Union shall, in accordance with the general principles common to the laws of the Member States, make good any damage caused by its institutions or by its servants in the performance of their duties'. This provision explicitly established the necessity to have a causal link between the unlawful conduct and the damage incurred.[479] However, analogously to the ARIO, there is neither an explicit test of causation that is advanced under the responsibility framework of the EU, nor is there a 'standard or uniform formulation of this requirement' under EU law.[480] Case law by the CJEU refers to the causality requirement under EU law in a number of different manners, including formulations that the damage incurred must be a 'sufficiently direct consequence'[481] of the unlawful conduct or that the unlawful conduct must

[477] Lenaerts, Maselis, Gutman and Nowak n 448 at §11.25–11.26; CJEU Judgment of 7 July 1987, *L'Etoile Commerciale 2. Comptoir National Technique Agricole (CNTA) v. Commission of the European Communities*, C-89/86 and C-91/86, ECLI:EU:C:1987:337 §16–21.

[478] Vezzani n 272 at 314–315.

[479] The notion of damage will not be elaborated upon *in casu*. In brief, it suffices to mentioned that damage must be 'actual and certain' and thus 'not hypothetical'. It may be reasonably assumed that unlawful returns of TCN's in violation of the *non-refoulement* principle, which presupposes a level of severity in the anticipated ill-treatment, will meet the standard for damages required under the action for damages. CJEU (General Court) Judgment of 25 October 2010, *Inuit Tapiriit Kanatami and Others v European Parliament and Council of the European Union*, T-18/10 R II, ECLI:EU:T:2010:448, §90; Fink n 27 at 228–231; Lenaerts, Maselis, Gutman and Nowak n 448 at §13.40.

[480] ibid §11.78.

[481] 'Il est de jurisprudence constante que la condition relative au lien de causalité exigée par l'article 288, deuxième alinéa, CE suppose l'existence d'un **lien suffisamment direct de cause à effet entre le comportement des institutions et le dommage** (arrêts du Tribunal du 24 octobre 2000, Fresh Marine/Commission, T-178/98, Rec. p. II-3331, point 118, et du 14 décembre 2005, Beamglow/Parlement e.a., T-383/00, Rec. p. II-5459, point 193), dont la preuve doit être rapportée par la requérante (voir arrêt du Tribunal du 24 avril 2002, EVO/Conseil et Commission, T-220/96, Rec. p. II-2265, point 41, et la jurisprudence citée)'. CJEU Judgment of 30 June 2011 (General Court Order), *Tecnoprocess Srl v Commission and EU Delegation to the Kingdom of Morocco*, T-264/09, ECLI:EU:T:2011:319, §120.

be the 'determining cause'[482] of the damage.[483] Lenaerts and others hold, that these terminological discrepancies do not necessarily point to different tests of causality.[484] Instead, the test for causality under EU law is generally understood as requiring that the damage must be the *direct consequence* of the unlawful conduct.[485] Insofar the damage is considered too remote of a consequence of the unlawful conduct, it will not be considered as having met the test for causation.[486] Finally, within a claim for damages, the burden of proof and consequently the accompanied standard of proof of the chain of causation, lies with the Applicant claiming the causal effect of the unlawful conduct by the EU.[487]

On the face of it, it appears that this test is less stringent than the 'but-for test' of causality that surfaces according to some interpretations of (shared responsibility) under the ARIO (see below). Practice, however, paints an entirely different picture. Although generally the existence of a causal link will be assessed on a case-by-case basis,[488] the threshold for the required causal link is strictly interpreted by the Court and in fact, *higher* than the 'but-for' test of causation.[489] This is evidenced inter alia in *Atlantic Container Line and Others v Commission*, where the Court of First Instance held that contrary to what the Applicants had claimed, it was *not* enough to assert that the unlawful conduct was a necessary condition for the damage to arise and that the 'but-for' test of causation had been met. Specially, the CFI held:

> 39. By submitting that the requisite causal link exists in the present case on the sole basis that, if the Commission had not adopted the TACA decision in their regard, they need not have provided the bank guarantees, the applicants in fact put forward a definition of causal link different from that which prevails in Community law. Such an argument is based on a definition to the effect that, for such a link to exist, **it is enough if the unlawful conduct constituted a necessary condition (a sine qua non) for the damage, in the sense that it would not have occurred without such conduct.**
>
> 40. However, **such a broad definition of the causal link is not supported by the Community case-law** on the second paragraph of Article 288 EC. As noted at paragraph 31 above, that

[482] 'The condition under the second paragraph of Article 340 TFEU relating to a causal link concerns a sufficiently direct causal nexus between the conduct of the institutions and the damage, the burden of proof of which rests on the applicant. The conduct complained of must therefore be the **determining cause of the damage** (see, to that effect, *Trubowest Handel and Makarov v Council and Commission*, cited above, paragraph 53 and case-law cited)'. CJEU Judgment of 31 March 2011, *Volker Mauerhofer v European Commission*, C-433/10P, ECLI:EU:C:2011:204, §127.

[483] See (and all sources cited therein): Lenaerts, Maselis, Gutman and Nowak n 448 at §11.78.

[484] ibid.

[485] The required test of causation is embedded in 340(2) TFEU and is additionally inspired by the general principles common to the laws of the Member States. CJEU Judgment of 31 March 2011, *Volker Mauerhofer v European Commission*, C-433/10P, ECLI:EU:C:2011:204, §127; CJEU (CFI) Judgment of 15 June 1999, *Ismeri Europa Srl v Court of Auditors of the European Communities*, T-277/97, ECLI:EU:T:1999:124, §100; Lenaerts, Maselis, Gutman and Nowak n 448 at §11.78.

[486] CJEU Judgment of 31 March 2011, *Volker Mauerhofer v European Commission*, C-433/10P, ECLI:EU:C:2011:204, §131–132; Lenaerts, Maselis, Gutman and Nowak n 448 at §11.78.

[487] CJEU (CFI) Judgment of 30 September 2003, *Atlantic Container Line AB and Others v European Communities*, T-191/98, ECLI:EU:T:2003:245, §1638. Lenaerts, Maselis, Gutman and Nowak n 448 at §11.78.

[488] ibid §11.80.

[489] ibid §11.79.

> provision limits Community liability to damage flowing directly, or sufficiently directly, from the conduct of the institution concerned which is complained of, which, in particular, precludes that liability from covering damage which arises only as a remote consequence of that conduct.[490]

If the 'but-for' test, where the unlawful conduct is a *sine qua non* for the damage to incur is not sufficient according to case law of the Court, what test is? In this same ruling the CFI recalled consistent case law which held that under (then) Community law, the incurred damage 'must be a sufficiently direct consequence of the act, constituting the **immediate cause of the damage suffered**'[491] (emphasis added). Bearing this in mind, to meet the causation requirement for a successful claim for damages, the Applicant would have to show that the damage flowed directly from the unlawful conduct, and exclusively from the unlawful conduct, without the chain of causation being 'broken by the Member State'.[492] This approach is implicitly confirmed by the Court in *Mauerhofer v European Commission*, where it held that the causal link may be considered as too remote when there is responsibility for the incurred damage resting also on other parties:

> even in the case of a possible contribution by the institutions to the damage for which compensation is sought, that contribution might be considered too remote because of some responsibility resting on others.[493]

Given the shared nature of the competences concerning IBM within the EU-*acquis* on BAM, as well as the executive-federalist dynamic between the Member States and the EU, there will always be some form of interaction in the implementation of measures taken in this field – be it through Member State implementation of EU measures or when acting conjointly in operational missions. In a setting of joint action where the EU has contributed to unlawful conduct resulting in damages, one can wonder how it will ever be possible to demonstrate that the underlying unlawful conduct by the EU is the immediate cause of the incurred damage.[494] When the damage is incurred on account of the implementation of EU measures, the Member States nevertheless remain at the helm of the implementation, thus diffusing the chain of causation between the underlying EU conduct, and the incurred damage, to the point where it becomes practically difficult to assert that the underlying act was the *immediate* cause for the damage. Alternatively, when the damage follows joint operational (unlawful) conduct by both Member States and the EU, which by its very nature is *joint*, the condition of '*immediate*' causation cannot be met, as the harm will inevitably occur as the result of the oftentimes unidentifiable contributions.

[490] CJEU (CFI) Order of 12 December 2007, *Atlantic Container Line and Others v Commission*, T-113/04, ECLI:EU:T: 2007:377, §39–40.

[491] See (and all cases cited therein): CJEU (CFI) Order of 12 December 2007, *Atlantic Container Line and Others v Commission*, T-113/04, ECLI:EU:T: 2007:377, §31.

[492] See also on the notion that the causation should be *exclusive* to the institution concerned, Craig and de Búrca n 143 at 631–632.

[493] CJEU Judgment of 31 March 2011, *Volker Mauerhofer v European Commission*, C-433/10P, ECLI:EU:C:2011:204, §132.

[494] ibid §131–132; Lenaerts, Maselis, Gutman and Nowak n 448 at §11.81.

b. Wrongful Conduct

i. The Lex Generalis *Rules*

Article 4 ARIO prescribes that in addition to attribution, there must be a breach of an international obligation for responsibility to be incurred. A breach of international law may occur 'regardless of the origin or character of the obligation concerned'.[495] The reference in Article 10 ARIO to the 'origin or character' of the obligation, entails that the obligation binding upon an IO may be deduced from 'a customary rule of international law, by a treaty or by a general principle applicable within the international legal order'.[496] In other words, obligations may arise vis-à-vis any subject of international law,[497] irrespective of the classification and nature of the primary norm.[498]

International obligations may likewise be deduced from the rules of the international organisation, which in line with Article 2(b) ARIO, include in particular 'the constituent instruments, decisions, resolutions and other acts of the organization adopted in accordance with those instruments, and established practice of the organization'.[499] Concerning this last point, Special Rapporteur Gaja observes that not necessarily *all* rules of the organisation may qualify as international obligations, pointing out that practice is divided on the matter.[500] Certain authors have rejected the proposition that rules of the organisation generate international obligations entirely,[501] whereas others have adopted a more nuanced approach holding that the rules of the organisation may encompass international obligations depending on the source and subject matter of such rules.[502] The ARIO do not purport to settle the matter.[503]

However, for the purpose of the present study and in line with the commentaries to Article 10 ARIO, the parallelism of the CFR with other international human rights treaties, containing in large part, reaffirmations of international human rights norms,[504] confirm that it contains international obligations, binding both upon the

495 Article 4 ARIO.

496 Comment 2 to Article 10 ARIO.

497 Comment 3 to Article 10 ARIO.

498 Comment 2 to Article 10 ARIO.

499 Article 2(b) ARIO; Comment 4 to Article 10 ARIO.

500 ILC, 'Third report on the responsibility of international organizations by Mr. Giorgio Gaja, Special Rapporteur' (UN Doc. A /CN.4/553) 13 May 2005, 11 §15–19; ILC Seventh Report n 272 at 81–82 §40–41.

501 ILC Third report n 500 at 81–82 §40–41.

502 Comment 5 to Article 10 ARIO; ILC Third report n 500 at 11–12 §18–23. Special Rapporteur Gaja argues in the *travaux préparatoires*, that ICJ case law appears to point in the direction that rules of the organization effectively encompass international obligations but acknowledges immediately thereafter that this holds true for the UN, but not automatically for other international organizations.

503 Comment 7 to Article 10 ARIO.

504 Recital 5 CFR; Article 53 CFR. See also: Allan Rosas, 'The Charter and Universal Human Rights Instruments' in Steve Peers, Tamara Hervey, Jeff Kenner, Angela Ward (eds), *The EU Charter of Fundamental Rights: A Commentary* (London, Bloomsbury, 2014) 1685–1686. The Charter does provide for *additional* fundamental rights that are not protected under the traditional, international human rights covenants and instruments. Sionaidh Douglas-Scott, 'The European Union and Fundamental Rights' in Robert Schütze and Takis Tridimas (eds), *Oxford Principles of European Union Law* (Oxford, Oxford University Press, 2018) 387. See for example: Freedom of the Arts and Sciences – Article 13 CFR; Freedom to Conduct a Business – Article 16 CFR; Workers' Right to Information and Consultation within the Undertaking – Article 27 CFR.

Member States, as well as the EU as a separate subject of international law.[505,506] This is in accordance with the observations made by the Special Rapporteur in the *travaux préparatoires* where he held that the ARIO apply 'to the extent that these rules have kept the character of rules of international law'.[507] Hence, in light of the symbiosis of the Charter with international human rights treaties, the CFR contains *international* human rights obligations owed by the EU.[508]

Articles 11 to 13 ARIO furthermore elaborate upon the specificities of a breach of an international obligation in a highly analogous manner to ARSIWA. In particular, Article 11 ARIO recalls that the obligation must have been binding upon the organisation at the time the conduct occurred. Article 12 ARIO governs a continuing breach and Article 13 ARIO addresses the notion of composite acts by the organisation amounting to a breach when considered together. However, as indicated by the commentaries and the preparatory works, the provisions have been transposed *verbatim* from ARSIWA with the sole adaptation being the addressees of such obligations (the organisation as opposed to states).

Two points warrant further attention. These points were raised in the preparatory works but did not appear (at the time) to be sufficiently relevant to be included in the text or the Commentary to the ARIO concerning a breach of an international obligation.

Firstly, in the *travaux préparatoires* the Special Rapporteur pointed out that compliance with international obligations may be difficult for IOs, particularly when such obligations require positive action by the organisation, which in certain cases can only be achieved through (majority) voting procedures.[509] Concerns were raised that the political unwillingness in voting procedures of the organisation may prevent compliance with such positive obligations.[510] The Special Rapporteur responded, however, by noting that the absence of political will in adhering to *positive* obligations is not a prerogative of, or an issue exclusive to IOs.[511] States are similarly confronted with political pushback and this does not exonerate states from their international obligations, nor should it exonerate IOs.[512] Likewise, the Special Rapporteur held that it would be 'strange to assume that international organizations cannot possess obligations to take positive actions'.[513]

A second and interesting observation in the preparatory works, is the implicit and fleeting reference by the Special Rapporteur to the 'common but differentiated responsibilities' of States and IOs in fulfilling international obligations. While the notion of 'common but differentiated responsibilities' is anchored in (international)

[505] Article 51 CFR – '1. The provisions of this Charter are addressed to the institutions, bodies, offices and agencies of the Union with due regard for the principle of subsidiarity and to the Member States only when they are implementing Union law'. See also: Douglas-Scott n 504 at 474, 395.

[506] 'The Charter is an internal set of rules that legally binds the EU … This applies both within the EU and to its external relations'. Douglas-Scott n 504 at 387.

[507] ILC Third report n 500 at 12 §22.

[508] Recital 5 CFR; Article 53 CFR. See also: Rosas n 504 at 1685–1686.

[509] ILC Third report n 500 at 9 §8; ILC Seventh Report n 272 at 82 §43.

[510] ILC Third report n 500 at 9 §8.

[511] ibid 9 §9.

[512] ibid 9 §9–10.

[513] ibid 9 §9–10.

environmental law, the underlying meaning of the notion is transposable *in casu* and unveils the most rudimentary and elemental argument of the current work. In the preparatory works, Special Rapporteur Gaja observes that it is not necessary to identify the various types of obligations that may arise for international organisations in achieving their international obligations. Yet, referring to the EU, the Special Rapporteur underscores that differentiated obligations may exist for the Member States and the EU in adhering to international obligations.[514] This suggests that different obligations for states and IO may exist in the fulfilment identical human rights *commitments*. The transposition of 'common but differentiated responsibilities' *in casu* refers to the idea that although Member States and IOs may be bound by the same international human rights commitment in theory, the *means* of achieving such commitments, or the obligations in and of themselves, may differ. This contention may appear self-evident on account of the functional speciality of IOs, is (implicitly) supported in doctrine,[515] and builds on the considerations developed in Chapter 3.

The ICJ in its Advisory Opinion on the *Interpretation of the Agreement of 25 March 1951 between the WHO and Egypt*, held that 'international organizations are subjects of international law and, as such, are bound by any obligations incumbent upon them under general rules of international law, under their constitutions or under international agreements to which they are parties'.[516] Applied specifically to the EU, this entails that it is bound by general rules of international law, including customary international (human rights) law, general principles of EU law, its constituent treaties (TEU, TFEU and CFR), as well as any other agreement to which it is a party. Furthermore, the rules of the organisation may arguably encompass a number of international obligations depending on their content and subject. This entails that a number of sources inform the EU's international obligations. But as argued in Chapter 3, these sources are tainted by a very significant and notable deficiency, particularly in the field of human rights. The (theoretical) normative human rights commitments by which the EU is bound, fail to identify precisely how IOs such as the EU – constrained practically and functionally by their specific mandate – can comply with these obligations.

This concern is indeed, of particular relevance with respect to the protection of human rights, as IOs are not typically the addressees of, or parties to international human rights instruments. The EU for example – besides having bound itself to the Charter directly and the ECHR indirectly – is not a contracting party to any international human rights treaty of a *general* nature, with the exception of the UN Convention on the Rights of Persons with Disabilities since 2010.[517] Traditionally, human rights instruments regulate(d) the dynamic between the state exercising (extra-)territorial jurisdiction and the individual under that states' jurisdiction.

[514] Special Rapporteur Gaja furthermore recalls that even if Member States are not the duty-bearers of a particular international obligation, they may still be bound to facilitate EU adherence through the duty of sincere cooperation. ILC Third report n 500 at 10–11 §14–15.

[515] Ahlborn n 287 at 52–53.

[516] ICJ Advisory Opinion of 20 December 1980, *Interpretation of the Agreement of 25 March 1951 Between the WHO and Egypt* §37.

[517] Rosas n 504 at 1687.

International human rights instruments were traditionally not developed with IOs in mind as the duty-bearers of its obligations. Instead, such treaties and instruments specifically identify States as the duty-bearers. Nevertheless, the EU is now bound by these same normative commitments to respect, fulfil and protect human rights. And precisely on this point a nuance is elemental. The very simple, albeit extremely crucial question must be posed, how and whether it is even desirable to transpose *verbatim*, the concretised human rights obligations that are addressed to States, to IOs? While the objectives international human rights commitments in theory are common and transversally applicable, the tools and methods by which such protection is achieved must be assessed in light of the nature of the duty-holder. This is not the same as saying that these different types of actors should or would be held to different standards of human rights compliance. It merely means that in the absence of identical tools and powers to meet human rights obligations as they apply to States, such differentiation should be accounted for when considering the EU's responsibility.

On the one hand, it cannot be claimed that an IO has the same tools and methods at its disposal to achieve and fulfil the positive obligations that have been developed under international human rights law for signatory States. Hence, should an IO then be bound by those positive obligations that presuppose and are contingent on the availability of such tools and methods? On the other hand, IOs, such as the EU, do have *other* powers and measures at its disposal that individual Member States do not have, which may steer the conduct of a single or multiple States in a particular direction – a direction that may ultimately result in human rights harms. Should the concretised human rights obligations (positive, negative, procedural and/or substantive) not be considered then, in light of these peculiarities that characterise IOs and the EU specifically?

It remains difficult, if not impossible, to contend that the positive and negative obligations under human rights law, which are both procedural and substantive in nature, under the Charter and international human rights law generally, should be analogous for Member States and the EU alike. The mere fact that the EU has legal personality, is a subject of international law, and is bound by (international) human rights law embodied in the Charter and customary international law, neither clarifies the contours of the concretised obligations borne by the EU, nor does it instruct as to the concrete rights that can be invoked by an individual vis-à-vis the EU.[518] Particularly in the field of human rights law, the enforceable negative, positive, procedural and substantive obligations have almost exclusively been interpreted, enacted and applied for States – the traditional duty-bearers of such obligations – and not yet in any meaningful manner for a highly integrated IOs such as the Union. In the *Reparations Advisory Opinion* by the ICJ, it was held that 'the subjects of law in any legal system are not necessarily identical in their nature or in the extent of their rights' and 'the legal personality and rights and duties (of an international organisation are not) the same as those of a state'.[519]

[518] Delgado Casteleiro n 27 at 14; Klein n 32 at 1034–1035; Klabbers n 106 at 284.

[519] ICJ Advisory Opinion of 11 April 1949, *Reparation for Injuries Suffered in the Service of the United Nations* 174, 178; Pellet n 32 at 46.

The question must thus be raised whether it is even possible to simply transplant the concrete obligations stemming from the applicable human rights standards that are applicable to Member States to the EU. In the ARIO's preparatory works, the Special Rapporteur implicitly and additionally hinted at potentially imposing 'obligations of means' on IOs, in ensuring respect for international obligations.[520] This could translate for example, to a due diligence obligation for the EU to ensure that human rights are respected in the enactment of EU measures through its own entities and its Member States. In fact, it could even be considered that a duty of care is somehow inherent to the human rights framework as it stands. The argument is made here however, that this is not sufficiently constitutionally embedded within the positive and negative obligations doctrine applicable to the EU. Under the current EU Human Rights Responsibility Regime, the determination of the scope of positive, negative (procedural and substantive) human rights obligations binding upon the EU is left entirely up to ad hoc post-facto appraisals by the EU Courts – to the detriment of legal certainty, legitimate expectations and the effectiveness of human rights protection (see Chapter 3). Simply put, if the positive and negative human rights obligations binding on the EU remain obscure and nebulous and without explicit constitutional foundations, how then can an individual rights-seeker successfully direct claims at the EU for neglect of those obligations in a manner that meets the requirements of the rule of law and the right to an effective remedy in particular?

In the alternative, it could be argued that the rights conferred upon individuals according to the Charter and international human rights law generally, are solely enforceable on (Member) States and were never intended to confer enforceable rights for individuals vis-à-vis the EU and its institutions, bodies, offices and agencies. Supposing that this latter assumption is correct, and a simple 'copy-and-paste manoeuvre' is not possible, this raises questions as to whether Article 51 CFR which identifies the EU as a duty-bearer of human rights, amounts to no more than abstract recognition of the requirement to refrain (obligation to respect, as opposed to the obligation to protect and fulfil) from acting in a manner that is inconsistent with fundamental rights, as opposed to being obliged to fulfil the positive (due diligence) obligations inherent to such rights. And precisely on this point there is tension between on the one hand the potential positive duties the EU must fulfil in keeping with its human rights commitments and on the other hand, the absence of conferred powers to regulate human rights generally (see Chapter 3).

It is interesting to note that the CJEU at times appears to follow the line of thinking whereby generalised obligations directed at Member States cannot simply be transposed to IOs such as the EU (albeit in a different type of procedure). The *ClientEarth* case provides some guidance in this respect.[521] The case concerned the Aarhus Convention[522] which was invoked by the Applicant ClientEarth, in order to

[520] Special Rapporteur Gaja furthermore recalls that even if Member States are not the duty-bearers of a particular international obligation, they may still be bound to facilitate EU adherence through the duty of sincere cooperation. ILC Third report n 500 at 1011 §14–15.

[521] CJEU Judgment of 16 July 2015, *ClientEarth and Pesticide Action Network Europe (PAN Europe) v European Food Safety Authority*, C-612/13 P, ECLI:EU:C:2015:489.

[522] Convention on access to information, public participation in decision making and access to justice in environmental matters [25 June 1998] ('the Aarhus Convention'); Council Decision 2005/370/EC [2005] OJ 2005 L 124, 1.

challenge Regulation 1049/2001 concerning public access to documents. Article 4(2) of Regulation 1049/2001 had been invoked by the European Commission in an attempt to prevent full access to studies concerning Member State compliance with environmental safeguards, which ClientEarth reasoned was at odds with Article 4(4) of the Aarhus Convention.[523] Although Member States and the EU alike, are party to the Aarhus Convention, the CJEU reasoned that 'that convention was manifestly designed with the national legal orders in mind, and not the specific legal features of institutions of regional economic integration, such as the European Union, even where those institutions can sign and accede to the Aarhus Convention, under Articles 17 and 19 thereof'.[524] Following this reasoning, the CJEU held that nothing in the invoked provisions by the Applicants could be construed as 'imposing a precise obligation on the EU legislature', which would result in the invalidation of Regulation 1049/2001.[525] In other words, within the realm of environmental law – similarly a shared competence between the EU and its Member States – it is held that being legally bound by the same agreement does not necessarily mean that the concrete obligations under such multilateral agreements are analogously applicable to the Member States and the EU.[526]

Although this case does not relate to IBM, subsequent cases concerning IBM suggest that the CJEU may be reluctant to simply transpose the substantive obligations of human rights under the CFR and the ECHR, to the EU, as these have all been traditionally and manifestly designed with States as the duty-bearers in mind.[527]

Furthermore, in *Cruciano Siragusa v Regione Sicilia*, the CJEU held that the objective of human rights protection by the latter 'is to ensure that those rights are not infringed in areas of EU activity, whether through action at EU level or through the implementation of EU law by the Member States. The reason for pursuing that objective is the need to avoid a situation in which the level of protection of fundamental rights varies according to the national law involved in such a way as to undermine the unity, primacy and effectiveness of EU law …'.[528] This suggests

[523] See general discussion on the judgment: Laurens Ankersmit and Benedikt Pirker, 'Review of EU Legislation under EU International Agreements Revisited: Aarhus Receives Another Blow' (*European Law Blog*, 17 November 2015) europeanlawblog.eu/2015/11/17/review-of-eu-legislation-under-eu-international-agreements-revisited-aarhus-receives-another-blow/.

[524] CJEU Judgment of 16 July 2015, *ClientEarth and Pesticide Action Network Europe (PAN Europe) v European Food Safety Authority*, C-612/13 P, ECLI:EU:C:2015:489, §40. See more recently: CJEU Judgment of 5 March 2024, Kočner v Europol, C-755/21 P, ECLI:EU:C:2024:202, §119.

[525] CJEU Judgment of 16 July 2015, *ClientEarth and Pesticide Action Network Europe (PAN Europe) v European Food Safety Authority*, C-612/13 P, ECLI:EU:C:2015:489, §40–43.

[526] CJEU Judgment of 16 July 2015, *ClientEarth and Pesticide Action Network Europe (PAN Europe) v European Food Safety Authority*, C-612/13 P, ECLI:EU:C:2015:489, §40. See on the matter (and sources cited therein): André Nollkaemper, 'Joint Responsibility between the EU and Member States for Non-Performance of Obligations under Multilateral Environmental Agreements' in Elisa Morgera (ed), *The External Environmental Policy of the European Union – EU and International Law Perspectives* (Cambridge, Cambridge University Press, 2012) 328.

[527] Unlike the Client Earth case, in *WS and others v Frontex* as well as in *Hamoudi*, the CJEU avoids assessing the merits of the human rights responsibility claim directed at the EU by pointing directly and indirectly to the responsibility of the Member States in effectuating border management, and how this entails that the complicit EU entities merely adopt a supporting or coordinating role. CJEU (General Court) 2023, *WS and others v Frontex* n 59; CJEU (General Court) 2023, *Hamoudi v Frontex* n 59.

[528] CJEU Judgment of 6 March 2014, *Cruciano Siragusa v Regione Sicilia – Soprintendenza Beni Culturali e Ambientali di Palermo*; C-206/13, ECLI:EU:C:2014:126; §31.

that the goal of CJEU review in matters concerning human rights is focused on balancing the objective of human rights protection and the objective of ensuring that the level of fundamental rights protection does not differ across the various Member States to the detriment of the internal market. Whilst this last objective is entirely defendable from an EU and market-centric vantage point, it raises concerns about the consistency of (international) human rights protection, particularly when the minimum level of protection enshrined in the ECHR is not entirely reconcilable with areas of EU action. These concerns are exacerbated by the *N v Staatssecretaris* Case, where the CJEU held that 'the explanations relating to Article 52 of the Charter indicate that paragraph 3 of that article is intended to ensure the necessary consistency between the Charter and the ECHR, "without thereby adversely affecting the autonomy of Union law and … that of the Court of Justice of the European Union"',[529] pointing again to the potential subsidiary nature of consistent *individual* fundamental rights protection when weighed up against EU policy in a given field. Of course, such observations should not be exaggerated, as the CJEU has been a driving force in ensuring human rights protection as concerns Member States compliance. Yet, the potential for inconsistency arises again, on account of the fact that there is pervasive uncertainty about the scope of obligations that are effectively binding on the EU.

The CJEU could provide ex post facto guidance on what the concrete (positive and negative) obligations are borne by the EU per individual provision or when raised in a particular dispute brought within the realm of its jurisdiction. The desirability of leaving the articulation and determination of this exclusively to the CJEU however is questionable, as hinted at by Advocate General Sharpston in *Zambrano*:

> if fundamental rights under EU law were known to be guaranteed in all areas of shared or exclusive Union competence, Member States might be encouraged to move forward with detailed EU secondary legislation in certain areas of particular sensitivity (such as immigration or criminal law), which would include appropriate definition of the exact extent of EU fundamental rights, rather than leaving fundamental rights problems to be solved by the Court on an ad hoc basis, as and when they are litigated.[530]

Leaving the determination of breaches of human rights obligations by the EU to ad hoc findings of the CJEU (and where possible, other adjudicatory mechanisms), poses a significant risk to the principles of legal certainty, legitimate expectations, the effectiveness of human rights, and the principle of legality which lay at the basis of the EU based upon the rule of law (see also Chapter 3). The formulation of Article 51 CFR seems to indicate that the question of the concrete obligations of Member States and the EU under the CFR arose when the Charter was drafted as Member States and the EU and its agencies are held to 'therefore respect the rights, observe the principles and promote the application thereof <u>in accordance with their respective powers</u> …'.[531] However, this generalised approach which implicitly

[529] CJEU Judgment of 15 February 2016, *J.N. v Staatssecretaris voor Veiligheid en Justititie*, C-601/15 PPU, ECLI:EU:C:2016:84, §47.
[530] Opinion Sharpston 2010, *Zambrano* n 140 at §169.
[531] Article 51 CFR.

acknowledges the *sui generis* nature and functional speciality of the EU, does not provide a specific answer to the substantive questions concerning how the EU as an IO is to meet its specific obligations under the CFR and international human rights law in practice. In view of the legal fog which taints the responsibility landscape, it is hard – if not impossible – to determine to what extent indeed the EU has committed a breach through act or omission, of its human rights obligations, when the obligations remain obscure.

ii. The Lex Specialis *Rules*

– Sufficiently Serious Breach of EU Law

For non-contractual EU responsibility to be established, there must be a breach of an EU obligation, irrespective of whether the norm is founded in primary EU law, secondary EU law or general principles of EU law.[532] The CJEU has clarified that for conduct to be considered a breach of EU law, the breach must be qualified as being 'sufficiently serious'.[533] The qualification of an unlawful act as being sufficiently serious was initially determined by reference to the amount of discretion retained by the EU and whether – mindful of this discretion – the EU had 'manifestly and gravely' overstepped the limitations of the rule of EU law concerned.[534]

Discretion of the EU is not assessed in a legal vacuum or in reference to a general domain of EU law, but is determined in relation to a specific situation requiring a case-to-case assessment by the CJEU.[535] This entails that the retained discretion by the EU will be determined by the peculiarities of the area of substantive EU law at stake, but likewise by overarching norms such as general principles and human rights.[536] The CJEU has confirmed that when assessing whether discretion is retained by the parties involved, it will only take into consideration discretion and limitations from an EU perspective. Conversely discretion that is limited by virtue of external (international or domestic) sources of

[532] Lenaerts, Maselis, Gutman and Nowak n 448 at §234.

[533] CJEU Judgment of 4 July 2000, *Bergaderm and Goupil v Commission*, C-352/98 P, ECLI:EU:C:2000:361, §42–43; Lenaerts, Maselis, Gutman and Nowak n 448 at §11.45.

[534] 'For the non-contractual liability of the Community to arise, a number of conditions must be met, including, where the unlawfulness of a legal measure is at issue, the existence of a sufficiently serious breach of a rule of law intended to confer rights on individuals. As regards that condition, the decisive criterion for establishing that a breach of Community law is sufficiently serious is whether the Community institution concerned manifestly and gravely disregarded the limits on its discretion. Where that institution has only considerably reduced, or even no, discretion, the mere infringement of Community law may be sufficient to establish the existence of a sufficiently serious breach (Case C-282/05 *P Holcim (Deutschland) v Commission* [2007] ECR I-2941, paragraph 47 and the case-law cited)' CJEU Judgment of 16 July 2009, *Commission of the European Communities v Schneider Electric SA*, C-440/07, ECLI:EU:C:2009:459 §160. Craig and de Búrca n 143 at 618; Fink n 27 at 207; Lenaerts, Maselis, Gutman and Nowak n 448 at §11.45.

[535] 'EU action needs a legal basis ('competence norm') in order to be lawful, but institutions are also constrained by non-competence-related legal obligations and rights under EU law ('body of law to comply with') in their exercise of conferred competence. The limits to discretionary powers therefore stem from other EU objectives stated elsewhere in the treaties, or norms protecting the interests of the Member States, other EU institutions or individuals' Anne Thies, *International Trade Disputes and EU Liability* (Cambridge, Cambridge University Press, 2013) 53–54. See also: Fink n 27 at 208–209.

[536] Fink n 27 at 208–209.

law, will not be considered.[537] Where much discretion is retained by the EU, only grave and manifest disregard for the limits on that discretion will amount to an unlawful act.[538] In the case where the EU has limited to no discretion, the mere violation of the provision may amount to an unlawful act in the context of an action for damages.[539] However, to determine whether the EU has much discretion or rather, is (significantly) limited in its ability to act, it is crucial to determine at the very least the scope of the concrete legal obligation binding upon the EU. This, however, is no easy feat, when attempting to distil the concrete human rights obligations and the retained discretionary power.

Discretion of the EU has consistently permeated as a crucial and oftentimes determinative criterion in determining whether an unlawful act has occurred.[540] However, it is not the sole criterion, nor does it upstage other factors any longer.[541] This is demonstrated by the fact that the CJEU has increasingly turned to factors such as the complexity of a case[542] (1), the clarity of the (concrete) binding legal obligations upon the Union[543] (2) and the intentional character of the act or omission[544] (3) to determine whether an act or omission was indeed unlawful or whether it could be considered excusable.[545] These factors are furthermore, neither cumulative nor exhaustive.[546] In the current analysis, the criterion of a clear and legally unambiguous provision of law particularly, may pose a problem in determining responsibility. In this respect Advocate General Geelhoed recalls in *Mediator v Lamberts* that the 'excusability depends on the clarity and the precision of the rule of law breached and, on the existence, and state of judgments of the Court'.[547]

The Charter does not encompass clear and actionable human rights obligations tailored to the EU. Although the CFR is directly binding upon the EU, these

[537] 'The discretion referred to in paragraph 38 above is that enjoyed by the Member State concerned. Its existence and its scope are determined by reference to Community law and not by reference to national law. The discretion which may be conferred by national law on the official or the institution responsible for the breach of Community law is therefore irrelevant in this respect' CJEU Judgment of 4 July 2000, *Salomone Haim v Kassenzahnärztliche Vereinigung Nordrhein*, C-424/97, ECLI:EU:C:2000:357 §40. Fink n 27 at 223.

[538] CJEU Judgment of 5 March 1996, *Brasserie du Pêcheur SA v Bundesrepublik Deutschland and The Queen v Secretary of State for Transport, ex parte: Factortame Ltd and others*, C-46/93 and C-48/93, ECLI:EU:C:1996:79, §51, 55; CJEU Judgment of 4 July 2000, *Bergaderm and Goupil v Commission*, C-352/98 P, ECLI:EU:C:2000:361, §43.

[539] CJEU Judgment of 4 July 2000, *Bergaderm and Goupil v Commission*, C-352/98 P, ECLI:EU:C:2000:361, §44; Fink n 27 at 221.

[540] Lenaerts, Maselis, Gutman and Nowak n 448 at §11.45.

[541] Craig and de Búrca n 143 at 620–622; Fink n 27 at 219.

[542] CJEU (CFI) Judgment of 26 January 2006, *Medici Grimm KG v Council of the European Union*, T-364/03, ECLI:EU:T:2006:28, §87.

[543] CJEU Judgment of 26 March 1996, *The Queen v H.M. Treasury, ex parte British Telecommunications*, C-392/93, ECLI:EU:C:1996:131, §43; CJEU Judgment of 17 October 1996, *Denkavit Internationaal and Others v Bundesamt für Finanzen*, C-283/94, ECLI:EU:C:1996:387, §51–52.

[544] CJEU (CFI) Judgment of 26 January 2006, *Medici Grimm KG v Council of the European Union*, T-364/03, ECLI:EU:T:2006:28, §87.

[545] CJEU Judgment of 19 April 2007, *Holcim (Deutschland) v Commission*, C-282/05, ECLI:EU:C:2007:226, §50. See also (and sources cited therein): Lenaerts, Maselis, Gutman and Nowak n 448 at §11.60.

[546] Fink n 27 at 221.

[547] Opinion of Advocate General Geelhoed of 3 July 2003, *Mediator v Lamberts*, C-234/02P, ECLI:EU:C:2003:394, §88–89.

commitments have not yet been meaningfully translated to actionable obligations on behalf of the EU. Assuming that human rights obligations as they apply to the EU Member States cannot be transposed *verbatim* to the EU in light of the EU's functional speciality, a determination of EU human rights responsibility is currently (in the absence of legislative developments) left to post-facto adjudication to determine whether the EU has or has not met its obligations under the human rights standards encompassed in the Charter.

If the determination of the scope of human rights obligations binding upon the EU is left to post-facto adjudication, this necessarily implies that the requirement of a violation of a clear and concrete binding legal obligation upon the EU cannot be met. This complexifies the right to reparation of individuals vis-à-vis the EU as there simply is no clear rule on how the EU, its institutions, bodies, offices, and agencies can meet the human rights commitments embedded in the CFR.[548] Within this same vein, it becomes a matter of adjudicatory discretion to determine when a breach was sufficiently serious to constitute an unlawful act capable of triggering damages under the EU *lex specialis* regime. The risk of self-referentialism by the CJEU may give rise to issues of misalignment, different conceptualisations of justice and the right to an effective remedy (Chapter 3).[549]

Case law precedents set by the CJEU in consecutive judgments on the topic, could to a certain extent remedy this conundrum, but this has not yet occured. In a limited number of cases, the CJEU has effectively found violations of human rights by EU institutions and/or servants.[550] However, in the limited number of cases such violations were found, the obligations had in fact been legislatively pre-determined. Generally, the CJEU appears to be a very staunch enforcer of Member State human rights compliance, but less so with respect to EU institutions, bodies, offices and agencies. This may be inferred from both *Kampffmeyer*,[551] as well as the Draft Accession Agreement, as well as … the recent *WS and others v Frontex* and the recent *Hamoudi v Frontex* case, according to which the EU can only incur responsibility in a subsidiary manner.[552] Arguably, the concrete legal obligations for the EU stemming from the human rights embedded in the CFR are purposely left vague. By not identifying them – as was the case in the *ClientEarth* case – a certain level of manoeuvring discretion, is retained. Particularly in fields such as borders, asylum and migration, where political stakes are high and contentious, this may provide the EU the required balance to reconcile political stances across the EU Member States. And while this may be understandable from a political perspective, this is simply

[548] Conversely, EU secondary legislation within the realm of borders, asylum and migration, containing clear and precise rules on how to abide by the underlying human rights norms are addressed explicitly to the Member States.

[549] CJEU Judgment of 26 March 1996, *The Queen v H.M. Treasury, ex parte British Telecommunications*, C-392/93, ECLI:EU:C:1996:131, §43; CJEU Judgment of 17 October 1996, *Denkavit Internationaal and Others v Bundesamt für Finanzen*, C-283/94, ECLI:EU:C:1996:387, §51–52.

[550] Fink, Rauchegger and De Coninck n 151.

[551] CJEU Judgment of 14 July 1967, *Firma E. Kampffmeyer and others v Commission of the EEC*, C-5, 7, and 13 to 24–66, ECLI:EU:C:1967:31.

[552] CJEU (General Court) 2023, *WS and others v Frontex* n 59; CJEU (General Court) 2023, *Hamoudi v Frontex* n 59.

not reconcilable with notions and principles of legality, legal certainty, effectiveness and the overarching rule of law from the perspective of the *individual* TCN. From the vantage point of the individual rights-seeker, this normative opaqueness again, frustrates any potential for an effective remedy for damages incurred at the hands of the EU or on account of its contribution to unlawful human rights conduct in asylum and migration policies.

For the sake of thoroughness, an action for damages may also concern the failure to act on behalf of the EU. However, crucial here is that there must have been a legal(ly enforceable) obligation upon the Union to take certain (positive) action for such responsibility to arise.[553] Again, absent any clarification on the positive human rights obligations binding upon the EU, claims for damages for a failure to act on behalf of the EU, will not be successful.

Finally, the condition of a breach of EU law articulated in *Bergaderm*, does not clarify whether fault is required for an act to be construed as an unlawful act (subjective liability), or whether the mere violation of a particular norm suffices (objective liability).[554] While Lenaerts and others hold that in earlier case law it was difficult to assess whether fault was an implicit requirement for unlawful conduct by the EU to give rise to reparations,[555] the aforementioned factors referenced by the CJEU in more recent case law do appear to add an element of subjectivity, further conflating the notions of subjective and objective liability.[556] On this point, Fink notes that the CJEU has consistently refuted the inclusion of an explicit fault-criterium but that it has added a *fault-like* criterium by taking into account precisely factors such as the complexity of a situation, the clarity of the imposed legal obligation as well as the intentional character of the act or omission committed by the Union.[557] In any event, for the purpose of the present inquiry, the conceptual nuances between 'fault' and 'fault-like' criteria are less relevant. As is the case under the *lex generalis* regime, there is no standardised method to determine when the subjective element of fault has been established.

– Rule Intended to Confer Rights

Contrary to the international rules on responsibility embedded in the ARIO, the EU-specific *lex specialis* regime responsibility holds that responsibility will only arise, when a rule of law was intended to confer rights on an individual. This condition has been subject to some debate and has appeared in the case law of the Court in various terminological variations, which in turn, inevitably results in additional ambiguity concerning its scope and meaning.[558] However, the CJEU has already clarified that the foregoing condition should not be equated to the rule concerned having direct effect.[559]

[553] Lenaerts, Maselis, Gutman and Nowak n 448 at §11.46.

[554] See on the evolution in the CJEU case law on objective and subjective liability: Lenaerts, Maselis, Gutman and Nowak n 448 at §11.41–11.46.

[555] ibid §11.42.

[556] ibid §11.45; Fink n 27 at 209.

[557] Fink n 27 at 209.

[558] See (and sources cited therein): Lenaerts, Maselis, Gutman and Nowak n 448 at §11.48.

[559] ibid §11.48.

It is hardly disputable that these human rights provisions in the Charter regulate the dynamic between the Member States and the EU vis-à-vis individuals and have been developed with the protection of the individual in mind.[560] This is indicative of the fact that the CFR intends to confer rights on individuals. However, as held by Ward, 'it would be a mistake to pick up the Charter and read it as if it contained a catalogue of judicially enforceable fundamental rights. It is a nuanced instrument, which features civil and political rights along with economic, social and cultural rights, while including some so-called third generation human rights such as environmental protection …'.[561] This is evidenced amongst other, by the fact that the Charter makes the distinction between principles and rights – the latter being considered as being judicially enforceable and the former considered as not.[562] Although the Explanations to the Charter provide a first indication of what Charter provisions are considered as constituting legally enforceable rights and what provisions may be considered as principles, this indication is by no means exhaustive and an assessment of what provisions in the Charter can be considered as conferring rights would have to be made for every single provision.[563] Over time, the CJEU has elaborated upon the matter somewhat on a case-by-case basis, by indicating what precise Charter provisions can be considered as legally enforceable, when prompted to do so. In line with the foregoing and based on recent case law of the CJEU, it is advanced that the *non-refoulement* principle can be considered as intending to confer rights on an individual.[564] Within the context of the *lex specialis* regime to establish international responsibility, it thus appears that this last condition will be met. Accordingly this will not be addressed in the illustrations.

iii. Interim Conclusions on the Rules for Independent Responsibility

The one definitive conclusion that may be distilled from the ARIO is that in its attempt to develop a set of rules for the independent responsibility of a heterogenous group of public actors, it has given rise to indeterminate and at times, conflicting rules.

As discussed, questions arise concerning attribution, causation, as well as concerning the scope of legal obligations.

It is not the individual components of the responsibility framework of the ARIO that are problematic – it is the totality of the framework. The ARIO are for the most part, a patch-work of open-ended, inconsistent and transposed provisions from the provisions on state responsibility. This does not mean that a responsibility

[560] Fink n 27 at 203, 206.
[561] Ward n 437 at 163.
[562] ibid.
[563] Fink n 27 at 203, 206–207.
[564] See for *non-refoulement* as a provision of EU law capable of conferring rights on an individual: CJEU Judgment of 24 February 2021, *M and Others v Staatssecretaris van Justitie en Veiligheid and T*, C-673/19, ECLI:EU:C:2021:127, §40; CJEU (Grand Chamber) Judgment of 14 May 2020, *FMS, FNZ, SA, SA Junior v Országos Idegenrendészeti Főigazgatóság Dél-alföldi Regionális Igazgatóság, Országos Idegenrendészeti Főigazgatóság*, Joined Cases C-924/19 PPU and C-925/19 PPU, ECLI:EU:C:2020:367, §118–165; CJEU Judgment of 19 March 2020, *LH v Bevándorlási és Menekültügyi Hivatal (Tompa)*, C-564/18, ECLI:EU:C:2020:218, §37; Fink n 27 at 207.

framework for the international responsibility of IO should be exclusively and strictly delineated and defined. Indeed, to a certain extent it is imperative even to retain flexibility in the conditionality for international responsibility of IOs, in light of their functional, constitutional and institutional heterogeneity. However, mindful of the increased recourse to cooperation under the *chapeau* of international organisations, an updated balance must be struck between legal guidelines on how to establish such responsibility and the differentiation across international organisations. The ARIO were drafted and established pre-emptively – anticipating analogous scenarios of unlawful conduct that would give rise to state responsibility, yet blind to the fact that the (human rights) obligations applicable to states, have not yet been settled for IOs. While this methodological approach may have been defendable at the time of the drafting, reality has now caught up with embryonic state of the ARIO, and legal certainty, the principle of effectiveness, the principle of legality and the right to an effective remedy, now require a fresh look at the grounds for responsibility, particularly for human rights violations, mindful of the lessons learned.

Although theoretically, the *lex generalis* under the ARIO do not necessarily provide any solace in determining responsibility vis-à-vis IOs, the ARIO also reference the *lex specialis*, which may very well constitute a more effective basis for international responsibility for unlawful conduct by international organisations, and *in casu* the EU.

At first glance, the rules on independent responsibility of the EU appear to be relatively straightforward in application. However, when inspecting the *Bergaderm* conditions and the application thereof, it becomes clear that a successful claim for damages is largely dependent upon a case-by-case assessment of each condition, with no legal certainty as to the scope and standard of assessment of these conditions. In addition to the already high threshold to establishing causation, establishing attribution requires consideration of both the division of competence, as well as the de facto genuine discretion accorded to the implicated actors in each concrete scenario – all of which differ depending upon the substantive area of EU law at stake. Furthermore, depending on whether questionable human rights adherence occurs within the *internal* sphere or within the context of *external* EU action, this will complicate the attribution question as it may affect de facto competence division and access to legal remedies. The foregoing is aggravated by the fact that, for conduct to be attributed to the EU and for this to potentially trigger responsibility, it is presupposed that obligations apply (and be enforceable) to *both* Member States and the EU. To date, it remains highly uncertain whether the Member States and the EU share congruent positive and negative obligations under (international) human rights instruments and sources. Without clarity in this regard, it is difficult to determine ex ante when the EU can be considered to have committed an unlawful act and leaves any determinations thereof reliant upon (successful) ex post litigation – to the detriment of legal certainty. Finally, the diverse sources of fundamental rights provisions united in the Charter, render it uncertain what rights in particular can be considered as being intended to confer rights on an individual.

The fragmentation and lack of consistency in the *lex specialis* conditionality for *independent* responsibility, again frustrates access to an effective remedy for TCNs seeking relief for human rights violations. How can a responsibility mechanism that is overwhelmingly determined by adjudicatory ex post facto control to determine the scope and limits of both the primary norm and the secondary norm, and tainted by scholarly and de facto ambiguity, meet standards of standards of legality, legal certainty and effectiveness? It is non-sensical to place the burden and high standard of proof upon the Applicant, where there is no indication what thresholds must be met as a *sine qua non* to establish international responsibility. Recall in this respect that causality under the EU responsibility paradigm encompasses, according to the Court, the notion of attribution, and the burden to demonstrate the already high threshold for causation under the EU-regime for responsibility, is placed upon the Applicant claiming the unlawful conduct. It is unlikely – absent precedent-setting judgements by the CJEU – that the conditionality for independent responsibility will ever be met in the field of IBM. Placing the burden and standard of proof on the Applicant *in casu*, in a vast land of judicial opaqueness, is akin to asking the Applicant to land a plane with a blindfold on: it is possible but will be extremely difficult to execute successfully.

The theoretical and conceptual ambiguity which flows from the *Lex Generalis* and *Lex specialis* rules for independent responsibility is compounded by the fact that in practice, the EU does not act alone in the field of IBM. Due to the shared nature of competences in IBM, a dynamic occurs between the Member States and the EU, where action taken within the field of borders, asylum and migration by both actors, can no longer be conceptually disjointed from each other. This sits uneasy with the traditional individualistic approach to responsibility. On the one hand, Member States may be bound to implement certain acts (with limited to no discretion) by (pre-emptive) measures taken by the EU. On the other hand, even where Member States retain significant (legislative) discretion to act, they will remain loosely bound to at least the duty of loyal cooperation and thus refrain from taking action that may jeopardise the effectiveness of Union legislation. While the conditions for independent responsibility under the *lex specialis* thus form part of the responsibility enigma, they alone do not suffice in solving the responsibility question because typically, actions within the realm of borders, asylum and migration are joint in nature, involving an interaction between various actors. Accordingly, a relational account of responsibility – paying tribute to such joint action – constitutes the next step in solving the puzzle of EU responsibility for contributions to human rights harms.

2. CONDITIONS FOR SHARED RESPONSIBILITY

This section discusses the conditions for shared responsibility between the EU and its Member States for joint and indissociable conduct, as governed by both international and EU law.

a. Introductory Remarks

In addition to independent responsibility of IOs, the ARIO have also anticipated scenarios where IOs work together in joint actions or operations, with other actors such as Member States and IOs. Such responsibility is defined by Lanovoy as responsibility for a *separate* wrongful act, which constitutes a 'separate trigger of responsibility (*fait générateur*) from the principal wrongful act it facilitates'.[565] Accordingly, responsibility does not arise for the principal wrongful act that is committed by the primary wrongdoer, but rather for the conduct *facilitating* the primary wrongful act.[566] Articles 14–18 ARIO encompass this type of joint legal responsibility and are considered as codifications of existing custom and progressive development of international law.[567] These provisions were developed with the intent of preventing situations whereby an IO could successfully circumvent one of its international obligations 'by availing itself of the separate legal personality of its members, whether States or other international organizations'.[568] Addressing such forms of concerted action ensures that the burden of responsibility would not rest solely upon the shoulders of the primary wrongdoer, which Nollkaemper notes would be problematic for two reasons.[569] Firstly, independent responsibility in a multi-actor context, does not sufficiently take into consideration diffusion of conduct.[570] The diffusion of conduct across various actors, may disincentive the various complicit actors from acting in accordance with international obligations in light of the fact that the diffusion of responsibility will likely hamper definitive determinations of responsibility.[571] Secondly, from the perspective of individual claimants against conduct of the IO, independent responsibility is not a suitable mechanism for reparations in multi-actor unlawful conduct, as it may be difficult to penetrate the diffused responsibility, to identify the perpetrator(s) of the unlawful conduct that resulted in (human rights) harm.[572] In line with these concerns, Nollkaemper concludes that 'If cooperative conduct in transnational law enforcement cannot be reduced to conduct of individual participating actors, responsibility needs to connect to the relationship between the individual actors. Individualizing responsibility may miss the point'.[573] By adopting provisions on shared responsibility, these concerns could theoretically be avoided.

[565] Lanovoy n 26 at 4.
[566] ibid 5.
[567] Lanovoy notes that the underlying premise of complicity may have acquired the status of custom, but that this has no bearing on the customary nature of the *constituent elements* of complicity. This aligns with one of the main themes of his monograph. Lanovoy holds that the principle of complicity holds validity as a source of international law, but that the diverging and ambiguous application thereof in practice, impair determinations of custom. In coming to this conclusion, Lanovoy builds upon the seminal works of Andreas Felder, Helmut Aust and Miles Jackson. Lanovoy n 26 at 6, 9. Jackson n 26; Helmut Aust, *Complicity and the Law of State Responsibility* (Cambridge, Cambridge University Press, 2011); Andreas Felder, *Die Beihilfe im Recht der völkerrechtlichen Staatenverantwortlickheid* (Zürich, Schulthess, 2007).
[568] ILC Seventh Report n 272 at p. 83 §47.
[569] André Nollkaemper, 'Shared responsibility for human rights violations: a relational account' in Thomas Gammeltoft-Hansen and Jens Vedsted-Hansen (eds), *Human Rights and the Dark Side of Globalisation – Transnational Law Enforcement and Migration Control* (Abingdon, Routledge, 2017) 29–30.
[570] ibid 30.
[571] Nollkaemper n 569 at 30.
[572] ibid.
[573] ibid 31.

i. Terminology

The ARIO's provisions on shared responsibility govern the indirect or secondary responsibility of an IO for its involvement in *facilitating* the primary breach of an international obligation.[574] Scholarship and practice interchangeably refer to such situations as resulting in secondary and ancillary,[575] complicit,[576] derivative,[577] indirect,[578] shared,[579] relational[580] or joint[581] responsibility.[582] Lanovoy notes that although there may be subtle differences in the concepts and terminology, ultimately these notions all refer to situations where the responsibility of an IO is considered for having facilitated a wrongful act by another actor – the principal wrongdoer.[583]

ii. Nature of Shared Responsibility

The inclusion of these provisions in the ARIO was not uncontroversial. This is first, (partially) because the ARIO were intended, as indicated by its Commentary,

[574] ILC, 'Fourth Report on the Responsibility of International Organizations by Mr. Giorgio Gaja, Special Rapporteur' (UN Doc. A /CN.4/564) 28 February, 12 and 20 April 2006, 114–115 §54; General Comment 2 to Chapter IV ARIO.

[575] Robert Kolb, *The International Law of State Responsibility* (Cheltenham, Edward Elgar Publishing, 2017) 215–230; James Crawford, *State Responsibility* (Cambridge, Cambridge University Press, 2013) 395–434.

[576] Lanovoy n 26; Jackson n 26.

[577] Derivative responsibility is used to denote the fact that the responsibility for the international organization would arise only after responsibility for the primary wrongful act by the principal wrongdoer is established. Lanovoy n 26 at 10.

[578] Voulgaris n 262.

[579] André Nollkaemper and Ilias Plakokefalos, 'The Practice of Shared Responsibility: A Framework for Analysis' in André Nollkaemper and Ilias Plakokefalos (eds), *The Practice of Shared Responsibility* (Cambridge, Cambridge University Press, 2017) 1–11.

[580] Nollkaemper n 569 at 27–52.

[581] Matthias Hartwig, 'International Organizations or Institutions, Responsibility and Liability' in Rüdiger Wolfrum (ed), *Max Planck Encyclopaedia in Public International Law* (Oxford, Oxford University Press, 2011) §25.

[582] For the purpose of completeness, it is relevant to mention that Lanovoy makes the argument that this type of responsibility should not necessarily be construed as being 'derivative' in nature for a number of reasons. Essentially, the argument is that by construing the responsibility of the international organization as derivative, this diminishes the gradation of involvement, the nature of the involvement, the potential remedial consequences associated to this responsibility and may have the impact of shifting the primary burden of responsibility upon the primary actor (the state for example), while (partially) absolving the complicit actor – *in casu* the international organization. Mindful of this, Lanovoy argues in favour of referring to this form of responsibility as shared or joint. Lanovoy n 26 at 10–11.

[583] Lanovoy n 26 at 4, 10. A more contemporary approach to shared responsibility expands the scope and definition thereof, however. This is predominantly done by the work under direction of André Nollkaemper. Nollkaemper defines this form of responsibility as referring to situations where a 'multiplicity of actors contributes to a single harmful outcome, and legal responsibility for this harmful outcome is distributed among more than one of the contributing actors'. Nollkaemper and Plakokefalos n 579 at 3. For the purpose of the present study, joint responsibility will function as an umbrella term that references both composite acts by different actors that result in one undivided injury, joint (unlawful) acts between the Member States and the EU that also result in one undivided injury, as well as any other dynamic that results in one undivided injury. The relevance of the terminological distinctions in joint responsibility is limited in the present study on account of the fact that the constituent elements to determine whether such responsibility has arisen, still require that attribution and an internationally wrongful act be established. Hence, the issues that arise with respect to the determination of attribution and an internationally wrongful act under *independent* responsibility remain applicable under any conceptualisation of joint responsibility. See on the topic (and sources cited therein): Nollkaemper n 526 at 330. Insofar the scope or concrete obligations differ depending on the context, these nuances will be highlighted.

to contain only 'secondary rules' (liability rules), which are concerned with allocating responsibility, as opposed to primary norms which concern the international obligations by which IOs are bound.[584] However, the provisions on shared responsibility in the ARIO contain elements of both, as a result of which these provisions can be considered as being of a pseudo-secondary nature.[585] On the one hand the provisions are indeed concerned with allocating responsibility in multi-actor scenarios. On the other hand, the responsibility that arises in accordance with these provisions, is not necessarily the result of a primary norm that was binding upon the international organisation and was violated accordingly. It is, rather, a subsidiary act that triggers the responsibility.

iii. Limited Practice

Much like in cases of independent responsibility for IOs, this second form of responsibility is plagued by limited practice.[586] However, the common thread concerning this form of joint responsibility, is that it considers the responsibility of an IO for its *fait générateur* facilitating a violation of an international obligation binding upon the primary actor.[587] The ARIO explain that this type of responsibility will arise when the IO is responsible for aiding or assisting (Article 14 ARIO), directing or controlling (Article 15 ARIO), coercing (Article 16 ARIO) (a) signatory State(s) unlawful conduct and finally, in case of circumvention of an international obligation by addressing decisions and authorisations to Signatory States.[588] Recent developments demonstrate that these identified variations of joint responsibility were only in an embryonic phase when incorporated in the ARIO. An analysis of the topic would thus not be complete without including the developments since, which are in large part, fruits of the labour conducted under the direction of Nollkaemper and which paved the path to the 2020 *Guiding Principles on Shared Responsibility in International Law*.[589] Building upon and clarifying the rules set forth in the ARIO, these developments adopt a more comprehensive approach to shared responsibility.[590] Nollkaemper defends this broader approach, as it does

[584] An extensive discussion on the topic goes beyond the ambit of the current research and does not necessarily bear any relevance to the questions posed *in casu*, as the present research is concerned rather with the application of the rules on responsibility as opposed to the nature of those rules. For an extensive discussion on topic, see: Voulgaris n 262 at 98; Lanovoy n 26; Jackson n 26.

[585] Voulgaris n 262 at 98; Lanovoy n 26 at 11.

[586] General Comment 1 to Chapter IV ARIO. Limited practice on the topic is complicated by the fact that in cases of such complicit conduct, adjudicatory bodies have not assessed the joint or complicit responsibility of the international organization on account of lacking jurisdiction *ratione personae*, particularly within the realm of fundamental rights protection. See for case law references: General Comment 4 to Chapter IV ARIO. See also: Lanovoy n 26 at 7, 11. Lanovoy notes that one of the reasons why practice is scant for responsibility is because of the fact that a cognitive and thus subjective element is added in the determination of responsibility, which is much harder to identify than objective responsibility. Nollkaemper n 569 at 29.

[587] General Comment 2 to Chapter IV ARIO; Lanovoy n 26 at 4.

[588] General Comment 1 to Chapter IV ARIO.

[589] Nollkaemper, d'Aspremont, Ahlborn, Boutin, Nedeski and Plakokefalos n 26 at 15–72.

[590] The Guiding Principles are broader in identifying shared responsibility (see below), but purportedly also as concerns the invocation of international responsibility by actors other than States and other international organizations. However, as aforementioned, despite not explicitly noting that individuals may

not limit shared responsibility to 'the individual actor that influences or is influenced by another actor, but rather the relationship, or the collectivity of actors who participate in the concerted action' as it is the 'relationship that influences the action of individual participants'.[591] Accordingly, the degree and intensity of the relationship will determine what actor and to what extent the complicit actor(s) are to be held responsible.[592]

iv. Modalities of Shared Responsibility

Despite the recent developments on the topic, to date, joint responsibility particularly for international human rights violations, remains underexplored.[593] However, common across the various conceptualisations of joint responsibility, is that there must be multiple actors implicated on the one hand (interdependent conduct), and a single harmful outcome on the other hand (interdependent outcome).[594] The interdependent conduct must have led – causally or not – to an interdependent outcome that could not have been achieved by one of the parties alone and that resulted in a single harmful result amounting to a violation of an (international human rights) obligation borne by one or more of the parties involved. Building on this limited (international and regional) practice,[595] Nollkaemper – based on similar distinctions in earlier scholarship – identifies three main forms of shared responsibility: concurrent responsibility[596] (1), cumulative responsibility[597] (2) and joint responsibility

invoke the international responsibility of an international organization, this is nevertheless implied in a number of provisions across the ARIO (see above). Nollkaemper, d'Aspremont, Ahlborn, Boutin, Nedeski and Plakokefalos n 26 at 20–21, 22.

[591] Nollkaemper n 569 at 32.

[592] ibid.

[593] Joint responsibility predominantly finds its inspiration in domestic legislation and has only been used sparsely in international legal instruments and case law. This was highlighted repeatedly in the *travaux préparatoires* to the ARIO. ILC Third report n 500 at p. 13–14 §28–29. Despite the absence of practice concerning joint responsibility, much scholarly work has been devoted to analysing this form of responsibility. For an extensive discussion on joint responsibility, see: Nollkaemper n 526 at 308–319.

[594] Nollkaemper n 569 at 31–34; Nollkaemper and Plakokefalos n 579 at 3; Ahlborn n 287 at 55.

[595] Nollkaemper n 569 at 32.

[596] **Concurrent responsibility:** A scenario where multiple actors commit separate and different wrongful acts, which would all have been sufficient in order to trigger the single (human rights) harm. Here the 'but-for' test of causality does not apply, as the separate acts and/or omissions, would have been sufficient to bring about the single injury. Instead, a test of causal sufficiency may be applied. An often-cited example of concurrent responsibility is the situation in which multiple states have rescue ships at their disposal, which they refrain from using in naval rescue missions, with fatal consequences as a result thereof. See: Nollkaemper n 569 at 39; Nollkaemper, d'Aspremont, Ahlborn, Boutin, Nedeski and Plakokefalos n 26 at 25–26 §7.

[597] **Cumulative responsibility**: A scenario where multiple wrongful acts or omissions accumulate to generate a single harmful outcome, but the acts or omissions taken separately wouldn't necessarily have given rise to that particular injury. This type of responsibility is to be distinguished from concurrent responsibility, as *in casu* the individual conduct may not have been sufficient to generate the single harm, as a result of which the separate conduct does not meet the causal sufficiency requirement. Instead, the single injury envisaged in this scenario, is the result of the *accumulated* separate conduct of the implicated parties. This form of joint responsibility includes instances where for example, a Member State returns a TCN to an unsafe third country and the EU and/or other Member States assist in this process. While the Member State returning the individual will be held to account for the return itself, the complicit parties can theoretically be held responsible for the wrongful act of aiding and assisting in the commission of a human rights violation. See: Nollkaemper n 569 at 39; Nollkaemper, d'Aspremont, Ahlborn, Boutin, Nedeski and Plakokefalos n 26 at 27 §9.

for one single wrongful act[598] (3).[599] While the latter presupposes joint responsibility stemming from a *single* wrongful act, the former two variations of joint responsibility, refer to scenarios of multiple wrongful acts (by multiple actors) that result in a single harmful result. The provisions of shared responsibility in the ARIO, fall within this second category of joint responsibility as discussed below.

What all of these forms of joint responsibility have in common, is that they presuppose the separability of the measures taken, culminating in a single harmful outcome.[600] In other words, 'the harm may be an indivisible totality that results from the addition of various contributions and the interaction between them',[601] and the wrongfulness of conduct must thus be separated conceptually from the responsibility that arises from that wrongful conduct. The indivisible harmful effect is determined by a factual test of causation.[602] Insofar the injury is the direct result of the single wrongful act, the actor to which this conduct is attributed will be held *independently* responsible, to the exclusion of shared responsibility. The wrongful act would have to be considered the 'single necessary and sufficient cause of a certain injury'.[603] However, in joint operational actions such as joint (military) operations it may prove difficult to disentangle the various acts and omissions that resulted in the violation, and evidentiary smokescreens which prevent disentanglement and distribution of responsibility may very well be purposely maintained to avoid legal ramifications for all parties involved.[604] In addition, the argument has been advanced that as human rights instruments traditionally have been adopted to regulate the dynamic between states and the individuals under their (territorial) jurisdiction, arguably, any violations thereof, would not be capable of being traced back to an IO.[605] Rather, States as the primary duty bearers then of such instruments, would be exclusively responsible.[606]

[598] **Single wrongful act:** Joint responsibility due to a single wrongful act by separate actors that generates one indivisible unlawful (human rights) outcome is also referred to as cooperative or individual responsibility. According to the commentaries to ARSIWA, a single wrongful act refers to 'a single course of conduct [that] is at the same time attributable to several [international persons] and is internationally wrongful for each of them'. The distinction of this type of shared conduct from the other forms of shared conduct is that is characterized by an individual contribution that is attributable to multiple actors. Insofar multiple actors conduct themselves in a closely coordinated manner, 'but engage in separate conduct, the situation is not one of shared responsibility for a single wrongful act but, rather, one of shared responsibility for multiple internationally wrongful acts that could concurrently or cumulatively cause the injury' (see below). See: Nollkaemper n 569 at 41; Comment 3 to Article 47 ARSIWA; Nollkaemper, d'Aspremont, Ahlborn, Boutin, Nedeski and Plakokefalos n 26 at 29–32.

[599] Principle 2; Comment 5–8 to Principle 2. See (and sources cited therein): Nollkaemper, d'Aspremont, Ahlborn, Boutin, Nedeski and Plakokefalos n 26 at 38-39.

[600] The separability of the complicit conduct should not be confused with the indivisibility of the harmful outcome.

[601] Comment 3 and 4 to Principle 2: Nollkaemper, d'Aspremont, Ahlborn, Boutin, Nedeski and Plakokefalos n 26 at 24; Nollkaemper n 569 at 33.

[602] Comment 4 to Principle 2: Nollkaemper, d'Aspremont, Ahlborn, Boutin, Nedeski and Plakokefalos n 26 at 24.

[603] ibid.

[604] Nollkaemper n 526 at 323.

[605] Nollkaemper n 569 at 33–34.

[606] The line of reasoning where the Member State is the sole duty-bearer of human rights obligations is rebutted by Nollkaemper on three grounds. Firstly, while a human rights violation may indeed be traced back to a state exercising jurisdiction, it is entirely possible that the state concerned, was aided and assisted by another actor such as an international organization. Secondly, in certain scenarios, a human rights violation is not the outcome of the conduct of a single state, but rather the result of the conduct

These practical considerations must be borne in mind when assessing the efficacy of the contemporary regime on shared responsibility.

b. The *Lex Generalis* Rules

The ARIO set out four scenarios of shared responsibility for IOs in relation to the conduct of a state.[607] These scenarios refer to aid or assistance by the IO in the unlawful conduct by a state (1); direction and control by an IO vis-à-vis a State over its unlawful conduct (2); coercion (3) and circumvention (4). The ARIO do acknowledge however, that shared responsibility is not limited to these four scenarios and that IOs may influence and affect state behaviour beyond these four scenarios.[608]

The scenarios envisaged by the ARIO concerning shared responsibility, 'do not affect attribution of conduct to the State which is aided or assisted, under the direction or control, or under coercion'.[609] This is underscored in the *travaux préparatoires*, where Special Rapporteur Gaja recalls that the ARIO are primarily concerned with the responsibility arising vis-à-vis IOs, while matters of attribution for unlawful conduct *to States* are dealt with by the ARSIWA.[610] The primary wrongful conduct will thus be attributed to the complicit State according to the rules in ARSIWA and the IO will be responsible for the secondary conduct which causally contributes or influences the primary wrongful act.[611] Bearing in mind the aforementioned typology elaborated upon in the 2020 Guiding Principles on Shared Responsibility in International Law, shared responsibility as developed by the ARIO is likely to be qualified as shared responsibility for the *same* unlawful conduct resulting in a single harm or, shared responsibility for *cumulative* conduct (as concurrent conduct will trigger independent responsibility instead).[612]

Prior to delving into the various grounds of shared responsibility in the ARIO, it is important to underscore that in developing the provisions on shared responsibility between states and IOs, the Special Rapporteur opted for an almost *verbatim* transposition of the ARSIWA provisions concerning state responsibility, with only

of a 'collectivity of states', particularly within extra-territorial operational settings. Finally, a distinction must be made between a singular human rights breach, as opposed to a global harm that detrimentally affects human rights on account an amalgam of conduct that is contrary to the human rights obligations borne by the complicit actors. The foregoing demonstrates that the supposition that human rights are owed solely in a binary dynamic between a duty-bearing state and the individual(s) under its jurisdiction is not tenable, particularly in light of transnational cooperative conduct involving multiple actors. Nollkaemper n 569 at 31-34.

[607] The inverse scenario of the responsibility of a state in connection with the act of an international organization, which also constitutes a form of shared responsibility, will not be discussed here, as the present analysis is concerned solely with the question of the responsibility of an international organization. For further insight into the matter, see Articles 58–61 ARIO, as well as the Third and Fourth Report by Special Rapporteur Gaja. ILC Third report n 500 at p. 13 §26; ILC Fourth Report n 574 at p. 114–124.

[608] General Comment 3 to Chapter IV ARIO.

[609] General Comment 2 to Chapter IV ARIO. This is reiterated a number of times in the *travaux préparatoires*, where the Special Rapporteur reaffirms, that questions of attribution concerning unlawful state conduct are determined in accordance with the ARSIWA.

[610] ILC Fourth Report n 574 at p. 114 §54.

[611] See (the analogy of state responsibility referenced in): General Comment 2 to Chapter IV ARIO.

[612] Again, depending on whether independent responsibility under the ARIO is considered as being exculpatory or not.

minor terminological alterations to extend the ARSIWA provisions to IOs.[613] While instances of cooperation and concerted action between States and IOs were on the rise, regulation of these forms of responsibility were in an embryonic phase. In the Third Report for example, the Special Rapporteur appeared to conflate the acts of 'direction and control' with 'circumvention' and with the exception of a single sentence, refrained from elaborating upon the notion of 'aid and assistance' or and 'coercion', at which point he held that these concepts would be dealt with in a later phase.[614] Yet in the Seventh Report, the Special Rapporteur again focused predominantly upon the notions of 'direction and control' and 'circumvention', while reiterating the parallelism for the notions of shared responsibility with the analogous provisions in the ARSIWA.[615] Finally, in the Eighth Report, the Special Rapporteur systematically addressed the provisions of shared responsibility that were to be incorporated in the ARIO, albeit only summarily addressing the contours of those provisions[616] as discussed below. Precisely because of the limited practice and the embryonic nature of shared responsibility between IOs and states for concerted action, the ARIO's practical value on this topic is contested.

i. Article 14 ARIO – Aid and Assistance

Aid and assistance concerns situations where an IO aids or assists a state 'in carrying out conduct which is unlawful for the latter, for example, by knowingly providing an essential facility or financing the activity in question … with a view to facilitating the commission of an internationally wrongful act'.[617] As aforementioned, the IO's responsibility thus arises for its conduct in *facilitating* the commission of the unlawful conduct. The international responsibility that arises for aid and assistance is thus conceptually limited to those acts that facilitate the primary unlawful act.[618]

The parallel provisions on shared responsibility in ARIO and ARSIWA explain that for aid and assistance to result in responsibility for the IO, three conditions must be fulfilled:[619] knowledge of the circumstances of the unlawful conduct (1), intent (2) and the opposability of the legal obligation (3) as dealt with in turn below.

The international organisation must firstly, have 'knowledge of the circumstances of the unlawful act'.[620] Hence, if the IO providing the aid and assistance is unaware of the unlawful conduct it is contributing to, it will not incur any responsibility. Crucially however, both provisions miss any further indication as to how such knowledge is to be determined.[621] This may be determined by the various standards

[613] ILC Third report n 500 at 13 §25–26; ILC Seventh Report n 272 at p. 82 §45.
[614] ILC Third report n 500 at 16–17 §43.
[615] ILC Seventh Report n 272 at 82–84 §45–54.
[616] ILC, 'Eighth Report on the Responsibility of International Organizations by Mr. Giorgio Gaja, Special Rapporteur' (UN Doc. A /CN.4/640) 14 March 2011, 90–92 §45–58.
[617] Comment 1 to Article 16 ARSIWA.
[618] Certain primary norms already contain provisions on the prohibition on aid and assistance. However, such provisions have typically been directed at scenarios of aid and assistance between states. Comment 2 to Article 16 ARSIWA.
[619] Comment 3 to Article 14 ARIO; Comment 3 to Article 16 ARSIWA.
[620] Comment 3 to Article 14 ARIO; Comment 3 to Article 16 ARSIWA.
[621] Comment 3 to Article 14 ARIO; Comment 4 to Article 16 ARIO.

and burdens of proof required by different adjudicatory bodies, yet the limited practice in this respect, falls short of providing any guidelines on the matter. In the Commentary to Article 14 ARIO an example is included of support provided by the UN Mission in the Democratic Republic in Congo (MONUC) to the Forces armée de la République démocratique du Congo (FARDC) and the risk the latter poses respect for international humanitarian law, human rights law and refugee law.[622] The Legal Counsel of the United Nations held specifically that:

> If MONUC has reason to believe that FARDC units involved in an operation are violating one or the other of those bodies of law and if, despite MONUC's intercession with the FARDC and with the Government of the DRC, MONUC has reason to believe that such violations are still being committed, then MONUC may not lawfully continue to support that operation but must cease its participation in it completely. [...] MONUC may not lawfully provide logistic or 'service' support to any FARDC operation if it has reason to believe that the FARDC units involved are violating any of those bodies of law. [...] This follows directly from the Organization's obligations under customary international law and from the Charter to uphold, promote and encourage respect for human rights, international humanitarian law and refugee law.[623]

If the foregoing example is indicative of the legal standard to determine whether an IO did or did not have knowledge of the circumstances surrounding the unlawful conduct, it appears that an element of reasonableness is required. If then it can be reasonably deduced that there are detrimental human rights consequences associated to the project or measures for which an IO provides support, this would be sufficient to conclude that the IO had knowledge of the circumstances of the unlawful act. In the Eighth Report, the Special Rapporteur acknowledges that in cases of financial and material support, it may be difficult to pre-emptively determine the means in which such support would be used.[624] However, if the organisation should be aware of certain human rights implications stemming from such projects, it should abstain from providing support at risk of otherwise being held responsible for aid and assistance under Article 14 ARIO.[625] Such scenarios immediately raise the question as to the legitimacy of financial and material assistance by the EU to the Libyan Coast Guard in light of the widespread and documented human rights abuses at the hands of the Libyan Coast Guard (see Chapter 7).

Secondly, aid and assistance must have been *intended* to facilitate the unlawful conduct by the state(s) and must additionally have contributed significantly to the unlawful conduct.[626] Although aid and assistance does not have to be essential, as this would otherwise entail that the IO and the implicated state(s) would be co-perpetrators (see above), the aid and assistance must meet a *de minimis* threshold

[622] Comment 6 to Article 14 ARIO.
[623] Comment 6 to Article 14 ARIO.
[624] ILC Eighth Report n 616 at p. 90–91 §46–49.
[625] In the discussions of the topic, certain States opted to include a 'presumption of knowledge', which would reverse the burden of proof and require from the international organization to rebut that they had reasonable knowledge of the potential (human rights) implications of a project for which it provided aid and assistance. However, this was considered as being too far reaching and omitted. Moreover, if the aid and assistance meets the opposability criterion, that inevitably already includes the 'presumption of knowledge' on behalf of the international organization. ILC Eighth Report n 616 at 90–91 §46–49.
[626] Comment 4 to Article 14 ARIO.

and cannot be negligible.[627] The parallel provision in the ARSIWA implies that there must be some form of causality between the aid and assistance and the unlawful conduct that it facilitated, albeit that this is not further elaborated upon.[628] Hence, the second condition of *intent* is again, fraught with obscurity and it remains up to a Court or tribunal confronted with such questions, to determine – without much guidance – when the subjective criteria of intent has been established.[629]

Finally, the opposability condition requires that the wrongful conduct by the state would also have been wrongful had it been committed by the IO itself.[630] In other words, both parties (the primary perpetrator and the IO aiding and assisting) must have been bound by the same obligations, for international responsibility to arise vis-à-vis the IO for aid and assistance.[631] However, the Commentaries and *travaux préparatoires* fail to address a crucial question with respect to the opposability criterion: to what extent must the implicated parties be bound *by the same concrete primary obligations* for the opposability requirement to be met? Does it suffice that the State and the international organisation providing the aid and assistance are bound by the same primary norms in the theory? Or, taking the example of the concrete negative and positive human rights obligations: does the opposability requirement entail that the actors must both be bound by the same concrete obligations stemming therefrom? On the one hand, the aforementioned statement by the Legal Counsel of the United Nations, indicates that it would suffice for the implicated parties to be bound by the same general framework or human rights commitments.[632] Yet, on the other hand, a valid argument is made regarding the functional speciality of international organisations and how this impacts the extent to which they are bound by concrete human rights obligations.

In any event, the fact that the Legal Counsel implies that the former scenario suffices for the opposability requirement to be met, does not necessarily have any bearing on how this opposability requirement is applied in practice. An additional observation is needed in this respect – if it is sufficient for the IO to be bound by the general (abstract) human rights obligations principles to fulfil the opposability condition, this does not say much about how the primary norm obligations are to be interpreted vis-à-vis IOs when assessing their independent responsibility. Taking the example of *non-refoulement*: if under the opposability requirement, it would be sufficient that both the state party responsible for the illegitimate return of a TCN and the international organisation aid and assisting in this return, to simply be bound

[627] ILC Eighth Report n 616 at 90 §45.

[628] Comment 5 to Article 16 ARSIWA.

[629] Use could be made of analogy reasoning in order to determine whether the element of 'intent' has been met, albeit that this again increases the potential for fragmentation concerning responsibility of international organizations, in light of their functional heterogeneity.

[630] Article 14(b) ARIO 'the act would be internationally wrongful if committed by that organization'.

[631] Comment 5 to Article 14 ARIO; Comment 6 to Article 16 ARSIWA. The rationale behind this provision, as explained in Comment 6 to Article 16 ARSIWA, is that 'a State is not bound by obligations of another State vis-à-vis third States. This basic principle is also embodied in articles 34 and 35 of the 1969 Vienna Convention. Correspondingly, a State is free to act for itself in a way which is inconsistent with the obligations of another State vis-à-vis third States. Any question of responsibility in such cases will be a matter for the State to whom assistance is provided vis-à-vis the injured State'.

[632] Comment 6 to Article 14 ARIO.

by the principled provision, this would fail to explain how and when under independent responsibility, the international organisation could be held responsible. Moreover, two different standards of obligations could theoretically arise – the standard to protect the *non-refoulement* by refraining from aid and assistance to a State engaged in such prohibited practices, which operates at a more abstract level and encompasses a negative obligation, as opposed to the standard under independent responsibility which may be somewhat more stringent and could encompass both negative and positive obligations on behalf of the IO. While this may in fact be something to strive towards in the interest of the individual, again, the ambiguity concerning the contours of the opposability requirement, reduce all the foregoing to mere conjecture.

What *can* be deduced with absolute certainty from the conditionality of aid and assistance as included in the ARIO, is that it is tainted by uncertainty: the IO must have had knowledge of the circumstances of the unlawful act, but no indications are given as to how such knowledge is to be determined. Similarly, there must be intent to facilitate the wrongful conduct by the state, albeit without any definitive guidelines as to when such intent is established. Finally, the opposability criterion does not explain the extent to which IO must bear the same obligations, absent which, there is again room for uncertainty and divergence in practice. The foregoing obscure elements, demonstrate again, that determinations and apportionment of shared responsibility under the ARIO will not necessarily yield a legally certain and effective methodology and rather, remains subject to the (potentially arbitrary) discretion of various legal regimes and adjudicatory bodies. And although the ARIO never sought to provide a finite, determinative set of rules, precisely because of the heterogeneity of IOs, the degree of indeterminacy facilitates the erosion of common baselines on IO responsibility. This, in turn, gives rise to inconsistencies that may be manipulated to avoid responsibility altogether.

ii. Article 15 ARIO – Direction and Control

Article 15 ARIO[633] addresses the apportionment of responsibility in scenarios in which an IO exerts direction and control over its members. Similar to Article 14 ARIO, this provision transposes its twin provision in ARSIWA (Article 17)[634] to the ARIO, with only minor modifications, to broaden its scope and render it applicable to IOs.[635] In addition, Article 15 ARIO similarly requires that the direction and control is exercised with *knowledge* of the circumstances of the unlawful conduct and likewise recalls the *opposability* condition.

[633] Article 15 ARIO: 'An international organization which directs and controls a State or another international organization in the commission of an internationally wrongful act by the State or the latter organization is internationally responsible for that act if: (a) the former organization does so with knowledge of the circumstances of the internationally wrongful act; and (b) the act would be internationally wrongful if committed by that organization'.

[634] Article 17 ARSIWA: 'A State which directs and controls another State in the commission of an internationally wrongful act by the latter is internationally responsible for that act if: (a) that State does so with knowledge of the circumstances of the internationally wrongful act; and (b) the act would be internationally wrongful if committed by that State'.

[635] Comment 1 to Article 15 ARIO.

The Commentaries to Article 15 ARIO, are rather limited and lack any definitive pronouncement on the type of conduct that will amount to direction and control to trigger responsibility of the IO. Instead, limited guidance is provided by indicating that the notion of control exceeds mere oversight and influence or concern, and that direction exceeds incitement to unlawful conduct.[636] Bearing in mind these *de minimis* factors, the Commentaries suggest that a binding decision taken by an IO, with limited to no margin of discretion on behalf of the implementing state, may amount to direction and control.[637] Similarly, depending on the factual circumstances, normative control exerted by the IO may amount to direction and control, albeit that this 'could not be regarded as a feature characterizing all the organisations that have the power to bind member States'.[638] The Special Rapporteur underlines in this regard, that there must be factual direction and control and only when normative control aligns with such factual control, will this be considered to trigger Article 15 ARIO.[639] Direction according to the Commentaries, is consequently construed as 'direction of an operative kind', whereas control is construed as 'domination over the commission of wrongful conduct and not simply the exercise of oversight'.[640] The mere ability to exert influence over the conduct of a state, will thus not amount to direction and control by the international organisation, and will not be 'a sufficient basis for attributing to it any wrongful acts'.[641]

The embryonic nature of shared responsibility is particularly visible in the preparatory works for Article 15 ARIO, which are characterised by ambiguity, lacking clear delineation on its scope and implicit and explicit overlap with other provisions.

On the one hand, the Special Rapporteur repeatedly observed in his Third,[642] Seventh[643] and Eighth[644] Report as well as in the Commentaries to Article 15 ARIO,[645] that an overlap between the responsibility for direction and control and circumvention (see below) is possible. However, the Special Rapporteur appeased any concerns on the matter, by holding that in any event, both provisions seek to assess the international responsibility of an organisation for its contribution in the unlawful conduct of a state.[646] Consequently, any overlaps are not problematic. Drawing further from this overlap between provisions on shared responsibility, the question could be raised (but is not addressed in the preparatory works), whether an IO could still be held responsible for its contributions to unlawful conduct under the provision of aid and assistance, if it does not meet the standards required for direction and control or

[636] Comment 4 to Article 15 ARIO; ILC Eighth Report n 616 at 91 §50.

[637] Comment 4 to Article 15 ARIO.

[638] Comment 4 to Article 15 ARIO; ILC Third report n 500 at 13, 15 §25–26, 35.

[639] ILC Third report n 500 at 15 §35.

[640] Comment 4 to Article 15 ARIO.

[641] Comment 6 to Article 17 ARSIWA. Note here that the Commentaries refer to the *attribution* of conduct on the basis of Article 17 ARSIWA, concerning direction and control.

[642] In the Third Report, the overlap is discussed indirectly. ILC Third report n 500 at 15–16 §35–39.

[643] ILC Seventh Report n 272 at 83 §46.

[644] ILC Eighth Report n 616 at 91 §51. The Russian Federation had suggested to remedy such overlaps, which was at the time, considered unnecessary by the Special Rapporteur.

[645] Comment 5 to Article 15 ARIO.

[646] ILC Eighth Report n 616 at 91 §51.

circumvention. As the Special Rapporteur did not exclude the possibility for overlap between responsibility based on direction and control, as opposed to responsibility on the basis of circumvention, it appears this question would have to be answered in the affirmative. Bearing this hypothesis in mind, the provisions of shared responsibility could subsequently be regarded as 'sliding scales of involvement', rather than an attempted typology of separate forms of contributions to unlawful conduct of states. This in turn, could have been beneficial for the purpose of more effectively establishing when an IO incurs responsibility.

Similarly, the Commentaries and Special Rapporteur do not address the relationship between the provision on direction and control, and the provisions on attribution for the purpose of establishing *independent* responsibility. The Commentaries and the *travaux préparatoires* on Article 15 ARIO elaborate upon the notion of 'direction and control', by indirectly linking it to Article 8 ARSIWA as a ground for attribution of unlawful conduct,[647] albeit that this does not necessarily clarify its scope. In the Commentaries to Article 8 ARSIWA, different tests of direction and control are presented by juxtaposing the *Military and Paramilitary Activities in and against Nicaragua* case and the *Tadić* case. The focus of the ICJ in the first case was on whether the United States exercised effective control over the contras by planning, directing and providing (financial) support to the extent that the contras could be considered as acting on behalf of the United States.[648] The ICJ found that although the US was responsible for its involvement and support to the contras, 'a general situation of dependence and support would be insufficient to justify attribution of conduct to the State'.[649] The Appeals Chamber in the *Tadić* case took a slightly different approach in determining whether there was direction and control, holding that such determinations will depend on factual circumstances which may vary from case to case, and that overall control was required, exceeding mere financing and logistical support.[650] The Commentaries to Article 8 ARSIWA conclude that 'it is a matter for appreciation in each case whether particular conduct was or was not carried out under the control of a State, to such an extent that the conduct controlled should be attributed to it', entailing that the matter is not resolved for responsibility sharing between states.[651] Given the implicit parallelism between Article 8 ARSIWA and the notions of direction and control in Article 15 ARIO, this same obscurity exists as to its scope. Furthermore,

[647] See for example the terminology used in the Commentaries to Article 17 ARSIWA, to which the Commentaries in Article 15 ARIO refer. Comment 6 to Article 17 ARSIWA. Note here that the Commentaries refer to the *attribution* of conduct on the basis of Article 17 ARSIWA, concerning direction and control. This confirms to a limited extent, that the rules on shared responsibility are indeed partly of a secondary nature. Moreover, it seems to indicate particularly in the case of direction and control, that the Commentaries conflate attribution under Article 15 ARIO, with the test of attribution that may arise under Article 6 and 7 ARIO.

[648] Comment 4 to Article 8 ARSIWA.

[649] Comment 4 to Article 8 ARSIWA.

[650] Comment 5 to Article 8 ARSIWA.

[651] Comment 5 to Article 8 ARSIWA. The fact that for both state responsibility and the responsibility of international organizations this has not been established, is not overwhelmingly problematic as such. However, in the latter case, it is problematic as the ambiguity concerning the scope and implications of 'direction and control' further compound the issues and obscurity that has arisen for the other conditions that must be met for international responsibility to arise.

the debate on the scope of 'direction and control' which refers to both a test of effective control and a test of overall control, is highly reminiscent of the same test for the purpose of attribution of conduct under Article 6 and 7 ARIO, albeit that this dynamic is simply not discussed by the Special Rapporteur. Simply put, the question is thus whether on the one hand, the tests for direction and control are effectively the same,[652] and secondly, what the implications are of a finding of direction and control vis-à-vis the existence of attribution.

In the hypothesis that the threshold for direction and control under Article 15 ARIO would be met, and the degree of direction and control is of the type that it constitutes normative control for example (as a result of which Members no longer have any margin of discretion),[653] would this entail that the latter would escape responsibility altogether? And would this entail, under the exculpatory approach to independent responsibility that the international organisation would subsequently be held independently responsible for the unlawful conduct, as opposed to the 'mere' facilitation thereof under Article 15 ARIO? If, of course, a non-exculpatory approach is adopted to independent responsibility, what then are the implications of a finding of direction and control under Article 15 ARIO – would both the international organisation and the complicit state be held independently responsible, and the organisation additionally responsible for facilitating the wrongful conduct? Moreover, as aforementioned, the obscurity of the opposability requirement complicates the effectiveness and applicability of Article 15 ARIO. Indeed, in the preparatory phases concerning Article 15 ARIO, the United States, the Russian Federation, Guatemala and Israel all raised criticisms with respect to the opposability requirement. The United States in particular, questioned specifically whether responsibility would be incurred by the international organisation, if it was not bound by the same [concrete] obligation as the state engaged in the unlawful conduct, which was highlighted by the Russian Federation, holding that 'some actions could be taken only by States and not by international organizations'.[654] The Special Rapporteur did not however, offer any guidance on this matter.

The foregoing prompt the question of the added value of this provision. While the foregoing questions may potentially be of a mere methodological nature, the absence of any discussion or clarity on the matter, evidence the seemingly artificial separation between shared and independent responsibility in the ARIO and complicates the (effective) application of its provisions. How are (international) courts and tribunals to apply these standards coherently and consistently when there remains so much ambiguity as to the scope and the dynamic of its provisions? It may very well be the case that the indeterminacy and incongruence that taints the respective responsibility frameworks may give rise to a race to the bottom and facilitate a responsibility gap.

[652] The Commentaries to Article 8 ARSIWA and Article 15 ARIO, indicate that the tests are at least in part different. Whereas the notions of direction and control are considered as being disjunctive under Article 8 ARSIWA, the Special Rapporteur leaves this open in Comment 4 and 5 to Article 15 ARIO.

[653] ILC Third report n 500 at 14 §31.

[654] ILC Seventh Report n 272 at 83 §45 n 80.

iii. Article 16 ARIO – Coercion

Article 16 ARIO holds that an IO will incur international responsibility if the unlawful conduct of the State '(a) would, but for the coercion, be an internationally wrongful act of the coerced state or international organization; and (b) the coercing international organization does so with full knowledge of the circumstances of the act'.[655] Again, the parallelism with its twin provision in Article 18 ARSIWA is emphasised,[656] entailing that the scope of coercion is elaborated upon in the Commentaries thereto. The Commentaries on coercion in ARSIWA, highlight the narrow scope of coercion[657] and define coercion as being 'deliberately exercised in order to procure the breach of one State's obligation to a third State'.[658] The responsibility is incurred in such scenarios, on account of the unlawful conduct stemming from the coercion – not the coercion itself per se, which may or may not be lawful.[659] It would not be sufficient for the obligation which is violated by the coerced state, to have been made more difficult to comply with.[660] Rather, the ground of coercion requires that the conduct of the coerced state leaves it 'no effective choice but to comply with the wishes …' of the IO to trigger its responsibility.[661] In fact, binding decisions adopted by IOs, requiring a particular conduct by its members will only exceptionally be considered as coercion.[662] However, the Commentaries on the topic neglect to elaborate upon the type of binding decisions that may give rise to responsibility based on coercion, evidencing the potential links with the provision of direction and control under Article 15 ARIO, and the grounds for attribution and independent responsibility under Article 6 and 7 ARIO, which remain unaddressed.

The provisions on coercion in both the ARIO and ARSIWA, emphasise that the ground of coercion, precludes the wrongful conduct of the coerced state.[663] As such, coercion is equated with the *force majeure*, entailing that the coerced state had no choice but to adopt the sought-after unlawful conduct by the international organisation.[664]

Analogous to preceding provisions, Article 16 ARIO requires that the IO had knowledge of the circumstances of the unlawful conduct. The same questions concerning the scope of the knowledge requirement similarly arise. However, contrary to the preceding provisions, the opposability requirement does not apply here. In other words, the unlawful conduct that is coerced by the IO does not necessarily have to be unlawful for adapted the IO itself.[665] The rationale behind this nuance is that the

[655] Article 16 ARIO.

[656] Comment 1 and 2 to Article 16 ARIO.

[657] Comment 3 to Article 18 ARSIWA.

[658] Comment 1 to Article 18 ARSIWA.

[659] In most cases, the coercion will, however, be unlawful. Comment 3 to Article 16 ARIO; Comment 1 and 3 to Article 18 ARSIWA; ILC Eighth Report n 616 at 91 §52.

[660] Comment 2 to Article 18 ARSIWA.

[661] Comment 4 to Article 16 ARIO; Comment 2 to Article 18 ARSIWA.

[662] Comment 4 to Article 16 ARIO.

[663] Comment 4 to Article 16 ARIO; Comment 2, 3 and 6 to Article 18 ARSIWA.

[664] Comment 4 to Article 16 ARIO; Comment 2, 3 and 6 to Article 18 ARSIWA.

[665] Comment 3 to Article 16 ARIO; Comment 6 to Article 18 ARSIWA. Note the terminological nuance in (a) of Article 16 ARIO, where it is held that the 'act would, but for the coercion, be an internationally wrongful act of the coerced state or the international organization' (emphasis added).

victim of the unlawful conduct by the coerced state would otherwise be deprived of any legal review or redress, if the IO coerces unlawful conduct that it itself is not bound by.[666]

Again, the Special Rapporteur only summarily addresses the dynamic of this provision with the other provisions on shared responsibility in the ARIO. In particular, the relationship between Article 16 ARIO on coercion is raised with respect to Article 17 ARIO on circumvention,[667] particularly when a binding decision by an IO constitutes both coercion and circumvention.[668] Reaffirming his earlier stance, the Special Rapporteur notes that any overlap between the aforementioned provisions, does not provide for any inconsistencies, as both provisions pursue the IO's international responsibility. Unlike the Commentaries concerning coercion in Article 18 ARSIWA, however, the Special Rapporteur does not elaborate upon how coercion by IOs may relate to the notions of the earlier provision concerning direction and control. The Commentaries to Article 18 ARSIWA suggest that the test for coercion adopts a higher threshold than the test for direction and control, as a result of which the coerced state is left no choice but to comply with the wishes of IO.[669] All other instances where it is made more difficult for a State to comply with its international obligations, would instead be caught by the preceding provisions of aid and assistance, and direction and control.[670] While this does seem to support the 'sliding scales of contributions' approach (see above), it is not clear whether this is what the Special Rapporteur had in mind when drafting the provisions on shared responsibility between organisations and its members in the ARIO. The Commentaries to the ARIO – particularly on direction and control – appear to already apply a very stringent test of direction and control. Under this test for direction and control, the responsibility of the IO would thus 'hinge on whether the organization's binding decision actually requires the wrongful act to be done, or whether the act is just one of the ways that a member State may select when implementing a decision'.[671] Without any further clarification on the topic, it is hard to determine how or where this form of control exercised by the IO over the (unlawful) conduct by the State, is to be differentiated from the control under Article 6 (normative control or competence) and 7 ARIO (effective control and/or overall authority and control), Article 16 (coercion) and 17 ARIO (circumvention – see below). This is particularly relevant here, as under the test for direction and control, the opposability requirement applies, whereas this is not the case under the test for coercion. But if conversely the test for both direction and control, as well as coercion (and potentially circumvention) amount to a highly analogous test in practice, any international court or tribunal confronted with a situation as such, will have to make a potentially arbitrary choice between the grounds for shared responsibility, which may have consequences on the potential reparations to which a victim would otherwise be entitled, given the different conditions that apply to invoke responsibility.

[666] Comment 3 to Article 16 ARIO; Comment 6 to Article 18 ARSIWA.
[667] Comment 5 to Article 16 ARIO.
[668] Comment 5 to Article 16 ARIO.
[669] Comment 4 to Article 18 ARSIWA.
[670] Comment 4 to Article 18 ARSIWA.
[671] ILC Third report n 500 at 14 §31.

More concretely – in the hypothesis that an IO adopts a decision, which requires (with no room to manoeuvre) unlawful conduct by a state, international responsibility of the IO may arise on the basis of direction and control (Article 15 ARIO). In the assumption that this ground would form the basis of such responsibility, the opposability requirement would have to be met. This would not be the case, however, if the international responsibility would be based upon the ground of coercion (Article 16). Moreover, if the ground of coercion is invoked, the coerced states' conduct would be precluded of wrongfulness, further limiting the means of reparation for the victim of the unlawful conduct. Hence, insofar the 'sliding scales of contribution' was not intended by the Special Rapporteur, any (international) court or tribunal faced with questions of shared responsibility may be left a (policy) choice between the grounds to establish the international responsibility of the IO. So, whereas the Special Rapporteur consistently holds that the overlap between provisions in the ARIO does not necessarily matter as they all seek the same result, in the present case it is argued, that the overlap and lacking clarity on the dynamic *does* matter. In fact, this is implicitly acknowledged in the Third Report, where the Special Rapporteur on the degree of involvement required for the threshold of aid and assistance to be met, holds that the degree of involvement will not necessarily affect the *existence* of the (shared) responsibility, but may affect the *content* of the responsibility,[672] namely who and to what extent will bear the burden of the reparations and consequences flowing from the international responsibility. It matters additionally, because the legal fog surrounding these provisions, allow adjudicatory bodies (unintended) leeway to adopt fragmented and potentially conflicting decisions on the (shared) responsibility of IOs. In turn, the absence on clarity on the matter, could in practice, detrimentally affect legal certainty, legitimate expectations, as well as the effectiveness of the right to a remedy against unlawful conduct by IOs.

iv. Article 17 ARIO – Circumvention

The final provision in the ARIO concerning shared responsibility between an IO and its member(s), concerns circumvention. An IO will incur responsibility when it circumvents its international obligations by '(a) by adopting a decision binding member States or international organizations to commit an act that would be internationally wrongful if committed by the former organization'. Similarly, an IO will incur international responsibility by '(b) authorizing member States or international organizations to commit an act that would be internationally wrongful if committed by the former organization and the act in question is committed because of that authorization'.[673] Here too, the opposability criterion does not need to be fulfilled, as circumvention refers to the scenario where an IO makes use of the separate legal personality of its members, to circumvent one of its own legal obligations, that does not necessarily need to be a legal obligation of the implementing state(s).[674] In other words, Article 17 ARIO 'does not make the international

[672] ILC Third report n 500 at 16–17 §43.

[673] Article 17 ARIO.

[674] Article 17(3) ARIO. *In casu*, it thus irrelevant whether the implementing state is also bound by the same obligation as the international organization is seeking to circumvent. This is the inverse scenario of

responsibility of the international organization dependent on the unlawfulness of the conduct of the member State or international organization to which the decision or authorization is addressed'.[675]

The rationale behind this provision was to prevent IOs from expressly making use of their members to achieve objectives that could otherwise not legally be achieved,[676] thus encompassing the subjective element of intent.[677] Interestingly, in the Eighth Report, the Special Rapporteur noted the reluctance of States to incorporate this subjective element, on account of the difficulty in demonstrating that such subjective intent was effectively present.[678] However, the element was nevertheless included and the Commentaries explain that intent is to be determined based on the factual circumstances, without any further guidance on how this is to be assessed.[679]

As aforementioned, Article 17 ARIO makes the distinction between (binding) adopted decisions by the international organisation on the one hand, and (non-binding) authorisations by the international organisations on the other hand. When the organisation has adopted a binding decision vis-à-vis its member(s), the unlawful conduct need not yet have occurred, as it can be reasonably assumed that the state will effectively implement the adopted decision.[680] In the case of authorisations, however, the circumvention must already have occurred for the organisation to incur international responsibility.[681] This is because, authorisation (without a request by the organisation) necessarily entails a level of discretion on behalf of the member State. The provision on authorisation was nevertheless deemed necessary to include, because the discretion retained by a member State, may only exist in theory and members may de facto be compelled to act in accordance with an authorisation by the international organisation.[682] For authorisation by the international organisation to trigger international responsibility, there must be a direct link between the unlawful conduct by the State and the authorisation provided by the organisation. The Commentaries explain that this will have to be determined taking into account the context in which the authorisation occurred.[683]

The terminological reference to 'authorisation' does not require that the rules of the organisation define such instructions or request as such – different terminology may apply and yet still be caught by Article 17 ARIO.[684] However, the use of the term 'recommendations' was contested, including explicitly by the European Commission,

Article 16 ARIO, where it is irrelevant whether the international organization is bound by the international obligation. Hence, international responsibility based upon Articles 14–16 ARIO are made contingent upon the unlawfulness of the conduct on behalf of the State, whereas, under the chapeau of Article 17 ARIO, the State does not need to be bound by the same obligation.

675 Comment 14 to Article 17 ARIO.

676 Comment 1 to Article 17 ARIO.

677 Comment 4 to Article 17 ARIO.

678 ILC Eighth Report n 616 at 91 §55.

679 Comment 4 to Article 17 ARIO.

680 Comment 5 to Article 17 ARIO.

681 Comment 7–8, 10 to Article 17 ARIO.

682 Comment 8 to Article 17 ARIO.

683 Comment 11 to Article 17 ARIO.

684 Comment 9 to Article 17 ARIO.

as this would otherwise have had the effect of broadening the scope of the international responsibility for IOs considerably.[685]

In any event, as aforementioned, the same questions concerning the applicable standards and overlap arise. Bearing in mind the vagueness of the rules on shared responsibility under the ARIO, we turn to the shared responsibility rules under EU law to see whether these rules can accommodate situations of cooperative conduct between Member States and the EU so as to give rise to EU responsibility.

c. The *Lex Specialis* Rules

i. A Developing Concept under EU Law

To date, practice and precedent on joint responsibility within the EU remains limited and fragmented.[686]

Craig and de Búrca identify two scenarios in which joint liability (responsibility) between Member States may be possible, while acknowledging that these two scenarios are by no means exhaustive.[687] On the one hand, there are the scenarios in which the EU has failed to prevent the unlawful conduct in the form of a breach of *EU law* by national authorities.[688] On the other hand, there are the scenarios in which the Member States implement unlawful EU legislation.[689] As will be portrayed, however, these scenarios constitute cases in which the duality of liability is acknowledged implicitly, but the focus is on the *consequences* of the responsibility.[690] In other words, the preceding step (following ARIO methodology) of ascertaining responsibility and apportioning this among the complicit actors, is not addressed.

Concerning the first scenario, the authors acknowledge that EU law does not preclude the apportionment of shared responsibility between Member States and the EU, as recognised in *Lütticke*.[691] However, there are significant hurdles in establishing shared responsibility, particularly in light of the European Commissions discretion in bringing infringement claims against Member State. Based upon Article 258 TFEU.[692] The CJEU has clarified, however, in the case of *Kampffmeyer* that insofar the European Commission adopts a formal measure *authorizing* illegal national action, it may result in EU responsibility.[693] The Commission authorisation

[685] ILC Eighth Report n 616 at 92 §56–57.

[686] There have been numerous attempts to strike out EU secondary legislation on the basis of non-compliance with EU human rights, or likewise contest national implementation of EU law on the basis of non-compliance with EU fundamental rights. However, none of these cases concern the responsibility of the EU as such. Furthermore, the overwhelming majority of these cases concern a preliminary ruling, with the exception of one annulment case. Additionally, all these cases concerned whether the secondary act or national implementing act constituted an illegitimate infringement of the right at stake, which particularly in preliminary references, will not be determined *in concreto*. In any event, these cases do not inform as to the scope of the concrete obligations that are imposed upon the EU. Craig and de Búrca n 143 at 434–435.

[687] ibid 634–635.

[688] ibid 634.

[689] ibid 635.

[690] Part Three – Content of the International Responsibility of an International Organization ARIO.

[691] CJEU Judgment of 28 April 1971, *Alfons Lütticke GmbH v Commission of the European Communities*, C-4/69, ECLI:EU:C:1971:40.

[692] Article 258 TFEU.

[693] CJEU Judgment of 14 July 1967, *Firma E. Kampffmeyer and others v Commission of the EEC*, C-5, 7 and 13-24/66, ECLI:EU:C:1967:13, 266.

in casu, had already been the subject of an annulment proceeding. More interestingly, the CJEU held that in order to avoid the applicants being 'excessively compensated for the same damage by the different assessment of two different courts applying different rules of law', the national court would have to rule upon the responsibility on behalf of Germany first. In other words, *Kampffmeyer* indicates that in this particular scenario, shared (ie non-exculpatory) responsibility is possible (albeit for different wrongful acts resulting in a single harm[694]), but subject to the implicit caveat that Germany was primarily responsible, with the EU incurring only residual liability (including *residual* duties of reparation).[695]

A second scenario which may give rise to shared responsibility, concerns the implementation by Member States of unlawful EU legislation. *Haegeman* by the CJEU illustrates this perfectly. This case concerned the implementation by national authorities of EU-mandated regulations. *In casu*, the CJEU held that 'Issues … which are raised during such a procedure as to the interpretation and validity of regulations establishing the Communities' own resources must be brought before the national courts which have at their disposal the procedure under Article 177[696] of the Treaty in order to ensure the uniform application of EU law'.[697] In essence, the CJEU held that even when the regulation compels national authorities to implement its provisions, and the implementation results in funds being relocated to the EU, the claims for compensation are first and foremost actionable before domestic courts, even when national authorities have been instructed to act in accordance with the interpretation of the EU institution.[698] The requirement to first address actions before national courts is rebutted in a limited number of scenarios, rendering direct action against the EU possible: when the interpretation of the EU institution, de facto constitutes an instruction (1);[699] when no action is available within the domestic jurisdiction (2);[700] and finally, where the EU act is directly the cause of the injury undergone by the applicant (3).[701]

[694] The European Commission erred by wrongful authorization of the Member State conduct, and the Member State erred by virtue of the primary unlawful conduct via the retention of protective measures vis-à-vis the import of maize, millet and sorghum. CJEU Judgment of 14 July 1967, *Firma E. Kampffmeyer and others v Commission of the EEC*, C-5, 7 and 13-24/66, ECLI:EU:C:1967:13, 259. This type of shared conduct falls neatly within the category of Article 14 ARIO concerning aid and assistance provided by the international organization to a Member State but could likewise possibly fall within the scope of Article 17 ARIO concerning circumvention by the international organization via authorization. It appears unlikely however, that the conditionality for either of these two grounds of shared responsibility could be met (see above).

[695] This type of apportionment of responsibility, where the Member State carries the primary responsibility and the EU only carries responsibility in a residual manner, resurfaces at different points, including in the Draft Accession Agreement for joint responsibility for unlawful human rights conduct. Craig and de Búrca n 143 at 635.

[696] Now Article 267 TFEU concerning the preliminary reference procedure.

[697] CJEU Judgment of 25 October 1972, *R. & V. Haegeman v Commission of the European Communities*, C-96/71, ECLI:EU:C:1972:88, 1015, §8.

[698] Craig and de Búrca n 143 at 636.

[699] CJEU Judgment of 15 January 1987, *Krohn & Co. Import-Export GmbH & Co. KG v Commission of the European Communities*, C-175/84, ECLI:EU:C:1987:8.

[700] CJEU (CFI) Judgment of 18 September 1995, *Detlef Nölle v Council of the European Union and Commission of the European Communities*, T-167/94, ECLI:EU:T:1995:169, §38.

[701] CJEU Judgment of 15 December 1977, *Firma Gebrüder Dietz v Commission of the European Communities*, C-126/76, ECLI:EU:C:1977:211.

What both of these scenarios demonstrate, is that a rule emerges according to which there must be prior exhaustion of internal remedies (ie before national courts) to assess the *Member State* liability and deal with matters of indemnification, *before* the EU's responsibility may be assessed and result in reparations.[702] This does not reveal much, however, on the *conditions* to establish joint responsibility and how such responsibility is to be apportioned. Rather, it treats joint conduct in the abovementioned scenarios as two separate matters, to be determined by separate courts altogether. If anything, the conclusion may be drawn that at least as concerns the substantive areas of law at stake in these cases, at the time, responsibility determinations were not *per se* exculpatory.[703] Furthermore, these cases have evidenced that at times, the CJEU conflates notions of attribution, causation and responsibility.

Notwithstanding the fact that the scenarios and cases aforementioned depart from the idea that there is indeed *shared* responsibility without explicitly and exhaustively delving into the manners in which such responsibility is to be apportioned,[704] several conclusions can nonetheless be drawn from the foregoing. Specifically, the following scenarios can be identified where the EU *could* incur responsibility for its complicit conduct in Member State action, with a principled rule on prior exhaustion of internal remedies, but without exhaustively clarifying *how* such responsibility would be determined:

Figure 2 Scenarios which may give rise to EU responsibility (J. De Coninck)

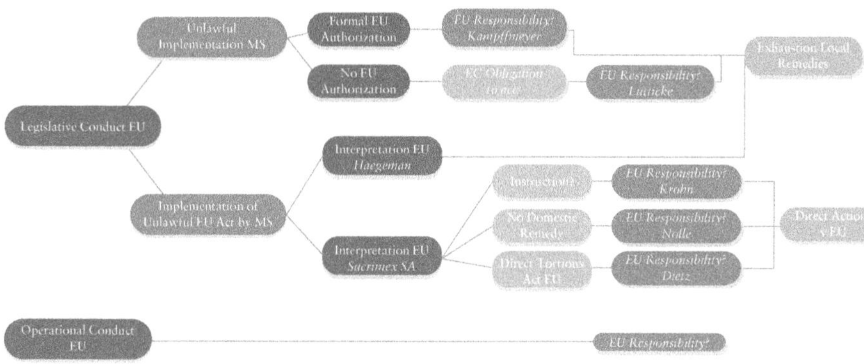

[702] CJEU (CFI) Judgment of 18 September 1995, *Detlef Nölle v Council of the European Union and Commission of the European Communities*, T-167/94, ECLI:EU:T:1995:169, §36.

[703] This isn't surprising, as the conduct by the Member States and that of the EU often differed, with on the one hand, the *implementing* act by the Member State and on the other hand the legal act by the EU that lays at the basis of the implementation of the Member States, or alternatively, the absence of intervention on behalf of the EU. Conceptually, these are all different acts – the enactment of a legal instrument (1), the (unlawful) implementation of a legal instrument (2) and the omission to intervene upon the unlawful implementation of a legal instrument by Member States (3).

[704] For the sake of thoroughness, it is necessary to note that in certain cases (*ia Kampffmeyer*) the damages claim stemmed from the already annulled European Commission authorization, thus making it redundant in that particular case for the CJEU to pronounce itself on the extent of EU responsibility.

As demonstrated, the CJEU has (implicitly) acknowledged the potential of shared responsibility *in theory* in a number of cases. However, these cases do not address the allocation of responsibility for operational joint conduct by the EU in concert with Member States. Furthermore, as the aforementioned cases are focused predominantly upon the consequences and the implementation of responsibility, these scenarios that theoretically confirm EU shared responsibility do not reveal much on how such responsibility is allocated in practice and what the *conditions* are for responsibility to arise.

ii. Shared Responsibility Beyond the CJEU

In different substantive areas of EU law, shared conduct and subsequent responsibility are handled in varying ways, sometimes blurring the lines between attribution and responsibility.[705] This is not surprising when the competence test of attribution is relied upon to establish EU responsibility.[706] As demonstrated, the competence test necessarily requires engaging with mutable power dynamics between the EU and its Member States depending on the substantive area of EU law at stake, and the nature of the competence (exclusive, shared or parallel competences).[707] The fact that competence division is not static as such,[708] and the fact that the division of competence is qualified by the overarching obligation of sincere cooperation (Article 4(3) TFEU), render it all the more difficult for external third parties to decipher which actor is competent to act in a given scenario, particularly where shared or parallel competences are at stake.[709] Consider the following examples:

Practice surrounding WTO disputes reveals that on the one hand, the WTO panels appear largely inclined to follow the EU in its application of what appears to be the exonerating/exculpatory normative control model for attribution[710] (and ensuing responsibility), whereby Member States are considered as (de facto or functional)

[705] Kuijper and Paasivirta n 267 at 64–65.

[706] It is argued that the EU in practice does not always adopt competence division, or declarations of competence in international agreements, as the decisive criterion to determine attribution. Heliskoski n 317 at 208.

[707] Paasivirta n 444 at 462–463.

[708] Rosas n 322 at 23; Kuijper and Paasivirta n 267 at 59.

[709] Paasivirta makes a compelling argument that, in light of these differing variations of competences and the – sometimes – absent explicit delineation or declaration of competence division, there is a duty of communication internationally on the Member States and the EU towards third parties within the context of mixed agreements. Paasivirta argues that such a duty of communication is to be read in tandem with the customary duty of international cooperation for settling disputes peacefully. This approach was first adopted under the *chapeau* of UNCLOS, which not only included a declaration of competence upon accession, but likewise provides under Annex IX provides that Parties to UNCLOS may request the international organization and its Members for information concerning the competence division in any particular situation, which the requested parties are then compelled to provide. Failure to provide the required information, in an uncontradictory manner and within a reasonable time frame, will result in *joint and several* liability. Paasivirta n 444 at 462–465.

[710] In *Airbus*, the WTO panel disregarded the exonerating/exculpatory normative and competence models on attribution altogether, holding that in cases where Member States are acting in parallel with the EU, without being subject to its authorization, they remain liable for their own conduct. WTO Panel Report of 30 June 2010, *European Communities and certain Member States: Measures Affecting Trade in Large Civil Aircraft*, WT/DS316/R, §7.174–7.175.

EU organs or agents.[711] Internally, however, the CJEU and Advocate Generals are somewhat more divided on the matter, with some adopting the normative control model on attribution, albeit not in its exculpatory form (eg, *Parliament v Council;* Advocate General Jacobs;[712] Advocate General Tesauro[713]), while others (Advocate General Mischo[714]) argue in favour of a combination of the (non-exonerating) competence model on attribution.

EU responsibility related to UNCLOS demonstrates what is commonly referred to as the 'proceduralisation of the EU's responsibility'.[715] Upon accession to UNCLOS, Annex IX thereof requires a declaration of competence of the powers that have been transferred by the States to the acceding IO. Article 6 of Annex IX UNCLOS subsequently holds that responsibility will be established in accordance therewith[716] thus explicitly relying on the competence model on attribution.[717] Additionally, Article 6(2) of Annex IX UNCLOS holds that any applicant in a dispute may request additional information concerning the division of competence for matters concerning the substance of UNCLOS. Failure to provide coherent information on this division, or failure to do so within the required timeframe, will give rise to *joint and several liability*, albeit that this responsibility would only be for failure to comply with Annex IX, and thus has no bearing on responsibility for the substantive violation of the UNCLOS.[718] Echoing HELISKOSKI and the ITLOS Advisory Opinion in *Case No. 21*, a declaration of competence is a procedural matter, that does not necessarily yield an effective determination of responsibility.[719]

The proceduralisation of EU responsibility also appears to spill over into recently concluded free trade agreements, concerning the investment chapters in particular.[720] Attribution and ensuing responsibility is determined – on request by the Applicant to a dispute – by the EU, relegating this determination to a purely internal EU level. The ad hoc provisions that describe this procedural mechanism, on the face of it, hold that an exonerating/exculpatory and broadly construed variation of the normative control model is to be applied, whereby Member States will only be held responsible if the subject matter falls exclusively within their purview.[721] Conversely, disputed measures that *include* the EU, will result in the EU acting as the respondent

[711] Contartese n 322 at 430; Kuijper and Paasivirta n 267 at 63.

[712] Opinion of Advocate General Jacobs of 2 March 1994, *Parliament v Council*, C-316/91, ECLI:EU:C:1993:872, §69. See also: Article 1 Fourth ACP-EEC Convention; Contartese n 322 at 424.

[713] Opinion of Advocate General Tesauro of 13 November 1997, *Hermès International (a partnership limited by shares) v FHT Marketing Choice BV.*, C-53/96, ECLI:EU:C:1997:539, §14.

[714] Opinion of Advocate General Mischo of 27 November 2001, *Commission of the European Communities v Ireland*, C-13/00, ECLI:EU:C:2001:643, §30.

[715] Delgado Casteleiro n 27 at 135–136.

[716] Contartese n 291 at 441. See also: Esa Paasivirta, 'The European Union and the United Nations Convention on the Law of the Sea' (2015) 38 *Fordham International Law Journal* 1059–1060.

[717] Contartese n 322 at 423, 436–441.

[718] Delgado Casteleiro n 27 at 135; Paasivirta n 444 at 465.

[719] ITLOS Advisory Opinion of 2 April 2015, *Case No. 21*; Contartese n 322 at 439, 443; Delgado Casteleiro n 27 at 146–150.

[720] Contartese n 322 at 450.

[721] See for example: Article 8.21 CETA ('determination of the respondent for disputes') Comprehensive Economic and Trade Agreement (CETA) between Canada, of the one part, and the European Union and its Member States, of the other part [2017] OJ L 11/23.

in the proceedings.[722] The terminology used in these provisions, lend support to a model for attribution and responsibility that *is* exculpatory. Interestingly, these provisions neither provide further clarification as to the scope of normative control required, nor do they explain when the EU can be considered as being implicated to warrant it acting as the (sole) respondent in responsibility proceedings. Crucially, practice appears to militate away from shared responsibility, avoiding situations where Member States and the EU are co-respondents in a dispute.[723]

Generally, multilateral environmental agreements (*hereafter* MEAs) 'do not contain express provisions on joint responsibility'.[724] Instead there is (also) a noticeable practice of declarations of competence, albeit that the content of such declarations and effectiveness thereof, vary considerably.[725] Practice suggests that such declarations are (generally) not sufficient in identifying to what party conduct should be attributed, or to what party responsibility will be attached.[726] In summary, as concerns environmental law, there appears to be a discernible shift away from the possibility of shared responsibility, in favour again of the trend of individualisation of responsibility.

An all-encompassing empirical study of the manner in which attribution and ensuing shared responsibility is approached in various domains of EU law goes beyond the ambit of the present inquiry.[727] However, the foregoing examples sought to provide initial insights into the varied approaches adopted to establish attribution and the manner in which this affects responsibility. What these initial insights suggest is that the tests of attribution that are applied depend first and foremost on which adjudicatory bodies are tasked with the determination of responsibility (internal as opposed to external adjudicatory bodies). Second, there is discernible variation in the attribution tests relied upon by different EU entities (e.g., European Commission as opposed to the CJEU). Thirdly, the tests of attribution and ensuing responsibility appear fragmented, which comes as no surprise as this may in part be the result of the differentiated nature of competence division in the EU. This last point reveals a driver for the differentiated and at times fragmented approach: in questions of *international* responsibility there are two questions that are essentially being asked. Firstly, who (the Member States, the EU or both) is responsible externally – a question largely of international law – and secondly, how is that external responsibility allocated between the EU and its Members – a question that is largely internal and drives at the heart of the autonomy of EU law. With so many moving parts surrounding one single responsibility question, fragmentation comes as no surprise. Interestingly, recent examples suggest that in a (deliberate?) move away from fragmentation, there is notable increased recourse to the proceduralisation and

[722] 'if the measures identified in the notice include measures of the European Union, the European Union shall be **the respondent**' (emphasis added). Article 8.21 CETA.

[723] Vezzani n 272 at 314.

[724] Nollkaemper n 526 at 326.

[725] ibid 321.

[726] ibid 341.

[727] For more recent work in EU law investigating integrated decision making and the questions of shared responsibility this may give rise to, see: Filipe Brito Bastos, Judging Composite Decision-Making – The Transformation of European Administrative Law (Hart Bloomsbury, 2024).

individualisation of EU responsibility through declarations of competence. However, for now the effectiveness of such declarations for the purpose of establishing attribution remains contested (see above). Furthermore, the opacity and fragmentation that characterises applicable tests of attribution within the EU's regulatory domains constitutes only element of the responsibility question. The question of attribution only answers which actors conduct may be attributed to and is a responsibility allocation rule. Even in the event that one or multiple definitive attribution rules existed for situations of shared conduct between the EU and its Member States, that does not answer the question of how a violation of human rights would ultimately be established, as developed under Chapter 3.

d. Interim Conclusions on Rules for Shared Responsibility

In summary, four large factors further complicate the already underdeveloped nature of the provisions of shared responsibility under the ARIO. Firstly, the undetermined scope and obscurity of the transversal condition on how to establish 'knowing intent' vis-à-vis the international organisation, entails that it will be difficult to meet the cumulative criteria to establish international responsibility. Secondly, the opposability requirement under Articles 14 and 15 ARIO directly correlates to the scope of the human rights norms applicable to IOs. While on the one hand, the argument is made that it suffices for the organisation to be bound *in theory* by human rights commitments for this opposability requirement to be met, the opposing argument is that the organisation would have to be bound by the same concretised human rights obligations inherent to the primary norm. Again, the absence of clarity on the matter, implies that the IO may continuously escape responsibility on account of not meeting the opposability criterion. Thirdly, causality is implicit throughout all the provisions on shared responsibility under ARIO. In all cases, there must be an established link with the secondary facilitatory act, without any indication as to which causality test must be adopted or when causality will be considered as sufficient to trigger the responsibility under Articles 14–17 ARIO. Finally, the dynamics and interplay between the provisions on shared responsibility are quite ambiguous. A literal, contextual and teleological reading of the ARIO and its *travaux préparatoires* does not necessarily shed any light on the matter. Conversely the preparatory works appear to complicate the matter, due in part to use of similar terminology in artificially divided and distinguished modes of shared responsibility.

These *défauts de jeunesse* are relevant to the question of systemic deficiencies in the EU's responsibility regime. Not only are the provision-specific issues problematic for legal certainty and the effectiveness thereof, but the totality of issues additionally results in a shared responsibility framework that is tainted by systemic and transversal lacunae to the detriment of the victim of unlawful conduct at the behest of the IO.

The EU's *lex specialis* on shared responsibility reveals that practice is scattered, and even within substantive areas of EU law, it is uncertain what mechanisms for the apportionment of attribution and responsibility are being used. In addition, particularly where use is made of procedural mechanisms for the apportionment of responsibility between the EU and the Member States (UNCLOS and investment disputes) the EU appears to move towards exonerating/exculpatory mechanisms of responsibility division in favour of the individualisation of responsibility. As a result, there is a discernible shift *away* from *shared* responsibility. This is supported by the increased use of the competence model for attribution (UNCLOS, Financial Responsibility Regulation, environmental law). Finally, within the overarching realm of fundamental rights protection, the EU has adopted a conservative approach to shared responsibility. This was demonstrated inter alia by the Draft Accession Agreement, where the EU would only act as a respondent in a subsidiary order. *Grosso modo* it can thus be deduced, that despite willingness to adopt conduct as its own and willingness to share responsibility under the WTO *chapeau*, the EU has taken a rather reluctant approach to shared responsibility, indicating that under the contemporary *lex specialis* framework, instead, the EU makes use of exonerating/exculpatory approaches to attribution and resulting responsibility.

While it is not inconceivable that this shift to the individualisation of responsibility occurs as a manifestation of responsibility following power, it nevertheless constitutes an oversimplification of power dynamics – particularly in cases of shared competences and concerted (operational) action between the EU and its Member States. While practice under UNCLOS, investment law and environmental law – all of which constitute shared competences – gravitates towards the individualisation of responsibility, the argument here is that within the realm of mixed agreements, but particularly within the context of operational action, joint responsibility is an effective (and necessary) tool to incentivise compliance with human rights, and to ensure access to remedies in line with the rule of law as defended by the EU.

In the preceding chapter we tackled the rules under both international (*lex generalis*) and EU law (*lex specialis*) that exist to establish EU responsibility (or IO responsibility more generally). Both under international and EU law, multiple tests of attribution exist. And while the sheer multiplicity of these tests likely accommodate multiple heterogenous IOs, the opacity and indeterminacy that taints these tests (eg, what is the degree of normative control; how to delineate competence-division, etc) significantly obstruct the ability of individuals to successfully lodge a claim against the EU.

Additionally, the dynamic between and alignment of these attribution tests is unclear (eg, are these tests exculpatory? How does attribution for independent responsibility relate to shared responsibility?). Causation is inherently required under the ARIO but is not further elaborated upon in those rules; under EU law the causation test is exceedingly high. The requirement under both international and EU law which holds that there must be unlawful conduct for a right to reparations to arise, runs into the issue of normative incongruence. And finally, shared responsibility under international and EU law is an unlikely avenue to obtain reparations, as this ground for responsibility remains conceptually obscure and indeterminate. This obscurity is exacerbated under EU law by the different approaches to shared responsibility across different areas of EU law and the perceived tendency *away* from EU shared responsibility in favour of individualization of responsibility (with only a subsidiary role for the EU).

From a theoretical perspective, any applicant seeking damages from the EU on account of its contribution to human rights harms is bound to encounter a debilitating number of difficulties, warranting the question whether the right to an effective remedy – that is to say a remedy that is accessible, effective and ensures procedural equality – can ever truly be met. Liability incongruence thus emerges when juxtaposing the existing rules to establish (human rights) responsibility of the EU (and IOs generally) on the one hand, and the opaqueness, indeterminacy, ambiguities and inconsistencies that are threaded into these rules, preventing access to a remedy on the other hand.

The question now arises as to how the EUs human rights responsibility regime applies to the enactment of IBM strategies. Contrary to the previously discussed areas of substantive EU law, the realm of borders, asylum and migration – particularly within the context of IBM – is characterised by legal instruments, *as well as* operational action.

Part III

EU Human Rights Responsibility in Practice

In the following chapters, we apply the EU's Human Rights Responsibility Regime to four IBM illustrations which have garnered much notoriety due to alleged EU complicity in human rights harms and violations of the *non-refoulement* principle specifically. To investigate the implications of the EU's human rights responsibility regime as comprehensively as possible within the constraints of this inquiry, these four illustrations were selected to cover each phase of the 'four-tier access control model' of IBM, covering both legislative measures by the EU, as well as operational conduct within and beyond EU territory.

However, any claims of EU responsibility for human rights harms, presuppose the applicability of human rights norms (under international and/or EU law) to the fact patterns. Having established that the illustrations of EU IBM will be tested against the *non-refoulement* principle, Chapter 5 will first introduce how and when adjudicatory jurisdiction triggers the applicability of the *non-refoulement* principle across the four illustrations, before delving into the concretised negative, positive, procedural and substantive human rights obligations stemming from the *non-refoulement* principle in a manner that integrates international and EU human rights law. Chapter 6 discusses visa regulation under EU law and its implications for *non-refoulement* and TCNs. Chapter 7 discusses Operation Sophia, bearing in mind that adjudicatory jurisdiction is limited here, as this constitutes an operation under the EU's Common Foreign and Security Policy, which is typically shielded from CJEU legal review. Chapter 8 discusses Frontex conduct in the Aegean Sea in concert with the Greek Coastguard, and Chapter 9 focuses on the informalisation of readmission agreements, focusing in particular on the EU-Turkey Statement as a paradigmatic and blueprint illustration of such informalisation.

5

Adjudicatory Jurisdiction and the Non-Refoulement *Principle*

EU CONDUCT IN all four illustrations will be assessed against the *non-refoulement* principle, which is not only firmly embedded in the EU's Charter of Human rights and European human rights law, but is also considered a rule of customary international law and is equally firmly embedded in international human rights law. The *non-refoulement* principle holds that individuals – irrespective of their legal status – may not be forcibly returned to a place where they are at risk of being subjected to severe ill-treatment.[728] This means that the duty-bearer is bound by a negative obligation to refrain from sending individuals back to a location where they could be subject to significant ill-treatment meeting a particular threshold. The multitude of international and European sources governing the *non-refoulement* principle have clarified the degree of protection this generates.[729] And while the protection is consistently comparable, it is not always identical.[730] The protection against *refoulement* under the Refugee Convention for example, is limited *ratione personae* to refugees,[731] while the protection against *refoulement* under the

[728] Eman Hamdan, *The Principle of Non-Refoulement Under the ECHR and the UN Convention Against Torture and Other Cruel, Inhuman or Degrading Treatment or Punishment* (Leiden, Brill, 2016) 1.

[729] The *non-refoulement* principle is considered customary international law. See on the topic: UN High Commissioner for Refugees, 'Note on International Protection: A/AC.96/951' (*UNHCR*, 13 September 2001) https://www.refworld.org/docid/3bb1c6cc4.html 5–6; ECtHR Concurring Opinion Judge Pinto De Albuquerque of 23 February 2012, *Hirsi Jamaa and others v Italy*, App no. 27765/09 (and sources cited therein). See also: Cathryn Costello and Michelle Foster, '*Non-refoulement* as Custom and *Jus Cogens?* Putting the Prohibition to the Test' in Maarten den Heijer and Harmen van der Wilt (eds), *Netherlands Yearbook of International Law 2015 – Jus Cogens: Quo Vadis?* (New York, Springer, 2016) 273. The *non-refoulement* principle is also embedded in Article 33 Refugee Convention and its Protocol; United Nations, *UN Convention against Torture* [10 December 1984] Treaty Series, vol. 1465, 85 (*hereafter* CAT); Organization of American States, *American Convention on Human Rights, 'Pact of San Jose'* [22 November 1969], the ICCPR and the ECHR.

[730] See Article 33 Refugee Convention, referring explicitly to the 'refugees': 'No Contracting State shall expel or return ("refouler") a refugee in any manner whatsoever to the frontiers of territories where his [or her] life or freedom would be threatened on account of his [or her] race, religion, nationality, membership of a particular social group or political opinion'. See also on the matter: Paul Weis, *The Refugee Convention, 1951 – The Travaux Preparatoires Analysed with a Commentary* (Cambridge, Cambridge University Press, 1995) 233–245.

[731] Elspeth Guild, 'Article 19 – Protection in the Event of Removal, Expulsion or Extradition' in Steve Peers, Tamara Hervey, Jeff Kenner, Angela Ward (eds), *The EU Charter of Fundamental Rights: A Commentary* (London, Bloomsbury, 2014) 547, 553; Manfred Nowak and Elizabeth McArthur, *The United Nations Convention Against Torture: A Commentary* (Oxford, Oxford University Press, 2008) 128–129.

UN Convention Against Torture and Other Cruel, Inhuman or Degrading Treatment or Punishment is limited *ratione materiae* to instances where the individual would be subjected to torture as defined therein.[732] Different still, the scope of protection for this same principle afforded by general human rights treaties is broader both *ratione personae* and *ratione materiae*. In line with Article 6 and 7 ICCPR, the principle of *non-refoulement* is defined as an 'obligation not to extradite, deport, expel or otherwise remove a person from their territory, where there are substantial grounds for believing that there is a real risk of irreparable harm', which is applicable to all individuals 'regardless of nationality or statelessness, such as asylum-seekers, refugees, migrant workers and other persons, who may find themselves in the territory or subject to the jurisdiction of the State party'.[733]

Similarly, the ECtHR has described the *non-refoulement* principle as prohibiting 'expulsion, extradition or any other measure to remove an alien … where substantial grounds have been shown for believing that the person in question, if expelled, would face a real risk of being subjected to treatment contrary to Article 3 in the receiving country. In such circumstances, Article 3 implies an obligation not to expel the individual to that country'.[734] Similarly to the ICCPR, the definition provided by the ECtHR imposes no limitation in terms of eligibility and no direct limitation as to the type of treatment.

The *non-refoulement* principle is firmly enshrined in the EU-*acquis*, including in primary law. Article 78(1) TFEU in particular, holds that 'The Union shall develop a common policy on asylum, subsidiary protection and temporary protection with a view to offering appropriate status to any third-country national requiring international protection and ensuring compliance with the principle of non-refoulement'.[735] This has been consistently translated into secondary BAM legislation in both the recitals, as well as operative clauses.[736] Articles 4, 18 and 19 CFR, additionally implicitly

[732] In fact, the scope of the *non-refoulement* principle in Article 3 CAT is limited solely to instances of torture as defined in Article 1 thereof and not including other instances of cruel, inhuman or degrading treatment. Nowak and McArthur n 731 at 128.

[733] Human Rights Committee, 'General Comment No. 31 – The Nature of the General Legal Obligation Imposed on States Parties to the Covenant' (*United Nations Human Rights Committee*, 29 March 2004) https://www.refworld.org/legal/general/hrc/2004/en/52451 §10 and 12.

[734] ECtHR (Grand Chamber) Judgment of 23 February 2012, *Hirsi Jamaa and others v Italy*, App no 27765/09, 33 §115. Maarten Den Heijer, 'Refoulement' in André Nollkaemper and Ilias Plakokefalos (eds), *The Practice of Shared Responsibility* (Cambridge, Cambridge University Press, 2017) 483. See for a more recent judgment on *non-refoulement* and expulsion at the border: ECtHR Judgment of 23 July 2020, *MK and others v. Poland*, Application nos. 40503/17, 42902/17 and 43643/17.

[735] Article 78(1) TFEU.

[736] Recital 36, Article 3(b) and Article 4 Regulation (EU) 2016/399 of the European Parliament and of the Council of 9 March 2016 on a Union Code on the rules governing the movement of persons across borders (Schengen Borders Code) [2016] OJ L77/1; Recital 3, Article 28, Article 35, Article 37, Directive 2013/32/EU of the European Parliament and of the Council of 26 June 2013 on common procedures for granting and withdrawing international protection (Asylum Procedures Directive) [2013] OJ L180/60; Recital 3, Recital 48, Article 21 Directive 2011/95/EU of the European Parliament and of the Council of 13 December 2011 on standards for the qualification of third-country nationals or stateless persons as beneficiaries of international protection, for a uniform status for refugees or for persons eligible for subsidiary protection, and for the content of the protection granted (Qualification Directive) [2011] OJ L337/9; Recital 3 Directive 2013/33/EU of the European Parliament and of the Council of 26 June 2013 laying down standards for the reception of applicants for international protection (Reception Conditions Directive) [2013] OJ L180/96; Recital 8, Article 4, Article 5, Article 9, Directive 2008/115/EC of the European Parliament and

and explicitly reaffirm the protection against *refoulement*.[737] The standard of protection against *refoulement* set in the CFR cannot be read independently of the standard provided for in the ECHR. Article 4 CFR – concerning the general prohibition on torture, cruel, inhuman and degrading treatment and or punishment – is considered as the *lex generalis* concerning *non-refoulement* and is the corresponding Charter provision to its counterpart in Article 3 ECHR.[738] In line with Article 52(3) CFR and the Explanations of the CFR, Article 4 must thus be interpreted and applied, in accordance with its corresponding provision in the ECHR, as well as in conformity with the case law on the matter by the ECtHR.[739] Article 19(2) CFR concerning *non-refoulement* specifically, constitutes the EU's *lex specialis* concerning the *non-refoulement* principle, which must also be read in conformity with the minimum standards imposed by Article 3 ECHR and its subsequent case law.[740] The ECtHR

of the Council of 16 December 2008 on common standards and procedures in Member States for returning illegally staying third-country nationals (Return Directive) [2008] OJ L348/98; Recital 84, Recital 103, Article 36, Article 48, Article 50, Article 71, Article 72, Article 73, Article 80, Article 86 Regulation of the European Parliament and of the Council on the European Border and Coast Guard and repealing Regulations (EU) No 1052/2013 and (EU) 2016/1624 (European Border and Coast Guard Regulation) [2019] OJ L295/1; Recital 3 Regulation (EU) No 604/2013 of the European Parliament and of the Council of 26 June 2013 establishing the criteria and mechanisms for determining the Member State responsible for examining an application for international protection lodged in one of the Member States by a third-country national or a stateless person (Dublin III Regulation) [2013] OJ L180/31. The textual references to the *non-refoulement* principle in primary and secondary Union legislation do not necessarily have any bearing on the enforceability and de facto protection thereof. See on this topic: ECtHR Judgment of 23 July 2020, *MK and others v Poland*, Application nos. 40503/17, 42902/17 and 43643/17, §180–181; ECtHR 2011, *MSS* n 197; Guild n 718 at 561. Jens Vedsted-Hansen, Céline Bauloz, Constantin Hruschka, Hana Lupačová, Dirk Sander, Louise Halleskov Storgaard, 'Judicial Analysis – Asylum procedures and the principle of *non-refoulement*' (*EASO Professional Development Series for members of courts and tribunals*, 9 August 2019) www.easo.europa.eu/sites/default/files/asylum-procedures-ja_en.pdf 30.

[737] The Explanations to the Charter confirm that Article 4 CFR corresponds to Article 3 ECHR, which ensures respect for the *non-refoulement* principle. In Article 18 CFR, *non-refoulement* is furthermore considered inherent to the right to asylum. Maarten den Heijer, 'Article 18 – Right to Asylum' in Steve Peers, Tamara Hervey, Jeff Kenner, Angela Ward (eds), *The EU Charter of Fundamental Rights: A Commentary* (London, Bloomsbury, 2014) §18.39, 535. On the connection between *non-refoulement* and the right to (access) asylum (international protection) procedures, see: ECtHR Judgment of 23 July 2020, *MK and others v. Poland*, Application nos. 40503/17, 42902/17 and 43643/17, §173, where the ECtHR held '173. The Court has further clarified that in all cases of removal of an asylum-seeker from a Contracting State to a third intermediary country without examination of the asylum request on the merits, regardless of whether or not the receiving third country is an EU Member State or a State Party to the Convention, it is the duty of the removing State to examine thoroughly the question of whether or not there is a real risk of the asylum-seeker being denied access, in the receiving third country, to an adequate asylum procedure, protecting him or her against refoulement. If it is established that the existing guarantees in this regard are insufficient, Article 3 implies a duty that the asylum-seeker should not be removed to the third country concerned (see Ilias and Ahmed, cited above, §134)'. Article 19 CFR furthermore builds on the protection derived from Article 4 CFR and Article 3 ECHR indirectly, and explicitly protects against *refoulement* by stating 'No one may be removed, expelled or extradited to a State where there is a serious risk that he or she would subjected to the death penalty, torture or other inhuman or degrading treatment or punishment'. See more generally on the matter: CJEU (Grand Chamber) Judgment of 21 December 2011, *N.S. and others v Secretary of State for the Home Department*, Joined cases C-411/10 and C-493/10, ECLI:EU:C:2011:865, §86. See also: Guild n 731 at 545.

[738] ibid 545.

[739] Article 6 TEU highlights the significance of the Explanations: 'the rights, freedoms and principles in the Charter shall be interpreted in accordance with the general provisions in Title VII of the Charter governing its interpretation and application and with due regard to the explanations referred to in the Charter, that set out the sources of those provisions …'. This is confirmed in Article 52 CFR.

[740] Explanations to the CFR: '19(2) corresponds to Article 3 of the ECHR as interpreted by the European Court of Human Rights'. This is confirmed in Article 52 CFR. See also: Mungianu n 27 at 128.

has been resolute in maintaining that the prohibition to return or expel an individual to a state where he or she may face treatment contrary to Article 3 ECHR, is absolute and is triggered as soon as this substantial/real risk exists.[741]

A comparative analysis of the *non-refoulement* principle under the ECHR and the *non-refoulement* principle protected under the EU-*acquis* on borders, asylum and migration reveals significant symbiosis and convergence. In both legal systems, *non-refoulement* (like all human rights) translates into concrete negative and positive (procedural and substantive) obligations. However, prior to any determination on the (compliance with the) negative and positive obligations stemming from the *non-refoulement* principle, adjudicatory jurisdiction must first be established, as 'the exercise of jurisdiction is a necessary condition … to be held responsible for acts or omissions imputable to it which give rise to an allegation of the infringement'.[742]

1. JURISDICTION

a. Jurisdiction under the ECtHR

Article 1 ECHR notes that the State Parties 'shall secure to everyone within their jurisdiction' the rights and freedoms – including the protection against *refoulement* – encompassed in the ECHR.[743] The ECtHR recalls that the jurisdictional competence of State Parties and thus the obligations stemming from the ECHR are essentially territorial,[744] albeit that extra-territorial jurisdiction may arise in exceptional circumstances.[745] The limited circumstances in which extra-territorial jurisdiction

[741] Guild n 731. Whereas the CJEU and the EU legislator have continuously echoed the absolute nature of the *non-refoulement* principle, a slightly different approach is adopted in assessing its applicability.

[742] ECtHR (Grand Chamber) Judgment of 23 February 2012, *Hirsi Jamaa and others v Italy*, App no. 27765/09, §113 (and sources cited therein) §70. See also: ECtHR Judgment of 8 July 2004, *Ilaşcu and others v Moldova and Russia*, App no. 48787/99, §311. See also: ECtHR (Grand Chamber) Judgment of 13 February 2020, *N.D. and N.T. v. Spain*, App nos 8675/15 and 8679/15, §102 (and sources cited therein). See similarly concerning the Inter-American Court System: IACtHR Advisory Opinion of 15 November 2017, *Opinión Consultiva Solicitada por la República de Colombia*, OC-23/17, §72.

[743] See also: ECtHR (Grand Chamber) Judgment of 13 February 2020, *N.D. and N.T. v. Spain*, App nos 8675/15 and 8679/15, §102. The notion of jurisdiction according to Article 1 ECHR is inspired by the notion of jurisdiction (see §109) under public international law but is not necessarily synonymous. The notion of jurisdiction under international law encompasses various forms of jurisdiction, namely: jurisdiction to prescribe (1), jurisdiction to enforce (2) and adjudicatory jurisdiction (3). As recalled by Milanovic, jurisdiction for the purpose of the ECHR refers to the authority of a State Party to regulate, by various means, the conduct of people. See: Marko Milanovic, *Extraterritorial Application of the Human Rights Treaties – Law, Principles, and Policy* (Oxford, Oxford University Press, 2011) 23–26, 99.

[744] ECtHR (Grand Chamber) Judgment of 13 February 2020, *N.D. and N.T. v. Spain*, App nos 8675/15 and 8679/15, §103; ECtHR 2001 *Banković* n 42 at §312. Jurisdiction is presumed to be established throughout all of the territory and will only be rebutted when a State is prevented from exercising authority over its own territory. ECtHR (Grand Chamber) Judgment of 8 April 2004, *Assanidze v Georgia*, App no. 71503/01, §137–139 and ECtHR Judgment of 8 July 2004, *Ilaşcu and others v Moldova and Russia*, App no. 48787/99 §312–313 and 333).

[745] This development started when the ECtHR ruled in the case of *Issa*, holding that a State may be liable for actions violating human rights of individuals under its authority and control, albeit outside of its state territory. This ruling appears to contradict the seminal case of *Banković*, where the Strasbourg

may arise were recently recalled by the ECtHR in *Güzelyurtlu and others v Cyprus and Turkey*[746] and reaffirmed in *Hanan v Germany*.[747] Such extra-territorial jurisdiction may be established where acts by State(s) (agents) give rise to (legal) effects outside the respective territory of the Contracting party, thus amounting to state-agent control,[748] which must be assessed on a case-by-case basis.[749] Alternatively, extra-territorial jurisdiction may arise where there is spatial effective control over territory abroad.[750] This may occur directly through the occupation of armed forces of territory abroad, including on-board vessels registered in or flying the flag of that state.[751] Indirectly, spatial effective control may be established, through subordinate

Court noted that jurisdiction as a general rule, is determined by territory and will only extend extra-territorially in (highly) exceptional cases to be determined on a case-by-case basis. ECtHR Judgment of 16 November 2004, *Issa and others v Turkey*, App no. 31821/96, 4 §2; ECtHR 2001 *Banković* n 42 at §61. In 2011, the Strasbourg Court further clarified and nuanced its findings from the *Banković* ruling and the subsequent cases that (implicitly) endorsed the personal model of attribution. Specifically, the Strasbourg Court held in *Al Skeini* (ECtHR (Grand Chamber) Judgment of 7 July 2011, *Al-Skeini and others v the UK*, App no. 55721/07, §130–142) that 'jurisdictional competence under Article 1 is primarily territorial' but in exceptional circumstances may result in extra-territorial applicability of the Convention. The two recognized circumstances of such extra-territoriality by the Strasbourg Court in *Al Skeini* are the instance of 'state agent authority and control' and 'effective control over an area'. In this case the ECtHR furthermore accepted that the ECHR rights may be 'divided and tailored' when applied extra-territorially, as a result of which a State party will be held to protect and safeguard Convention rights extra-territorially that are relevant to the individual concerned (§136–137). Hence, despite the – at first glance – seemingly inconsistent approach to (spatial) jurisdiction taken by the Strasbourg Court, ensuing case law has incrementally evidenced a more expansive interpretation of jurisdiction for the purpose of triggering the ECHR. This trend was reaffirmed less than a year onwards with the *Hirsi* judgment, where the Court recognized the applicability of the Convention with respect to border management measures taken on high seas and on-board Italian military vessels. (ECtHR (Grand Chamber) Judgment of 23 February 2012, *Hirsi Jamaa and others v Italy*, App no. 27765/09, §76–82). In *Jaloud* several years later, the Strasbourg Court went even further regarding the extra-territorial applicability of the ECHR, holding that the extra-territoriality will be determined on a case-by-case basis, mindful of the case-specific facts, and that *in casu* the death of Mr Jaloud as a result of being shot at in a vehicle passing a checkpoint 'under the command and direct supervision of a Netherlands Royal Army Officer' was sufficient to establish jurisdiction in respect of the Netherlands (See for example: ECtHR (Grand Chamber) Judgment of 20 November 2014, *Jaloud v the Netherlands*, App no 47708/08, §152). See on the matter: Milanovic n 743 at 99–103.

[746] ECtHR (Grand Chamber) Judgment of 29 January 2019, *Güzelyurtlu and others v Cyprus and Turkey*, App no. 36925/07, §178–187.

[747] ECtHR (Grand Chamber) Judgment of 16 February 2021, *Hanan v Germany*, App no. 4871/16, §132–145. See for a more general discussion on the various forms of (extra-)territorial jurisdiction: Seunghwan Kim, 'Non-refoulement and Extraterritorial Jurisdiction: State Sovereignty and Migration Controls at Sea in the European Context' (2017) 30 *Leiden Journal of International Law* 1, 49; Milanovic n 743.

[748] ECtHR (Grand Chamber) Judgment of 29 January 2019, *Güzelyurtlu and others v Cyprus and Turkey*, App no 36925/07, §180; ECtHR (Grand Chamber) Judgment of 20 November 2014, *Jaloud v the Netherlands*, App no. 47708/08, §152; ECtHR (Grand Chamber) Judgment of 23 February 2012, *Hirsi Jamaa and others v Italy*, App no 27765/09, §127; ECtHR (Grand Chamber) Judgment of 7 July 2011, *Al-Skeini and others v the UK*, App no. 55721/07, §136, 149–150; ECtHR Judgment of 24 June 2008, *Isaak v Turkey*, App no. 44587/98, §121–125. State-agent control is interchangeably referred to as 'personal jurisdiction'. Milanovic n 743 at 173, 188.

[749] ECtHR (Grand Chamber) Judgment of 13 February 2020, *ND and NT v Spain*, App nos 8675/15 and 8679/15, §102–111; ECtHR (Grand Chamber) Judgment of 23 February 2012, *Hirsi Jamaa and others v Italy*, App no 27765/09, §70–82; ECtHR 2001 *Banković* n 42 at §67.

[750] ECtHR 2020, *M.N. and others v Belgium* n 34 at §103.

[751] See (and cases cited therein): ECtHR (Grand Chamber) Judgment of 29 January 2019, *Güzelyurtlu and others v Cyprus and Turkey*, App no 36925/07, §179; ECtHR (Grand Chamber) Judgment of 29 March 2010, *Medvedyev and others v France*, App no 3394/03, §64. This latter case confirms that military coercive action on high seas may trigger jurisdiction and thus the extraterritorial application of the ECHR.

local administrations, that 'survive as a result of the Contracting State's military and other support', irrespective of whether the State exercises influence over all policies and actions by the subordinate local administration.[752] In addition to state-agent control and spatial effective control, which exceptionally result in extra-territorial jurisdiction, the ECtHR has recognized that where such 'clear jurisdictional links' have *not* been established, extra-territorial jurisdiction may also arise, on account of the 'existence of special features'.[753] The ECtHR has held that it is not required to define such special features *in abstracto*, allowing for a case-by-case assessment of whether such special features are present in a case, which warrant extra-territorial jurisdiction.[754] One of the elements that has been relevant in the determination of whether special features apply is whether a Member State has initiated investigations into possible violations of human rights abroad *by virtue of domestic law*, with the caveat that the mere initiating of investigations, is not necessarily enough to trigger extra-territorial jurisdiction.[755]

As demonstrated by a number of ECtHR cases within the realm of *non-refoulement* in particular, the notion of jurisdiction to trigger the applicability of the ECHR has also incrementally shifted away from being predominately territorial and has been increasingly understood in a broader, extra-territorial manner. In *Hirsi*, the ECtHR explicitly confirmed that in Search and Rescue (SAR) operations which involve the boarding of the rescued individuals on naval vessels, jurisdiction is established, rendering the Convention provisions applicable, including *non-refoulement*, even when such operations occur on high seas.[756] The Strasbourg Court held that 'Italy cannot circumvent its "jurisdiction" under the Convention by describing the events at issue as rescue operations on the high seas. In particular the Court cannot subscribe to the Government's argument that Italy was not responsible for the fate of the applicants on account of the allegedly minimal control exercised by the authorities over the parties concerned'.[757] With this judgment, the Strasbourg Court solidified its stance on extraterritorial jurisdiction in exceptional circumstances, holding that a degree of control – to be assessed on a case-by-case basis – over an individual, may be sufficient to trigger the enforceability of the ECHR, and a border control measure

[752] ECtHR (Grand Chamber) Judgment of 29 January 2019, *Güzelyurtlu and others v Cyprus and Turkey*, App no 36925/07, §179.

[753] ECtHR (Grand Chamber) Judgment of 16 February 2021, *Hanan v Germany*, App no. 4871/16, §132–136. See for an overview of the relevant case law on 'special features' which may trigger extra-territorial jurisdiction: ECtHR (Grand Chamber) Judgment of 29 January 2019, *Güzelyurtlu and others v Cyprus and Turkey*, App no 36925/07, §182–187. Notably, the case law suggests that such special features are not limited to situations of armed conflict but may likewise arise in other cases such as medical negligence: ECtHR Judgment of 22 May 2014, *Gray v Germany*, App no 49278/09.

[754] ECtHR (Grand Chamber) Judgment of 16 February 2021, *Hanan v Germany*, App no. 4871/16, §136; ECtHR (Grand Chamber) Judgment of 29 January 2019, *Güzelyurtlu and others v Cyprus and Turkey*, App no 36925/07, §190.

[755] ECtHR (Grand Chamber) Judgment of 16 February 2021, *Hanan v Germany*, App no 4871/16, §134–136.

[756] ECtHR (Grand Chamber) Judgment of 23 February 2012, *Hirsi Jamaa and others v Italy*, App no 27765/09, §73–75, 76–82.

[757] ibid §79.

'the effect of which [was] to prevent migrants from reaching the borders of the State or even to push them back to another State, constitute[d] an exercise of jurisdiction within the meaning of Article 1 of the Convention'.[758]

The foregoing was furthermore endorsed by the Vice-President Mr Jacques Barrot of the European Commission as recorded by the ECtHR in *Hirsi*, who held that 'border surveillance activities conducted at sea, whether in territorial waters, the contiguous zone, the exclusive economic zone or on the high seas, fall within the Schengen Borders Code and that in line with ECtHR case law, this constitutes extra-territorial jurisdiction (potentially) triggering the responsibility of the Contracting party.[759] Arguably, such an (extra-)territorial-jurisdictional link may not be necessary to render the Charter applicable vis-à-vis the Union and its Members, as Article 51 CFR holds that the Charter is addressed to the 'institutions, bodies, offices and agencies of the Union' and the Member States insofar they are implementing Union law (see Chapter 3).

The concept of jurisdiction within the context of border management specifically, was recently elaborated upon in the Grand Chamber judgment of *ND and NT v. Spain* before the Strasbourg Court, where the applicants attempted to irregularly enter Spain via the Melilla enclave.[760] *In casu*, Spain invoked an exception to (territorial) jurisdiction, arguing that the three fences at the Melilla enclave, constitute an 'operational border' with the objective of preventing irregular entry into Spain by TCNs and as a result of which it had limited its territorial jurisdiction.[761] Specifically, Spain held that, as a result of the introduction of this border, territorial jurisdiction could only be triggered once an individual had crossed the third and final fence.[762] This view was endorsed by a number of States, including France, that argued that according to the case facts, the interception of the applicants by Spanish authorities before reaching the final fence, had been too brief and limited to constitute a form of control liable of triggering jurisdiction under the ECHR.[763] In addition, Italy and Belgium as intervening parties, recalled that the measures taken by the Spanish authorities stemmed from EU law, in an attempt to securitise the Union external border. The implication was thus that under EU legislation, the applicants could not be considered

[758] ibid §180.

[759] ibid §34.

[760] ECtHR (Grand Chamber) Judgment of 13 February 2020, *ND and NT v Spain* App nos 8675/15 and 8679/15. See also for a recent case concerning jurisdiction under the ECtHR: ECtHR (Grand Chamber) Judgment of 16 February 2021, *Hanan v Germany*, App no 4871/16. For discussions of *Hanan v Germany*, see: Marko Milanovic, 'Extraterritorial Investigations in *Hanan v. Germany*; Extraterritorial Assassinations in New Interstate Claim Filed by Ukraine against Russia' (*EJIL:Talk*, 26 February 2021) www.ejiltalk.org/extraterritorial-investigations-in-hanan-v-germany-extraterritorial-assassinations-in-new-interstate-claim-filed-by-ukraine-against-russia/; Dominik Steiger, '(Not) Investigating Kunduz and (Not) Judging in Strasbourg? Extraterritoriality, Attribution and the Duty to Investigate' (*EJIL:Talk*, 25 February 2020) www.ejiltalk.org/not-investigating-kunduz-and-not-judging-in-strasbourg-extraterritoriality-attribution-and-the-duty-to-investigate/.

[761] ECtHR (Grand Chamber) Judgment of 13 February 2020, *ND and NT v Spain* App nos 8675/15 and 8679/15 §91.

[762] ibid.

[763] ibid §95.

to fall under Spanish jurisdiction.[764] The Strasbourg Court resolutely refused the invoked exception to territorial jurisdiction, holding in particular that it could not identify 'any constraining *de facto* situation or objective facts capable of limiting the effective exercise of the Spanish State's authority over its territory at the Melilla border …'.[765] The Strasbourg Court recalled that internal law (*in casu* European Union law) 'may not be invoked as justification for failure to perform a treaty' in line with Article 27 VCLT, and furthermore recalled that

> the special nature of the context as regards migration cannot justify an area outside the law where individuals are covered by no legal system capable of affording them enjoyment of the rights and guarantees protected by the Convention which the States have undertaken to secure to everyone within their jurisdiction [see *mutatis mutandis, Hirsi Jamaa and Others*, cited above, §178]. As a constitutional instrument of European public order, the Convention cannot be selectively restricted to only parts of the territory of a State by means of an artificial reduction in the scope of its territorial jurisdiction. To conclude otherwise would amount to rendering the notion of effective human rights protection underpinning the entire Convention meaningless.[766]

This view was similarly endorsed by the United Nations High Commissioner for Human Rights, who held more generally that border control measures do not escape the notion of jurisdiction.[767]

Finally, questions of jurisdiction arose in the cases of *MK and others v Poland*, and *MN and others v Belgium* before the ECtHR. In *MK and others v Poland*, on the point of extra-territorial jurisdiction, the Polish government argued that by immediately returning the applicants for international protection at the Polish border, the interaction had been of an extremely limited nature and duration, as a result of which jurisdiction had not been established. The ECtHR refuted this line of argumentation, however, and reaffirmed its earlier stance, by holding that 'whenever a State, through its agents operating outside its territory, exercises control and authority over an individual, and thus jurisdiction, it is under an obligation to secure to that individual, the rights and freedoms … of the Convention that are relevant to his or her situation.'[768] In addition, the ECtHR held that because the events occurred at official border checkpoints, a presumption of jurisdiction was established, which *in casu* was not rebuttable on account of the short duration of the interaction between the applicants and the border officials.[769] This case is interesting, as it was delivered shortly after the case of *MN and others v Belgium*, which is highly analogous to the *X and X* decision by the CJEU (see Chapter 6). Whereas in *MK and others v Poland*, the ECtHR appeared ready to accept jurisdiction, as the individuals were near the Polish border (at a border checkpoint), explicitly asking for international protection, proclaiming a risk of direct or indirect *refoulement* upon return,[770] in *MN and*

[764] ibid §96–97.
[765] ibid §108.
[766] ECtHR (Grand Chamber) Judgment of 13 February 2020, *ND and NT v Spain*, App nos. 8675/15 and 8679/15 §105, 109–110.
[767] ibid §101.
[768] ECtHR Judgment of 23 July 2020, *MK and others v Poland*, Application nos. 40503/17, 42902/17 and 43643/17, §128, 130–130.
[769] ibid §129–132.
[770] ibid §130.

others v Belgium, the ECtHR was not inclined to accept extra-territorial jurisdiction. This is somewhat peculiar as in the latter case, the Applicants sought to obtain access to international protection procedures, by going through legal pathways. Crucially, the Applicants attempted to obtain visas – albeit via administrative proceedings – at the Belgian embassy in Beirut.[771] In this latter case, the ECtHR held that no special connection could be established between the Applicants and Belgium, capable of triggering extra-territorial jurisdiction, and that the Applicants had freely presented themselves at the Belgian embassy, and thus were at all times, free to leave.[772]

When comparing and contrasting these last two cases, along with the case of *Güzelyurtlu*, it appears that the ECtHR is (implicitly) making a distinction between *administrative* proceedings and *legal* proceedings for the purpose of determining whether extra-territorial jurisdiction has been established.[773] The case of *MK and others v Poland* concerned requests for international protection, capable of affecting the *legal* status of the individuals concerned, whereas *MN and others v Belgium* concerned a request for visas, for the purpose of obtaining access to procedures in Belgium, which in turn could ultimately affect the legal status of the individual concerned. If that is indeed the distinction being pursued by the ECtHR, it can be questioned whether this would not have the perverse effect of facilitating *more* irregular travel to the EU's external border, instead of facilitating legal travel for the purpose of obtaining international protection.

In any event, it appears that the ECtHR is continuously engaging in a balancing exercise. On the one hand, the Strasbourg Court seeks to ensure that rights affected by Contracting States abroad, remain 'practical and effective' rather than 'theoretical and illusory'. On the other hand, the ECtHR remains vigilant that recognition of extra-territorial jurisdiction does not 'excessively broaden the scope of application of the Convention'.[774] Interestingly, this has resulted in some peculiar distinctions in its case law, as evidenced by the distinct approaches adopted in *MK and others v Poland* and *MN and others v Belgium,* the coherence of which, is questionable.

b. Jurisdiction under the CFR

The relevance of the ECtHR's evolution on extra-territorial jurisdiction lies in the fact that contrary to the ECHR, the CFR does not contain a jurisdictional clause *territorially* limiting the applicability of the CFR(see Chapter 3).[775] Hence, the question

[771] ECtHR 2020, *MN and others v Belgium* n 34 at §118.
[772] ibid §119, 122.
[773] ibid §118.
[774] ECtHR (Grand Chamber) Judgment of 16 February 2021, *Hanan v Germany*, App no. 4871/16, §135.
[775] See on the matter: Opinion of Advocate General Wathelet of 13 September 2016, *Council v Front Polisario*, C-104/16 P, EU:C:2016:677, §270. Here, the Advocate General could be argued to be applying a conjunctive reading of the 'applicability of EU law' and the 'exercise of effective control'. Whether this is applied in practice remains to be seen. See for a discussion: Peter Van Elsuwege, 'The nexus between the Common Commercial Policy and human rights: implications of the Lisbon Treaty' in Michael Hahn and Guillaume Van der Loo (eds) *Law and Practice of the Common Commercial Policy – The first 10 years after the Treaty of Lisbon* (Brill 2020) 423–427. See also: Angela Ward, 'Article 51 – Scope' in Steve Peers, Tamara Hervey, Jeff Kenner, Angela Ward (eds), *The EU Charter of Fundamental Rights: A Commentary* (London, Bloomsbury, 2014) 1422 §51.23.

must be asked in what way the CFR is limited in its applicability to the Member States and the EU, if not limited territorially? Milanovic notes that human rights treaties lacking an explicit clause delineating the (territorial) applicability thereof, can either be interpreted as being entirely territorially limited, or territorially entirely unlimited.[776] In addition, he advances the argument that a third, more integrated approach is possible, whereby a distinction is made in the positive and negative human rights obligations that are applicable extra-territorially.[777]

True to the assertion made by Milanovic that there is no need for a one-size-fits-all approach to human rights treaties[778] – which appears particularly appropraite given the heterogeneity across various international organizations – it would be incorrect to assume that the CFR does not encompass any EU-specific provisions clarifying its jurisdictional applicability. The jurisdictional limitations for the Charter are spread out across the Charter itself, and consist of rights-specific limitations,[779] as well as overarching jurisdictional provisions as set out in Articles 51–53/54 of the Charter.[780] The latter provisions are oftentimes referred to as the horizontal clauses, which function as a precondition to its applicability. In addition, Protocol No 30 must be taken into regard when assessing the applicability and enforceability of the Charter (see Chapter 3).[781]

These EU and Charter-specific jurisdictional rules are the direct consequence of the constitutional dynamic between the Member States and the EU, and the division of competences in particular.[782] In fact, the drafting history of these articles, support a narrow interpretation of jurisdiction, limiting the applicability of the Charter to matters falling 'within the scope of application of EU law' (see Chapter 3).[783] Article 51(1) CFR clarifies the applicability of the Charter by holding that Charter provisions 'are addressed to the institutions, bodies, offices and agencies of the Union with due regard for the principle of subsidiarity and to the Member States only when they are implementing Union law'. This provision has not been without controversy, however, both as concerns the proviso 'institutions, bodies, offices and agencies of the Union', as well as the provision that Member States are bound by the Charter 'only

[776] Milanovic n 743 at 227.

[777] Specifically, he argues that within an extra-territorial setting, the negative obligations inherent to fundamental rights would apply (namely, the 'obligation to respect'), whereas it is arguably more difficult to require compliance with *substantive* positive obligations extra-territorially where no effective (spatial) control is established, without risking upsetting the feasibility of fundamental rights protection extra-territorially. He thus proposes an integrated approach that is tailored to the particular case as concerns the compliance with substantive positive human rights obligations but does not elaborate upon the particularities of such a mechanism of extra-territorial fundamental rights protection. Milanovic n 743 at 227.

[778] ibid 227.

[779] See for example: Article 16 CFR (freedom to conduct a business); Article 28 (the right of collective bargaining and action); Article 35 CFR (right to health care) – all of which are subject to the condition that they must be in accordance with national laws and practices.

[780] See more generally (and sources cited therein): Ward n 775 at 1415–1416.

[781] Protocol (No. 30) on the application of the Charter of Fundamental Rights of the European Union to Poland and to the United Kingdom [2008] OJ C 115/313; Anthony Arnull, 'Protocol 30' in in Steve Peers, Tamara Hervey, Jeff Kenner, Angela Ward (eds), *The EU Charter of Fundamental Rights: A Commentary* (London, Bloomsbury, 2014) 1595–1612.

[782] Ward n 775 at 1422.

[783] Opinion Sharpston 2010, *Zambrano* n 110 at §156; Ward n 775 at 1428–1429.

when they are implementing Union law', which taken together have given rise to a number of questions and a number of cases that clarify its scope.[784] The Explanations explain the former to a certain extent, by stating that 'the expression 'bodies, offices and agencies' is commonly used in the Treaties to refer to all the authorities set up by the Treaties or by secondary legislation', which suggests that a broad interpretation should be adopted when identifying the relevant entities set up under Union law that are bound by the Charter.[785] This does not, however, address the question of the enforceability of Charter rights vis-à-vis CFSP operations and entities, which may escape judicial review by the CJEU on account of Article 24(1) TEU[786] despite incremental attempts by the Court to remedy the potential absence of judicial review in this respect (see Chapter 7).[787] In addition, it remains unclear … what the legal implications are of such a broad conceptualization of the first phrase in Article 51(1) CFR, particularly concerning Union naval missions, such as EUNAVFOR MED Operation Sophia or its successor, EUNAVFOR MED Operation Irini, that could arguably also escape judicial review by the CJEU.[788]

The obligation of Member States to respect and protect the Charter provisions, 'only when they are implementing Union law', has resulted in a number of cases which purportedly clarify when a Member State is effectively considered to be implementing Union law, and appear to favour – contrary to the drafting history – a broader interpretation of Article 51 CFR. The terminological insertion of the word 'only' evinces the initial reluctance of Member States to be bound by the Charter for matters that fall outside the scope of EU legislation and appears to point to a restrictive reading of Article 51(1).[789] This means that for Member States, the CFR does not contain self-standing rights (see Chapter 3).[790] Rather, these rights can only be invoked together with provisions or rights stemming from the ambit of Union law.[791] The CJEU does not appear to be inclined to follow a restrictive reading of jurisdiction, however, as in the seminal case of *Åkerberg Fransson* it held that in mixed cases, concerning both national measures and matters falling within the scope of EU law, the Member States will be considered to be implementing Union law for the purpose of triggering the applicability of the Charter.[792] Furthermore, in *NS v Secretary of State*, the CJEU held that even where Member States retain discretion under EU law to adopt (national) measures, the Member

[784] Craig and de Búrca n 143 at 408–418.

[785] Opinion Sharpston 2010, *Zambrano* n 110 at §163; Article 51 – Explanations to the CFR.

[786] 'The Court of Justice of the European Union shall not have jurisdiction with respect to these provisions, with the exception of its jurisdiction to monitor compliance with Article 40 of this Treaty and to review the legality of certain decisions as provided for by the second paragraph of Article 275 of the Treaty on the Functioning of the European Union'.

[787] Graham Butler, *Constitutional Law of the EU's Common Foreign and Security Policy* (Oxford, Hart, 2019) 147, 168–169.

[788] Heliskoski n 380 at 144.

[789] Ward n 775 at 1424.

[790] Vladislava Stoyanova, 'The Right to Life Under the EU Charter and Cooperation with Third States to Combat Human Smuggling' (2020) 21 *German Law Journal* 445.

[791] ibid.

[792] CJEU (Grand Chamber) 2013, *Åkerberg Fransson* n 138 at §20–21; Di Federico n 148 at 28–29.

States are still acting within a larger Union framework and are thus caught by Article 51(1) CFR.[793] These cases were later elaborated upon in the *TSN* ruling by the Court, which recalls the scenarios in which a Member State can be considered to be implementing Union law.[794] Article 52(3) CFR builds upon this jurisdictional guidance, by requiring for corresponding rights in the Charter and in the ECHR, the ECHR and its corresponding case law, functions as a normative baseline (see Chapter 3). In other words, rights in the Charter that correspond to rights in the ECHR, can never fall below the minimum standards set by the ECHR and the ECtHR. Finally, Article 53 CFR holds that nothing therein 'shall be interpreted as restricting or adversely affecting human rights and fundamental freedoms as recognised, in their respective fields of application, by Union law and international law and by international agreements to which the Union or all the Member States are party, including the European Convention for the Protection of Human Rights and Fundamental Freedoms, and by the Member States' constitutions'. This provision reiterates that in the interpretation and applicability of the CFR, the reconcilability of the latter with international human rights and domestic constitutions instruments must be duly regarded.

c. Interim Conclusions

Despite the jurisdictional limitations as to how the CFR applies, the absence of a comprehensive (territorial-) jurisdictional clause in the CFR raises unresolved questions. For instance – in the cases of *external* border management measures, such as Frontex-mandated operations, or military operations such as former EUNAVFOR MED Operation Sophia (see *infra*), which took and continue to take place on high seas and thus *outside* of the direct (maritime) territory of EU Member States, it is uncertain to what extent the Charter applies.[795] Although it has been established that third parties may invoke the protection of the Charter even when located outside of the EU,[796] this does not clarify whether and to what extent the EU and Member States (when they are implementing Union law), are bound by concrete obligations of the CFR. Similarly, the current limited jurisdictional provisions do not clarify the applicability of the Charter to more informal EU measures in the realm of borders, asylum and migration, such as amongst others, the infamous EU-Turkey Statement, action plans, mobility partnerships, or memoranda of understanding – which all contribute to the shaping of border management policies extraterritorially.[797] Part of the latter question could be considered solved by the *Ledra Advertising*

[793] CJEU (Grand Chamber) Judgment of 21 December 2011, *NS and others v Secretary of State for the Home Department*, Joined cases C-411/10 and C-493/10, ECLI:EU:C:2011:865, §68. Conversely, the CJEU declined jurisdiction in *X and X v Belgium* despite the fact that the contested provision (Article 25 of the Visa Code) provides Member States with discretion to deviate from the requirements of the Visa Code for humanitarian reasons. CJEU (Grand Chamber) 2017, *X and X v Belgium*, n 34 §45.

[794] CJEU Judgment of 19 November 2019, *Terveys- ja sosiaalialan neuvottelujärjestö (TSN) ry v Hyvinvointialan liitto ry and Auto- ja Kuljetusalan Työntekijäliitto AKT ry v Satamaoperaattorit ry*, C-609/17, ECLI:EU:C:2019:981, §45–50.

[795] Ward n 775 at 1423.

[796] CJEU Judgment of 21 April 2016, *Council v Bank Saderat*, C-200/13P, ECLI:EU:C:2016:284, §47.

[797] Stoyanova n 790 at 443–444.

case by the CJEU. As held by both the Advocate General Wahl and the CJEU, 'the Charter is addressed to the EU institutions, including, as the Advocate General has noted in point 85 of his Opinion, when they act outside the EU legal framework'.[798] However, subsequent cases, such as the *NF v European Council* case suggest a slightly approach stricter informal acts to adjudicatory jurisdiction over, particularly in the realm of borders, asylum and migration.[799] By adopting a different approach to the determination of when the EU is implicated as an actor in measures falling outside of the EU legal framework, the jurisdictional applicability of the CFR may thus be affected. Mindful of these scenarios, the case law evolution on jurisdiction before the ECtHR, as well as the CJEU may very well affect how and when the CFR is considered to apply, particularly when looking to ensure that the minimum protection flowing from the ECHR and its case law for corresponding rights (such as the *non-refoulement* principle) remain respected.[800]

Once jurisdiction has been established and the protection against *refoulement* is thus triggered under the ECHR and the CFR, a number of specific obligations would have to be met, for the *non-refoulement* principle to be complied with by virtue of international and EU law. These concrete obligations are translated into negative and positive obligations and may encompass both procedural and/or substantive obligations.

2. THE PROHIBITION OF *REFOULEMENT*

As aforementioned, the *non-refoulement* principle as protected by the Charter and Union law generally, cannot be read independently of other (international) standards and in line with art. 52(3) CFR, must be interpreted and applied in conformity with its corresponding provision and case law from the ECHR and ECtHR.[801] Echoing this, Moreno-Lax

[798] CJEU Judgment of 21 April 2016, *Ledra Advertising Ltd.*, Joined Cases C-8/15P, C-9/15P and 10/15P, ECLI:EU:C2016:701, 7. It remains to be seen, however, whether this finding may be extrapolated more generally.

[799] The point at stake in *Ledra Advertising* concerned whether the right to property as encompassed in the CFR could be deemed violated by the European Commission and the European Central Bank for their contribution to a memorandum of understanding that both institutions had a role in. Although in this case, and by virtue of a textual interpretation, the CJEU holds as a matter of fact that the Charter is applicable to the EU institutions even when acting outside of the EU legal framework, it is unlikely that the CJEU intended for this to be an irrebuttable principle on the application of the CFR. In 2018, the CJEU appears to have taken a slightly different approach to assigning authorship to the EU in the realm of asylum and migration for informally concluded arrangements, by holding that it lacked jurisdiction with respect to the infamous EU-Turkey Statement, and this despite involvement of the European Council in the realization thereof and despite it having been concluded outside of the EU legal order. CJEU (General Court) Order of 28 February 2017, *NF v Council*, T-192/16, ECLI:EU:T:2017: 128, §46–79 and CJEU Order of 12 September 2018, *NF v European Council*, Joined Cases C-208/17P to C-210/17P, ECLI:EU:C:2018:705.

[800] Ward takes a different perspective on the matter and claims that the evolution on the application of fundamental rights and the Charter specifically within the Union, renders all other jurisdictional rules encompassed in general international human rights law irrelevant. This could be questioned, as the Explanations to the CFR hold explicitly that 'In any event, the level of protection afforded by the Charter may never be lower than that guaranteed by the ECHR' (§4 to the explanation to Article 51 CFR), which – following both a textual and a teleological interpretation – entails that regard would have to be had for the case law on jurisdiction by the ECHR for affected fundamental rights with an extra-territorial component.

[801] See for example, Article 78(1) TFEU, which explicitly notes the obligation to read the *non-refoulement* principle in line with the Refugee Convention.

holds that the 'aggregate-standards approach' entails that the *non-refoulement* principle under EU law must be read in line with international law, and the ECHR in particular.[802] These sources thus help identify the negative and positive obligations stemming inherent to the *non-refoulement* principle.[803]

Generally, the *non-refoulement* principle as conceptualised under Article 3 ECHR, constitutes an exception to the general rule whereby States retain the prerogative to 'control the entry, residence and expulsion of aliens'.[804] Although

[802] Moreno-Lax n 17 at 238–241.

[803] As concerns the *non-refoulement* principle embedded in Article 33 of the Refugee Convention, it is necessary to note that this provision distinguishes itself from the *non-refoulement* principle embedded in the Charter and the ECHR on a number of levels. Firstly, the prohibition of *refoulement* under the Refugee Convention is not based upon the prohibition of torture or inhuman treatment, but rather limited to those individuals who are considered refugees in line with Article 1(A)(2) of the Refugee Convention. This protection is accorded to anyone who fears persecution pursuant to one (or more) of the five grounds enumerated in Article 1. Secondly, the *non-refoulement* principle according to Article 33 Refugee Convention may not be invoked when there are reasonable grounds to believe that the person concerned constitutes a danger to the security of the residing state. This exclusion from the *non-refoulement* prohibition, is the main distinction between the Refugee Convention and the unlimited protection accorded against *refoulement* under the ECHR, the Convention against Torture, the ICCPR and consequently the CFR, which pursue absolute protection against *refoulement* irrespective of the status or conduct of the person concerned. This could raise the idea that protection under the Refugee Convention is generally more limited than the protection under the aforementioned human rights treaties, as can explicitly and implicitly be read in cases by the Strasbourg Court case law itself. It could be argued that from an EU perspective, a similar exclusion is found in Article 12 and Article 17 of the Qualification Directive, which allows for the exclusion of certain individuals from refugee status and/or subsidiary protection where they pose a significant threat to the state concerned on account of their behaviour. Whereas this may seem counterintuitive in light of the absolute nature of Article 3 ECHR, it is crucial to recall that the acquisition of a particular protection status (such as under the Qualification Directive) is not to be equated to the absolute prohibition of *refoulement* under the ECHR – *non-refoulement* and the acquisition of a particular international protection status, constitute two sides of the same coin. See on the matter: ECtHR Judgment of 26 July 2005, *N. v Finland*, App no. 38885/02, §159; ECtHR Judgment of 2 May 1997, *D v the United Kingdom*, App no. 30240/96, §48; ECtHR Judgment of 17 December 1996, *Ahmed v Austria*, App no. 25964/94, §40–41. De Weck argues that the difference in protection standards is not very pronounced, as there are forms of persecution against which the Refugee Convention provides protection, which may not reach the severity threshold to trigger the *non-refoulement* prohibition under general human rights provisions. See: Fanny De Weck, *Non-refoulement under the European Convention on Human Rights and the UN Convention against Torture – The Assessment of Individual Complaints by the European Court of Human Rights under Article 3 ECHR and the United Nations Committee Against Torture under Article 3 CAT* (Leiden, Brill, 2017) 47. In addition, Hamdan points out that the protection afforded is more limited under the CAT, as this is limited materially to acts of torture, whereas the protection against *refoulement* afforded under the ECHR encompasses protection against torture, as well as cruel, inhuman and degrading treatment or punishment. Hamdan n 728 at 23–24; 27–28, 38, 67. See also: European Agency for Fundamental Rights, 'Handbook on European Law Relating to Asylum, Borders and Immigration' (*FRA – Council of Europe*, 26 June 2013) https://fra.europa.eu/sites/default/files/handbook-law-asylum-migration-borders-2nded_en.pdf. On the principle of *non-refoulement* as customary international law, it has been observed that certain states that are specially affected (in line with the seminal *North Sea Continental Shelf* case), are *not* bound by the Refugee Convention despite hosting large numbers of international protection seekers. Yet, these States continue to abide by the principle, thereby affirming its existence via state practice as a norm of custom, in addition to the overwhelming number of states that are signatories to the Refugee Convention, as well as more general human rights treaties which implicitly and explicitly protect the *non-refoulement* principle. See: Mungianu n 27 at 100–102; Vedsted-Hansen, Bauloz, Hruschka, Lupačová, Sander, Storgaard n 736 at 27–31.

[804] ECtHR (Grand Chamber) Judgment of 28 February 2008, *Saadi v Italy*, App no. 37201/06, §124. On the prerogative of States to control entry into sovereign territory: ECtHR (Grand Chamber) Judgment of 21 November 2019, *Ilias and Ahmed v Hungary*, App no. 47287/15, §125; ECtHR (Grand Chamber) Judgment of 23 March 2016, *FG v Sweden*, App no. 43611/11, §111; De Weck n 803 at 17.

the *travaux préparatoires* are not conclusive as to whether the *non-refoulement* obligation was inherent to Article 3 ECHR from the very start, it is clear that the provision seeks to holistically prevent all forms of significant ill-treatment.[805] More concretely, the ECHR protects against removal where a real risk exists that the person removed will be subjected to treatment that amounts to torture, or cruel, inhuman and degrading treatment or punishment, upon arrival in the country of origin or a third country, irrespective of whether this is the result of an act or omission on behalf of the receiving state.[806] The Strasbourg Court has refrained from categorizing the type of ill-treatment which could trigger the *non-refoulement* obligation, focusing rather on the *effect* of the measure. In other words, the Strasbourg court determines whether the (envisaged) ill-treatment will meet the minimum severity threshold, to be assessed on a case-to-case basis, mindful of whether the envisaged ill-treatment will result in irreparable harm.[807] In making such determinations the Strasbourg Court neither makes a distinction between physical and/or mental ill-treatment, nor does it require that such acts are perpetrated by public officials.[808]

Although the first case in which deportation was considered as giving rise to a violation of Article 3 ECHR dates back to 1961, it was only in 1989 when the ruling in *Soering v United Kingdom* was delivered. In this case the ECtHR effectively found a violation of Article 3 "*based on the consequences of a removal*".[809] More than that, the case was innovative as it considered for the first time, the extraterritorial application of Article 3 ECHR, and recognised the violation of a human right, not on account of an already committed violation, but rather, on the basis of the existence of a *possible future violation* pursuant to the expulsion of the individual concerned.[810] The latter is inherent to *refoulement* cases, as such cases typically concern *hypothetical* violations that will occur once the expulsion has been effectuated, irrespective of the legal basis for, or the type of expulsion.[811] Such hypothetical violations do not engage the responsibility of the receiving state, but rather the state

[805] De Weck n 803 at 17–18.

[806] On the expulsion to the country of origin or a third country: ECtHR (Grand Chamber) Judgment of 21 November 2019, *Ilias and Ahmed v Hungary*, App no. 47287/15, §128. On the indifference or an omission on behalf of a duty-bearer, see ECtHR (Grand Chamber) Judgment of 21 January 2011, *MSS v Belgium*, App no. 30696/09, §253, 263. See also: Hamdan n 728 at 82.

[807] ECtHR Judgment of 18 January 1978, *Ireland v the United* Kingdom, App no. 5310/71, §162. See also: Hamdan n 728 at 39–41.

[808] ECtHR Judgment of 30 April 2013, *Kochieva and others v Sweden (admissibility)*, App no 75203/12, §30; ECtHR Judgment of 2 March 2010, *Al-Saadoon and Mufdhi v the United Kingdom*, App no 61498/08, §144. On the (irrelevance of the) perpetrator of the ill-treatment, see: ECtHR (Grand Chamber) Judgment of 4 November 2014, *Tarakhel v Switzerland*, App no 29217/12, §104; ECtHR Judgment of 11 January 2007, *Salah Sheekh v the Netherlands*, App no 1948/04, §147. See also: Hamdan n 728 at 90; Jurisconsult, 'Guide on the Case-law of the Convention – Immigration' (*European Court of Human Rights*, 30 May 2020) rm.coe.int/court-case-law-guide-immigration-eng/16809f1556 15–21.

[809] ECtHR Judgment of 7 July 1989, *Soering v the United Kingdom*, App no 14038/88; De Weck n 791 at 18.

[810] De Weck n 803 at 19.

[811] Article 3 ECHR applies to *inter alia* extradition, expulsion or deportation. ECtHR (Grand Chamber) Judgment of 21 November 2019, *Ilias and Ahmed v Hungary*, App no 47287/15, §126. See also: 'The act of refoulement may consist in expulsion, extradition, deportation, removal, informal transfer, "rendition", rejection, refusal of admission or any other measure which would result in compelling the person to remain

that is responsible for the expulsion measure.[812] A violation of the *non-refoulement* principle is generally raised by reference to Article 3 ECHR,[813] but has also been raised in relation to a number of *other* Convention rights, with the most notable examples being Article 2 ECHR concerning the right to life[814] and Article 4 Protocol 4 ECHR concerning collective expulsions.[815]

Within the EU legal order, the protection afforded against *refoulement* is highly similar to the standards set under the ECHR and ensuing case law, on account of the fact that Article 4 CFR, and Article 19(2) CFR correspond to Article 3 ECHR, including *non-refoulement* in particular.[816] Recall that Article 52(3) CFR requires that for corresponding rights in the CFR and the ECHR, the minimum standard of protection shall be that of the ECHR and the respective case law stemming therefrom. The foregoing was confirmed by the CJEU which held first in its grand chamber judgment in *Elgafaji*, that Article 3 ECHR (concerning *non-refoulement*) 'forms part of the general principles of Community law, observance of which is ensured by the Court …'.[817] The *NS* case reaffirmed the obligation to interpret and apply EU law

in the country of origin' – ECtHR Concurring Opinion Judge Pinto De Albuquerque of 23 February 2012, *Hirsi Jamaa and others v Italy*, App no 27765/09 60. In a more recent case, the ECtHR held that '185. … these reasons have led the Court to interpret the term "expulsion" in the generic meaning in current use ("to drive away from a place") [see *Khlaifia and Others*, cited above, §243, and *Hirsi Jamaa and Others*, cited above, §174], as referring to any forcible removal of an alien from a State's territory, irrespective of the lawfulness of the person's stay, the length of time he or she has spent in the territory, the location in which he or she was apprehended, his or her status as a migrant or an asylum-seeker and his or her conduct when crossing the border. The Court has also used the term in the context of Articles 3 and 13 of the Convention [see, for example, *JK and Others v Sweden*, App no 59166/12, §78–79, 4 June 2015, and *Saadi*, cited above, §95, 124–25], and especially with regard to the removal of aliens at the border … 186. **As a result, Article 3 of the Convention and Article 4 of Protocol No. 4 have been found to apply to any situation coming within the jurisdiction of a Contracting State, including to situations or points in time where the authorities of the State in question had not yet examined the existence of grounds entitling the persons concerned to claim protection under these provisions** … 187. In the Court's view these considerations, which formed the basis for its recent judgments in *Hirsi Jamaa and Others, Sharifi and Others and Khlaifia and Others* [all cited above], concerning applicants who had attempted to enter a State's territory by sea, have lost none of their relevance. There is therefore no reason to adopt a different interpretation of the term "expulsion" with regard to forcible removals from a State's territory in the context of an attempt to cross a national border by land. Nevertheless, it should be specified that this approach follows from the autonomous interpretation of Convention terms' (emphasis added). ECtHR (Grand Chamber) Judgment of 13 February 2020, *ND and NT v Spain*, App nos. 8675/15 and 8679/15, §185. See also: Nuala Mole and Catherine Meredith, *Asylum and the European Convention on Human Rights* (Strasbourg, Council of Europe Publishing, 2010) 23; De Weck n 803 at 20.

[812] Hamdan n 728 at 22.

[813] See for an extensive discussion on the matter: De Weck n 803 at 23–33.

[814] De Weck n 803 at 22–23.

[815] See amongst other the most notable cases: ECtHR Judgment of 21 October 2014, *Sharifi and others v Italy and Greece*, App no. 16643/09; ECtHR (Grand Chamber) Judgment of 23 February 2012, *Hirsi Jamaa and others v Italy*, App no. 27765/09, §207; ECtHR Judgment of 5 February 2002, *Conka and others v Belgium*, App no. 51564/99, §63. See also: De Weck n 803 at 32–33. Hamdan n 728 at 93–102.

[816] Mungianu n 27 at 113–116; FRA Handbook n 803 at 64–66.

[817] CJEU (Grand Chamber) Judgment of 17 February 2009, *Elgafaji v Staatssecretaris van Justitie*, C-465/07, ECLI:EU:C:2009:94, §28. "In that regard, while the fundamental right guaranteed under Article 3 of the ECHR forms part of the general principles of Community law, observance of which is ensured by the Court, and while the case-law of the European Court of Human Rights is taken into consideration in interpreting the scope of that right in the Community legal order, it is, however, Article 15(b) of the Directive which corresponds, in essence, to Article 3 of the ECHR. By contrast, Article 15(c) of the Directive is a provision, the content of which is different from that of Article 3 of the ECHR, and the interpretation of which must, therefore, be carried out independently, although with due regard for fundamental rights, as they are guaranteed under the ECHR'.

in accordance with inter alia the ECHR.[818] While the minimum standard of protection must be respected, the EU and its Member States when acting in the scope of Union law, may provide more extensive protection (insofar this does not affect the unity, effectiveness and primacy of Union law and does not endanger the Union autonomous legal order) (see Chapter 3).[819] When asked in *NS* whether the corresponding provisions concerning *non-refoulement* and asylum in the Charter provide for more extensive protection than the corresponding Article 3 ECHR, the CJEU maintained the same level of protection, rather than interpreting its twin provision in the Charter more broadly.[820] Consequently, Mungianu argues that Article 4 and Article 19(2) CFR correspond to Article 3 ECHR and foresee in an *identical* level of protection as concerns the *non-refoulement* principle.[821]

Although the prohibition of *refoulement* appears straightforward enough, gradually the Strasbourg Court has clarified what concrete negative and positive (substantive and procedural) obligations must be respected for the *non-refoulement* principle to be complied with, as discussed below.[822] Identifying these concrete obligations is crucial in determining whether the Member States and/or European Union (institutions, bodies, agencies and offices) have violated human rights commitments in the implementation of IBM.

a. Negative Obligations

Firstly, the *non-refoulement* principle encompasses the negative obligation to refrain from the 'removal, transfer, rejection or refusal of admission of a person'[823] where

[818] CJEU (Grand Chamber) Judgment of 21 December 2011, *NS v Secretary of State for the Home Department and ME and others v Refugee Applications Commissioner and Minister for Justice, Equality and Reform*, C-411/10 and C-493/10, ECLI:EU:C:2011:865, §78.

[819] Comment to Article 52(3) in the Explanations to the CFR; Mungianu n 27 at 120–122, 126; Peers and Prechal n 182 at 1494–1496.

[820] CJEU (Grand Chamber) Judgment of 21 December 2011, *NS v Secretary of State for the Home Department and ME and others v Refugee Applications Commissioner and Minister for Justice, Equality and Reform*, C-411/10 and C-493/10, ECLI:EU:C:2011:865, §112–115.

[821] Mungianu n 27 at 128. Arguably, Article 4 and Article 19(2) CFR do foresee in more extensive protection in that it provides protection against *refoulement* in cases of indiscriminate violence, albeit for applicants of subsidiary protection as held by Article 15 Qualification Directive. This is the case where the degree of indiscriminate violence is so high in the country of return, as a result of which the applicant for subsidiary protection is relieved of the obligation to demonstrate that the individual circumstances warrant the application of the *non-refoulement* principle. However, in the case where this was raised, the CJEU did not rely upon Article 3 ECHR in its assessment of whether the *non-refoulement* principle should apply and noted that Article 15(c) Qualification Directive concerning indiscriminate violence, does not correspond to Article 3 ECHR. CJEU (Grand Chamber) Judgment of 17 February 2009, *Elgafaji v Staatssecretaris van Justitie*, C-465/07, ECLI:EU:C:2009:94, §28. See also: Mole and Meredith n 811 at 45. On a different note, it has been argued that general principles that protect fundamental rights have not been rendered redundant on account of the Charter of Fundamental Rights, and conversely, may prove to provide more extensive protection than the corresponding protection standards afforded for corresponding rights in the Charter and ECHR. See on the matter: Opinion of Advocate General Trstenjak of 8 September 2011, *Maribel Dominguez v Centre informatique du Centre Ouest Atlantique and Préfet de la région Centre*, C-282/10, ECLI:EU:C:2011:559, §158; Mungianu n 27 at 110–111.

[822] Hamdan n 728 at 21–22.

[823] See also: concurring opinion Judge Pinto De Albuquerque and the sources cited therein concerning the extra-territorial application of *non-refoulement* – ECtHR Judgment of 23 February 2012, *Hirsi Jamaa and others v Italy*, App no. 27765/09, 64.

substantial grounds exist, demonstrating an individualised, real risk of being subjected to treatment that may amount to torture, cruel, inhuman or degrading treatment or may result in his or her livelihood being at stake, and this irrespective of the legal basis for the removal.[824] The foregoing includes de facto *refoulement*, which refers to a situation where a person fleeing from such ill-treatment is forced to return 'as a direct and immediate result of the measures taken by the State party', irrespective of whether such return measures were founded in law or not, as long as the actions (or omissions) by the sending state are crucial to the chain of events that led to the return of the individual concerned.[825] In addition, States will be held responsible for *indirect refoulment*, when a person is returned to an intermediary third state and a risk is established that upon arrival in the intermediary state, the individual will be returned to a third (receiving) state, where he or she will be subjected to ill-treatment in violation of Article 3, without the intermediary state conducting a meaningful or effective assessment of the risk upon return to the third country.[826] The prohibition of *indirect refoulement* gains importance particularly where the intermediary state is not a State Party to the ECHR.[827]

Contrary to the *non-refoulement* prohibition in the Refugee Convention (see above), the prohibition under the ECHR is absolute, and cannot be negated on account of the safety concerns posed by the individual concerned, nor the undesirability of his or her presence.[828] The foregoing was explicitly confirmed in the *Chahal* case by the Strasbourg Court[829] and reiterated in the landmark *Saadi* decision, which now functions as a precedent for the Strasbourg Court in *non-refoulement* cases.[830] Political assurances by the receiving State do not alleviate this prohibition.[831] As aforementioned, the *non-refoulement* principle can be triggered even when

[824] De Weck n 803 at 19–20; Hamdan n 728 at 106–107.

[825] ECtHR (Grand Chamber) Judgment of 13 February 2020, *ND and NT v Spain*, App nos. 8675/15 and 8679/15, §185; ECtHR Concurring Opinion Judge Pinto De Albuquerque of 23 February 2012, *Hirsi Jamaa and others v Italy*, App no. 27765/09 p. 60; ECtHR Judgment of 7 July 1989, *Soering v the United Kingdom*, App no. 14038/88, §91 ('it is liability incurred by the extraditing Contracting State by reason of its having taken action which has as a direct consequence the exposure of an individual to proscribed ill-treatment'.); ECtHR Judgment of 20 March 1991, *Cruz Varas and Others v Sweden*, App no. 15576/89, §76; Kees Wouters, *International Legal Standards for the Protection from Refoulement* (Cambridge, Intersentia, 2009) 318. See also: Hamdan n 728 at 107.

[826] ECtHR Judgment of 21 November 2019, *Ilias and Ahmed v Hungary*, App no. 47287/15, §134. See also (and sources cited therein): Den Heijer n 734 at 485–486; Hamdan n 728 at 113.

[827] ibid 112; ECtHR 2011, *MSS* n 197 at §358; ECtHR (Grand Chamber) Judgment of 23 February 2012, *Hirsi Jamaa and others v Italy*, App no 27765/09, §147.

[828] ECtHR (Grand Chamber) Judgment of 15 November 1996, *Chahal v the United Kingdom*, App no 22414/93; ECtHR (Grand Chamber) Judgment of 29 January 2008, *Saadi v United Kingdom*, App no 13229/03; ECtHR Judgment of 17 December 1996, *Ahmed v Austria*, App no. 25964/94; Guild n 731 at 561; Mole and Meredith n 811 at 23. Similarly, as concerns the Convention Against Torture, the prohibition of *refoulement* is likewise considered to be absolute. See Article 2(2) UN Convention against Torture (UN General Assembly, *Convention Against Torture and Other Cruel, Inhuman or Degrading Treatment or Punishment*, 10 December 1984, United Nations, Treaty Series, vol. 1465, 85). See also: Hamdan n 728 at 22–23.

[829] ECtHR (Grand Chamber) Judgment of 15 November 1996, *Chahal v the United Kingdom*, App no 22414/93, §80; Hamdan n 728 at 28.

[830] ECtHR (Grand Chamber) Judgment of 29 January 2008, *Saadi v United Kingdom*, App no 13229/03, §137. See also: Hamdan n 728 at 33–34.

[831] Guild n 731 at 561.

the individual concerned has not yet reached the territory to ask for international protection – be it at the land border or at sea, irrespective of whether international protection was explicitly asked.[832] The ECtHR clarifies the latter by holding that responsibility may arise when action has been taken 'which has as a direct consequence the exposure of an individual to the risk of pro-scribed ill-treatment',[833] irrespective of whether the risk of ill-treatment directly or indirectly stems from the authorities of the receiving state.[834]

Article 78 TFEU functions as a *chapeau* for asylum policy in the Union, which must be implemented in complaince with the *non-refoulement* principle.[835] The obligation to respect the *non-refoulement* principle, was explicitly incorporated in Article 21(1) of the Qualification Directive, which holds that Member States are to respect the *non-refoulement* obligation 'in accordance with their international obligations'.[836] In line therewith, Union legislation combines the standards set in the Refugee Convention and the ECHR regarding *non-refoulement* in Article 9 Qualification Directive, holding that in order to acquire refugee status, the feared ill-treatment must be 'sufficiently serious by its nature or repetition to constitute a severe violation of basic human rights …'. Analogously to the protection against *refoulement* under the ECtHR, Union legislation does not limit or exclude certain forms of treatment that may trigger the *non-refoulement* obligation, as evidenced by the open-ended nature of Article 9(2) Qualification Directive, which provides a non-exhaustive list of grounds that may be demonstrative of ill-treatment capable of triggering the *non-refoulement* obligation.[837] Analogously to ECtHR case law concerning *non-refoulement*, Article 6 Qualification Directive confirms that the actors of the persecution or serious harm may be the receiving state authorities directly or non-state actors.[838] Despite the many similarities, and contrary to the ECHR, EU law

[832] ECtHR (Grand Chamber) Judgment of 23 February 2012, *Hirsi Jamaa and others v Italy*, App no 27765/09, §73–75. The foregoing is not nullified by the recent judgment of the Strasbourg Court in *ND and NT v Spain*, which concerned alleged violations of the prohibition of collective expulsion as protected under Article 4 Protocol 4 ECHR. In paragraph 128 of that case, the Strasbourg Court held that the complaints under Article 3 ECHR were inadmissible on account of the fact that the Applicants did not face a risk concerning a violation of Article 3 ECHR in Morocco and had either requested asylum at very late stage or not at all. ECtHR (Grand Chamber) Judgment of 13 February 2020, *ND and NT v Spain*, App nos 8675/15 and 8679/15, §105, 109–110.

[833] ECtHR (Grand Chamber) Judgment of 23 February 2012, *Hirsi Jamaa and others v Italy*, App no. 27765/09, §11; ECtHR (Grand Chamber) Judgment of 29 January 2008, *Saadi v United Kingdom*, App no 13229/03.

[834] ECtHR Judgment of 11 January 2007, *Salah Sheekh v the Netherlands*, App no 1948/04, §147; Mole and Meredith n 811 at 28.

[835] Provisions on *non-refoulement* can be found in a number of secondary legislative documents regulating the CEAS, albeit that there have been consistent issues pertaining to this principle in the application of these provisions.

[836] Vedsted-Hansen, Bauloz, Hruschka, Lupačová, Sander, Storgaard n 736 at 26–29.

[837] The CJEU recalled that the standard of ill-treatment that gives rise to subsidiary protection does not necessarily correspond to the standard set by Article 3 ECHR with respect to refugee status, as these types of international protection are not identical. See: CJEU (Grand Chamber) Judgment of 17 February 2009, *Elgafaji v Staatssecretaris van Justitie*, C-465/07, ECLI:EU:C:2009:94, §28.

[838] Article 6 Qualification Directive.

does provide for a number of (strict) exceptions to the non-refoulement principle (see article 17 and 21 qualification directive).[839]

The prohibition against removal will only be triggered where a significant and individualised risk of ill-treatment exists upon return to a third country or a country of return. The case law of both the CJEU and the ECtHR has developed significantly in this respect, clarifying that when such a significant and individualised risk *does not* exist, the *non-refoulement* principle cannot be deemed applicable. While this is a straightforward and sensical assertion, it begs the question what the threshold is to establish when a significant and individual risk of ill-treatment upon return, triggers the applicability of the negative obligation of the *non-refoulement* principle. This question is particularly relevant in light of the recourse to Safe Third Country (STC) designations within the EU legal order.

In accordance with Article 33, Article 38 and/or Article 39 of the Asylum Procedures Directive, a third country may be designated as a safe third (European) country, when a number of conditions have been met. Where these conditions have been met, EU Member States may consider an application for international protection from an individual coming from such countries, as inadmissible (Article 33(2)(c) *in juncto* Article 38 Asylum Procedures Directive) or decide to assess the application only partially on the merits (Article 39 Asylum Procedures Directive). An inadmissibility decision based on an STC designation departs from the rebuttable presumption that the individual will not face a significant and individualised risk upon return to the third country, entailing that the *non-refoulement* principle will not be triggered or considered applicable. To be qualified as a STC, a third state must provide both *de jure* and *de facto* equivalent (not identical) procedural and substantive protection.[840] This is reminiscent of the aforementioned 'equivalent protection doctrine' adopted by the ECtHR, as well as the recourse to similar recognition within an intra-EU context pursuant to the Dublin arrangements and the Aznar Protocol.[841]

The CJEU has elaborated upon the requirements to be met in order to be designated as a STC, holding in particular that the exhaustive conditions for inadmissibility concerning applications from a STC, are cumulative.[842] Advocate General Bobek,

[839] Jelena Ristik, 'The Right to Asylum and the Principle of *Non-Refoulement* Under the European Convention on Human Rights' (2017) 13 *European Scientific Journal* 117.

[840] Jens Vedsted-Hansen, 'Asylum Procedures Directive 2013/32/EU – Article 38' in Kay Hailbronner and Daniel Thym (eds), *EU Immigration and Asylum Law – A Commentary* (Munich, Verlag CH Beck, 2016) 1363; Pieter Boeles, Maarten den Heijer, Gerrie Lodder and Kees Wouters, *European Migration Law* (Cambridge, Intersentia, 2014) 281.

[841] The (rebuttable) presumption of EU Member States as safe countries of return, was inherent to the 1990 Dublin Convention, as well as the Aznar Protocol. The latter holds specifically that, 'Given the level of protection of fundamental rights and freedoms by the Member States of the European Union, Member States shall be regarded as constituting safe countries of origin in respect of each other for all legal and practical purposes in relation to asylum matters'. In addition, the designation of *third countries* as safe on account of procedural and substantive equivalence dates back to the first Asylum Procedures Directive, as evidenced by Article 25 and Article 27 (Council Directive 2005/85/EC of 1 December 2005 on minimum standards on procedures in Member States for granting and withdrawing refugee status [2005] OJ L 326/13).

[842] CJEU (Grand Chamber) Judgment of 14 May 2020, *FMS, FNZ, SA, SA Junior v Országos Idegenrendészeti Főigazgatóság Dél-alföldi Regionális Igazgatóság, Országos Idegenrendészeti Főigazgatóság,*

as followed by the CJEU in the *Tompa* judgment, has described these conditions as consisting of principles, (national) rules and safeguards *vis-à-vis* the individual applicants for international protection. First and foremost,

> the Member State must be satisfied that explicitly stated principles will be respected vis-à-vis the given applicant. They are: that life and liberty are not threatened on account of race, religion, nationality, membership of a particular social group or political opinion; that there is no risk of serious harm as defined in Directive 2011/95/EU; respect for the principle of non-refoulement in accordance with the Geneva Convention; respect for the prohibition of removal, in violation of the right to freedom from torture and cruel, inhuman or degrading treatment as laid down in international law; and the existence of a possibility to request refugee status and, if found to be a refugee, to receive protection in accordance with the Geneva Convention.[843]

These conditions of *principle* elaborated on by Advocate General Bobek appear to point to the requirement of substantive equivalent protection that must be provided in the third country of return or origin. Next, national *rules* must foresee in a particular methodology to determine the relationship of a STC vis-à-vis an *individual* applicant and provide national rules that incorporate the requirement of a special connection between the individual and the country of return (Article 32(2)(a) Asylum Procedures Directive).[844] Finally, the Member States must foresee *safeguards*, which permit individual applicants for international protection to contest inadmissibility decisions.[845] Crucially, under the EU-*acquis* on borders, asylum and migration, national designations of a country (of return or origin) as safe, remains a *rebuttable* assumption at all times.

The ECtHR thus far, has implicitly acknowledged the legitimacy of STC designations in accordance with the Asylum Procedures Directive, nevertheless underscoring that the 'assessment of whether there are substantial grounds for believing that the applicant faces a real risk of being subjected to treatment in breach of Article 3 must necessarily be a rigorous one'.[846] The ECtHR does make the explicit distinction, however, between returns of individuals without a substantive assessment on the merits to *third countries*, as opposed to *countries of origin*.[847] Return of individuals to a country of *origin*, will inevitably require an assessment on the merits and the risks associated to the return. Return to a STC that is *not* the country of origin (ie not based on the merits) will, conversely, focus predominantly on the effective access to an asylum procedure in that third country. Where the guarantees are insufficient

Joined Cases C-924/19 PPU and C-925/19 PPU, ECLI:EU:C:2020:367, §149–153; CJEU (Grand Chamber) Judgment of 19 March 2019, *Ibrahim and others*, Joined Cases C-297/17, C-318/17, C-319/17 and C-438/17, ECLI:EU:C:2019:219, §76; CJEU Judgment of 19 March 2020, *LH v Bevándorlási és Menekültügyi Hivatal (Tompa)*, C-564/18, ECLI:EU:C:2020:218, §36, 40–41.

[843] Opinion of Advocate General Bobek of 5 December 2019, *LH v Bevándorlási és Menekültügyi Hivatal (Tompa)*, C-564/18, ECLI:EU:C:2019:1056, §43.

[844] CJEU Judgment of 19 March 2020, *LH v Bevándorlási és Menekültügyi Hivatal (Tompa)*, C-564/18, ECLI:EU:C:2020:218, §37–39.

[845] ibid.

[846] ECtHR (Grand Chamber) Judgment of 21 November 2019, *Ilias and Ahmed v Hungary*, App no 47287/15, §127.

[847] ibid §130.

in the STC that individuals will have access to adequate asylum procedure protecting the individual against *refoulement*, 'Article 3 implies a duty that the asylum seekers should not be removed to the third country concerned'.[848] The ECtHR furthermore underscores that STC designations do not relieve sending Member States of the burden of proof (shared with individual applicants), to rigorously assess the conditions of return and accessibility to the adequate asylum procedures *propriu motu* in the third country.[849]

In sum, there is convergence between the case law of the CJEU and ECtHR concerning the designation of third countries as safe, and the procedural (positive) obligations associated to such designations. Only where all the cumulative and exhaustive conditions have been met, may the sending Member State consider the negative obligation of the *non-refoulement* respected.

b. Positive Obligations

The *non-refoulement* principle additionally encompasses positive obligations of a *substantive* and a *procedural* nature, which are inextricably connected to the compliance with the aforementioned negative obligation.

The nature of the positive obligation may differ depending on the country to which the individual TCN is being returned.[850]

If returned to the country of origin, the expelling Member State will be required by virtue of a *substantive* positive obligation, to investigate the conditions of return from both a generalised perspective, as well as an individual perspective. The ECtHR has clarified that the burden of proof lies firstly upon the individual claiming anticipated ill-treatment in the country of return. Secondly, there rests upon the Contracting party a 'duty to investigate, of its own motion, any situation of need for international protection, especially when, as the Court has stressed, the facts which constitute the risk to the applicant "were well known before the transfer of the applicant and were freely ascertainable from a wide number of sources".'[851] In other words, the burden of proof is shared between the individual applicant and the Member State, entailing that State authorities are under an positive substantive obligation to investigate individually, any claim for international protection. Particularly when systematic human rights violations are widely known to occur in the country of return, there exists a heightened burden upon the Contracting party to *take* measures to assess whether such a risk upon return exists, irrespective of whether international protection has been explicitly requested.[852] According to

[848] ibid §134.

[849] ibid §141.

[850] ECtHR Judgment of 23 July 2020, *MK and others v Poland*, App nos 40503/17, 42902/17 and 43643/17, §171.

[851] ECtHR Concurring Opinion Judge Pinto De Albuquerque of 23 February 2012, *Hirsi Jamaa and others v Italy*, App no 27765/09, §11. See also: ECtHR (Grand Chamber) Judgment of 21 November 2019, *Ilias and Ahmed v Hungary*, App no 47287/15, §141; Moreno-Lax n 17 at 424.

[852] ECtHR Judgment of 11 July 2000, *Jabari v Turkey*, App no 40035/98, §38–40.

ECHR case law, this requires a rigorous assessment by the sending state of the foreseeable consequences as result of removal not only of the general situation of the receiving State,[853] but equally so, of the individual and personal circumstances of the individual(s) concerned.[854]

Alternatively, if the individual is returned to a third country (ie *not* the country of origin) the expelling State must ensure that upon return to the third country, the TCN will not face a risk of subsequently being *transferred* to a third country where such a risk of ill-treatment exists without an assessment of such risks by the intermediary country.[855] Such foreseeable risks must be assessed prior to removal.[856] Insofar a case is brought before the ECtHR and the removal has not yet been effectuated (for example, on account of interim measures taken pending the removal proceedings), the assessment by the Strasbourg Court will occur at the time of the Courts' examination.[857] Throughout its case law, the Strasbourg Court has clarified that the vulnerable status of individuals in the receiving State, may give rise to heightened burden on the sending State to verify whether returning the individuals concerned would result in a violation of Article 3 ECHR.[858]

In addition to the duty to investigate direct and indirect claims of anticipated ill-treatment upon return, State authorities are under a two-fold positive procedural obligation. On the one hand, the expelling State must ensure that the domestic procedures whereby claims for international protection are investigated, are not of an automated and mechanical nature, and ensure that the factual basis for such claims are diligently investigated.[859] General presumptions that a third country or the country of return is a 'safe third country' must be sufficiently substantiated for such determinations to be considered in compliance with Article 3 ECHR.[860] In line with the foregoing, the Strasbourg Court has also read – in reference to the right to an effective remedy enshrined in Article 13 ECHR – a procedural positive obligation to foresee in the possibility of suspensive appeal against return decisions, where claims have been raised regarding anticipated ill-treatment triggering Article 3 ECHR

[853] ECtHR Judgment of 23 March 2016, *F.G. v Sweden*, App no 43611/11, §114.

[854] ECtHR (Grand Chamber) Judgment of 23 February 2012, *Hirsi Jamaa and others v Italy*, App no 27765/09 §116–118 (and cases cited therein); ECtHR Judgment of 11 July 2000, *Jabari v Turkey*, App no 40035/98, §38–39; ECtHR Judgment of 30 October 1991, *Vilvarajah and others v the United Kingdom*, App nos 13163/87; 13164/87; 13165/87; 13447/87; 13448/87, §108.

[855] ECtHR (Grand Chamber) Judgment of 23 February 2012, *Hirsi Jamaa and others v Italy*, App no 27765/09, §130; ECtHR Judgment of 8 June 2006, *Lupsa v Romania*, App no 10337/04, §147.

[856] ECtHR Judgment of 20 March 1991, *Cruz Varas and Others v Sweden*, App no 15576/89, §76; Hamdan n 715 at 204.

[857] ECtHR Judgment of 4 February 2005, *Mamatkulov and Askarov v Turkey*, App nos 4682799 and 46951/99, §76; Hamdan n 728 at 204–205.

[858] See (and sources cited therein): ECtHR Judgment of 23 March 2016, *FG v Sweden*, App no 43611/11, §113.

[859] ECtHR Judgment of 21 November 2019, *Ilias and Ahmed v Hungary*, App no. 47287/15, §137; ECtHR Judgment of 15 March 2018, *AEA v Greece*, App no. 39034/12, §68–71; ECtHR Judgment of 11 July 2000, *Jabari v Turkey*, App no. 40035/98, §40. See also: UNHCR, 'UNHCR Manual on Refugee Protection and the ECHR' (*UNHCR*, 1 August 2006) www.unhcr.org/publications/legal/3ead312a4/unhcr-manual-refugee-protection-echr-updated-august-2006.html.

[860] ECtHR Judgment of 21 November 2019, *Ilias and Ahmed v Hungary*, App no 47287/15, §163.

upon return.[861] Secondly, if returning an individual to a purportedly 'safe third country', the expelling State must ensure that the individual has access to adequate international protection proceedings in that third country.[862]

As aforementioned, these same positive obligations are similarly embedded in the conceptualization of *non-refoulement* under EU law. In fact, whereas the ECtHR has repeatedly affirmed that the signatory states retain the right to determine who may or may not enter their respective territories, and that the ECHR does not provide a self-standing right to asylum,[863] the EU does have competences in border management, asylum and migration. In view of this competence, it need not surprise that the Union legislator has taken more affirmative action in regulating the different aspects of claims for international protection, including the positive obligations that are inherent to the *non-refoulement* principle.

Conceivably, the negative obligation to not expel or return an individual to a country of return where he or she may face ill-treatment, cannot be effectively complied with if the individual concerned is not first provided the opportunity to make such a claim according to certain standards.[864] This was explicitly confirmed in the *European Commission v Hungary* infringement case before the CJEU, where it was held that the effectiveness lodging an application for international protection, with the objective of preventing an unlawful return, is imperative to the effectiveness of the right to asylum as protected by Article 18 CFR.[865] In other words, to ensure that an individual is not wrongfully expelled to a country where there is a risk of significant ill-treatment, the individual concerned must have the opportunity to voice that such risk exists. Mindful of the fact that the claims for international protection are inextricably connected to protecting the *non-refoulement* principle, the Union legislator has (unlike the ECtHR) explicitly incorporated the positive obligations that facilitate the protection of the *non-refoulement* principle in secondary legislation, in particular in the Asylum Procedures Directive.[866] It has been argued that these concrete substantive and procedural obligations in Union legislation are a translation of the aforementioned rigorous scrutiny standard that the ECtHR requires to be in compliance with the *non-refoulement* principle.[867]

[861] ECtHR Judgment of 15 March 2018, *AEA v Greece*, App no. 39034/12, §68–71; ECtHR Judgment of 11 July 2000, *Jabari v Turkey*, App no 40035/98, §50.

[862] ECtHR Judgment of 23 July 2020, *MK and others v Poland*, App nos 40503/17, 42902/17 and 43643/17, §172.

[863] ECtHR Judgment of 23 February 2012, *Hirsi Jamaa and others v Italy*, App no. 27765/09, §130; ECtHR Judgment of 8 June 2006, *Lupsa v Romania*, App no 10337/04, §113.

[864] The ECtHR (implicitly) acknowledges that the acquisition of an international protection status as regulated under EU law and the *non-refoulement* principle constitute two sides of the same coin. ECtHR (Grand Chamber) Judgment of 13 February 2020, *ND and NT v Spain*, App nos 8675/15 and 8679/15, §102 and 182.

[865] CJEU (Grand Chamber) Judgment of 17 December 2020, *European Commission v Hungary*, C-808/18, ECLI:EU:C:2020:1029, §102.

[866] Article 6–29 Asylum Procedures Directive. These provisions elaborate upon, inter alia, the right to a personal interview (Article 14), access to the procedure for international protection (Article 6), the right to remain pending the international protection proceedings (Article 9).

[867] Vedsted-Hansen, Bauloz, Hruschka, Lupačová, Sander, Storgaard n 736 at 85.

Furthermore – although the *non-refoulement* principle gives rise to a self-standing residence right – Article 9 Asylum Procedures Directive does hold explicitly that pending an application for international protection, throughout the examination of this application and during the (time frame to make an) appeal against a decision on the application for international protection, the applicant(s) have a substantive right to remain in the country where the application has been made.[868] This is not to be equated to the Member States being under a positive obligation to provide residence rights to applicants of international protection.[869] However, Member States *are* under the positive substantive obligation to ensure that the applicant has the possibility of remaining within respective Member State territories throughout the procedure of the application and any suspensive appeals against decisions concerning the application for international protection.[870]

Union legislation additionally requires that to be able to comply with the negative obligation under the *non-refoulement* principle, the Member State authorities are under a positive substantive obligation to ensure that personnel tasked with the examination of the applications for international protection, are adequately trained.[871] This requires *inter alia* that said individuals are sufficiently capable of making individualised, objective and impartial assessments of the claims for international protection[872] and have sufficient knowledge of the applicable (legal) standards that must be respected throughout a procedure for international protection.[873] In addition, Member States must ensure that personnel tasked with the applications for international protection have access to expert advice pertaining to various aspects of such claims, such as medical expert advice and psychological advice.[874] Personnel tasked with the examination of such claims must also be provided up to date information on the general situation in the various countries of origin, which must likewise be available for those tasked with the re-examination of claims for international protection throughout appeal proceedings.[875] Finally, throughout the examination of the applications and appeals against decisions following such applications, the Member States must ensure that there are rules and practices in place that regulate the translation of the necessary documents, so that the applicant can make him or herself understood.[876] This last requirement serves as a prerequisite in order to comply with the right to an effective remedy as safeguarded under Article 47 CFR and Article 13 ECHR.[877]

[868] There are two exceptions to this right to remain – in the case of subsequent applications or alternatively, in the case of surrender or extradition of the applicant. However, even in these exceptional circumstances, the Member States remain under an obligation to respect the *non-refoulement* principle. Vedsted-Hansen, Bauloz, Hruschka, Lupačová, Sander, Storgaard n 723 at 82.

[869] Article 9(1) Asylum Procedures Directive: 'That right to remain shall not constitute an entitlement to a residence permit'.

[870] Vedsted-Hansen, Bauloz, Hruschka, Lupačová, Sander, Storgaard n 736 at 87.

[871] Article 10(3) Asylum Procedures Directive.

[872] Article 10(3)(a) Asylum Procedures Directive.

[873] Article 10(3)(c) Asylum Procedures Directive.

[874] Article 10(3)(d) Asylum Procedures Directive.

[875] Article 10(3)(b) and Article 10 (4) Asylum Procedures Directive.

[876] Article 10(5) Asylum Procedures Directive.

[877] Vedsted-Hansen, Bauloz, Hruschka, Lupačová, Sander, Storgaard n 736 at 85.

Concerning the decision on an application for international protection, EU law imposes the substantive positive requirement that this be motivated in fact and in law, and that the applicant(s) receive sufficient information on how to proceed in appealing such decisions.[878]

Finally, the Asylum Procedures Directive sets forth a number of *procedural* additional guarantees that the Member States must comply with, to ensure adherence the *non-refoulement* obligation, including *inter alia* linguistic guarantees (Article 12 Asylum Procedures Directive), the requirement of a personal interview so the applicant(s) may explain why there is a significant risk upon return to the country of origin or a third country (Articles 14–17 Asylum Procedures Directive),[879] and a medical examination (Article 18 Asylum Procedures Directive).[880]

c. A Matter of Interpretation?

When interpreting human rights, these rights must always be interpreted in a manner to respect, protect and fulfil the pursued objectives of the human rights provisions,[881] so that the rights concerned are not 'theoretical and illusory',[882] but practical and effective.[883] This is fortified by the fact that the ECHR as well as the CFR encompass an anti-abuse provision, holding that nothing in the respective documents may be construed in such a manner so as to impair the essence of the rights encompassed therein.[884] Finally, the precautionary principle and the principle of effectiveness, require an interpretation by the Member States of the *non-refoulement* principle that encompasses a negative duty not to impede the protection stemming from this

[878] Article 11 Asylum Procedures Directive. See also: Vedsted-Hansen, Bauloz, Hruschka, Lupačová, Sander, Storgaard n 736 at 86–87.

[879] See: CJEU Judgment of 16 July 2020, *Milkiyas Addis v Bundesrepublik Deutschland*, C-517/17, ECLI:EU:C:2020:579.

[880] Vedsted-Hansen, Bauloz, Hruschka, Lupačová, Sander, Storgaard n 736 at 87–101.

[881] Opinion of Advocate General Mengozzi of 7 February 2017, *X and X v Belgium*, C-638/16, ECLI:EU:C:2017:93, §158; ECtHR Judgment of 3 June 2010, *Gäfgen v Germany*, App no 22978/05, §123.

[882] Opinion of Advocate General Mengozzi of 7 February 2017, *X and X v Belgium*, C-638/16 PPU, ECLI:EU:C:2017:93, §158; ECtHR judgment of 26 April 2016, *Murray v Netherlands* App no 10511/10, §104; ECtHR (Grand Chamber) Judgment of 23 February 2012, *Hirsi Jamaa and others v Italy*, App no 27765/09, §130; ECtHR judgment of 1 June 2010 (version corrected on 3 June 2010), *Gäfgen v Germany*, App. No. 22978/05 §123; ECtHR Judgment of 8 June 2006, *Lupsa v Romania*, App no 10337/04, §60.

[883] See inter alia: ECtHR (Grand Chamber) Judgment of 13 February 2020, *ND and NT v Spain*, App nos. 8675/15 and 8679/15 §171; Hamdan n 728 at 17–18.

[884] Article 53 CFR: 'Nothing in this Charter shall be interpreted as restricting or adversely affecting human rights and fundamental freedoms as recognised, in their respective fields of application, by Union law and international law and by international agreements to which the Union or all the Member States are party, including the European Convention for the Protection of Human Rights and Fundamental Freedoms, and by the Member States' constitutions'; Article 54 CFR: 'Nothing in this Charter shall be interpreted as implying any right to engage in any activity or to perform any act aimed at the destruction of any of the rights and freedoms recognised in this Charter or at their limitation to a greater extent than is provided for herein'; Article 53 ECHR: 'Nothing in this Convention shall be construed as limiting or derogating from any of the human rights and fundamental freedoms which may be ensured under the laws of any High Contracting Party or under any other agreement to which it is a party'.

principle, and the positive obligation to take measures to ensure the effective protection thereof,[885] consistent with the international and national standards concerning *non-refoulement*.[886]

d. Interim Conclusions

The interpretation of the *non-refoulement* principle by the ECtHR and the CJEU reveals that the EU legislator has explicitly incorporated the 'rigorous standard' approach adopted by the ECtHR in its case law on *non-refoulement*. More concretely, the EU legislator has explicitly incorporated the positive (procedural and substantive) obligations in secondary legislation, that must be met for the *non-refoulement* principle to be complied with and/or not triggered. On this last point, the EU legislator as affirmed by the CJEU, has set in place a framework to determine when and how a third country may be considered as a *safe* third country, as a result of which the *non-refoulement* principle cannot be considered to apply. Of the utmost importance here, is the fact that (all of) these positive obligations are predominantly, if not exclusively directed at Member States.[887] This is interesting, because by virtue of Article 19 *in juncto* Article 52(3) CFR, the *non-refoulement* principle is also binding on the EU. Of course, the argument can be made that the absence of clarification on the positive and negative obligations on the EU in secondary legislation is informative of the fact that the EU cannot be a duty-bearer of the *non-refoulement* principle, particularly because of the shared nature of competence division in borders, asylum and migration. However, such reasoning presupposes that the EU as an entity separate from the Member States, cannot meaningfully conduct itself politically, legislatively and operationally, in a manner that could detrimentally affect the protection against *refoulement*. Bluntly worded – such reasoning is flawed. As evidenced by the operational measures taken under the *chapeau* of CSDP missions such as Operation Sophia and its successor, Operation Irini, the EU as a sui generis IO *is* meaningfully implicated in measures that have the return of individuals to (potentially) unsafe third countries as an effect. Similarly, instruments under EU law (formal or informal) having legal effects vis-à-vis individuals seeking international protection, may likewise affect the manner in which *non-refoulement* is effectuated. In scenarios where the return of individuals is not the exclusive result of (solitary) Member State action, but rather, the result of operational and/or political action including the EU, the question may be raised how the positive and negative obligations inherent to the *non-refoulement* principle apply to the EU, so as to ensure that its safeguards remain practical and effective, as opposed to theoretical and illusory.

[885] Moreno-Lax n 17 at 395, 421.
[886] Vedsted-Hansen, Bauloz, Hruschka, Lupačová, Sander, Storgaard n 736 at 26.
[887] See for example Articles 35–39 of Section III Asylum Procedures Directive concerning first countries of asylum and (European) safe third countries, which are exclusively directed at Member States, and not the EU.

Figure 3 Concretized Obligations under the non-refoulement principle

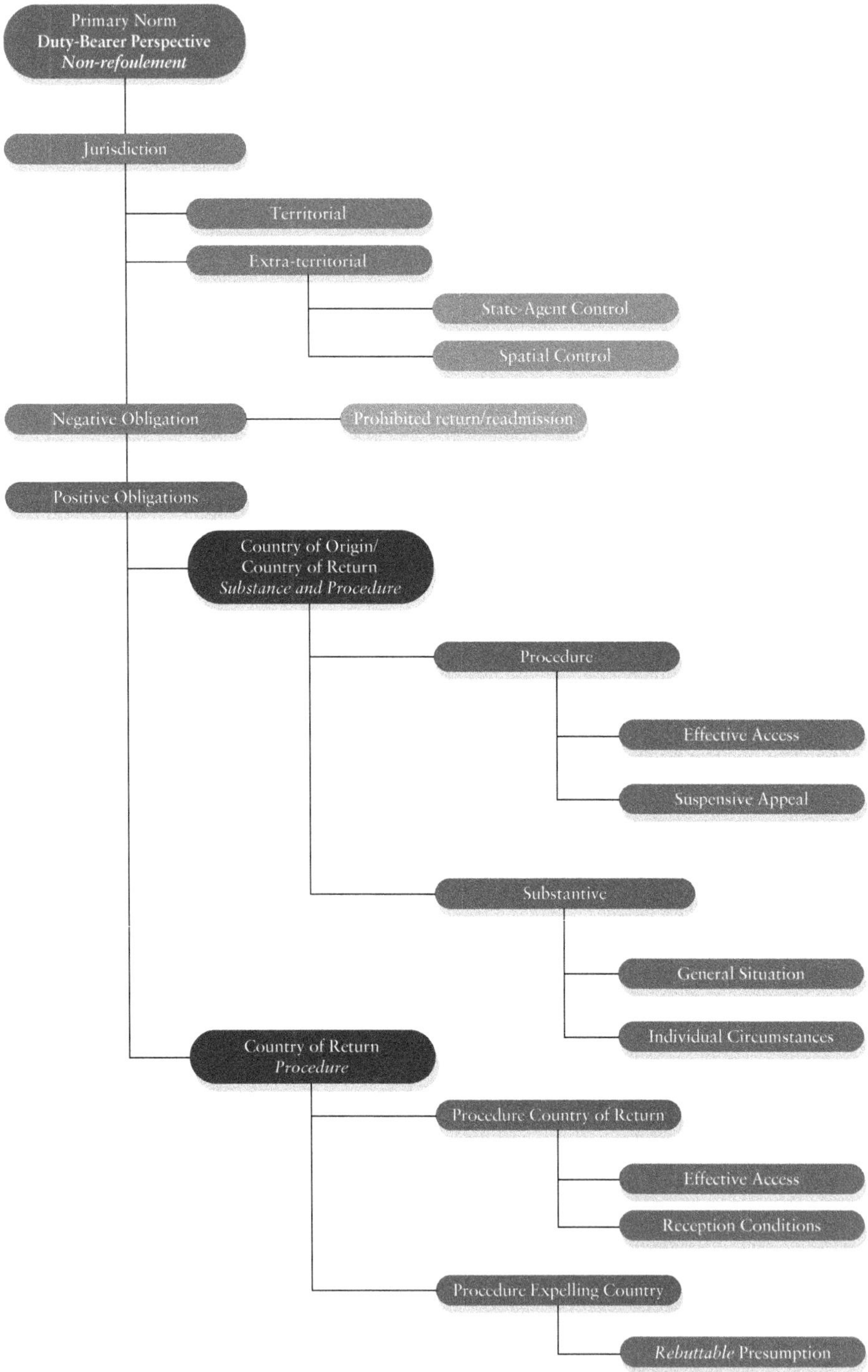

6

Measures in Third Countries

THE FIRST TIER of IBM concerns measures that are taken within and in cooperation with third countries, such as the implementation of a common visa policy.[888] The EU Visa Code defines a 'visa' as an 'authorization issued by a Member State with a view to (a) transit through or an intended stay in the territory of the Member States … (b) transit through the international transit areas of airports of the Member States'.[889] As a pre-border measure of control, visas under EU law fulfil the dual function of the 'facilitating legitimate travel and tackling illegal immigration'.[890] In laymen's terms, visas thus constitute an authorization to enter EU Member State territory obtained by a TCN, *prior to* physical entry to its territory. As a result, the pre-emptive controls of eligibility for entry of TCNs occur first and foremost in the countries of origin and affect *legal* travel to the EU. This perfectly captures the externalisation of IBM, via the 'de-localization of entry checks', which externalizes and shifts the controls for entry, to third countries.[891]

Where does the *non-refoulement* prohibition factor into anticipatory controls in third countries and how could this potentially trigger EU responsibility? These two questions will be addressed in what follows. However, from the onset, what differentiates the discussion on the EU common visa policy, from the other topics under discussion (concerning other tiers of IBM), is that it concerns legislative action by the EU, which is subsequently implemented by the Member States. Recall in this respect that the CJEU has already acknowledged in *Lütticke* that shared responsibility *may* arise where the EU has failed to prevent the unlawful implementation of EU law by Member States, or alternatively, insofar Member States have implemented an unlawful EU legal act, as discussed in *Haegeman* (see Chapter 4). Recalling the scenarios in which responsibility may arise for the EU, the question that must thus be borne in mind throughout this first discussion, is firstly, whether the legislative instruments at the heart of the EU common visa policy constitute unlawful EU legal acts, capable of generating EU responsibility with the ensuing obligation for reparations, or alternatively, whether the unlawful implementation thereof by the Member States has triggered an obligation upon the EU to *prevent* unlawful MS implementation, thus triggering its responsibility under Article 340 TFEU.

888 Recital 11 EBCG Regulation.
889 Regulation (EC) No 810/2009 of the European Parliament and of the Council of 13 July 2009 establishing a Community Code on Visas (Visa Code).
890 Recital 3 Visa Code.
891 Moreno-Lax n 17 at 82.

1. LEGAL FRAMEWORK AND CONTEXT

For the purpose of the present analysis the two most relevant legislative instruments are the Visa Regulation[892] and the Visa Code, which will be dealt with in turn.

The Visa Regulation sets forth the conditions and criteria for the inclusion of third countries on the blacklist (countries from which nationals would have to be in possession of valid visa to travel to the EU) and the white list (countries of which nationals do not have to have a valid visa to travel to the EU).[893] Inclusion on either list requires a case-by-case assessment, mindful of considerations such as illegal (irregular) migration flows, EU relations with the country at stake, economic considerations and public policy and security considerations, to name a few.[894] A recurring and dominant determinant for the inclusion (or exclusion) from either list, was and continues to be the surge of irregular migration stemming from the third state.[895] Simply put, insofar there are risks of surges of irregular migrants from a particular country, such states are typically placed on the blacklist, thus requiring its nationals to obtain visas prior to travel to the EU, as an attempt to *curb* irregular migration.[896] Despite pursuing the objective of legitimate travel and curbing irregular travel, such visa requirements appear to have the inverse effect on the movement of individual TCNs and on respect for *non-refoulement*.[897]

The EU's visa regime adopts the following logic: third states that *do not* give rise to significant irregular migratory flows are typically retained on the white-list or have procured visa liberalisation regimes. Conversely, third states that *do* give rise to irregular migratory flows are typically placed on the blacklist and subjected to visa requirements. Such visa impositions may be relinquished or eased if the

[892] Regulation (EU) 2018/1806 of the European Parliament and of the Council of 14 November 2018 listing the third countries whose nationals must be in possession of visas when crossing the external borders and those whose nationals are exempt from that requirement [2018] OJ L 303/39 (*hereafter* Visa Regulation).

[893] Moreno-Lax n 17 at 89.

[894] ibid; Steve Peers, *EU Justice and Home Affairs Law: Volume I: EU Immigration and Asylum Law* (Oxford, Oxford University Press, 2016) 194–195.

[895] This is likewise evidenced by the suspension mechanism enshrined in Article 8 of the Visa Regulation. This provision allows for visa liberalization arrangements to be temporarily suspended, inter alia due to surges in irregular migratory flows (see below).

[896] Recital 3 Visa Code. Peers nuances this slightly by holding that the common EU visa policy has undergone a wave of liberalization. Accordingly, the EU has been more willing to waive visa requirements vis-à-vis neighbouring countries, despite migratory pressures stemming therefrom, in the interest of safeguarding strong relations with its neighbours. Such visa liberalization arrangements were established with Moldova, Ukraine and Georgia. Peers n 894 at 194; European Commission, 'Visa Liberalisation with Moldova, Ukraine and Georgia' (*Migration and Home Affairs*) ec.europa.eu/home-affairs/what-we-do/policies/international-affairs/eastern-partnership/visa-liberalisation-moldova-ukraine-and-georgia_en.

[897] The limited efficacy of the EU visa arrangements from an individual TCN perspective does not preclude its efficacy of visa arrangements as a powerful tool in bilateral arrangements of the EU with its neighbours and third states more generally. See on the topic: Peter Van Elsuwege and Zvezda Vankova, 'Migration and Mobility in the EU's Eastern Neighborhood: Mapping Out the Legal and Political Framework' in Francesca Ippolito and Federico Casolari (eds), *Bilateral Relations in the Mediterranean* (Cheltenham, Edward Elgar Publishing, 2020) 176–177.

third state facilitates readmission of its nationals and TCNs that have arrived in Europe irregularly.[898] On first reading, the EU's visa regime appears to benefit those states that facilitate regular travel, while imposing a carrot and stick approach for those third states that have more difficulties in managing migratory flows from their borders. But does this really address the question of irregular migratory flows and how does this relate to *non-refoulement*?

Recital 18 of the Visa Regulation holds that significant increases of irregular migratory flows and/or inefficient application of readmission arrangements will result in a (temporary) suspension of the visa waiver.[899] Third states that generate larger migratory flows, including individuals seeking international protection, are thus subjected to visa requirements. But how does this impact TCNs that are seeking international protection in the EU? Individuals fleeing their country of origin, or a third country, typically cannot avail themselves to visa procedures for a plethora of reasons, which is aggravated by the difficulties experienced by TCN protection-seekers in effectively gaining *access* (legally and practically) to visa procedures. Counterintuitively, and mindful of the fact that one of the reasons for visa requirements is to curb irregular migratory flows, there are only generic references and fleeting references to international human rights law and refugee law in the Visa Regulation. The Visa Code thus imposes visa restrictions on regular travel, while confining and directing TCN protection-seekers precisely to the irregular movement that the Visa Code purports to combat, without any clarifications on how the human rights of TCN protection-seekers are to be safeguarded, under the visa arrangements. This externalises the burden of border management to the third state. By cooperating on readmission and tightening border controls in third countries, visa restrictions may be lifted, albeit to the detriment of TCNs looking for international protection and in favour of a policy of consensual containment. Put bluntly, the visa regime works for those that are not in need of international protection and condemns those that are in need of international protection.

In addition to the Visa Regulation, the Visa Code sets out harmonized rules on the visa issuing procedure.[900] The Visa Code harmonizes the rules and procedure to obtain short-term visas for the purpose of 'transit through or intended stays in the territory of the Member States not exceeding three months in any six-month period',[901] and must be read in tandem with the aforementioned Visa Regulation.[902] Again, only generic references to human rights adherence surface, without explicit

[898] Salvatore Fabio Nicolosi, 'Refashioning the EU Visa Policy: A New Turn of the Screw to Cooperation on Readmission and to Discrimination?' (2020) 22 *European Journal of Migration* 467–491.

[899] Recital 18, 19, 23, as well as Article 8(2) Visa Regulation. Notably, recital 28 of that same regulation, requires the European Commission to take into account 'the situation of human rights in that third country and the possible consequences of the visa exemption for that situation'. However, this same obligation is not reiterated in the operative provisions concerning the suspension mechanism.

[900] Recital 2 and 3 Visa Code.

[901] Article 1(1) Visa Code.

[902] Recital 25 and Article 1(2) Visa Code.

safeguards for TCN protection-seekers.[903] As Moreno-Lax points out, this is indicative of the fact that no tailored provisions exist for TCN protection-seekers, who are in fact subsumed in the more general framework for the obtaining of visas for the purpose of regular travel.[904]

Although there is no explicit reference to international protection-seekers in the Visa Code, two provisions could theoretically be relevant: Article 19(4)[905] and Article 25 Visa Code both refer to humanitarian grounds and international obligations of Member States in applying the Visa Code. On the basis of these provisions it was considered by some that Article 25 Visa Code was instilled as a safety valve for international protection-seekers.[906] This provision allows national authorities, by way of derogation from the general framework under the Visa Code, to provide a visa to a TCN protection-seeker, 'a) when the Member State concerned considers it necessary on humanitarian grounds, for reasons of national interest or because of international obligations'. When a visa would otherwise be refused on the grounds of Article 32 Visa Code, Article 25 Visa Code thus authorizes Member States to provide a visa to comply with international obligations and/or humanitarian grounds.

Two inconsistencies arise regarding the application of Article 25 Visa Code. Firstly, the provision is terminologically incoherent and potentially contradictory, as on the one hand the Member States have discretionary power to provide limited territorial visas (LTV's) based upon Article 25 Visa Code, while on the other hand, Article 25 Visa Code explicitly refers to *international obligations* (such as the *non-refoulement* principle) rebutting any notion of discretion.

Secondly, this terminological inconsistency is aggravated by Article 19 Visa Code, concerning the *admissibility* of a visa application. Article 19(4) Visa Code holds that, 'By way of derogation, an application that does not meet the requirements set out in paragraph 1 may be considered admissible on humanitarian grounds or for reasons of national interest'. It is notable that Article 19 Visa Code omits any reference to the Article 25 Visa Code, which further compounds the legal obscurity for international protection-seekers. Following a textual interpretation of the Visa Code, it is unclear whether the admissibility requirements of Article 19 Visa Code can be considered met in case of *non-refoulement*-related international obligations. Crucially, a decision on admissibility, whereby an application for a(n) (LTV) visa is refused, cannot be contested and is therefore not legally reviewable.[907] The right to appeal a decision on the *merits* is provided in Article 32(3) Visa Code. The right to an appeal against an *admissibility* decision, however, is not provided by the Visa Code.

[903] Recital 29 Visa Code requires generic compliance with fundamental rights. Article 13 Visa Code requires the obtaining of biometric identification parameters to happen in compliance with human rights law.

[904] Moreno-Lax n 17 at 95, 100, 106. See more generally on the imbalance of the sought-after objective of curbing irregular migration in the EU's eastern neighbourhood and the absence of protection for TCN protection-seekers: Van Elsuwege and Vankova n 897 at 173, 181.

[905] Article 19(4) Visa Code: '4. By way of derogation, an application that does not meet the requirements set out in paragraph 1 may be considered admissible on humanitarian grounds or for reasons of national interest'.

[906] Peers n 894 at 179.

[907] Annalisa Meloni, 'Visa Code Regulation (EC) No 810/2009)' in Kay Hailbronner and Daniel Thym (eds), *EU Immigration and Asylum Law – A Commentary* (Munich, Verlag CH Beck, 2016) 152.

The European Commission notes in this respect that a right to appeal would not necessarily achieve anything, as a negative admissibility decision does not preclude future visa applications.[908] Yet a crucial nuance is missed here. It is precisely the vulnerable status of TCN protection-seekers, which may obstruct compliance with the admissibility requirements. These requirements include presenting a completed application form in accordance with Article 11 and Annex 1 Visa Code, which requires information that international protection-seekers – *because* of their vulnerable status – will not be able to provide.[909] For example, the Annex 1 application form requires details including the address of the place of accommodation in the Member State, employer details, identification of the type of travel documents, and dates of intended departure. Yet, individuals seeking to escape particular forms of ill-treatment warranting international protection status, will typically not have such information readily available, which may reflect negatively on the obligatory application form for the purpose of the *admissibility* of the application, against which no appeal is possible. It is thus argued that the generic use of this application form, in effect, renders it more difficult for protection-seekers to effectively leave the third country in a regular manner, for the purpose of asking international protection.

Hence, the limited provisions which could be invoked by TCN protection-seekers concerning the *merits* of a visa application (Article 25 and 32 Visa Code) and the *admissibility* of a visa application (Article 19 Visa Code) on account of international obligations, are formulated in such a manner that the scope is unclear, its legal enforceability limited, and a textual interpretation yields legal inconsistencies and contradictions.

Simply put, to curb irregular migration flows from the most affected countries, visa requirements were instilled, albeit without acknowledging the vulnerable status of TCN protection-seekers. In both the admissibility and the merits phases of the visa application process, TCN protection-seekers are confronted with practical (time constraints, accessibility to consulates and embassies), procedural[910] and legal (terminological inconsistences and a high threshold for conditionality) difficulties, which obstruct the legitimate travel envisaged by the common EU visa policy. As a result, the envisaged objective of curbing irregular migration is not met – quite the contrary. TCN protection-seekers are left the choice between an impractical system which fails to accommodate their particularly vulnerable status and prevents access to international protection procedures, and the option of irregular movement. In other words, the common visa policy appears to operate (as concerns TCN protection-seekers) as a decoy vis-à-vis third states, purportedly to curb irregular migration, which it does not actually address, and conversely prompts further irregular travel of TCN protection-seekers. In turn, visa formalities are … 'remedied' through readmission agreements with third states aimed at (semi-) automated returns of TCN protection-seekers, in return for waiving or the decreasing of visa restrictions.[911]

[908] ibid.

[909] The application form in Annex 1, requires details on the duration of the stay, envisaged return, accommodation details etc – details that TCN protection-seekers on account of their status and the nature of their anticipated stay, will typically not be able to provide.

[910] See for example Article 14 Visa Code on the (non-exhaustive list of) required supporting documents for a visa application.

[911] See for example: Van Elsuwege and Vankova n 897 at 167–169.

This brings to the fore the central question of this chapter: how does the common EU policy on visas relate to the principle of *non-refoulement*? One of the most illustrative cases on this point concerns the *X and X v Belgium* judgment,[912] and will be the point of study *in casu*, as it perfectly illustrates the issues arising for the protection of *non-refoulement* when applying the Visa Code.

2. TRACING HUMAN RIGHTS IMPLICATIONS

The infamous *X and X* case by the CJEU, concerned the application for short stay visa with limited territorial validity[913] (LTV) on the basis of the Visa Code. The Applicant, a father of three minors, who had been documented as having been tortured, travelled from Aleppo, Syria to Beirut, Lebanon in order to request an LTV for himself and his family members upon arrival at the Belgian consulate. The objective of this visa was to travel to Belgium, where, upon arrival he intended to ask for international protection. The request for an LTV was based upon Article 25 Visa Code, which again, holds that:

> A visa with limited territorial validity shall be issued exceptionally, in the following cases: (1) (a) when the Member State concerned considers it necessary on humanitarian grounds, for reasons of national interest or because of international obligations

This request was refused on several occasions and ultimately resulted in a preliminary reference procedure before the CJEU. The questions asked by the Belgian judiciary to the CJEU were three-fold and asked in essence: whether providing the LTV based upon Article 25 Visa Code *de facto* amounts to requesting a long-term visa (which currently is not governed by the Visa Code or EU law generally and remains a Member State competence) (1);[914] what the scope of the reference to 'international obligations' is under Article 25 Visa Code and whether this includes references to the CFR, the ECHR and the Refugee Convention (2);[915] and what the margin of discretion is for the Member States under Article 25 Visa Code (3).[916]

Unlike Advocate General Mengozzi, who opined that there *was* an obligation upon the Belgian state pursuant to Article 25 Visa Code, to deliver an LTV to the Applicants,[917] the CJEU concluded that it could not rule on the matter. Despite the fact that the applicability of the Visa Code to the proceedings was not contested by the parties, the CJEU found that the Visa Code solely foresees in the delivery of short-term visas not exceeding the duration of three months. In a burst of fictitious judicial ingenuity, the CJEU concluded that based upon the facts, it appeared that the Applicants were attempting to obtain a long-term visa by requesting an LTV under

[912] Highly analogous proceedings were also brought before the ECtHR. ECtHR 2020, *M.N. and others v Belgium* n 34.

[913] As opposed to a 'universal' visa which would provide access to the entire territory of the European Union. LTVs principally only provide access to the Member State which granted the visa.

[914] CJEU *X and X* n 59 at §44–45.

[915] ibid §28.

[916] ibid §28.

[917] Opinion of Advocate General Mengozzi of 7 February 2017, *X and X v Belgium*, C-638/16PPU, ECLI:EU:C:2017:93.

the Visa Code. The CJEU held that the objective of the Applicants was thus *not* to ask for a short-term LTV visa as governed by EU law and held that as such questions were governed by national law, the provisions of the Charter did not apply,[918] and the CJEU could not provide any additional interpretation on the matter.[919] Absent having taken an irregular route to Europe, it is unclear what other – if any – regular routes were available to the Applicants in seeking international protection. What is then the rationale behind Article 25 Visa Code, if not to ensure that potential victims of severe ill-treatment are not subjected to measures of *non-entrée* – measures which fall squarely within the scope of the *non-refoulement* principle? Is the objective of Article 25 Visa Code not precisely to prevent turning individuals away that are at risk of significant ill-treatment upon return and provide them instead with legal pathways to apply for international protection? It is highly questionable why this provision with its reference to international obligations, and the generic underpinnings of requisite respect for fundamental rights, was inserted at all, if not to provide access to asylum proceedings in a legal manner. Instead, absent any legal means to reach EU territory, this ruling and application of the Visa Code promotes the inverse of its objective to facilitate legal migration and prevent irregular migration. Rather, it facilitates recourse to irregular mobility. How then does this translate into responsibility, if at all?

In casu, departing from the *X and X* case, there is thus a binding interpretation by an EU institution (the CJEU) of a purportedly lawful EU legal instrument (the Visa Code), implemented by a Member State (Belgium) resulting in human rights harms in substance and which has not yet previously been assessed by either the CJEU or the ECtHR. This makes for a particularly difficult set of circumstances to determine whether the EU can be held responsible for its contribution therein, particularly in line with the fact that the instructions came on behalf of the CJEU.

3. RESPONSIBILITY IN PRACTICE

On a preliminary note, it is important to underscore that with its preliminary ruling in *X and X* the CJEU is not condoning the application of its interpretation in the relevant domestic proceeding in a manner that violates international or EU law. The CJEU is decidedly not saying that the Belgian judiciary and relevant authorities should conduct themselves in a manner that violates the *non-refoulement* principle. Yet, at the same time, the CJEU's reticence in engaging in a merit-based assessment of the meaning and scope of Article 25 Visa Code gives rise to a set of circumstances that permits the Belgian authorities to engage in a measure of *non-entrée*, notwithstanding the established personalized risk of ill-treatment of the applicant. And while the Applicant is free to file a new application against the Belgian authorities, including before the ECtHR against Belgium's implementation of this interpretation, this is where the relationship between the ECtHR and the CJEU (as discussed in Chapter 3) gains relevance. *In casu*, Belgium retains discretion in how the interpretation by the CJEU is

[918] CJEU *X and X* n 59 at §45.
[919] ibid §42–47.

implemented. In fact, the CJEU has noted that the matter falls squarely within Belgian competence and thus cannot be tested against the EU's human rights regime. This in turn, means that the 'equivalent protection' doctrine is unlikely to be invoked in the present case. This does not mean, however, that the ECtHR or domestic courts would not be inspired or impacted by the CJEU's ruling in the *X and X* case – quite the contrary. While the degree to which the ECtHR is impacted by the CJEU is hard ascertain in absolute and definitive terms, it is notable that in a subsequent proceeding before the ECtHR on quasi-identical facts, the ECtHR too declined to rule on the merits of the question, relegating the question back towards the Member State authorities.[920] Unlike the CJEU, the ECtHR declined to rule on the merits on the basis of (the lack of extra-territorial) jurisdiction. The implication of a combined reading of *X and X v Belgium* and the subsequent case of *MN and others v Belgium* is thus that there are no regular pathways available to the individuals concerned from abroad, to request international protection as protected under either regime, which essentially condemns the applicants in both cases to irregular pathways in their search for international protection. With the CJEU refusing to interpret the scope of Article 25 Visa Code which appears to be intended to govern the aforementioned set of facts, and the ECtHR adopting its cautious and conciliatory approach to questions of borders, asylum and migration, in which it explicitly cites the *X and X* ruling,[921] the CJEU's contribution in reducing available regular routes for international protection, in the reduction of irregular migration and in the ossification of measures of *non-entrée* under EU law, is clear.

a. The EU *Lex Specialis* Applied

i. Independent Responsibility

– Causal Conduct Attributable to the EU

While it is clear that the CJEU judgment in *X and X* is attributable to the CJEU and the CJEU alone, and the determination of attribution is not problematic in this particular case, the condition of causation is. Couched in 'interpretative' terms (as the CJEU cannot *apply* its interpretation to the facts giving rise to the preliminary reference proceeding, and this is left instead, to national authorities), the CJEU preliminary ruling requires implementation by the Member States. Hence, an intervening act is required (by the national authorities), breaking the chain of causation between the CJEU decision and the harms incurred by the Applicants and making the connection between the harm and the contribution by the CJEU too remote. Presupposing thus, that jurisdiction would be established, from the onset one of the cumulative conditions for a successful action for damages will not be met.

[920] The ECtHR did not rule on the matter on account of the fact that extra-territorial jurisdiction could not be considered established in this particular case, entailing that here too there was no assessment of the merits of the claim. Essentially this closed any access to regular routes for the purpose of obtaining international protection, thereby prompting the individuals concerned to find alternative (irregular) modes of travel in search of international protection. ECtHR 2020, *M.N. and others v* Belgium n 34 at §112.

[921] ibid §124.

– Sufficiently Serious Unlawful Conduct

In the (unlikely) assumption that the General Court would nevertheless establish jurisdiction, attribution and causation, it would then have to be demonstrated that the conduct of the EU institution (*in casu* the preliminary ruling) constituted a 'sufficiently serious breach of an EU obligation'. This condition is assessed not only by reference to the retained discretion by the CJEU *in casu*, but likewise by reference to whether the conduct was grave and manifest as determined *inter alia* by the complexity of the case, previous judicial precedent, and the inexcusability of the unlawful conduct.

Leaving any subjective assessments of the ruling in *X and X* aside, the complexity of the question of responsibility is unprecedented. With its preliminary ruling, the CJEU essentially reverts the question back to the Member State, by refusing to engage in an interpretation of Article 25 Visa Code. As the Member State had been clear in its refusal to provide access to Belgian territory through a humanitarian visa, which was furthermore consolidated by the ECtHR's finding in *MN and others v Belgium*, the Applicants were subjected to a measure of *non-entrée* and condemned to find alternative (irregular) routes to ask for international protection.

Any action for damage alleging the EU's responsibility for its contribution to the refused humanitarian visa before the EU's General Court, would require assessing the CJEU's interpretation of a highly contentious legal question[922] to determine whether the latter is legally responsible or complicit in the experienced harms: this would have been a first of its kind and has simply not yet occurred in IBM.[923] Furthermore, as the preliminary ruling is arguably delivered as an interpretation and does not actually purport to apply unlawful human rights interpretations to the case at hand, it does not seem likely that the condition of 'grave and manifest' will be met.

– Interim Conclusions

Bearing the foregoing in mind, and the fact that the CJEU has already provided an interpretation on the facts at stake, it is unlikely that the General Court would openly hold the CJEU responsible for its contribution to preventing access to international protection procedures vis-à-vis the Applicants, thereby also being at odds with the finding in *MN and others v Belgium* before the ECtHR. While such open disagreement is not excluded, it would add tension to an already politically heated area of EU law, thereby diminishing the chances of individuals obtaining damages despite being deprived of the essence of the *non-refoulement* obligation, by being refused legal access to international protection proceedings.

[922] There were 16 intervening Member States in the *X and X* procedure.

[923] Such procedures have occurred within the realm of competition law, whereby the European Union, represented by the Court of Justice of the European Union was ordered to pay EUR 588 769.18 in damages to Kendrion NV for failure to respect the obligation to adjudicate within a reasonable time. CJEU (General Court) Judgment of 1 February 2017, *Kendrion NV v European Union*, T-479/14, ECLI:EU:T:2017:48. In light of the shared nature of the competence *in casu* however, it seems less likely that such actions would be successful.

ii. Shared Responsibility

Recalling the typology identified by Craig and de Búrca (see Chapter 4), the case of the humanitarian visas can be brought under the scenario of a purportedly lawful EU act (the Visa Code) which is implemented in violation of the *non-refoulement* obligation that is legally binding upon the Member States and the EU alike, following a binding interpretation by the CJEU in the preliminary reference proceeding.

In light of the limited discretion that Member States have in disregarding the interpretations provided by a preliminary reference proceeding, and the duty of loyal cooperation enshrined in Article 4(3) TEU, it needs no further explanation that Member States are quite constrained in their discretion to disregard the interpretation afforded by the CJEU in the explanation of Article 25 Visa Code and its implications more generally. The case of *Kampffmeyer* acknowledges that where formal EU measures are adopted, authorizing unlawful (human rights) conduct, this may trigger responsibility. However, crucially, this only (implicitly) provides for residual responsibility for the EU's institutions and does not elaborate upon how the responsibility would arise. The latter entails that recourse must be had back to the general conditions for responsibility to arise under the action for damages of Article 340 TFEU. In other words, the absence of additional provisions on shared responsibility, entail that a successful action for damages will only arise when insofar the conditions of attribution, causation, and a sufficiently serious unlawful act or omission violating a rule of law that was intended to confer rights upon the individual is demonstrated. As has just been demonstrated, the success of an application as such, relies wholeheartedly on the willingness of the General Court, to set a precedent which would ultimately result in open conflict with the CJEU. Though this is not *a priori* excluded, it is likely to be avoided in such highly politicized cases. Finally, it is crucial in this respect that the burden and extremely high threshold of proof is placed with the Applicant.

Turning then to the concrete examples (see above), where shared responsibility has been implicitly and explicitly addressed by international adjudicatory mechanisms and the CJEU, the Applicant is none the wiser. The examples demonstrate that depending on the substantive area of law, the application of the competence model of attribution will differ based on the exercise of the competence, and the margin of discretion retained by the parties. Furthermore, at times declarations of competence have been relied upon to determine attribution, which as noted by Heliskoski fails to meet the objective of clear delineations of competence and thus attribution. Finally, use is increasingly made of internal mechanisms to determine what actor in a multi-actor situation including the Member States and the EU, is responsible for unlawful conduct. Arguably, this has already occurred *in casu*, as (1) the CJEU held that the matter falls entirely within national law and (2) the idea that the CJEU was complicit in the facilitating of a violation of the *non-refoulement* principle has not yet been addressed, thus sidestepping any assessment of whether there was any unlawful conduct.

iii. Interim Conclusions on the EU Lex Specialis *Applied*

Bearing these observations in mind, it appears unlikely that the *lex specialis* both for independent and shared responsibility *in casu* provides for any meaningful legal review and thus the responsibility of the EU, capable of meeting the standards of legal certainty, effectiveness, and legality, despite the fact that the *effect* of the measure results in a violation of the positive obligations of the *non-refoulement* principle under international and EU law *non-refoulement*.

b. The *Lex Generalis* Applied

i. Independent Responsibility

– Attribution

In casu the conduct under analysis is the preliminary ruling by the CJEU which facilitated the continued refusal by the Belgian (and other Member States) authorities to provide a humanitarian visa to the Applicants for the purpose of then requesting international protection upon arrival in Belgium. For the purpose of attribution under the *lex generalis* regime, this brings the conduct of the CJEU under Article 6 ARIO. Article 6 ARIO holds that the conduct of organs and/or agents of the IO will be attributed to the latter. In accordance with Article 13(1) TEU the CJEU does in fact constitute one of the organs of the EU embedded in its architectural framework. Hence, at least as concerns attribution for independent responsibility under the ARIO, no significant obstacles exist for the purpose of establishing responsibility.

– Internationally Wrongful Act

Unlike the *lex specialis* regime, internationally wrongful conduct is not conditioned on more concrete parameters such as whether the violation is sufficiently serious. Moreover, the notion of causality – though implicit throughout the entirety of the ARIO (see above), does not prescribe a particular test. In fact, the 2020 Guidelines on Shared Responsibility affirm that no definitive test of causality exists in international law.[924] Arguably, this thus provides more potential for the Applicants to assert the international responsibility of the EU under the *lex generalis* regime.

Yet, this brings the analysis back to one of the most crucial points under discussion – can it definitively be determined by way of positive law, that the CJEU erred in law and thus committed or contributed to unlawful human rights conduct? Can it be held that its ruling in the preliminary reference proceeding violated a concrete obligation under the primary norm of *non-refoulement*? Much of this depends on how *non-refoulement* is operationalized. *Non-refoulement* is considered on the one hand, by the effect of a given line of conduct on an individual TCN. On the other hand, *non-refoulement* (and potential violations thereof) is also considered on account of the concrete positive and negative obligations it gives rise to for its duty bearers.

Figure 4 Duty-bearer and TCN perspectives on *non-refoulement* (De Coninck)

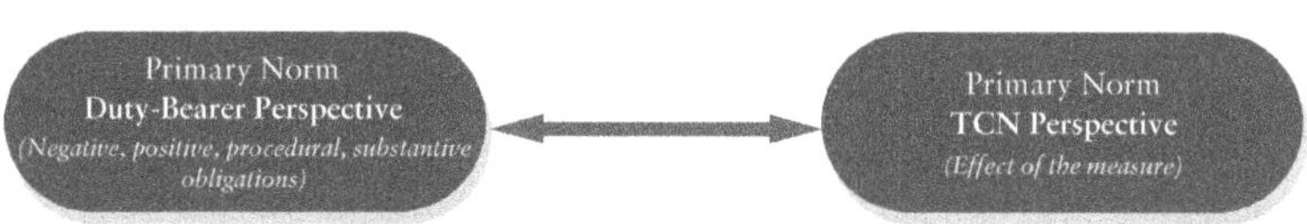

[924] Nollkaemper, d'Aspremont, Ahlborn, Boutin, Nedeski and Plakokefalos n 26 at 23 §5.

When considering *non-refoulement* from the perspective of the individual, the effect of the measure of *non-entrée* may be considered to constitute a violation of the *non-refoulement* principle, as the Applicants are prevented from accessing international protection proceedings and required to return to their country of origin where they are at risk of being subjected to ill treatment (torture) reaching the required threshold to trigger the *non-refoulement* principle. It is crucial in this respect that neither the CJEU nor the ECtHR ruled on the substance or merit of the *non-refoulement* claim. If one looks at the requirements and thresholds required for *non-refoulement* to be triggered, the Applicants (on substance) had a very compelling claim for international protection: the father had already been subject to torture (individualized circumstance)[925] which was uncontested throughout the proceedings. Furthermore, the Applicants were in a situation of indiscriminate violence threatening their lives due to an internal armed conflict, which is governed by subsidiary protection under Article 15 EU Qualification Directive.

Yet, when looking at the question of responsibility from the perspective of the duty-bearer, it is difficult under positive law to construe a human rights obligation binding on the CJEU which it violated by omitting to intervene on behalf of the Applicants. Indeed, while the essence of the *non-refoulement* principle was disregarded and resulted in experienced harm for the Applicant – which in part can be attributed to the fact that the CJEU acquiesced to the decisions by the Belgian authorities – it is implausible that the CJEU was bound by a legally enforceable human rights obligation to act differently in the present circumstances. Absent any pre-determined concrete (positive) due diligence obligation in that respect, the EU *in casu* cannot incur any responsibility for its contribution through acquiescence, notwithstanding the fact that the prohibition of *non-refoulement* did in fact become theoretical and illusory for the individuals concerned.

ii. Shared Responsibility

Finally, mindful of the fact that the current scenario encompasses a dynamic between both the CJEU and the Member States, the provisions in the *lex generalis* on shared responsibility may prove to be of some use. Although the CJEU did not rule on the substance of the claim, thereby precluding the conclusion that *on substance* it followed the Belgian authorities in their assessment, the mere fact that the CJEU read Article 25 Visa Code, as not requiring a humanitarian LTV to be accorded when there is a significant risk of ill-treatment upon return and held that the matter fell within domestic purview even though the parties agreed that the question was governed by Art. 25 Visa code, may be construed as 'aid and assistance' in line with Article 14 ARIO. It seems unlikely that the acquiescence by the CJEU could be construed as direction and control (Article 15 ARIO), coercion (Article 16 ARIO) or circumvention (Article 17 ARIO) for the purpose of shared responsibility as the Member States were left with sufficient discretionary powers to rule differently on the LTV request by the Applicants. Consequently, it cannot be held that the CJEU was conducting

[925] CJEU *X and X n* 59 §19–28.

itself with 'knowing intent' to attempt to procure a breach of the *non-refoulement* principle, by the Belgian state.

Despite the theoretical availability of Article 14 ARIO, the Applicants would be immediately confronted with the opposability condition, as well as the condition of knowing intent – which seem near impossible to meet. On the one hand, the opposability requirement cannot be met insofar there is no clarity as to the scope of the opposability criterion: does it suffice that the entities (Member State and the organization) are bound by the same human rights commitment, or must they be bound by the same concretized obligations (positive and negative)? If the latter is the case, the opposability condition is even more difficult to meet as there is simply no *ex-ante* determination of how the concrete obligations of the *non-refoulement* principle translate into actionable claims vis-à-vis the EU. Furthermore, absent any determination of *how* the condition of knowing intent is to be determined, it is again, left to the court to decide in an *ex post facto* manner without any guidance, whether the CJEU and by extension the EU, acted in a manner to deliberately facilitate unlawful human rights conduct by the Belgium authorities.

c. Interim Conclusions on Responsibility for Measures in Third Countries

What the foregoing demonstrates, is that the attempt to make use of existing and lawful instruments to facilitate legal access to international protection procedures, was struck down. This in and of itself drives a stake in the heart of the objective of the Visa Code *tout court*. Side-stepping the security-centric and externalisation approach that lies at the heart of the EU common policy on visas, how can the objective of facilitating legal migration, and reducing irregular migration be met, when one of the united ways in which TCN protection-seekers may obtain any *legal* access to international protection procedures are obstructed? Already, TCN protection-seekers, vulnerable on account of their particular status, are subsumed by the larger group of TCN's under the EU visa regime generally. By depriving them of the effectiveness of the sole procedural provision in the Visa Code – Article 25 on humanitarian LTVs – the individuals concerned arguably are pushed into seeking irregular forms of entry to gain access to international protection proceedings. Moreno-Lax captures this perfectly by holding that:

> This tendency to generically assimilate protection seekers to the wider category of migrants, creating then pseudo-exceptions, appealing to fundamental rights safeguards in general but without providing detailed guarantees, is a pattern repeated in other common rules regarding visa requirements and issuing condition.[926]

In short, there are EU legislative instruments for the purpose of authorizing entry and stay in EU Member States for TCNs, with no procedural or substantive effective safeguards for TCN protection-seekers, thereby hampering access to legal pathways for international application proceedings. This is compounded by the fact that the

[926] Moreno-Lax n 17 at 87.

CJEU has now provided a precedent, which squarely places the responsibility for compliance with *non-refoulement* in the hands of the Member States, providing them with ample discretion to refuse LTVs requested on the basis of international obligations. One may then ask how this shifting of responsibility is reconcilable with the overarching duty to respect the *non-refoulement* prohibition entrenched not only in the CFR, but likewise recognised as customary international law, and arguably has attained the status of *jus cogens*. Despite the principled application of the norm *in casu* and the (contested) involvement of the EU by virtue of the Visa Code full of inherent inconsistencies and the CJEU furthermore compounding those inconsistencies, neither the *lex specialis* nor the *lex generalis* regime provide plausible avenues of legal recourse that would be effective in identifying the responsibility of the latter.

7

Operational Cooperation with Third Countries

THE SECOND ILLUSTRATION concerns recently terminated EU naval operation EUNAVFOR MED Operation Sophia aimed at curbing irregular migratory flows and bringing a halt to human trafficking and smuggling.[927] The interrelated questions of (lacking) effective access to remedies for TCNs and the extent to which the EU as an actor can be held responsible for unlawful human rights conduct stemming from such CFSP/CSDP military operations, have largely remained underexplored. Although there have been cases before the CJEU concerning the first EU naval mission – EUNAVFOR Somalia Operation Atalanta (Operation Atalanta) – these cases did not concern an application for damages on account of unlawful human rights conduct.[928] Conversely, Operation Sophia sparked (much) controversy due to its human rights implications on individual TCNs, yet surprisingly has not given rise to any meaningful legal review concerning the damage resulting therefrom.[929] These allegations prompt an inquiry into the procedural and substantive obstacles that arise for individuals seeking (legal) redress flowing from the Operation. Identifying these obstacles will help determine the degree to which a legal responsibility gap tarnishes CSDP military missions for complicity in human rights harms.[930]

[927] Operation Sophia was recently terminated in its entirety. Its tasks have been incorporated in CSDP mission EUNAVFOR MED Operation Irini (Operation Irini). This new mission has as the objective the implementation of the UN arms embargo on Libya. Additionally, it has taken over the former Operation Sophia tasks of conducting information gathering and aerial surveillance to control irregular migratory flows and the countering of human smuggling and trafficking in the area. Hence, the considerations on aerial surveillance and resulting de facto push- and pull-backs, similarly apply to Operation Irini. Council of the European Union Council Decision (CFSP) 2020/472 of 31 March 2020 on a European Union Military Operation in the Mediterranean (EUNAVFOR Med Irini) [2020] OJ L101/4.

[928] CJEU Judgment of 24 June 2014, *European Parliament v Council*, C-658/11, ECLI:EU:C:2014:2025 (*Mauritius*). Advocate General Hogan has posited in his recent opinion in *Bank Refah Kargaran v Council* that an action of damages may be possible against CFSP-mandated restrictive measures taken on the basis of Article 215 TFEU, but this consideration is currently limited to restrictive measures referenced in Article 275(2) TFEU. Opinion of Advocate General Hogan of 28 May 2020, *Bank Refah Kargaran v Council*, C-134/19P, ECLI:EU:C:2020:396, §63.

[929] The limited case law precedent may be attributed to the fact that use is made of the Athena mechanism (which has individual legal personality) and/or (amicable) alternative dispute mechanisms. See on the topic: Heliskoski n 380 at 136–142.

[930] CJEU Judgment of 23 April 1986, *Les Verts*, C-294/83, ECLI:EU:C:1986:166, §23–24.

After briefly recalling Operation Sophia's mandate, the objectives, its legal peculiarities and its command-and-control structures, the focus of this chapter will shift to the human rights concerns that have arisen within the context of the Operation, with a particular focus on the use of aerial intelligence-gathering which facilitate *de facto* push-backs in the Mediterranean. The section subsequently applies the EU's Human Rights Responsibility Regime to EU conduct stemming from Operation Sophia highlighting in particular, the procedural and substantive pitfalls that hamper access to legal review on an international level (*lex generalis*) and on an EU level (*lex specialis*). It is crucial to recall that the CJEU in matters concerning the EU's Common Foreign and Security Policy - which includes its Common Security and Defence Policy - has very limited adjudicatory jurisdiction. The following analysis nevertheless engages in a substantive application of the EU's Human Rights Regime mindful of this limited jurisdiction.

1. MANDATE, OBJECTIVES, LEGAL FRAMEWORK AND COMMAND STRUCTURES

Operation Sophia was the second naval operation of its kind and pursued the dismantling and disruption of the business model of smuggling and trafficking of TCNs across the Mediterranean.[931] Enacted under the EU's Common Security and Defence Policy (CSDP), Operation Sophia fits neatly within the second tier of the 'four-tier access control model' of IBM, due to its cooperation with Libyan authorities.[932] Such cooperation consisted of training of the Libyan Coast Guard (LYCG), and importantly, through the transmission of location-data of distressed vessels obtained through aerial surveillance in the Mediterranean to the LYCG. By transmitting location-data of distressed vessels to the LYCG, Operation Sophia contributed to push- and pull-backs effectuated by the LYCG.

Operation Sophia was launched with the prevailing objective of the 'disruption of the business model of human smuggling and trafficking networks in the Southern Central Mediterranean …'[933] in an attempt to securitize the external EU border and save lives at sea.[934] To achieve its objectives, the mission was structured in three different phases.[935] The first phase was limited to detection and monitoring of migration networks by patrolling and information-gathering on high seas.[936] Phase two not only permitted 'boarding, search, seizure and diversion on … of vessels suspected of being

[931] See Recitals 2, 5, 7, 8, 9 and Article 1 Council Decision 2015/778.

[932] Moreno-Lax n 17 at 27–41.

[933] Council Decision 2015/778 and Council Decision 2015/972.

[934] Eugenio Cusumano, 'Migrant Rescue as Organized Hypocrisy: EU Maritime Missions Offshore Libya Between Humanitarianism and Border Control' (2019) 54 *Cooperation and Conflict* 12.

[935] Article 2 Council Decision 2015/778; Giorgia Bevilacqua 'Exploring the Ambiguity of Operation Sophia Between Military and Search and Rescue Activities' in Gemma Andreone (ed), *The Future of the Law of the Sea* (New York, Springer, 2017) 171–172; Graham Butler and Martin Ratcovich, 'Operation Sophia in Uncharted Waters: European and International Law Challenges for the EU Naval Mission in the Mediterranean Sea' (2016) 85 *Nordic Journal of International Law* 3, 235.

[936] Article 2 (2)(a) Council Decision 2015/778; Butler and Ratcovich n 935 at 248.

used for human smuggling or trafficking …' on high seas (Phase 2A) but also permitted similar measures within the territorial and internal waters of a third state – *in casu* Libya (Phase 2B).[937] The third and final phase – subject to consent of the coastal State or authorization via a Security Council Resolution – allowed for the mission to take 'all necessary measures against a vessel and related assets, including through disposing of them or rendering them inoperable, which are suspected of being used for human smuggling or trafficking …'.[938]

The legal basis for military (naval) Operation Sophia is found in Article 42–43 TEU, embedded within the EU's Common Foreign and Security Policy. These provisions clarify the varying aspects of CSDP-military operations, including the scope, the objectives and mandate. This framework governs civilian and military assets for the purpose of engaging in peace-keeping missions and the strengthening of international security, among others.[939] In adopting military measures, unanimity is required by the Council, following proposals advanced by the High Representative of the EU for Foreign Affairs and Security Policy. The establishment of a military (naval) operation is the result of a Council decision, with limited input by other EU institutions.[940] Though not a legislative act, Council decisions are formally considered an act of the EU, rather than the outcome of a collaboration between the Member States.[941]

Recourse to a CSDP military mission and its corresponding legal basis, has immediate ramifications for the delineation of competences and the legal recourse available against conduct resulting therefrom. Although CSDP competence is constitutionally embedded in the EU-*acquis*,[942] it remains of a *sui generis* nature,[943] as can be derived from the fact that CFSP/CSDP measures are not included in the explicit typology of conferred competences in Articles 3–6 TFEU.[944] The *sui generis* nature of CFSP/CSDP competences, is furthermore highlighted by the fact that these competences are 'subject to specific rules and procedures'[945] also different from the competences embedded in Articles 3–6 TFEU. Due to these idiosyncrasies, competence in CFSP/CSDP has been referred to as 'non-pre-emptive shared competence'[946] which, mindful of the relevance of competence for the purpose of attribution under the *lex specialis* and the *lex generalis*, has implications on responsibility determinations.

Another feature of the EU's CSDP that impacts the ability to hold the EU responsible for contributions to human rights harms is the restricted legal review capacity

[937] Article 2(2)(b)(i) and (ii) Council Decision 2015/778.
[938] Article 2(2)(c) Council Decision 2015/778.
[939] Naert n 372 at 670–671.
[940] Butler and Ratcovich n 935 at 239.
[941] Naert n 372 at 672; Frederik Naert, 'Responsibility of the EU Regarding its CSDP Operations' in Malcolm Evans and Panos Koutrakos (eds), *The International Responsibility of the European Union – European and International Perspectives* (Oxford, Hart, 2013) 335–336.
[942] Butler n 787 at 40–41.
[943] ibid.
[944] Rosas n 332 at 34, 40.
[945] Article 24(1) TEU.
[946] Butler n 787 at 40–41; Delgado Casteleiro n 27 at 233.

of the CJEU.[947] Despite incremental and case-specific widening of CJEU jurisdiction in the field, the precise contours of such 'crippled conferral' of legal review capacity cannot yet be definitively determined and the extent of adjudicatory jurisdiction enjoyed by the CJEU, is ultimately left to the Court itself to determine.[948] While an extensive analysis of the foregoing falls outside the ambit of the current contribution, it is crucial that the (mutable) nature of the competence division in CSDP and the (limited) availability of legal review before the CJEU are both informative of and determinative for the availability and effectiveness of legal recourse for individual TCN's against unlawful EU conduct flowing from Operation Sophia.

EU military operations are multi-actor operations[949] involving Member States, EU institutions and sometimes third parties, and teeter on the interface of distinct legal orders.[950] Accordingly, the command-and-control structures – particularly the military chain of command *in theatre*[951] – may differ across various missions. This is relevant as the manner in which military command is exercised throughout the mission will affect to what actor unlawful human rights conduct is attributed.

The Council exercises *political and strategic* command and is responsible for key decision-making via Council decisions. Such decisions may include provisions

[947] Article 24(1) TEU: 'The Court of Justice of the European Union shall not have jurisdiction with respect to these provisions, with the exception of its jurisdiction to monitor compliance with Article 40 of this Treaty and to review the legality of certain decisions as provided for by the second paragraph of Article 275 of the Treaty on the Functioning of the European Union'.

[948] "For a recent opinion on the question of CFSP jurisdiction before the CJEU, see: Opinion of Advocate General KS and KD of 23 November 2023, KS, KD v Council of the European Union, European Commission, European External Action Service and European Commission, C-29/22 P and C-44/22 P, ECLI:EU:C:2023:901. See on the broadening of scope of CJEU jurisdiction in CFSP/CSDP: Peter Van Elsuwege and Joyce De Coninck, 'Action for damages in relation to CFSP decisions pertaining to restrictive measures: A revolutionary move by the Court of Justice in Bank Refah Kargaran' (*EU Law Analysis*, 9 October 2020) eulawanalysis.blogspot.com/2020/10/action-for-damages-in-relation-to-cfsp.html; Peter Van Elsuwege, 'Upholding the Rule of Law in the Common Foreign and Security Policy: H v. Council' (2018) 54 *Common Market Law Review*. See more generally on CJEU jurisdiction in the realm of CFSP/CSDP: Butler n 787 at 155, 157; Inge Govaere, 'To Give or to Grab: The Principle of Full, Crippled and Split Conferral of Powers Post-Lisbon' in Marise Cremona (ed), *Structural Principles in EU External Relations Law* (Oxford, Hart, 2018) 70, 79; Rosas n 332 at 39–40; Wessel and den Hertog n 278 at 344.

[949] The Operation Headquarters of Operation Sophia for example, were manned by 159 individuals in 2016 including 99 individuals from the host state (Italy) and individuals from the following Member States: Austria, Belgium, Bulgaria, Cyprus, Czech Republic, Estonia, Finland, France, Germany, Greece, Hungary, Latvia, Lithuania, Malta, the Netherlands, Poland, Portugal, Slovenia, Spain, Sweden, the United Kingdom. In addition, there was a Frontex Liaison officer. Operation Commander Op Sophia EEAS, 'EUNAVFORMED – Operation Sophia Six Monthly Report: June 22nd to December 31st, 2015' (*EEAS*, 29 January 2016) wikileaks.org/eu-military-refugees/EEAS/EEAS-2016-126.pdf 9.

[950] Notably, from an international perspective, Operation Sophia triggers the applicability of the non-intervention principle, as well as international maritime legal provisions on the right to visit (vessels at sea) and the duty to rescue at sea that are encompassed in UNCLOS. See generally on the interplay of various areas of substantive international law concerning Operation Sophia: Daniel Ghezelbash, Violeta Moreno-Lax, Natalie Klein, Brian Opeskin, 'Securitization of Search and Rescue at Sea: the Response to Boat Migration in the Mediterranean and Offshore Australia' (2018) 67 *International and Comparative Law Quarterly* 2, 315; Bevilacqua n 935; Butler and Ratcovich n 935. Fink n 27 at 66–67; Daniel Fiott, 'Military CSDP Operations: Strategy, Financing, Effectiveness' in Steven Blockmans and Panos Koutrakos (eds), *Research Handbook on the EU's Common Foreign and Security Policy* (Cheltenham, Edward Elgar Publishing, 2018) 116, 117; Tom Dannenbaum, 'Dual Attribution in the Context of Military Operations' in Ana Sofia Barros, Cedric Ryngaert and Jan Wouters (eds), *International Organizations and Member State Responsibility* (Leiden, Brill, 2016) 403.

[951] Naert n 372 at 674–675.

concerning legal responsibility, which may be further elaborated upon in additional planning documents such as the Operational Plan (*hereafter* OPLAN). In its work, the Council is supported by a number of entities[952] including the High Representative and the European External Action Service (EEAS),[953] particularly in the preparatory phases of CSDP-missions.[954] The Council is additionally aided by a number of preparatory bodies including the Political and Security Committee (PSC) and the EU Military Committee (EUMC).[955] Specifically, the PSC exercises political control, determines strategic direction of the mission and oftentimes exercises the authority to take decisions concerning planning documents (such as the OPLAN),[956] alterations of the (military) chain of command and the rules of engagement.[957]

The *military chain of command* (ie *operational control*) is determined on a case-by-case basis,[958] as the EU lacks standing military headquarters or contingents at its disposal, making it reliant on voluntary Member State contributions per specific mission.[959] Military command is identified as encompassing operational control. Through a 'transfer of authority' or alternatively, a 'reversal of authority', the Operation Commander of a CSDP-mission is provided *operational command and control* of the mission by the Member States and the EU. Operational command and control is defined as being 'authority delegated to a commander to direct forces assigned so that the commander may accomplish specific missions or tasks which are usually limited by function, time or location'.[960] This includes the responsibility for the drafting and the implementation of the OPLAN, which details the particularities of the Operation and may include provisions on legal responsibility, the drafting and enacting of the rules of engagement and strategic direction.[961] Further operational control is exercised by the Force Commander,[962] who acts under the authority of the Operation Commander and is appointed by the Council or the PSC.[963] The military chain of command is legally significant as it may influence whether the EU can or cannot be held responsible for conduct under Operation Sophia.

952 Naert n 941 at 317.

953 Naert n 372 at 672. See also: Fergal O'Regan Anthony, Elpida Apostolidou, 'Report on the European Ombudsman's meeting with the European External Action Service in case 935/2018/EA concerning the handling of requests for access to EUNAVFOR MED Operation Sophia's documents' (*European Ombudsman*, 28 November 2018) www.ombudsman.europa.eu/en/report/en/106975 3.

954 Naert n 372 at 672. See also: Report European Ombudsman EUNAVFOR MED n 953 at 3.

955 ibid.

956 Planning documents are typically: Crisis Management Concept (1), Strategic Options (2), Concept of Operation (3), and an Operational Plan (4) From the outset it must be noted that these documents are not legal by nature and thus cannot be subject to annulment proceedings before the CJEU. For a detailed discussion see: Naert n 941 at 319.

957 Naert n 941 at 318.

958 Fiott n 950 at 112, 114.

959 Naert n 372 at 674–675.

960 See Annex A and §8–9, 11, 19, 28–29: European External Action Service, 'EU Concept for Military Command and Control' (*EUMC*, 23 April 2019) data.consilium.europa.eu/doc/document/ST-8798-2019-INIT/en/pdf; Naert n 941 at 320.

961 Naert n 941 at 319–320; Report European Ombudsman EUNAVFOR MED n 953.

962 Naert n 372 at 674–675.

963 Operational control should not be conflated with the retained *full command* by the Member States over seconded officers in military contingents, resulting in criminal and disciplinary Member State jurisdiction. Naert n 372 at 674–675.

2. TRACING HUMAN RIGHTS IMPLICATIONS

The human rights concerns notwithstanding,[964] Operation Sophia's achievements have been widely lauded, as the Operation contributed to the saving of more than 45,000 lives through its Search and Rescue missions.[965] In addition, it contributed to the apprehension of 148 suspected smugglers and traffickers, as well as the neutralisation of 549 assets.[966] Operation Sophia's final mandate was extended until 30 September 2019, albeit with the withdrawal of certain Member States' support, the temporary suspension of the deployment of naval vessels and instead, with an enhanced focus on the use of aerial surveillance.[967] Following this final extension, the EU decided to permanently cease all Operation Sophia activities and instead has launched a new CSDP mission in the Mediterranean – EUNAVFOR MED Irini.[968] The objective of this mission is the implementation of the UN arms embargo on Libya. Additionally, it has taken over the former tasks of Operation Sophia, concerning the conducting of information gathering and aerial surveillance to control irregular migratory flows and to combat human smuggling and trafficking in the area.[969] Accordingly, any issues concerning the determination of responsibility that arise in the context of Operation Sophia, will likely resurface under the framework of Operation Irini.

Despite the EU's self-congratulatory appraisal of the operation, Operation Sophia resulted in the deflection of unsafe vessels,[970] significant human rights harms, and fits within the 'contactless control' paradigm as developed by Moreno-Lax and Giuffré.[971] The authors explain that this paradigm is a novel variant of the 'deterrence paradigm', which seeks the elimination of any physical contact with TCNs attempting to reach the EU's external border of the EU, so as to prevent any jurisdictional nexus from being established which would otherwise trigger the obligations inherent to the human rights norms by which the EU and the Member States are bound.

[964] See concerning inter alia aerial surveillance, documented cases 7 and 11 in Annex 2 '*Communication to the Office of the Prosecutor of the International Criminal Court – EU Migration Policies in the Central Mediterranean and Libya*' (*Statewatch*, 3 June 2019) www.statewatch.org/media/documents/news/2019/jun/eu-icc-case-EU-Migration-Policies.pdf. See also more generally: Human Rights Watch, 'EU/Italy/Libya: Disputes Over Rescues Put Lives at Risk – Allow European Rescues, Agree on Safe Disembarkation' (*Human Rights Watch*, 25 July 2018) www.hrw.org/news/2018/07/25/eu/italy/libya-disputes-over-rescues-put-lives-risk; Zach Campbell, 'Europe's Deadly Migration Strategy' (*Politico*, 2019) www.politico.eu/article/europe-deadly-migration-strategy-leaked-documents/. For scholarship on the matter, see: Giuffré and Moreno-Lax n 71 at 85, 90; Moreno-Lax n 17; Ghezelbash, Moreno-Lax, Klein, Opeskin n 950 at 334.

[965] Strategic Review Operation Sophia 2018 5, 25.

[966] ibid.

[967] Virginie, Battu, 'Press Release – EUNAVFOR MED Operation Sophia: mandated extended until 30 December 2019' (*European Council – Council of the European Union*, 29 March 2019) www.consilium.europa.eu/en/press/press-releases/2019/03/29/eunavfor-med-operation-sophia-mandate-extended-until-30-september-2019/.

[968] Council of the European Union 'Council Decision on a European Union military operation in the Mediterranean (EUNAVFOR MED Irini)' (Council of the European Union, 25 March 2020) data.consilium.europa.eu/doc/document/ST-6414-2020-INIT/en/pdf.

[969] European Council – Council of the European Union, 'Press Release – EU Launches Operation IRINI to Enforce Libya Arms Embargo' (*European Council – Council of the European Union*, 31 March 2020) www.consilium.europa.eu/en/press/press-releases/2020/03/31/eu-launches-operation-irini-to-enforce-libya-arms-embargo/.

[970] See generally n 964.

[971] Giuffré and Moreno-Lax n 71 at 84, 93–95.

Two clear examples evidence the 'contactless control' policy pursued by the EU through Operation Sophia: the transmission of coordinates pinpointing the location of distressed vessels in the Mediterranean carrying TCNs, to the LYCG (1) and the training of the LYCG by those involved in Operation Sophia (2). Together, these measures put flesh to the bones of the consensual containment policy pursued by the EU, which seeks to prevent TCNs – through cooperation between the EU, the Member States and third parties (*in casu* Libya) – from leaving Libyan territory and prevent TCNs from obtaining access to international protection proceedings on EU territory.

By communicating coordinates of the location of distressed vessels carrying TCNs to the LYCG,[972] the EU eliminated any corporeal effective control over the individuals concerned, thereby limiting – if not severing – the jurisdictional nexus that would otherwise trigger the applicability of the ECHR and arguably the CFR. The transmission of these coordinates to the LYCG (without the deployment of EU naval assets to perform search and rescue operations), forms a component of concerted action between the EU, Member States and third parties, facilitating the return of individuals to situations of significant ill-treatment in violation of the *non-refoulement* principle through prohibited push and pull-backs, albeit in a manner that is not directly captured under the current conceptualization of the obligations under the *non-refoulement* principle. In other words, by outsourcing the obligation to rescue vessels to the LYCG, the EU's Operation Sophia eschews any legal obligations to intervene and prevented TCNs from applying for international protection.

This contactless control policy is complemented by the training of the Libyan Coastguard. The EU's objective *in casu* is to contribute to the development of a LYCG capable of exercising border management in such a manner that they are capable of *preventing* departure of TCNs, preventing TCNs from exercising their right to leave a country and preventing their access to procedures for international protection abroad.[973] However, it has been (repeatedly) established that the LYCG is not only aware of and facilitates smuggling and trafficking practices, but there have been numerous instances of active involvement by Libyan Coastguard officers in smuggling and trafficking networks, as well as armed violence directed at TCN's attempting to leave Libya.[974] Leaked EEAS, Frontex and Operation Sophia reports explicitly acknowledge these practices, yet have not prompted the EU to halt its dealings with the LYCG in the context of the Operation or to impose further conditionality to their cooperation.[975]

[972] See generally n 964; Strategic Review Operation Sophia 2018 5, 13–15, 19.

[973] Giuffré and Moreno-Lax n 71 at 15; Ghezelbash, Moreno-Lax, Klein, Opeskin n 950 at 334–335.

[974] Campbell n 964; Human Rights Watch, 'EU: Shifting Rescue to Libya Risks Lives' (*Human Rights Watch*, 19 June 2017) www.hrw.org/news/2017/06/19/eu-shifting-rescue-libya-risks-lives.

[975] See generally: Yasha Maccanico, 'Anti-Migration Cooperation between the EU, Italy and Libya: Some Truths' (*Statewatch*, March 2020) www.statewatch.org/media/documents/analyses/no-356-some-truths-about-libya.pdf. See also on this topic, UN sanctioning of a Libyan Coast Guard members for involvement in human trafficking and smuggling: Ayman al-Warfalli, 'Sanctioned Libya Coastguard Commander Say Hits migrants to Protect Them' (*Reuters*, 19 June 2018) www.reuters.com/article/us-europe-migrants-libya-exclusive-idUSKBN1JF2HL. European Operational Headquarters EUNAVFOR MED Operation Sophia, 'Monitoring Report' (*Monitoring Mechanism Libyan Coast Guard and Navy*, February 2018) www.politico.eu/wp-content/uploads/2019/02/ENFM-Monitoring-of-Libyan-Coast-Guard-and-Navy-Report-October-2017-January-2018.pdf 29; Operation Commander Op Sophia EEAS, 'EUNAVFORMED – Operation Sophia Six Monthly Report: June 22nd to December 31st 2015' (*EEAS*, 29 January 2016)

The reconcilability of the containment, contactless control and deterrence policy with the *non-refoulement* principle is dubious at best. In line with the ECtHR in its *Hirsi* judgment, when determining whether the *non-refoulement* principle has been respected, regard is not only had to the concrete positive and negative obligations, but likewise the *effect* of the measure. In other words, even if the operation solely consists of training the Libyan Coastguard or the transmission of location-coordinates, the effect of which is to prevent departure and access to international protection procedures, such conduct nevertheless raises significant compliance issues. In accordance with ECtHR case law, the obligation to respect rights, such as the *non-refoulement* obligation, does not solely require the authorities themselves to respect those rights and obligations stemming therefrom, but 'also has the consequence that, in order to secure the enjoyment of those rights and freedoms, those authorities must prevent or remedy any breach at subordinate levels'.[976] This appears to include an implicit due diligence obligation to ensure that the essence of those rights remain respected. Following this rationale, a policy aimed at actively preventing the attempt at escape from places where individuals run the risk of being subjected to torture, inhuman or degrading treatment or punishment and international protection procedures, is at odds with the *non-refoulement* principle. It has furthermore been consistently affirmed that Libya cannot be deemed a safe third country, which undermines the legitimacy of any blanket policy enabling collective pull-backs or push-backs to Libyan territory.[977]

Assuming the EU's Operation Sophia and the transmission of location-coordinates coordinates of distressed vessels in the Mediterranean to the LYCG[978] is not reconcilable with the *non-refoulement* principle – can the EU effectively be held legally responsible by individual TCNs for its contribution to human rights harms stemming therefrom? If so, why has this not yet triggered legal review procedures for the EU's involvement therein?

3. RESPONSIBILITY IN PRACTICE

a. The EU *Lex Specialis* Applied

i. Independent Responsibility

In *Bergaderm* the Court held 'that Community law confers a right to reparation where three conditions are met: the rule of law infringed must be intended to confer rights on individuals; the breach must be sufficiently serious; and there must be a

wikileaks.org/eu-military-refugees/EEAS/EEAS-2016-126.pdf 7; Ghezelbash, Moreno-Lax, Klein, Opeskin n 950 at 334–335; Campbell n 964.

[976] ECtHR (Grand Chamber) Judgment of 8 April 2004, *Assanidze v Georgia*, App no. 71503/01, §146.

[977] ECtHR (Grand Chamber) Judgment of 23 February 2012, *Hirsi Jamaa and others v Italy*, App no. 27765/09; Giuffré and Moreno-Lax n 71 at 17.

[978] See concerning aerial surveillance, documented cases 7 and 11 in Annex 2: *Communication to the ICC*, 224 and 226; Strategic Review Operation Sophia 2018, 5, 13–15, 19 (see above).

direct causal link between the breach of the obligation resting on the State and the damage sustained by the injured parties'.[979]

– Causal Conduct Attributable to the EU

Two factors must be considered in determining whether there is a causal link between the attributable conduct of aerial surveillance under Operation Sophia, and the resulting push- and pull-backs to Libyan territory. On the one hand, there is the requirement that the causal link meets the *sine qua non* test, meaning that the damage would not have occurred 'but for the' conduct attributable to the EU and that the damage is the immediate result of the acts (of aerial surveillance) by the EU. On the other hand, the – though not explicitly named in the *Bergaderm* judgment – the test of attribution must be met.

Multiple parties were implicated in specific lines of conduct under Operation Sophia: the EU which has mandated Operation Sophia via the Council and resulting Council Decisions; the Member State contingents which are implicated in Operation Sophia's tasks; and finally, Libya as the push- and pull-backs of distressed vessels are implemented by the LYCG.

With respect to the causality requirement, as previously hinted at, the multiplicity of actors renders it unlikely that an applicant will succesfully meet the threshold of 'immediate causality' required under the *lex specialis* concerning EU responsibility. Not only are multiple Member States involved in obtaining and processing aerial surveillance, but it also cannot be definitively determined what party (Member States or the Operation Commander under the authority and control of the Council) retains operational command at the time coordinates of distressed vessels are transferred to the LYCG as the OPLAN is in any event, confidential and may encompass (multiple) transfer(s) of authority. Consequently, the operational control over the conduct at stake is diffused amongst several actors, without any certainty at any given point, who assumed operational control for the transmission of the coordinates that ultimately resulted in return to Libyan shores. Moreover, the LYCG is likewise involved in such operations, rendering the question of causality even more diffused. Recall in this respect that the Court acknowledged explicitly that:

> even in the case of a possible contribution by the institutions to the damage for which compensation is sought, that contribution might be considered too remote because of some responsibility resting on others.[980]

Arguably, the CJEU intended to hold that for unlawful conduct by the EU to give rise to a successful claim for damages, it would have to be the 'exclusive' cause of the damage. Irrespective of this assertion, however, *in casu*, it cannot be held that the return of TCNs to Libya was the *immediate* and/or *direct* result of the transmission

[979] CJEU Judgment of 4 July 2000, *Bergaderm and Goupil v Commission*, C-352/98 P, ECLI:EU:C:2000:361, §42. Lenaerts, Maselis, Gutman and Nowak n 448 at §11.38. See also: Fink n 27 at 186.

[980] CJEU Judgment of 31 March 2011, *Volker Mauerhofer v European Commission*, C-433/10P, ECLI:EU:C:2011:204, §132.

of the coordinates to the LYCG. Hence, although this act of communicating coordinates of distressed vessels may be considered as a *necessary* condition of the incurred damage, it cannot be said to be the immediate and direct cause, in light of the (operational) involvement of other parties – notably various Member States, Frontex and the LYCG.

Even in the unlikely event that jurisdiction is established, and the causation threshold is met, the fact remains that for EU responsibility to arise, the conduct of transmitting coordinates would have to be attributable to the EU as a necessary condition for a successful claim for damages (see above). This in turn, requires an analysis of the division of competences under the *lex specialis*.

As aforementioned, the precise contours of CFSP/CSDP measures have yet to be definitively determined. Depending on whether the competences are deemed (non-pre-emptive) shared competences or not, the margin of discretion on behalf of the Member States may differ, as will the 'genuine discretion' in the implementation of the tasks under Operation Sophia.[981] In addition, the principle of loyal cooperation as enshrined in Article 4(3) TEU and Article 24(3) TEU may also have the effect of impacting the discretion Member States have in the enactment of CSDP missions generally.[982] Given this ambiguity, it becomes difficult to determine *ex ante* to what entity an act should be attributed. The CJEU has shed some light on the matter in *H v Council*. *In casu* it held that *operational* command and control in the European Union Police Mission in Bosnia and Herzegovina, was in hands of the Head of Mission, as instructed by the Civilian Operation Commander. The Civilian Operation Commander, in turn, was under the control of the PSC, which falls under the control of the Council, as a result of which the CJEU concluded that the operational (effective) control was retained by the Council and any alleged acts pursuant to this control were to be attributed to the Council.[983] However, the mission at stake concerned a civilian mission, as opposed to the *military* nature of Operation Sophia. In addition, the particularities of each CSDP mission are determined in reference to their specific needs and objectives in the Council decisions by which they are established (see above). While *H v Council* may thus be indicative of the fact that operational measures falling under military operational command and control would be attributed to the Council, this is by no means set in stone or determinative for Operation Sophia and may very well depend on which Court is being asked to rule on the question of attribution. In fact, in a domestic German case concerning CSDP military Operation Atalanta, the contested act of transferring suspects of piracy, was attributed to the German authorities, leaving open the question of attribution to the EU.[984]

For Operation Sophia the division of competences (and responsibility) for lines of conduct via the (military) chain of command and control is determined by the OPLAN, which – given the military nature of the Operation – remains confidential

[981] Delgado Casteleiro n 27 at 29; Kuijper and Paasivirta n 267 at 59.

[982] Delgado Casteleiro n 27 at 29; Wessel and den Hertog n 278 at 344.

[983] CJEU (Grand Chamber) Judgment of 19 July 2016, *H v Council of the European Union and Others*, C-455/14P, ECLI:EU:C:2016:569, §50–55, 66–68.

[984] Oberverwaltungsgericht Nordrhein-Westfalen Judgment of 18 September 2014, 4 A 2948/11 openjur.de/u/731026.html; Heliskoski n 380 at 149–150.

(see above). Additionally, this chain of command may be subject to change, via transfers of authority throughout the Operation.[985] Without insight and transparency into this chain of command and control at any particular moment *in theatre* and the extent to which Member States retained 'genuine discretion' to act without being under orders by the Council, it thus becomes extremely difficult – unless compelled to do so by national authorities *ex ante* – to determine whether conduct is to be attributed to the Member States or the EU or both. Moreover, even in the unlikely event that domestic courts, regional courts, or international courts, including the CJEU, were to pronounce themselves on the matter of attribution, there is considerable divergence on allocation of attribution and/or responsibility across substantive areas of EU law, leaving it to be anyone's best guess, whether adjudicatory mechanisms would be more inclined to exonerate Member States of their responsibilities, in favour of attribution to the EU, vice versa, or neither. Recall in this respect that whereas the European Commission argued in favour of the application of a normative control model for attribution in the preparatory phases of the ARIO, which appears to resurface in WTO practice, this approach was not deemed appropriate for UNCLOS-related matters, disputes arising from investment agreements and environmental matters, where use was instead made of declarations of competence and intricate applications of the competence model for attribution. Disregarding both models, the EU then appeared to pursue – albeit in the realm of human rights protection – the internalized 'proceduralization' of attribution and ensuing responsibility to the EU.

The foregoing suggests that both causation and attribution will pose significant obstacles in holding the EU legally responsible for its cooperation giving rise to significant human rights harms.[986]

– Sufficiently Serious Breach of EU Law

Secondly, for non-contractual responsibility of the EU arise, a breach of EU law must be established, irrespective of whether the breached norm is founded in the EU's constituent treaties, EU legislation, or general principles of EU law,[987] the breach must be qualified as 'sufficiently serious'.[988] The qualification of conduct as being sufficiently serious was initially determined by reference to the amount of discretion retained by the EU and whether – mindful of this discretion – the EU had 'manifestly and gravely' overstepped the limitations of the rule of law concerned.[989] This means that when the EU has limited discretion in the enactment of a rule, the mere violation of the rule will be sufficient to result in a breach liable of giving rise to damages.[990] Discretion

[985] Fiott n 950 at 115.

[986] Fiott n 950 at 29.

[987] CJEU Judgment of 11 July 2007, *Jose Maria Sison v Council of the European Union*, T-47/03, ECLI:EU:T:2007:207, §234; Lenaerts, Maselis, Gutman and Nowak n 448 at §11.49–11.51.

[988] CJEU Judgment of 4 July 2000, *Bergaderm and Goupil v Commission*, C-352/98 P, ECLI:EU:C:2000:361 §42–43.

[989] Lenaerts, Maselis, Gutman and Nowak n 448 at §11.45.

[990] ibid §11.45.

of the EU is not assessed in a legal vacuum or in reference to a general domain of EU law, but is instead assessed on a case-by-case basis.[991]

In addition to the criterion of 'genuine discretion',[992] the CJEU has increasingly relied on factors such as the complexity of a case[993] (1), the clarity of the (concrete) binding legal obligations upon the EI[994] (2) and the intentional character of the act or omission[995] (3) to determine whether conduct was indeed unlawful or whether it could be considered excusable.[996] Recall here that the normative incongruence (Chapter 3) is hardly reconcilable with the criterion of a clear and legally unambiguous provision of law in determining whether the act of transmitting coordinates to the LYCG can effectively be considered as a breach of EU law by an EU entity capable of giving rise to damage.

Irrespective of the *nature* of the competence accorded to the EU within the realm of CSDP – Member States have transferred powers to the EU to enact measures and policies giving rise to Operation Sophia, triggering Article 51 CFR, which holds that the provisions to be protected in the Charter 'are addressed to the institutions and bodies of the Union …', as a result of which it is directly bound by the *non-refoulement* principle in Article 19 CFR.

As previously argued however, the legal obligation of the EU to adhere to the *non-refoulement* principle in theory (under Article 19 CFR *in juncto* Article 51 CFR), does not clarify the concrete obligations – procedural and substantive, as well as negative and positive – that must be met by the EU to comply with this legal commitment.[997] While it is clear that the EU's contribution (transmission of location-coordinates) to Operation Sophia, resulted in the pull-backs of distressed vessels to Libya while actively preventing TCNs access to international protection proceedings, disregards the essence of the *non-refoulement* principle from the perspective of the individual,[998] it remains hard to contend that this *ipso facto* entails a violation of positive EU human rights law obligations that is sufficiently serious to warrant damages.

[991] Fink n 27 at 208–209.

[992] ibid 219.

[993] CJEU (CFI) Judgment of 26 January 2006, *Medici Grimm KG v Council of the European Union*, T-364/03, ECLI:EU:T:2006:28, §87.

[994] CJEU Judgment of 26 March 1996, *The Queen v HM Treasury, ex parte British Telecommunications*, C-392/93, ECLI:EU:C:1996:131, §43; CJEU Judgment of 17 October 1996, *Denkavit Internationaal and Others v Bundesamt für Finanzen*, C-283/94, ECLI:EU:C:1996:387, §51–52.

[995] CJEU (CFI) Judgment of 26 January 2006, *Medici Grimm KG v Council of the European Union*, T-364/03, ECLI:EU:T:2006:28, §87.

[996] CJEU Judgment of 19 April 2007, *Holcim (Deutschland) v Commission*, C-282/05, ECLI:EU:C:2007:226, §50. See also (and sources cited therein): Lenaerts, Maselis, Gutman and Nowak n 448 at §11.60.

[997] Klein n 32 at 1034–1035; Klabbers n 106 at 284.

[998] Recall in this respect that fundamental rights must be interpreted in a manner so that they are not 'theoretical and illusory' but rather 'practical and effective' (see above). Opinion of Advocate General Mengozzi of 7 February 2017, *X and X v État belge*, C-638/16PPU, ECLI:EU:C:2017:93, §158; ECtHR judgment of 26 April 2016, *Murray v Netherlands* App. No. 10511/10, §104; ECtHR Judgment of 23 February 2012, *Hirsi Jamaa and others v Italy*, App no. 27765/09, §130; ECtHR judgment of 1 June 2010, *Gäfgen v Germany*, App. no. 22978/05 §123 and ECtHR Judgment of 8 June 2006, *Lupsa v Romania*, App no. 10337/04, §60.

Recalling the concrete obligations inherent to the *non-refoulement* principle to Operation Sophia, it is hard to conceive how the EU could abide for example, by the procedural *positive* obligation of a 'duty to investigate, proprio motu, any situation of need for international protection …'.[999] This precisely because the prerogative of border control – including determinations and duties of investigation of the grounds for international protection – remain integral to the sovereignty of States.[1000] Similarly, it is uncertain how the EU can abide by the *negative* obligation to refrain from sending individuals back to Libya without having any actual border guards at its disposal, as the contingents under Operation Sophia are actually Member State contingents. Notably, the act of acquiring and communicating location-coordinates – though the effect may be the same – cannot be equated to the physical act of pushing or pulling individuals back to Libya in violation of the *non-refoulement* principle under positive EU law.

Hence, even in the assumption that the conditions of causation and attribution can be considered met, can it be held that the (mere) transmission of location-coordinates to the LYCG effectively meet the severity threshold of prohibited returns under the *non-refoulement* principle? From a purely positivist legal perspective, this is unlikely as the EU is not formally bound by an obligation to not cooperate with its EU Member States and third states for the purpose of IBM.

An argument could be constructed here, that the contribution by Operation Sophia to such push- and pull-back proceedings, though not explicitly foreseen under the current framework, violates the duty to respect (negative obligation), fulfil and protect (positive obligations) (see above). Similarly, the argument could be made that by contributing to a push- or pull-back operation through the communication of location coordinates to the LYCG, the EU has violated a due diligence obligation or even committed a data processing violation. However, the CJEU has not (yet) affirmed whether these obligations can be derived from the *non-refoulement* principle as it applies to the EU, or its scope, much less whether this would meet the qualification of 'sufficiently serious'. Hence, we are left with a scenario where the EU and its Member States are indissociably contributing to a situation of automated returns TCNs to Libya, whereby the individuals concerned are stripped of the possibility to request international protection, albeit without the ability to identify what concretised EU obligation(s) have been violated by the EU to be able to generate damages. In other words, although courts and tribunals have not yet interpreted the *non-refoulement* principle through the lens of indirect causal contributions such as the present scenario, the practice of coordinate transmission under Operation Sophia, clearly entails a due diligence violation on the one hand to *prevent* violations of *non-refoulement* and on the other hand, to *ensure* access to international protection proceedings. However, until a precedent-setting judgment interprets and

[999] ECtHR Concurring Opinion Judge Pinto De Albuquerque of 23 February 2012, *Hirsi Jamaa and others v Italy*, App no. 27765/09 §11; Moreno-Lax n 17 at 424.

[1000] ECtHR (Grand Chamber) Judgment of 23 February 2012, *Hirsi Jamaa and others v Italy*, App no. 27765/09, §113 (and sources cited therein).

articulates the concrete *non-refoulement* obligations of the EU and IOs generally, the scope and enforceability of such obligations remain conjecture.

Consequently, in the absence of *ex ante* (legislative) or *post facto* precedent-setting clarification by the Court, the second condition of a sufficiently serious breach of EU also cannot reasonably be met by individual applicants seeking redress for prohibited returns to an unsafe third country.

– Interim Conclusions

When applying the EU *lex specialis* for independent responsibility, four conditions must be met – three of which are explicitly noted in Article 340 TFEU and clarified in *Bergaderm*, and one – attribution – considered as implied by these conditions. It is quickly evident that the threshold for causation imposes an extremely difficult and practically impossible standard for Applicants to meet, given the situation of diffused albeit concerted conduct, characterized by evidentiary smokescreens as a result of the confidentiality of the OPLAN and the indissociable nature of joint EU military operations. Moreover, the interpretation and application of the substantive and procedural, positive and negative obligations flowing from the *non-refoulement* principle have (thus far) never been developed bearing in mind the functional speciality of IOs such as the EU. Accordingly, it cannot be definitively established without a degree of arbitrariness when and how the EU has violated concrete obligations under the *non-refoulement* principle. And so long it is not clear what the scope is of such obligations and who bears those burdens in practice, it will likewise be impossible to determine to whether the breach is sufficiently serious and to what actor the alleged breach of EU law must be attributed to. This latter point is furthermore complicated by the fact that attribution under the EU law (the *lex specialis*) may be determined by the application of the competence model in the strict (competence in the letter of the law), the broad sense (competence as applied), or altogether different models of attribution across different areas of substantive EU law. These findings are not exclusive to Operation Sophia and may be extrapolated to other instances of joint military conduct, as the issues in the application of the EU *lex specialis* responsibility regime, are not confined to IBM. While the issues surrounding adjudicatory jurisdiction in CFSP/CSDP measures are case-specific, the other obstacles that Applicants face for a successful claim for damages are inherent to the responsibility regime as such (eg an extremely high causation threshold, imprecise tests of attribution, ambiguous and incomplete delineation of concrete human rights obligations, absence of *ex ante* determinations of apportionment of responsibility) and *not* specific to the case study of conduct within Operation Sophia.

Mindful of the fact that three out of four conditions under the purported EU *lex specialis* can only be met in case of extreme judicial creativity and activism, mindful of the fact that this does not yet solve the issue of CJEU jurisdiction for CFSP/CSDP-related damages claims, and mindful of the fact that it is uncertain whether findings of attribution exonerate other complicit parties, it is necessary to assess further avenues for responsibility.

ii. Shared Responsibility

Shared responsibility could stem from cooperative conduct, where the Member States and the EU commit one single unlawful act which results in one single injury (1); from concurrent conduct where the Member States and EU commit separate and different unlawful acts (or omissions) which were independently sufficient to generate the single injury, but conjointly result in a single harm or injury (2); or from cumulative conduct, in which separate and distinct unlawful acts, which in and of themselves would not have been sufficient to generate the single injury, taken together create the harm for which relief is sought (3).

The transmission of coordinates pinpointing the location of distressed vessels through Operation Sophia to the LYCG, could theoretically be brought under any one of these three forms of conduct, depending on how the obligations under the *non-refoulement* are construed. If *non-refoulement* is construed broadly, entailing that actions (or inaction) of duty-bearers cannot result in the return of individuals to an unsafe third country, the inaction of the EU and/or transmission of coordinates of distressed vessels could arguably be considered as a violation thereof, alongside the active push- and pull-backs of the LYCG. In this case the EU, the Member States and the LYCG could all be perceived as complicit actors in cooperative conduct that results in a single harm (scenario 1). Insofar a more nuanced and narrow approach to *non-refoulement* is adopted, whereby the concrete obligations stemming from the principle are taken into consideration, it is more likely that the act of transmitting coordinates to the LYCG will fall under either concurrent or cumulative conduct giving rise to a single harm. Under concurrent conduct (scenario 2), this would require – for shared responsibility to be established – that the act of transmitting coordinates through Operation Sophia with the intent of outsourcing search and rescue duties and the refusal of access to international protection procedures, would have to have been sufficient to cause the harm in and of itself, and constitutes a breach of an EU rule. Under cumulative conduct, it would suffice that the conduct of the transmission of coordinates would amount to unlawful conduct and taken together with the (unlawful) conduct of other complicit parties, would result in the single harm (scenario 3).

However, irrespective of this theoretical and academic categorization, it is clear that without the precise determination of the scope of the concretised obligations by which the EU is bound, it cannot be definitively determined whether the EU has effectively violated this standard through the transmission of coordinates to the LYCG, under the EU *lex specialis*. Even in the event that this conduct was to be considered a violation of an undefined positive (due diligence) obligation to respect and protect the *non-refoulement* principle (see above), the question of apportionment of attribution and responsibility arises including the exculpatory nature of such determinations. Whether it functions in an exculpatory manner, will first be determined by whether the EU and the Member States are effectively bound by the same or distinguishable concrete obligations under the *non-refoulement* principle. If they are bound by the same obligations, and the applied apportionment works in an exculpatory manner, then either the Member States or the EU would be held responsible. Insofar apportionment is not exculpatory, shared responsibility would theoretically be possible. Different still, if they are not bound by the same concrete obligations, it would theoretically also be possible to hold both the EU and the Member States responsible. However, whether this theoretical shared responsibility between the EU and the Member States would be possible in practice, is not certain.

Recall in this respect that shared responsibility under the EU *lex specialis* is determined in large part by the area of substantive EU law at stake: while under the WTO-regime, the general consensus suggests that the EU exercises normative control over its Member States even where the Member States adopt national measures to comply with EU law, and thus assumes responsibility, UNCLOS disputes and investment disputes tend to follow an internal procedure and/or declarations of competence, to establish (seemingly exculpatory) apportionment of responsibility. Under *international* human rights law, it appears that the EU does not exclude the possibility of shared responsibility, as demonstrated by the Draft Accession Agreement. However, such shared responsibility would only be possible following an internal procedural assessment on the matter. Applied *in casu* it is thus possible that there would be shared responsibility, but in light of the general tendency to apply exculpatory mechanisms of responsibility under the EU *lex specialis* it is unlikely, and uncertain upon which grounds such shared responsibility would be based.

Grosso modo, the EU *lex specialis* does not provide for a self-contained regime, and any findings of responsibility would inevitably be made based upon a number of hypothetical factors that significantly tilt the balance in favour of Member State responsibility. In other words, given the absence on legal provisions for shared responsibility (in IBM), the CJEU is relatively free to determine how to go about the apportionment of responsibility, despite the fact that the EU is clearly contributing to a policy of outsourcing and externalisation of immigration control, in violation of the essence of the *non-refoulement* principle from the perspective of the individual. Drawing from analogous situations of shared conduct across EU law, it is suggested that it is unlikely that the CJEU would find that the EU could be held responsible for unlawful conduct *in casu*. This because its contribution to the push- and pull-backs of TCNs would be considered too tenuous to meet the causality threshold, which is furthermore complicated by the fact that attribution of unlawful conduct would have to be determined according to the competence model requiring a factual assessment of the retained 'genuine discretion' as determined in a confidential military OPLAN. Furthermore, shared responsibility can only occur when the parties involved perform identifiable and acts (or omissions) that constitute unlawful conduct – which *in casu* cannot be determined, or at least remains subject to discretion of post facto control by the judiciary.

In light of this obscurity and the potential arbitrariness stemming from the EU *lex specialis*, recourse may be had to the *lex generalis* to remedy any lacunae that arise in the EU-specific responsibility paradigm.

b. The *Lex Generalis* Applied

The *lex generalis* hold explicitly that the *lex specialis* referenced in Article 64 ARIO, do not prevail over the general provisions on IO responsibility nor do they nullify them (see above). Furthermore, Article 32 ARIO recalls that the internal rules of the organization cannot be invoked as a means to circumvent international responsibility. This entails that insofar the *lex specialis* do not provide a self-contained regime, recourse can be had to the *lex generalis*. Mindful thereof, the ARIO hold that IOs can be held independently responsible (Articles 6–13 ARIO) or can be held jointly responsible for concerted conduct with Member States (Articles 14–17 ARIO). Both will be addressed in turn.

i. Independent Responsibility

For an IO such as the EU to be held independently responsible for violations of human rights, two cumulative conditions must be met: conduct must firstly be attributable to the organization and secondly, the conduct must constitute a breach of an international obligation. As will be shown, the same issues that arose in the application of the EU's (*lex specialis*), resurface within the ARIO (*lex generalis*) responsibility framework, preventing a finding of EU responsibility for its contribution to acts that led directly to the push- and pull-backs of TCNs to Libyan territory.

– Attribution

Conduct will be attributed to IOs according to four potential scenarios (see above): when the conduct was committed by an agent or organ of the organization (Article 6 ARIO); when the individual/entity responsible for the conduct is 'at the disposal of the organization' (Article 7 ARIO); *ultra vires* acts of organs and agents will be attributed to the organization (Article 8 ARIO); when the organization acknowledges conduct as being its own (Article 9 ARIO).

Applying Article 6 ARIO to the situation at hand, does not resolve questions of attribution, as under positive (EU and international) law, it is undecided whether the Member States – when enacting EU IBM policy – are under sufficient normative control generally to be considered as *de facto* organs or agents of the EU. Moreover, the EU's military operations – despite the formal involvement of the Council – are the coordinated effort of EU entities, several Member States, and external third parties. Under a strict understanding of what constitutes an organ or agent, which appears to encompass only EU institutions, bodies, offices and agencies, it is unlikely that Member States would be considered as such. Bearing in mind that currently only WTO disputes give rise to the qualification of Member States as *de facto* organs (instead of *de iure* organs or agents) of the EU, Article 6 ARIO does not function as a suitable basis to attribute conduct to the EU stemming from a joint operation.

The competence model, argued by some as also being inherent to the test of attribution under Article 6 ARIO (see Chapter 4), requires competence according to the letter of the law and for that competence to have been exercised by the IO, for wrongful conduct to be attributed to the latter. Again, in the case of CSDP measures generally, it is unclear to what extent the EU has competence (in theory and in practice) and to what extent the Member States retain 'genuine discretion' in the conduct mandated by Operation Sophia to communicate the coordinates of the locations of distressed vessels to the LYCG (see above). Although the EU is responsible via its Operation Commander for the *operational* control of a mission, it is entirely possible for a 'reverse transfer of authority' to occur, whereby operational control is transferred back to a Member State. Whilst all relevant arrangements in this respect may to a certain extent be documented in the *confidential* OPLAN, this is not subject to external scrutiny, rendering it difficult – if not impossible – to determine at any given point who retains operational control over the mission, or measures taken within the context of the mission. Concretely and from an entirely practical perspective it is thus difficult in practice to determine which entity has *de facto* operational control – not to mention 'genuine discretion' – over a particular measure taking place within the context of the Operation. Attempts to uncover the chain of command as stipulated in OPLANs for IBM and attempts to enchance transparency have been met with reticence by the CJEU and have typically resulted in a successful invocation of the 'security exception'. In other words, while in theory one could ask the CJEU to have the OPLAN chain of command be revealed, this typically is refused on the objection that it would jeopardize the security of the operation.[1001]

Similar issues arise when attempting to establish attribution in accordance with Article 7 ARIO, which was drafted with the intent of covering scenarios such as the operational action at stake. For attribution to occur vis-à-vis the organization in this context, the organization would have to exert a certain level of effective control over the latter. However, doctrinal debate remains as to whether this level of control should amount to *effective control* as opposed to *ultimate normative control* – a question which currently remains unresolved, albeit that scholarship tends to lean towards the test of effective control. Applying this again to Operation Sophia: in view of the specific characteristics thereof and the modes of cooperation and command and control, which may switch hands throughout the course of the operation, and which may or may not be encompassed in the OPLAN, it is again difficult to determine who effectively has ultimate normative control and/or effective control concerning any particular measure taken within the context of the Operation. Much would have to be determined on a case-to-case basis. Yet again, while the chain of command is typically relayed in the OPLAN, reticence in making at least this component of the OPLAN transparent, frustrates a clear determination of what party any given act should be attributed to.

These same issues arise when attempting to establish attribution based upon Article 8 ARIO, for ultra vires conduct. Finally, the application of Article 9 ARIO, whereby attribution is acknowledged by the organization, is wholly dependent upon the latter. In light of the discernible trend under substantive areas of EU law (with the exception of WTO-disputes), to avoid instances of joint responsibility and EU responsibility specifically, this provision does not provide an adequate basis for attribution that is reflective of the actual conduct of the EU in the operationalisation of Operation Sophia.

In view of the foregoing, many of the same issues concerning attribution under the *lex specialis* also arise under the *lex generalis*. This does not surprise, as similar

[1001] CJEU (General Court) 2019 *Izuzquiza and Semsrott n* 48.

models to determine attribution are explicitly and implicitly relied upon by different entities to resolve disputes of joint conduct. This renders attribution as a constituent element of human rights responsibility of the EU difficult to establish.

– Internationally Wrongful Act

The second condition for independent responsibility to arise, is the violation of an international obligation by which the organization was bound. This condition remains problematic under the *lex generalis* as it did under the *lex specialis*, prompting again the question as to whether it is desirable and/or tenable to hold the EU and Member States to abide by corresponding positive and negative obligations under international human rights law.

ii. Shared Responsibility

In addition to independent responsibility, an IO could theoretically be held jointly responsible for conduct by a Member State insofar the organization aided or assisted the latter (Article 14 ARIO), directed and controlled conduct by the Member State (Article 15 ARIO), or coerced the Member State into conduct, which would have amounted to a violation of international obligation, had it been committed by the organization itself (Article 16 ARIO) (see above). Finally, an organization can also be held responsible if it circumvented its own obligations by directing a decision or authorization at a Member State for conduct that again, would have been deemed a breach of an international obligation binding upon the organization (Article 17 ARIO).

For joint responsibility to arise under these provisions, the IO must have been aware of the harm it was contributing to and an (undefined) test of causality must be met. As indicated however, the ARIO, in both its commentaries and its *travaux préparatoires* do not provide any definitive clarity of how 'knowing intent' and 'causality' should be applied *in casu*. Arguably, by transmitting the coordinates of the locations of distressed vessels to the LYCG – which has been widely condemned for its unlawful human rights conduct – the EU was reasonably aware of the fact that it was contributing to the unlawful pull and push-backs of TCN's to Libyan territory.[1002]

However, even if the conditions of knowing intent and (undefined) causality could be considered met under the provisions of shared responsibility, this does not address the most crucial issue common to all the forms of shared responsibility under the ARIO – the requirement that the facilitated conduct by the Member State would have constituted unlawful conduct had it been committed by the IO. Under Article 14 and 15 ARIO, this constitutes the 'opposability criterion', whereas under Article 16 and 17 ARIO, it is not required that the conduct also constituted unlawful conduct from the vantage point of the Member States. In any of the four scenarios

[1002] See similarly: Mauro Gatti, 'The Gendarmes of Europe of Europe: Southern Mediterranean States and the EU's Partnership Framework on Migration' in Francesca Ippolito and Federico Casolari (eds), *Bilateral Relations in the Mediterranean* (Cheltenham, Edward Elgar Publishing, 2020) 158, 160.

envisaged by the ARIO, it is thus imperative to know what concrete human rights obligations were binding upon the IO, to trigger the provisions of shared responsibility. Consequently, the same issues remain concerning the determination of a breach of a legal obligation binding upon IO in the field of human rights protection, as precise contours of the substantive positive and negative obligations remain ambiguous. Applied again to Operation Sophia and the transmission of location-coordinates, it is uncertain under the contemporary framework whether the EU violated any positive or negative (due diligence) obligations by which it was bound by transmitting the coordinates to the LYCG. Again, the argument can be made here that the requirement to interpret human rights as being practical and effective as opposed to theoretical and illusory, entails that in any event, the EU is bound by a due diligence obligation to respect, protect and fulfil the *non-refoulement* principle. However, it would remain at the discretion of a court to establish the merit of such lines of argumentation in an ex post facto assessment. Finally, the *lex generalis* framework as it stands, does not offer any clarification as to whether the responsibility mechanism functions in an exculpatory manner or not, or the dynamic and scope between the tests for shared responsibility and independent responsibility. While it is thus theoretically possible for an IO to incur human rights responsibility, precisely due to all the discretionary leeway under the *lex generalis* regime, it likewise entails that there is leeway for fragmentation and legal uncertainty.

Again, it appears that despite the available theoretical grounds upon which the EU and its institutions can be held responsible for human rights violations in the field of asylum and migration and Operation Sophia specifically, these grounds remain just that – theoretical.

c. Interim Conclusions on Responsibility for Cooperation with Third Countries

In attempting to hold the EU responsible for its contribution to human rights harms throughout the course of Operation Sophia, a number of structural obstacles arise, hampering effective recourse against its conduct. Firstly, as concerns attribution, it appears that both within the *lex specialis* (EU action for damages) as well as the *lex generalis* (ARIO) regime, issues arise on account of the fact that to date, there is no certainty as to what parameters must be applied to determine to what entity conduct must be attributed. It is currently not certain to what extent Member States can be viewed as organ or agents of the Union, much less how to define when an entity is considered an organ or agent. Moreover, no certainty exists as to how effective control is to be assessed. Indeed, scholarship seems to lean in the direction of military command and control in the context of military missions. However, this line of reasoning has not been followed steadfast in practice, requiring thus a case-to-case assessment to make determinations of attribution under both responsibility frameworks. The particular case of CSDP military missions, renders the foregoing even more complex, as much of the command-and-control structures are elaborated upon in the OPLAN, which is confidential and may be subject to change throughout the course of the mission. Absent any coercive requirement to disclose such information or declarations of responsibility by the implicated parties – which has traditionally successfully been challenged – it thus becomes unfeasible under both responsibility regimes for individual TCN protection-seekers to establish what entity is responsible for any given measure taken within the context of Operation Sophia.

The determination of an unlawful act or omission further complicates the international responsibility question given the functional and heterogenous legal personality of international organisations. The differing nature and limited functional personality thereof make it difficult – particularly in the field of international human rights law – to distil concrete positive, negative, substantive and procedural obligations from the rights accorded to individual protection-seekers. Recalling that traditionally human rights have regulated the dynamic between States and the individual, this has as a consequence that it is hard to determine when – if at all – an IO such as the EU has effectively violated a human right through either an act or omission.

At best, a TCN could rely on a set of overriding (EU) general principles to contest unlawful acts at the behest of the Union within the context of Operation Sophia. The precautionary principle and the principle of effectiveness could, for example, be invoked to require the EU to adhere to the negative duty to refrain from actions that impede the protection of the *non-refoulement* principle. However, in this last scenario a case-by-case assessment would again be required – by potentially diverging national courts in view of the limited jurisdiction of the CJEU in CFSP/CSDP-related matters – to the detriment of legal certainty and legitimate expectations. Hence, despite being bound to respect human rights within the context of the Operation and operations of a similar sort in theory, it is doubtful that these commitments can be enforced and safeguarded in practice for TCNs.

8

Measures at the EU External Border

In what follows, the EU's Human Rights Responsibility Regime – *lex specialis* and *lex generalis* – will be applied to the third limb of IBM, namely, border control measures adopted *at* the EU's external border. Despite the primary responsibility for the management of the external EU border resting with the Member States, the shared nature of the IBM is evinced by the role exercised by the European Border and Coast Guard Agency (*hereafter* Frontex[1003])[1004] as consolidated in Article 7 of the 2019 European Border and Coast Guard Regulation (*hereafter* EBCG Regulation).[1005] The question of Frontex responsibility for contributions to human rights harms in effectuating this shared role, remains at the forefront of discussions concerning IBM. This is in part attributed to the events that unfolded in the Aegean Sea as unveiled by *Bellingcat*, which document Frontex involvement in prohibited push-backs, as well as the result of the enhanced executive powers acquired by Frontex pursuant to the 2019 European Border and Coast Guard Regulation.

Consecutive legislative reforms over the course of the past 15 years have resulted in an increased and significant transfer of powers from the Member States to Frontex, for the purpose of contributing to the EU's external border management. The progressive development of Frontex into a Europeanized border and coast guard, has brought about – in the most recent legislative reforms – the power for Frontex to recruit its own border guards[1006] with an envisaged capacity of 10,000 operational staff,[1007]

[1003] The legislative reform concerning Frontex in 2016 purportedly adopted a new rhetoric concerning Frontex, including an improved name – *the European Border and Coast Guard Agency*, as opposed to its previous name *the European Agency for the Management of Operational Cooperation at the External Borders of the Member States of the European Union*. However, these terminological adaptations did not have any bearing on the substantive changes made to the framework within which Frontex was and continues to be embedded. For the sake of clarity and to avoid confusion between the Agency (Frontex) and the European Border and Coast Guard as an aspect of Frontex as an Agency, the present work will continue to refer to the Agency as Frontex. Recital 3 EBCG Regulation. See on the 2016 reform: Herbert Rosenfeldt, 'Establishing the European Border and Coast Guard: All-new or Frontex reloaded?' (*EU Law Analysis*, 16 October 2016) eulawanalysis.blogspot.com/2016/10/establishing-european-border-and-coast.html.

[1004] Melanie Fink has extensively discussed the application of the EU *lex specialis* to Frontex operations, albeit *prior* to the EBCG Regulation. As such, differences may arise as a result of the changes to Frontex in the 2019 reform. See for her findings: Fink n 27.

[1005] EBCG Regulation.

[1006] Philippe De Bruycker, 'The New Pact on Migration and Asylum: What It Is Not and What It Could Have Been' (*EU Migration Law Blog*, 15 December 2020) eumigrationlawblog.eu/the-new-pact-on-migration-and-asylum-what-it-is-not-and-what-it-could-have-been/.

[1007] Recital 5 EBCG Regulation.

to send liaison officers to third countries for the purpose of 'contributing to the prevention and fight against illegal immigration and the return of returnees',[1008] and has conferred 'executive powers' to Frontex operational staff to 'effectively address existing and future operational needs for border and return operations in the Union and third countries, including a rapid reaction capacity to face future crises'.[1009]

Recent events have propelled demands for Frontex and EU responsibility, in part because of alleged complicity in unlawful push- and pull-backs of TCN's within the Aegean Sea, from Greece back to Turkey.[1010] These events have resulted in a request by the European Commission for an extraordinary meeting of the Frontex Management Border on the topic of allegations of these push-backs,[1011] an investigation by the European Ombudsman to investigate the effectiveness of the internal complaints mechanism of Frontex,[1012] and a debate in the Civil Liberties Committee of the European Parliament on the topic.[1013] These initiatives resulted in outcries by the general public following very concrete events involving Frontex at the external Greek border dating from March 2020 to August 2020,[1014] but likewise following the earlier annual report by the Frontex Consultative Forum composed of representatives of the European Asylum Support Office, the EU Agency for Fundamental Rights, UNHCR, the Council of Europe and the International Organization for Migration, which voiced concerns with respect to Frontex human rights adherence.[1015] In addition, an investigation has been initiated by the European Anti-Fraud Office (OLAF) for alleged misconduct by the Agency and a European Parliament Frontex Scrutiny Working Group has been established, which started factfinding investigations in March 2021 concerning alleged human rights violations by Frontex in the exercise of its mandate. All of these developments ultimately gave rise to Fabrice Leggeri resigning from his post as the Frontex Executive Director in 2022.

These initiatives all have in common that they do not amount to legal review capable of yielding legal remedies. Instead, they serve as (potential) pathways

[1008] Article 77 EBCG Regulation.
[1009] Recital 5 EBCG Regulation.
[1010] Nick Waters, Emmanuel Freudenthal and Logan Williams, 'Frontex at Fault: European Border Force Complicit in 'Illegal' Pushbacks' (*Bellingcat*, 23 October 2020) www.bellingcat.com/news/2020/10/23/frontex-at-fault-european-border-force-complicit-in-illegal-pushbacks/. See also for a doctrinal discussion: Niamh Keady-Tabbal and Itamar Mann, 'Pushbacks as Euphemism' (*EJIL:Talk!*, 14 April 2021) www.ejiltalk.org/pushbacks-as-euphemism/?utm_source=mailpoet&utm_medium=email&utm_campaign=ejil-talk-newsletter-post-title_2.
[1011] European Commission, 'Extraordinary Meeting of Frontex Management Board on the Alleged Push Backs on 10 November 2020' (*European Commission – Migration and Home Affairs*, 11 November 2020) ec.europa.eu/home-affairs/news/extraordinary-meeting-frontex-management-board-alleged-push-backs-10-november-2020_en.
[1012] European Ombudsman Inquiry of 10 November 2020, *Own Initiative Inquiry about the European Border and Coast Guard Agency (Frontex), and Its Internal Complaint Mechanism*, Cas OI/5/2020/MHZ, www.ombudsman.europa.eu/en/opening-summary/en/134799.
[1013] European Parliament 'MEPs to grill Frontex director on agency's role in pushbacks of asylum-seekers' (*European Parliament News*, 30 November 2020) www.europarl.europa.eu/news/en/press-room/20201126IPR92509/meps-to-grill-frontex-director-on-agency-s-role-in-pushbacks-of-asylum-seekers.
[1014] Bellingcat Report n 1010.
[1015] Frontex Consultative Forum, 'Seventh Annual Report: Frontex Consultative Forum on Fundamental Rights' (*Frontex*, 1 October 2020) www.statewatch.org/news/2020/october/eu-advice-of-frontex-consultative-forum-on-fundamental-rights-still-falls-on-deaf-ears/.

towards broader (political) accountability for Frontex.[1016] What remains absent from these procedures, is recourse to effective *legal review* of Frontex conduct, capable of yielding legal remedies for potentially affected TCNs. While indeed, a number of different direct applications have since been lodged before the CJEU in an attempt to establish Frontex responsibility,[1017] these proceedings have not yet given rise to a merit-based review of Frontex's conduct in contributing to human rights harms stemming from its cooperation in IBM.[1018] By applying the *lex specialis* and the *lex generalis* responsibility mechanisms to the conduct of Frontex in the Aegean sea, the following analysis will determine whether the same (or different) issues arise in attempting to establish responsibility vis-à-vis Frontex (as an agency of the EU), and the EU more generally.

1. LEGAL FRAMEWORK AND CONTEXT

a. Legal Basis and Competences

Established in 2004, Frontex was initially entrusted with the task of supporting the correct implementation of the Schengen Border Code and the coordination of Member State initiatives concerning border management.[1019] However, in view of increasing migratory pressures and associated challenges, the competences and structure of Frontex have changed incrementally since, resulting in the establishment of

[1016] The notion of responsibility should be distinguished here from the broader concept of (political) accountability. See for a general discussion (and sources cited therein): Merijn Chamon, 'Transparency and Accountability of EU Decentralised Agencies and Agencification in Light of the Common Approach on EU Decentralised Agencies' in Sacha Garben, Inge Govaere en Paul Nemitz (eds), *Critical Reflections on Constitutional Democracy in the European Union* (Oxford, Hart, 2019) 247–248; Mathias Koenig-Archibugi, 'Accountability' in Jacob Katz Cogan, Ian Hurd and Ian Johnstone (eds), *The Oxford Handbook of International Organizations* (Oxford, Oxford University Press, 2018); Arne Vandenbogaerde, *Towards Shared Accountability in International Human Rights Law. Law, Procedures and Principles* (Cambridge, Intersentia, 2016) 36–38; Alain Pellet, 'The Definition of Responsibility in International Law' in James Crawford, Alain Pellet, Simon Olleson, Kate Parlett (eds), *The Law of International Responsibility* (Oxford, Oxford University Press, 2015) 8–11; Chittharanjan Felix Amerasinghe, *Principles of the Institutional Law of International Organizations* (Cambridge, Cambridge University Press, 2009) 385–386.

[1017] See n 59.

[1018] Conversely, there has been a case before the General Court on the matter of transparency requirements regarding border operations in which Frontex is involved. However, the General Court ruled *in casu* that 'that the defendant institution or agency, when dealing with a request for disclosure of certain information, is not required to reveal in the statement of reasons for the contested act information the effect of which would be, if that information were disclosed, to undermine the public interest covered by the exception relied on by that institution or agency'. Frontex has now initiated proceedings against the Applicants for the purpose of obtaining 'excessive' legal fees, which the Defendants in this second case argue, will have a 'chilling effect' on any future attempts at legal review of Frontex action. CJEU (General Court) 2019 *Izuzquiza and Semsrott n* 48 at §112; Arne Semsrott and Luisa Izuzquiza, 'Frontex Is Taking Us to Court' (FradDenStaat – Freedom of Information Investigations, 2 December 2020) fragdenstaat.de/en/blog/2020/12/02/frontex-costs-court-transparency/; Arne Semsrott and Luisa Izuzquiza, 'General Court Rules on Frontex: Less Transparency at EU Borders' (FradDenStaat – Freedom of Information Investigations, 27 November 2020) fragdenstaat.de/en/blog/2019/11/27/frontex-judgement-luxemburg-transparency/.

[1019] Sergio Carrera and Leonard den Hertog 'Whose Mare? Rule of Law Challenges in the Field of European Border Surveillance in the Mediterranean' (*CEPS*, 27 January 2015) www.ceps.eu/ceps-publications/whose-mare-rule-law-challenges-field-european-border-surveillance-mediterranean/6.

the European Border and Coast Guard Agency in 2016.[1020] Whilst initially heralded as a new EU Agency, a closer look unveils that the EBCG Agency was no more than the successor of Frontex, with enhanced and new competences.[1021] The 2016 European Border and Coast Guard Regulation built on this momentum and introduced a number of novelties, placing greater emphasis on the securitization of the EU's external border through Frontex-coordinated measures. In addition to the supporting and coordinating role Frontex exercised in the context of joint operations, the Frontex Regulation 2016 allowed the Agency to take initiative in cases requiring urgent action when Member States fell short in providing appropriate measures to deal with increased migratory pressures.[1022] Equally noteworthy, was the enhanced supportive role Frontex exercised at hot-spots. This enhanced role allowed Frontex to provide support in screening and registration of TCNs, as well as in the provision of relevant information concerning access to international protection proceedings.[1023]

The latest legislative reform of Frontex in 2019, solidifies the trend of increased (operational) powers for Frontex, and the increased focus on securitization of border management, as it provides Frontex with a EBCG standing corps envisaged to reach 10,000 members.[1024] Furthermore, the latest reform endows Frontex with executive powers, as well as enhanced powers to collaborate directly (independently) and indirectly (via cooperation with Member States and/or the EU), with third states.[1025]

In tandem with the increased powers afforded to Frontex, an increasingly louder outcry for corresponding human rights safeguards emerged – virtually non-existent at time of the initial establishment of Frontex in 2004. Accordingly, over the course of the following decade, albeit in a fragmented manner, human rights protection was gradually introduced into the Frontex architecture, with the enactment of entities such as the Fundamental Rights Strategy and Action Plan, the Consultative Forum, a Fundamental Rights Officer and finally, as of 2016, a Fundamental Rights Complaint Mechanism.

Notwithstanding these legislative reforms and the increase in conferred powers to Frontex, the EBCG Regulation continues to highlight the shared nature of competences in IBM (see below). It is crucial, however, to underscore that the legislatively embedded shared nature of the competence, is neither infallible, nor does it convey conduct *in theatre*. The distinction between competence division according to the letter of the law, and the manner in which this competence is exercised is evidenced in the EBCG Regulation itself. While on the one hand it is reaffirmed that Member States remain exclusively responsible (and competent) for the determination of who may enter Member State territory, the EBCG Regulation foresees in the possibility for statutory staff of an operational Frontex team, to make decisions on entry or refusal of entry, including decisions on whether visas should or should not be issued (see below).

[1020] Article 1 Frontex Regulation 2016.
[1021] Rosenfeldt n 1003.
[1022] Article 19 Frontex Regulation 2016.
[1023] Article 18 Frontex Regulation 2016.
[1024] Annex I EBCG Regulation. See also: Lilian Tsourdi, 'The New Pact and EU Agencies: an Ambivalent Approach Towards Administrative Integration' (*EU Immigration and Asylum Law and Policy*, 6 November 2020) eumigrationlawblog.eu/the-new-pact-and-eu-agencies-an-ambivalent-approach-towards-administrative-integration/.
[1025] Article 77(3) EBCG Regulation.

Hence, *de iure* competence division established in the EBCG Regulation, is not necessarily demonstrative of how such competence will be applied and implemented in practice. The relevance of this nuance lies in the fact that *de facto* competence division, in addition to the retained discretion by the Member States in a Frontex operation, will determine whether a given course of (unlawful human rights) conduct may be attributed to the Member States, Frontex or both.

i. Mandate

Amid the myriad of tasks and roles accorded to Frontex in line with the EBCG Regulation,[1026] two roles in particular, merit additional attention in light of the implications this may have on questions of responsibility for unlawful human rights conduct. On the one hand, there is the role Frontex plays in determining whether there is a need for urgent action at the EU external border, and on the other hand, there is the role that Frontex plays in the deployment of operational teams.

In the first case requiring urgent action at the EU external border, the Council – following a proposal by the European Commission – may mandate Frontex with the authority and obligation to adopt measures to address the situation of urgency.[1027] Such situations may arise when a Member State has failed to implement measures proposed by the Management Board of Frontex, pursuant to a vulnerability assessment, or alternatively when Member States have failed to request assistance and/or are simply not taking action.[1028] In such situations the EU may, *proprio motu* via the Council, instruct the Member States on how to proceed, regardless of their approval therewith. The role Frontex (and the EU) plays here is significant within the context of questions of attribution as such instructions significantly limit the discretion retained by Member States, which is a determining factor for the attribution of conduct to a particular entity (see below).

Secondly, Frontex has also been conferred the more visible task of deploying operational teams for operations intended to provide technical and operational support to the Member States in the management of the external border. These operations may vary tremendously according to the sought-after objectives (eg, return operations, joint operations at sea) and implicate a large number of different actors including but not limited to, Frontex, EU institutions and other EU agencies, the Member States (host Member States and participating Member States), as well as external third parties such as other IOs and/or third countries. The mere multiplicity of contributors to Frontex operations inevitably complicate questions of attribution and any determination of potential ensuing responsibility, precisely because of the diffusion of conduct across these different actors (see below).

ii. Structure and Organization

Frontex is comprised of two categories of staff: *statutory* staff and *operational* staff (see chart below). The latter constitute the European Border and Coast Guard

[1026] Recital 3 EBCG Regulation.
[1027] Recital 56–57, Article 42 EBCG Regulation.
[1028] Article 42 EBCG Regulation.

(*hereafter* EBCG) as a standing corps. Both are discussed briefly below, as the categorization of the staff members may, again, impact attribution in questions of human rights responsibility.

Figure 5 Categorization of Frontex staff (De Coninck)

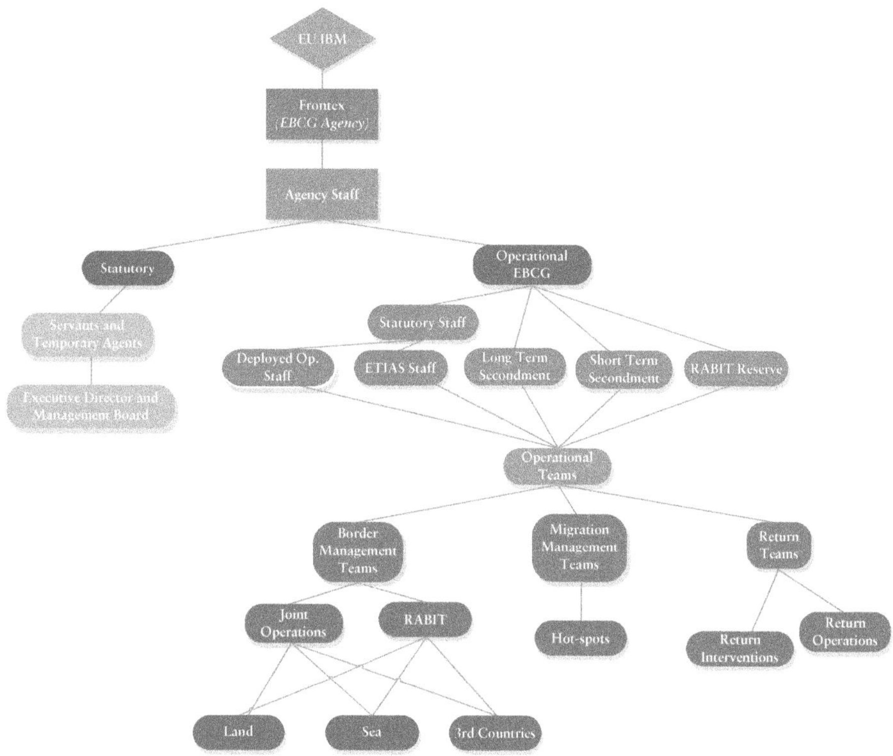

– (Non-Deployed) Statutory Staff

Article 99 EBCG Regulation addresses the administrative and management structure of Frontex, which is composed of the Management Board (1), the Executive Director (2), the Deputy Executive Directors (3), the Fundamental Rights Officer (4) and the Consultative Forum which acts as an advisory body (5).

The Management Board is composed of 1 representative of each Member State and two representatives of the European Commission, all of whom have one vote,[1029] with the exception of the Executive Director who not have a vote in the Management Board.[1030] Among the tasks and decisions to be taken by the Management Board, some of the most crucial are the appointment of the Executive Director

[1029] Article 101 EBCG Regulation. Typically, decisions by the Management Board require an absolute majority, albeit that in certain cases, such as the adoption of decisions concerning vulnerability assessments, a two-thirds majority is required. See Article 100(d) EBCG Regulation.
[1030] Article 105 EBCG Regulation.

(upon suggestion by the European Commission)[1031] and the decisions on whether to conduct vulnerability assessments in Member States.[1032] As aforementioned, these vulnerability assessments may ultimately give rise to Frontex-mandated border management operations, regardless of consent of the Member State involved.

The Executive Director represents the Agency but is independent in his or her functions[1033] and – despite the fact that this function does not provide voting power within the Management Board – exercises significant powers in the execution of Frontex operations. Specifically, the Executive Director drafts the OPLAN for each operation, which details among others, the command-and-control structures of operations, legal review and specific instructions for the teams.[1034] After the OPLAN has been drafted, the Executive Director and host Member State must agree on its contents before the OPLAN becomes binding upon the Agency, the host Member State and the participating Member States in the operation.[1035] Any changes to the OPLAN can only be effectuated in agreement between the Executive Director and the host Member State. This is of relevance to the question of responsibility, as this suggests that any unlawful conduct stemming from such operations, is a shared responsibility between the Member States and Frontex.

The Fundamental Rights officer is appointed by the Management board, following consultation with the Consultative Forum.[1036] The Fundamental Rights Officer is tasked with among others the development of a fundamental rights strategy, the monitoring of fundamental rights adherence by the Agency, and the communication of any violations of fundamental rights to the Executive Director.[1037]

The Consultative Forum functions as an advisory body established by the Agency, which may be consulted by the Executive Director and the Management Board on any matter concerning fundamental rights.[1038] Due to the nature of the tasks, overlaps with the tasks of the Fundamental Rights Officer are not unthinkable.

Finally, the internal complaints mechanism is noteworthy. Though not a managerial or administrative body, this mechanism merits mention as it may receive any complaints concerning unlawful human rights conduct by the Agency. Notably however, the Fundamental Rights Officer will determine the admissibility of such claims[1039] and assess whether such claims are sufficiently substantiated and involve concrete fundamental rights concerns.[1040] However, no indications are given as to when a complaint may be considered as sufficiently substantiated. Moreover, where a complaint is deemed admissible and substantiated regarding a team member of either the host Member State or the home Member State of a Frontex operation, the Member State concerned will ensure the appropriate ensuing disciplinary, criminal

[1031] Article 107 EBCG Regulation.
[1032] See for a full and seemingly exhaustive lists of the tasks of the Management Board – Article 100 EBCG Regulation.
[1033] Article 106 (1) EBCG Regulation.
[1034] Article 38 EBCG Regulation.
[1035] Article 38(3) EBCG Regulation.
[1036] Article 100(2)(z) EBCG Regulation.
[1037] For a non-exhaustive list of tasks see: Article 109 EBCG Regulation.
[1038] Article 108 EBCG Regulation.
[1039] Article 111(4) EBCG Regulation.
[1040] Article 111(3) EBCG Regulation.

and or civil responsibility procedure, to be followed up by the Fundamental Rights Officer and the Agency more generally.[1041] Crucially, the internal complaints mechanism is not a forum for legal review of Frontex conduct and does not preclude (in theory) an application for damages before the CJEU.[1042]

– Operational Staff

Operational conduct by Frontex, may be categorized in five different types of operations, namely: *joint operations* (1); *rapid border intervention operations* (*hereafter* RABIT) (2); *operations in hot-spots* (3); *return operations* (4); and finally, *return interventions* (5). For the purpose of these operations, three types of teams may be established: border management teams (for joint operations and RABIT operations), migration management teams (for operations in hot-spots) and finally return teams (for return operations and interventions). These three categories of teams may be comprised of any combination of operational staff, which together constitute the European Border and Coast Guard Standing Corps (*hereafter* EBCG). The EBCG staff is divided again, in four categories, including statutory staff (1), long-term seconded staff by Member States (2), short-term seconded staff by Member States (3) and finally, RABIT reserve (4). These staff members all have different legal regimes by which they are bound and depending on the secondment, carry the nationality of any of the Member States involved in a particular operation. Again, there is an interplay of different legal regimes governing the potential consequences attached to potentially unlawful human rights conduct by the staff members during any given operation.

Within this vein, it is interesting to cast a glance at the *deployed* statutory staff members under the EBCG. These staff members – when deployed to areas for operational action – enjoy a wide variety of powers,[1043] including the controversial 'executive power', of which the scope and limitations are not clearly delineated by the EBCG Regulation.[1044] More concretely, these statutory staff members are endowed with the power to refuse or authorize entry into EU territory in accordance with the Schengen Border Code,[1045] may function as escorts in return operations,[1046] may make determinations in visa issuance[1047] as well as conduct finger-printing activities.[1048] In addition, these statutory staff members may act as liaison officers in third countries, where they may cooperate with third countries on the topic of preventing irregular migratory flows to the EU external border.[1049] However, the EBCG Regulation does not elaborate upon how such liaison officers may effectuate this cooperation and what the limits are (if any) of their ability to cooperate with third countries.

[1041] Article 111(7) EBCG Regulation.
[1042] Article 98 EBCG Regulation.
[1043] Article 55 EBCG Regulation.
[1044] Instead, the scope and limitations are determined within the confidential OPLAN's, in line with Article 38(3)(d) and 82(2) EBCG Regulation, which differ for each operation.
[1045] Article 55 (b) and (c) EBCG Regulation.
[1046] Article 55 (b) and (c) EBCG Regulation.
[1047] Article 55 (e) EBCG Regulation.
[1048] Article 55 (g) EBCG Regulation.
[1049] Article 77(3) EBCG Regulation.

When juxtaposed with the supposedly exclusive prerogative of EU Member States to determine who may or may not enter its territory, there is seemingly a disconnect. If Member States effectively retain the exclusive responsibility in determining who may or may not be granted access to their territory,[1050] how then, can the statutory operational staff of the EBCG be accorded seemingly undefined 'executive powers', as well as the power to decide upon entry and return of individuals as stipulated in the EBCG Regulation? This also sits uneasy with the retained sovereignty of non-implicated Member States (Member States *not* involved in a particular operation), who have not necessarily consented to this de facto shift of competence in the AFSJ without internal borders.

Article 55(7) EBCG Regulation does establish a list of actions that require 'executive powers' but neither explains how such 'executive powers' are triggered, nor the scope or duration of such executive powers. Instead, the particularities of such 'executive powers' appear to be the result of bi- and multi-lateral agreements adopted within the context of the OPLAN. Indeed, Article 38(3)(d) and Article 82(2) EBCG Regulation in turn, explain that 'a description of the tasks, including those requiring executive powers' should be included in the (confidential) OPLAN. What these provisions fail to clarify however, is *how* the apportionment of conduct and subsequent responsibility will be established when human rights issues occur in the exercise of executive powers. Although recital 58 EBCG Regulation acknowledges that any damage occurring as the result of the exercise of 'executive powers' *should* result in Agency liability, it is not explained whether this would constitute exculpatory responsibility (i.e. to the exclusion of the implicated Member State(s)), or rather, shared responsibility together with the implicated Member States (for the same or different contributions to a single human rights harm). And precisely this question, is crucial when applying the EU's human rights responsibility regime (according to the *lex generalis* and the *lex specialis*) to conduct by Frontex.

In addition to the statutory EBCG staff, Member States may also second individuals on a long-term basis for a period of 24 months which may be prolonged for 12–24 months, or alternatively for a short secondment of four months, which may also be extended. Again, the provisions governing long-term and short-term secondment, do not develop apportionment of conduct and responsibility in case of unlawful human rights conduct in the execution of these operations. Finally, Article 58 EBCG Regulation holds that the Member States shall contribute additional operational staff for RABIT when the first three categories of staff have already been deployed. Again, this provision does not address the notion of responsibility.

The tasks and powers of the members of the operational teams, which are distinct from the tasks and powers of the statutory members of the operational teams, are elaborated upon in Article 82 EBCG Regulation. However, this provision does not provide clarification as to what the operational staff members are permitted to do (in contrast to the list of permitted actions by the statutory staff members). Rather, the provisions recall that the powers and tasks borne by the teams in Frontex-mandated operations are limited by the required authorization of the home Member State, and the relevant provisions of EU, international and domestic law (Article 82(3)

[1050] Article 7(2) EBCG Regulation.

EBCG Regulation), in particular concerning fundamental rights (Article 82(4) EBCG Regulation). It furthermore elaborates upon the uniforms to be worn by the teams in operations (Article 82(6) EBCG Regulation), and the use of force together with the right to carry service weapons (Article 82(7)–(9) EBCG Regulation). Finally, the provision clarifies that the operational teams may consult relevant databases for the purpose of executing the tasks and objectives set out in the OPLAN, which seemingly determines in greater detail what the precise tasks are of the implicated teams.

Indeed, Article 43 EBCG Regulation holds that the instructions to the teams shall be 'in accordance with the operational plan', which sets out (among others) the objectives of the deployment, 'a description of the tasks, including those requiring executive powers', responsibility arrangements, special instructions for the teams, the command-and-control structures of the deployed operation, the terms of cooperation with third countries and incident reporting along with an evaluation scheme including benchmarks to assess whether the objectives have been met. The OPLAN thus encompasses the concrete tasks of the deployed teams, as well as more detailed provisions on the apportionment of responsibility. In sum, the OPLAN – which differs for every operation – seemingly contains all the relevant information and building blocks for the purpose of establishing responsibility.

The particularities of the OPLAN are governed by Article 38 EBCG Regulation, which is applicable to all Agency operations.[1051] The OPLAN is drawn up by the Executive Director[1052] and requires the agreement of both the Executive Director together with the host Member State of an operation. Interestingly, the Management Board, in which the Executive Director has no voting power, does not appear to be involved in the drafting, the agreement on or the execution of the OPLAN. Rather, the only implicated parties are the Executive Director, the host Member State and participating Member States as concerns its implementation.[1053] In fact, any adaptions to the OPLAN throughout the course of an operation, requires the consent of the Executive Director and the host Member State.[1054] Interestingly, where absolute majority voting is required for any and all decisions taken within the Management Board of Frontex in which the Executive Director does not have a right to vote,[1055] conversely, decisions concerning the OPLAN appear not to require any consent other than that of the Executive Director and the host Member State. Put plainly, it is peculiar that precisely those operational measures that may give rise to fundamental rights concerns in the execution of Frontex operations, are determined in detail in a confidential OPLAN, with limited to no oversight, dictating the precise instructions and responsibility-chains to operational teams engaged in such operations, by the executive director who is for all means and purposes an EU representative and one or more Member State representative. This is not to say that there is no merit to the finding of the General Court whereby it held that Frontex could not be obliged to disclose information where 'the effect (of which) would be, if that information were disclosed, to

[1051] Article 38(5) EBCG Regulation.
[1052] Article 38(2) EBCG Regulation.
[1053] Article 38(3) EBCG Regulation.
[1054] Article 38(4) EBCG Regulation.
[1055] Article 105 EBCG Regulation.

undermine the public interest'[1056] of its conduct, in light of the 'particularly sensitive and essential nature of the public interests concerned'. In laymen's terms – insofar the information contained in the OPLAN could undermine the effectiveness of a Frontex-mandated operation, indeed, disclosure thereof in its entirety should be avoided. However, such operational confidentiality is a far cry from transparency on what (executive) tasks are to be exercised by the operational teams, how the command-and-control structures are organized in theory, and how apportionment of responsibility will be determined. Nuance is required here, particularly in light of the fact that only two entities are involved in the adoption of the OPLAN (Executive Director and the host Member State), without clarity on the legal status of the OPLAN and available judicial recourse against its contents and implementation. If nothing else, the shared role in the approval suggests shared responsibility.

b. Command Structures and Responsibility Apportionment

As indicated, the command-and-control structures (and ensuing responsibility-provisions) for Frontex-mandated operations are largely determined by the specific OPLANs drafted according to the specificities of each individual operation. Moreover, the command-and-control structures will inevitably vary depending on the implicated parties in any given operation. Hence, operations may or may not include *inter alia* any number of participating Member States, (including seconded individuals), as well as IOs, third countries and EU institutions, bodies, offices or agencies. Article 84(2) and Article 98 EBCG confirm that the provisions on liability and disciplinary action[1057] do not preclude concurrent legal review before the CJEU, including an action for damage against the Agency for unlawful (human rights) conduct in the execution of its operations.[1058] However, prior to applying the responsibility framework to the Frontex operational action, certain observations are necessitated.

Firstly, the EBCG Regulation appears to endorse the notion of shared responsibility, as evidenced by the numerous references thereto in the recitals and operative provisions.[1059] This is implicit in the fact that the Executive Director and the host Member State must both agree on the contents of the OPLAN. Similarly, the oversight provided by the Management Board, which is made up out of representatives of all Member States and two representatives of the European Commission, highlight the joint nature of the operations occurring under the *chapeau* of Frontex. However, upon closer inspection, it becomes evident that the textual references to 'shared responsibility', do not (necessarily) refer to the apportionment of legal responsibility pursuant to operational unlawful conduct, but rather to the shared nature of the competence of border management and IBM, between Frontex and the Member States *in abstracto*. This is supported by the assertion that IBM 'should be implemented as

[1056] CJEU (General Court) 2019 *Izuzquiza and Semsrott n* 48 at §64 and 112.

[1057] A discussion of the criminal liability and disciplinary action *vis-à-vis* individual staff members falls beyond the scope of the present contribution and will not be discussed here.

[1058] See also: Recital 104 EBCG Regulation which holds that the internal complaint mechanism of Frontex does not preclude legal action before the CJEU or other adjudicatory or administrative mechanisms.

[1059] See inter alia Recital 12, 20, 42, 84, 112, as well as Article 7 EBCG Regulation.

a shared responsibility of the Agency and the national authorities responsible for border management" while "Member States retain the primary responsibility for the management of their borders'.[1060] In addition, the EBCG Regulation does not hesitate to repeatedly underline that the Member States retain *primary* responsibility, whereas the Agency only supports and coordinates – highly reminiscent of the approach adopted in the Draft Accession Agreement (see above). In fact, only in the specific case where statutory staff exercise executive powers, *can* the Agency consider itself responsible according to the rules of the organization – this does not reveal much however, concerning the nature of such liability.[1061] Conversely, the EBCG Regulation recalls that the division of competences remain unaffected thereby, and the Member States accordingly remain responsible for their adherence to international agreements, including the ECHR.[1062]

Mindful of the foregoing, including the various command-and-control and responsibility structures at play, it appears that the EBCG Regulation pursues shared responsibility as a matter of principle. Somewhat paradoxically, the EBCG Regulation only foresees in responsibility vis-à-vis the Agency in a subsidiary manner, and only explicitly where statutory staff exercise 'executive powers' in an unlawful manner. The Regulation does not foresee in Frontex responsibility for the facilitating of unlawful (human rights) conduct. Having identified the most relevant provisions in the EBCG Regulation on responsibility, the analysis now turns to two examples where Frontex has been documented as being involved in unlawful push-backs together with the Greek Coast Guard in June and August 2020.

2. TRACING HUMAN RIGHTS IMPLICATIONS

On 13 March 2020, amid COVID-19 restrictions across the EU, Greece requested the deployment of two Frontex-mandated Rapid Border Intervention Teams (RABIT) to de-escalate and deflect migratory flows from Turkey and prevent entry to TCNs seeking international protection.[1063] These RABIT operations resulted in the deployment of 100 additional operational staff on the Greek and Turkish land and sea border, totalling approximately 600 Frontex operational staff deployed in Greece.[1064] This followed immediately after the decision of Greece in early March 2020 to suspend asylum applications for one month on the basis of Article 78(3) TFEU concerning emergency situations,[1065] and allegations of a black site

[1060] Recital 12 EBCG Regulation.
[1061] Recital 58 and Article 7(4) EBCG Regulation.
[1062] Recital 20 EBCG Regulation.
[1063] Matthias Monroy, 'Frontex Launches New Operations in Greece' (*Statewatch*, 14 March 2020) www.statewatch.org/news/2020/march/frontex-launches-new-operations-in-greece/.
[1064] ibid.
[1065] Diana Naoum, 'Greece Restarts Suspended Asylum Procedure – Country's 30-Day Hold on Right to Claim Asylum Not Renewed' (*Human Rights Watch*, 5 June 2020) www.hrw.org/news/2020/06/05/greece-restarts-suspended-asylum-procedure; ECRE, 'Violations Continue in Greece, EU Says Asylum Procedures Cannot be Suspended' (*European Council on Refugees and Exiles*, 13 March 2020) www.ecre.org/violations-continue-in-greece-eu-says-asylum-procedures-cannot-be-suspended/.

in Northern Greece where TCNs were being detained, stripped of belongings and expelled back to Turkey without the ability to request international protection.[1066]

These events culminated in several reported deaths and widespread allegations of human rights abuses in the form of violence and push-backs by both Greek authorities and complicit Frontex-deployed guards. Nevertheless, no Serious Incident Reports were filed with Frontex, and Frontex denied all involvement therein, despite its deployment of the RABIT in March 2020. Repeated calls by the European Commission in October 2020, to investigate claims of illicit push-backs by Frontex, of seaborne TCNs seeking asylum in Greece, failed to sway the Agency into assessing these purported violations of *non-refoulement*.[1067] The refusal by Frontex to address the matter in substance, prompted an additional inquiry in November by the European Ombudsman into the efficacy of the Frontex's internal complaint mechanisms, for human rights violations occurring in the exercise of its powers,[1068] as well as questioning by the European Parliament (see above).

In light of these events, investigative journalists in a joint investigation between Bellingcat, Lighthouse Reports, Der Spiegel, ARD and TV Asahi, identified six distinct incidents over the course of March 2020 to August 2020, in which Frontex complicity (together with Greece) in unlawful push-backs of TCNs back to Turkey in the Aegean Sea, was documented.[1069] The joint investigation unveils that the push-backs generally took place in one of two ways.[1070] On the one hand there was the practice of effectively blocking passage and entry to unworthy sea vessels travelling from Turkey to Greece through physical blockades or the disabling of the engine on the sea vessel.[1071] On the other hand, there was the practice of detaining TCNs and subsequently returning and abandoning them on unseaworthy vessels without an engine in the middle of the Aegean sea.[1072] While it is notoriously difficult at sea to ascertain what party is responsible for what conduct due to involvement of multiple vessels of the Greek Coast Guard and others,[1073] for two out of the six aforementioned incidents, there is explicit video footage implicating Frontex in these *de facto* push-backs.[1074]

[1066] Matina Stevis-Gridneff, Patrick Kingsley, Haley Willis, Sarah Almukhtar and Malachy Browne, 'We Are Like Animals: Inside Greece's Secret Site for Migrants' (*New York Times*, 10 March 2020 – updated 4 December 2020) www.nytimes.com/2020/03/10/world/europe/greece-migrants-secret-site.html.

[1067] European Commission, 'Extraordinary Meeting of Frontex Management Board on the Alleged Push Backs on 10 November 2020' (*European Commission – Migration and Home Affairs*, 11 November 2020) ec.europa.eu/home-affairs/news/extraordinary-meeting-frontex-management-board-alleged-push-backs-10-november-2020_en.

[1068] European Ombudsman Inquiry of 10 November 2020, *Own Initiative Inquiry about the European Border and Coast Guard Agency (Frontex), and Its Internal Complaint Mechanism*, Case OI/5/2020/MHZ, www.ombudsman.europa.eu/en/opening-summary/en/134799.

[1069] Bellingcat Report n 1010 at 5.

[1070] ibid.

[1071] ibid.

[1072] ibid, Matina Stevis-Gridneff, Patrick Kingsley, Haley Willis, Sarah Almukhtar and Malachy Browne, 'We Are Like Animals: Inside Greece's Secret Site for Migrants' (*New York Times*, 10 March 2020 – updated 4 December 2020) www.nytimes.com/2020/03/10/world/europe/greece-migrants-secret-site.html.

[1073] This is aggravated by the unavailability of transponder information, which was either not registered, not turned on or out of range. Bellingcat Report n 1010 at 19.

[1074] For the methodology on gathered evidence on all six incidents, see: Bellingcat Report n 1010 at 3–4, 6. For the other four incidents, 'Frontex assets were recorded as being within a certain range', albeit that the

The joint investigation concludes that concerning two incidents, taking place on 8 June and 15 August, it can be established that Frontex was not only aware of the push-backs on account of visual proximity to the push-backs, it appears from video-footage and image-capturing that a Frontex-asset actively participated in a push-back by physically preventing access to Greek territory for an unseaworthy vessel carrying TCNs.[1075] Concerning the incident on 8 June in particular, which took place off the coast of Lesbos, there is video footage of Frontex-vessel MAI1103 physically blocking passage to a dinghy carrying TCNs, with staff members onboard the Frontex-vessel communicating with the TCNs onboard. Subsequently, the MAI1103 was recorded as coming in even closer proximity to the dinghy at sufficient speed to generate waves, which is 'especially dangerous due to the overloaded and unseaworthy nature of the dinghies.'[1076] Upon arrival by the Greek Coast Guard, the Frontex vessel ultimately left the scene.[1077]

Recalling the negative obligation to refrain from any acts (or omissions) that result in the return of individuals to a territory where there is a real risk of significant ill-treatment upon arrival, and the corresponding positive obligations, to at least provide TCNs with the ability to submit a request for international protection,[1078] these incidents suggest that the *non-refoulement* principle was disregarded, at the very least from the perspective of the right-holders. Moreover, the joint conduct in the Aegean Sea on 8 June appears to negate the enforceable legal obligation to respect, protect and fulfil the principle of *non-refoulement*, in violation of international law and the CFR (see above). Similarly, this documented conduct by Frontex, appears to disregard recital 84 and 103, as well as Article 7(2), 48(1), 50(3), and Article 80 of the EBCG Regulation which holds that 'The European Border and Coast Guard shall guarantee the protection of fundamental rights in the performance of its tasks under this Regulation ....in particular the principle of non-refoulement'. Mindful of these concrete incidents, what prevents determinations of responsibility of Frontex as an EU agency, for complicity in human rights harms at sea?

3. RESPONSIBILITY IN PRACTICE

From the outset, it is important to underline that operational conduct taken within the remit of Frontex operations, will (to a certain extent) be differently assessed than operational action under CFSP/CSDP operations such as Operation Sophia. While the expanded scope of Frontex competences also permit the Agency to operate within

authors argue that it is difficult, given nature of the operation as being joint and the technical equipment employed by the Greek Coast Guard and Frontex, that Frontex was not aware of the unfolding push-backs.

[1075] Bellingcat Report n 1010 at 10–19.

[1076] ibid 15.

[1077] ibid 15.

[1078] ECtHR (Grand Chamber) Judgment of 23 February 2012, *Hirsi Jamaa and others v Italy*, App no. 27765/09, §114–121; ECtHR Concurring Opinion Judge Pinto De Albuquerque of 23 February 2012, *Hirsi Jamaa and others v Italy*, App no. 27765/09 §11. See also: ECtHR (Grand Chamber) Judgment of 21 November 2019, *Ilias and Ahmed v Hungary*, App no. 47287/15, §141; Moreno-Lax n 17 at 424.

the external dimension of EU law, and accordingly cooperate with CFSP/CSDP operations, as well as engage with third-party actors via binding and non-binding arrangements, the focus of this study will be on the operational conduct of Frontex within the internal dimension of EU law. This entails that the operational conduct discussed *in casu* will not be affected by the limited judicial review of the CJEU in CFSP/CSDP measures, and the conduct will not be characterised by arrangements between Frontex and third parties.

What is common, however, across these modes of operational action, is the OPLAN. Many of the findings pertaining to the (confidentiality of the) OPLAN within the discussion of Operation Sophia, will thus also be relevant in the present discussion.

a. The EU *Lex Specialis* Applied

i. Independent Responsibility

Having established that the Charter is fully applicable to the events that occurred in the Aegean Sea, and applies to Frontex, the *lex specialis* for independent responsibility will be applied, as well as the *lex specialis* for shared responsibility to determine whether any responsibility may be apportioned to Frontex, for its (indirect) involvement in acts that resulted in the push-back of individuals towards Turkey. It is interesting to note that, contrary to the (limited) provisions regarding responsibility for operational conduct by Operation Sophia according to the respective Council Decisions, the EBCG Regulation provides an intricate interplay of provisions which have direct and indirect ramifications on the potential of holding the Agency responsible.

– Causal Conduct Attributable to the EU

A cursory reading of the EBCG Regulation suggests that shared responsibility prevails in the determination of responsibility stemming from Frontex conduct, albeit with the caveat that Member States bear *primary* responsibility for IBM generally, and the *exclusive* (ie exonerating/exculpatory) responsibility for return and entry decisions (see above). However, when applied in practice a number of concerns arise. As aforementioned, decisions concerning entry and return may also be taken by statutory Frontex staff members throughout an operation in accordance with its ad hoc executive powers. Such decisions may entail (exclusive?) responsibility of the Agency based on recital 58 and Article 7(4) EBCG Regulation if found to be a breach of EU law. Crucially however, the determinations of the scope and extent of such executive powers, and the arrangements between the Agency and the host Member State are detailed in a confidential OPLAN, which differs per specific operation. Applied to the events of 8 June and 15 August, it cannot be determined, without insight into the OPLAN, what party was entitled to undertake specific acts and there is no indication as to whether shared responsibility was envisaged, or rather, exculpatory independent responsibility.

Furthermore, determinations of attribution of conduct differ across various areas of substantive EU law (eg use of the normative control model of attribution in the broader sense (WTO law);[1079] the competence model via the use of declarations of competence and an analysis of de facto competence division (UNCLOS, investment, environmental law),[1080] as well as procedural (internal) mechanisms to determine to what party an act should be attributed[1081]). With respect to Frontex mandated measures in the enactment of IBM, it appears that this fluctuating and haphazard approach continues. Whereas on the one hand, shared responsibility and underlying attribution appear to be pursued, this is quickly offset – again – by the reference to the primary responsibilities of the Member States, in line with their competences. Additionally, the provisions concerning responsibility of the Agency for unlawful human rights conduct are continuously cushioned with implicit and explicit references to the divisions of power.[1082] The generic reference that the EBCG 'shall ensure that no person, in contravention of the principle of non-refoulement, be forced to disembark in, forced to enter, or conducted to a country' but solely in the 'the performance of its tasks' loses significance as the EBCG Regulation repeatedly recalls that its tasks are predominantly of a supporting and subsidiary nature vis-à-vis the primary role adopted by the Member States in the implementation of IBM.[1083] Such stand-alone provisions are not problematic as such, but when taken as a whole – embedded in secondary legislation which consistently underscores the primary responsibilities of the Member States involved in Frontex operations – this leads to the conclusion that conduct will be attributed to the Agency in only highly exceptional cases. This, however, stands in stark contrast with the nebulous executive powers accorded to deployed statutory staff members of the EBCG, and appears to be at odds with the actions and role of Frontex staff *in theatre*.

The sole scenario in which the EBCG Regulation explicitly foresees in attribution (and ensuing responsibility) to the Agency, is in the case of executive power exercised unlawfully by a deployed statutory staff member of the EBCG standing corps. Bearing in mind that the determination of when and how such executive powers may be used, is documented in the OPLAN, and bearing in mind that *in casu* the recorded actions by the Frontex vessel MAI1103 are not necessarily the direct result of deployed statutory staff members exercising their executive powers, it becomes highly unlikely that attribution vis-à-vis the Agency can be established to this particular fact pattern.

In addition to the requirement of attribution, causality would have to be established between Frontex-mandated conduct, and the ensuing damage. In this regard, consistent case law has held that, the incurred damage 'must be a sufficiently direct consequence of the act, constituting the immediate cause of the damage suffered'.[1084] Consequently, to meet the causation requirement for a successful claim for damages,

[1079] Contartese n 322 at 430; Kuijper and Paasivirta n 267 at 62.

[1080] Contartese n 322 at 423, 436–441.

[1081] Contartese n 322 at 450.

[1082] See for example: Recital 20 EBCG Regulation. See also: Article 80 EBCG Regulation 'The European Border and Coast Guard shall guarantee the protection of fundamental rights in the performance of its tasks under this Regulation in accordance with Union law …'.

[1083] Article 80(2) EBCG Regulation.

[1084] See (and all cases cited therein): CJEU (CFI) Order of 12 December 2007, *Atlantic Container Line and Others v Commission*, T-113/04, ECLI:EU:T: 2007:377, §31.

an individual TCN would have to show that the damage flowed directly (and exclusively?) from the unlawful conduct, without the chain of causation being 'broken by the Member State'.[1085] This rule of causation makes it exceedingly difficult, if not impossible, to identify Frontex conduct as the 'immediate' cause of the damage. In instances of shared conduct, the immediacy requirement thus poses significant obstacles to the burden and standard of proof from the perspective of the TCN. This approach is implicitly confirmed by the CJEU in *Mauerhofer v European Commission*, where it held that the causal link may be considered as too remote when there is responsibility for the incurred damage resting also on other parties:

> in the case of a possible contribution by the institutions to the damage for which compensation is sought, that contribution might be considered too remote because of some responsibility resting on others.[1086]

The extremely high threshold for causality requiring not only that the conduct is a *sine qua non* for the damage to arise, but moreover and a direct and potentially exclusive result thereof, remains a near impossible requirement for the Applicant to meet bearing the burden and standard of proof. Not only were multiple vessels involved in the specific events on 8 June and 15 August, on 8 June, upon arrival of the Greek Coast Guard, the Frontex vessel eventually left the scene. Accordingly, under the causality standard required by the CJEU, the causality would be too diffused between various acts of both the Frontex vessel and other vessels present, to successfully establish the requisite causal link. This despite the fact that Frontex, which was recorded on video as involved and in close enough proximity to communicate with the TCNs aboard the dinghy, was instrumental in effectuating the push-back to Turkey. Meeting this high casuality test is furthermore problematized as the EU's general court appears to conflate causation and attribution.

In summary, significant obstacles arise in establishing causal conduct that can be attributed to Frontex. These obstacles are furthermore compounded by the fact that the evidentiary burden, and standard of proof are of such a high threshold that for cases of unlawful human rights conduct involving joint action by the EU or its agencies, it simply cannot be met, as causality will inevitably be too diffused precisely because of the joint nature of the actions.

– Sufficiently Serious Breach of EU Law

Secondly, for non-contractual responsibility of the EU arise, an unlawful act (or omission) must have been committed in violation of a norm of EU law, irrespective of whether the norm is founded in the EU's constituent treaties, EU legislative acts or general principles of Union law.[1087] The CJEU has clarified that for an unlawful act to be established under the EU regime on non-contractual responsibility, the violation

[1085] See also on the notion that the causation should be *exclusive* to the institution concerned, Craig and de Búrca n 143 at 631–632.

[1086] CJEU Judgment of 31 March 2011, *Volker Mauerhofer v European Commission*, C-433/10P, ECLI:EU:C:2011:204, §132.

[1087] CJEU Judgment of 11 July 2007, *Jose Maria Sison v Council of the European Union*, T-47/03, ECLI:EU:T:2007:207, §234; Lenaerts, Maselis, Gutman and Nowak n 448 at §11.49–11.51.

must be qualified as 'sufficiently serious'.[1088] Recall that to be qualified as sufficiently serious unlawful conduct, initially such determinations happened by reference to the amount of discretion retained by the EU and mindful of said discretion, whether the EU had 'manifestly and gravely' overstepped the limitations of the rule of law concerned.[1089] Accordingly, when the EU enjoys little to no discretion, the mere violation of a rule of law will suffice in the qualification of an unlawful act.[1090] Discretion of the EU is not assessed in a legal vacuum or in reference to a general domain of EU law, but instead, it is assessed with regard to the specific circumstances at hand. This underscores that the determination of whether an unlawful act has taken place relies entirely on a case-by-case evaluation by the CJEU.[1091]

Again, the recurring question resurfaces here as to whether it is even possible to simply transpose the concrete obligations stemming from the applicable human rights standards directed at the Member States to the EU.

As hinted at, it is crucial to note that throughout the EBCG Regulation, the shared nature of the responsibilities of the Agency and the Member States are underscored and the Regulation consistently recalls the requirement to conduct Frontex actions and operations in complete compliance with the international human rights standards by which it is bound, including in particular, the *non-refoulement* obligation. However, the conjoint reference to the division of competences, the primary responsibility of Member States in all substantive determinations of entry and return, the subsidiary and supplementary nature of the Frontex action in the realm of IBM, are reminiscent of the terminology employed in the Charter, whereby the level of human rights protection, neither alters the division of competences, nor may it affect the autonomy, unity, effectiveness and primacy of EU law. Bearing this in mind, the requirement that legal obligations binding the EU, and by extension Frontex, must be sufficiently clear, combined with the nebulous *de facto* competence division (in theory) provides sufficient ambiguity to refute the claim that any concrete positive or negative obligations that could be considered binding upon the Agency, were effectively breached in a manner that is sufficiently serious. Legally speaking, making sure individuals cannot approach internal Greek waters through the generation of waves, has not been considered as being a breach of the *non-refoulement* principle under its negative or positive obligations. Hence, notwithstanding its contribution to the eventual push-back, it is unlikely that a breach would be established *in casu*.

The argument that human rights, including the *non-refoulement* principle, must be interpreted in a manner that is practical and effective, encompasses a (positive) due diligence obligation upon the Agency to prevent illegitimate returns and to ensure that the requisite safeguards are being implemented by Member State, is valid. To date however, such line of argumentation has yet to be brought before the CJEU in a claim for damages against Frontex, entailing that it is too soon to assess whether this could solve (part of) the conundrum of the transposability of concrete human rights obligations to the EU.

[1088] CJEU Judgment of 4 July 2000, *Bergaderm and Goupil v Commission*, C-352/98 P, ECLI:EU:C:2000:361 §42–43; Lenaerts, Maselis, Gutman and Nowak n 448 at §11.45.
[1089] Lenaerts, Maselis, Gutman and Nowak n 448 at §11.45.
[1090] ibid.
[1091] Fink n 27 at 208–209.

ii. Shared Responsibility

In the particular case of 8 June, there is clear interaction between the Frontex vessel MAI1103 and the Greek Coast Guard which arrived on the scene after the MAI1103 had already been documented in physically preventing access to Greek territory, without abiding by the positive obligations under the *non-refoulement* principle vis-à-vis the individuals aboard the dinghy. At the very least, the Frontex vessel kept the dinghy in its location, by subjecting it to waves generated by the speed and movement of its own vessel, until the Greek Coast Guard took over and proceeded to continuing the push-back. A factual analysis of this incident casts no doubt over the fact that both parties are complicit in preventing the TCNs from requesting international protection and the push-back of these individuals towards Turkish shores. In fact, under the typology of shared responsibility advanced by Nollkaemper and the 2020 Guiding Principles of Shared Responsibility in International Law, these acts form aspects of cumulative conduct, which theoretically could give rise to cumulative responsibility. The act of not providing the TCNs onboard with the possibility to request international protection despite being able to communicate with them, arguably amounts to a violation of the positive (procedural) obligation by which Frontex is bound under *non-refoulement*. However, this will only be considered an unlawful act if this positive obligation is considered as effectively transposable to Frontex. The ensuing act of pushing the vessel back further into the Aegean Sea by the Greek Coast Guard, is a *separate* unlawful act, which violates the negative obligation under the *non-refoulement* principle. These two distinct unlawful acts, both culminated into the single harm of the individuals concerned, namely the return to a country where ill-treatment has been widely documented vis-à-vis TCNs and at the very least is notorious for indirect refoulement.

However, as aforementioned, EU law does not explicitly (or implicitly) adopt this typology of shared responsibility, much less attach any legal consequences to it. In the absence of legislative or judicial guidance on how to apportion responsibility in a multi-actor operational context, and bearing in mind the significant discrepancies across substantive EU law involving the EU as an entity separate from its Member States in mixed agreements (see above), any determinations of responsibility will inevitably entail recourse back to the traditional conditions for a successful application for damages (see above), which in and of themselves present the Applicants with significant obstacles that prevent effective access to legal remedies for unlawful conduct by Frontex. Again, the question arises whether the ARIO framework could potentially provide any additional relief.

b. The *Lex Generalis* Applied

i. Independent Responsibility

– Attribution

The normative control model on attribution, which may either be interpreted broadly or strictly, on the face of it, provides a sufficient model for attribution of conduct to

Frontex. Indeed, according to the rules of the organization[1092] Frontex is an agency and thus a body of the EU[1093] entailing that its conduct theoretically may be attributed thereto. Furthermore, as it is an EU body having 'legal personality and exercising implementing powers that are conferred upon it' by the EBCG Regulation while enjoying technical and operational independence along with legal, administrative and financial autonomy,[1094] a claim for damages may effectively be directed at it for unlawful human rights conduct throughout one of its operations.

Crucially, however, practice concerning the EU has shown that although international adjudicatory bodies apply the normative control model for attribution, this is not necessarily the case internally: the EU institutions and the CJEU specifically appear far more inclined (with the exception of WTO-disputes) to apply a stringent version of the competence model. Applying this competence model would entail that an assessment would need to be made of the retained 'genuine discretion' by the Member State and in all likelihood result in the finding that the conduct (analysed as a whole – including the physical blockade and ensuing push-back) was attributable to Greece, which arguably retained sufficient discretion to refrain from the push-back.

Moreover, Article 6 ARIO on attribution was never intended to cover operational matters. Instead, such operations fall within the purview of Article 7 ARIO (see above). Hence, despite the deceptive simplicity of applying Article 6 ARIO to the current actions of Frontex in the Aegean Sea, everything would depend upon the legal bases that are invoked in an *ex post facto* proceeding to establish attribution. If the normative control model under Article 6 ARIO is accepted as the legal basis to establish attribution, no significant issues would arise insofar this model of attribution is not exculpatory. If, however, the normative control model of attribution is exculpatory this would mean that the wrongful conduct would be attributed to Frontex and absolve the Member State (Greece) or vice versa. Given Greece's involvement in the execution of the operation, as well as the retained primary responsibility of the Member States in the implementation of the EBCG Regulation, attribution of the push-back to Frontex seems implausible.

However, in the event that Article 7 ARIO is applied to determine attribution, in light of the operational nature of the events that occurred on 8 June and 15 August, it may be far more difficult to establish who precisely exercised effective control over the situation, whereby TCNs were physically prevented from requesting international protection and subsequently pushed back to Turkey, precisely as such arrangements are determined by the OPLAN.

– Internationally Wrongful Act

The line of argumentation concerning the transposability of concrete positive and negative obligations, both substantive and procedural, remains unchanged here. Without certainty as to the scope of the obligations (negative, positive, procedural and substantive) stemming from the *non-refoulement* principle as they apply to the

1092 Article 93(1) EBCG Regulation.
1093 Recital 105 EBCG Regulation; Article 93(1) EBCG Regulation.
1094 Recital Clause 105 EBCG Regulation.

EU and Frontex, *in casu* the EU entities continue to retain sufficient leeway in demonstrating that it could not be bound by specific obligations of the *non-refoulement* principle that were developed specifically for and tailored to Member States.

ii. Shared Responsibility

At this point it has become clear that the obstacles for Applicants that were previously discussed in theory and in practice under the *lex specialis* and *lex generalis* regime for independent responsibility within the context of operational conduct in the implementation of IBM, will likewise resurface under the ARIO's provisions on shared responsibility.

While arguably the conduct by Frontex *in casu* could be construed as constituting either 'aid or assistance' under Article 14 ARIO, or circumvention of its own obligations via 'authorization' under Article 17 ARIO, the effectiveness of these provisions in ascertaining responsibility of Frontex is doubtful at best.

For responsibility under Article 14 ARIO to arise, an Applicant would need to prove that the opposability requirement is met, entailing that both the Member State *and* the EU are effectively bound by the *same* legal obligation. Depending on how broadly or narrowly this requirement is construed (see above), the functional speciality of the EU prevents the transposition of concrete human rights obligations that are applicable to Member States to the EU and Frontex specifically. Hence if the opposability requirement is understood strictly, requiring thus that both parties are bound by the same *specific and concrete* human rights obligations (flowing from the *non-refoulement* principle), the EU could evade any shared responsibility. If on the other hand, the opposability requirement is approached in a broad manner, whereby it is solely required that the parties concerned are bound by the same legal commitment (in theory), this condition may be met. Crucially however, this will depend on how the opposability criterion is interpreted in a post facto adjudicatory setting.

Moreover, Article 14 ARIO requires that 'knowing intent' is established, without definitive guidelines however, on the required threshold for the standard of proof that an Applicant would need to meet to demonstrate 'knowing intent'. Arguably, in light of the widespread documentation that Greece has frequently violated the *non-refoulement* principle through push-backs, and in light of the proximity and cooperation between the MAI1103 Frontex vessel and the Greek Coast Guard, this requirement would prove less of an issue in this particular case. However, as Frontex merely prevented access to the internal Greek waters, and the subsequent conduct by the Greek Coast Guard is the result of its own discretion, the threshold of the evidentiary burden is instrumental in being able to establish 'knowing intent'. The absence of any delineation of this evidentiary threshold, again appears to disadvantage individual Applicants seeking to establish Frontex responsibility.

In sum, depending on the how the conditions for Article 14 ARIO are applied in practice, this legal basis may provide Applicants with a potential avenue for the purpose of establishing responsibility vis-à-vis Frontex. Much however, will be contingent on how strict or broad the opposability criterion is construed, as well as how strict or broad the evidentiary threshold is construed.

Under Article 17 ARIO IOs incur responsibility insofar it is demonstrated that the latter circumvented its *own* legal obligations by authorizing Members to undertake action that would be considered unlawful had it been conducted by the organization itself. Under Article 17 ARIO the opposability criterion thus does not need to be met, entailing that it must only be demonstrated that the conduct by the Member State would have been unlawful had it been executed by the IO. Such authorization may take the form of binding and non-binding decisions. While this thus appears to be an alternative manner in which to hold the EU and Frontex specifically, responsible for its conduct in the Aegean Sea, in practice, this is far more complicated. Again, the evidentiary smokescreens as a result of the confidential OPLAN, entail that it is difficult (if not impossible) to discern whether Greece had obtained any authorization on behalf of Frontex, to engage in push-backs of the TCNs concerned. The absence of protest on behalf of Frontex as the events unfolded, could arguably be construed as entailing that the Frontex and by extension the EU, had acquiesced to Greece engaging in conduct giving rise to human rights harms. *In casu*, such acquiescence (and arguably, implicit) authorization would thus stem from the condoning of the actions by Frontex. However, the ARIO do not elaborate upon the required standard of proof to be met by individual Applicants in demonstrating that States were authorized by an organization to engage in unlawful conduct. Again, positive law does not provide any definitive guidelines and leaves the determination of responsibility under Article 17 ARIO entirely up to *post facto* adjudicatory assessments, which will inevitably be affected by the forum in which such disputes are raised. In turn, this may give rise to fragmentation and legal uncertainty in the adjudication of responsibility stemming from multi-actor operations involving Member States and the EU.

c. Interim Conclusions on Responsibility for Control Measures at the EU External Border

Notwithstanding the exponentially more significant references to the obligation to respect the *non-refoulement* principle in the EBCG Regulation, the conditionality for responsibility to arise under the *lex specialis* as well as the *lex specialis* regime, appear to yield the same difficulties in the present circumstances. Issues concerning causality, attribution, and the determination of sufficiently serious unlawful conduct resurface in an analogous manner as they did with respect to operational action stemming from Operation Sophia. Arguably, this is more problematic in light of the nature of the events, the proximity, the increased demands for responsibility but most of all, in light of the extensive (generic) reference to fundamental rights adherence. The EBCG Regulation weaves human rights protection in the Frontex architecture by way of textual references, yet upon closer inspection, this appears to be no more than a legal mirage, as the enforceability thereof vis-à-vis Frontex and the EU remains subject to seemingly unsurmountable obstacles.

9

Return and Readmission Agreements with Third Countries

THE EU HAS repeatedly underlined that effective IBM and an effective BAM policy is contingent on an effective return policy. While a number of legislative reforms of the Return Directive have sought to render returns more effective in practice, the fact remains that frequently, returns of individuals found to be staying on EU territory irregularly are simply not effectuated.[1095]

In large part, returns and readmission currently are executed through bilateral (in)formal arrangements between Member States and third countries,[1096] which already have exhibited signs of flawed human rights compliance as demonstrated in *Khlaifia v Italy*.[1097] Quoting the precedent-setting *Hirsi Jamaa* ruling, the ECtHR recalled that any form of collective return of individuals to a state of return, without individualized assessments of their applications for protection and without the opportunity to submit reasons against their return, necessarily violates the ECHR.[1098] This finding is neither affected by bilateral (informal) arrangements, nor by (informal) EU-mandated arrangements to that end.[1099] Indeed, Article 3(5) TEU

[1095] See inter alia: Communication from the Commission to the European Parliament and the Council on a more effective return policy in the European Union – a renewed action plan [2017] COM(2017) 200 final, 2. See for a general discussion: Katharina Eisele, 'The EU's Readmission Policy: of Agreements and Arrangements' in Sergio Carrera, Juan Santos Vara and Tineke Strik (eds), *Constitutionalising the External Dimensions of EU Migration Policies in Times of Crisis – Legality, Rule of Law and Fundamental Rights Reconsidered* (Cheltenham, Edgar Elgar Publishing, 2019) 147–148.

[1096] Van Elsuwege and Vankova n 897 at 163–177; Federico Casolari, 'The Unbearable 'Lightness' of Soft Law: on the European Union's Recourse to Informal Instruments in the Fight against Illegal Immigration' in Francesca Ippolito and Federico Casolari (eds), *Bilateral Relations in the Mediterranean* (Cheltenham, Edward Elgar Publishing, 2020) 219–223; Javier A. González Vega, '*Non-Refoulement* at Risk? Asylum's Disconnection Mechanisms in Recent EU Practice' in Sergio Carrera, Juan Santos Vara and Tineke Strik (eds), *Constitutionalising the External Dimensions of EU Migration Policies in Times of Crisis – Legality, Rule of Law and Fundamental Rights Reconsidered* (Cheltenham, Edgar Elgar Publishing, 2019) 91.

[1097] ECtHR (Grand Chamber) Judgment of 15 December 2016, *Khlaifia and others v Italy*, App. No. 16483/12.

[1098] ibid §238.

[1099] ibid §242. In this Grand Chamber ruling no violation was established, despite the Court coming to another conclusion in the previous Chamber ruling. However, the Court recalled its steadfast principles that bilateral or multilateral arrangements cannot cancel out the obligation to ensure that prior to expulsion, individuals are accorded an opportunity to submit reasons for their application for international protection and/or against return decisions directed at them. In this case the prohibition of collective expulsion was at stake. However, this provision goes hand-in-hand with the *non-refoulement* principle, which constitutes the normative underpinning for the prohibition of collective expulsion as evidenced by the

and Article 21 TEU require that the EU in its international arrangements with the wider world, regardless of the type of measures at stake, upholds fundamental rights and the rule of law.[1100] Yet, despite the requirement to sufficiently mainstream human rights protection in such formal and informal readmission and return arrangements, Ippolito argues that much of this human rights protection remains rhetorical, as opposed to effective.[1101] The potential for unlawful human rights conduct is aggravated when such (formal and informal) bilateral or multilateral arrangements envisaging accelerated and simplified readmission procedures, are concluded with states commonly referred to as 'failed states' such as Libya.[1102]

Concurrently with bilateral arrangements between Member States and third states on the topic of readmission and return, the EU too, has become a notable partner of third states for this same purpose. Although initially focused on formal readmission agreements,[1103] the technical difficulties associated to forging formal cooperation between the EU Member States and third countries proved no easy feat in light of political sensitivities in the relations of the partners and the formalities of the Article 218 TFEU procedure on international agreements.

The 'informalisation of EU migration relations with third countries'[1104] characterizes the adopted approach by the EU following the migratory surge in 2015.[1105] In addition to the Global Approach to Migration (*hereafter* GAM)[1106] which had already been adopted by the EU in 2005 with the intent of addressing the root causes of

Hirsi Jamaa ruling repeatedly referenced by the ECtHR *in casu*. For a discussion see: Izabella Majcher, *The European Union Returns Directive and its Compatibility with International Human Rights Law – Analysis of Return Decision, Entry Ban, Detention and Removal* (Leiden, Brill, 2020) 649–650.

[1100] Article 3(5) TEU and Article 21(1) TEU. See also: Stefan Oeter, 'Article 21 – The Principles and Objectives of the Union's External Action' in Hermann-Josef Blanke and Stelio Mangiameli (eds), *The Treaty on European Union (TEU) – A Commentary* (New York, Springer, 2013) 839. See also on the *requirement* to uphold human rights within the external (informal) dimension of BAM: Francesca Ippolito, 'The Rhetoric of Human Rights in EU External Relations in the Mediterranean' in Francesca Ippolito and Federico Casolari (eds), *Bilateral Relations in the Mediterranean* (Cheltenham, Edward Elgar Publishing, 2020) 274–278.

[1101] ibid 278.

[1102] González Vega n 1096 at 92.

[1103] Currently, the EU has concluded an approximated 20 readmission agreements focusing on reciprocal rights and obligations for the EU and third countries in order to facilitate return of irregularly residing TCNs in the European Union. As aforementioned, the reciprocated nature of such agreements, may result in visa facilitation and/or waiving vis-à-vis the implicated third countries. Van Elsuwege and Vankova n 887 at 167; Juan Santos Vara, 'Soft International Agreements on Migration Cooperation with Third Countries: a Challenge to Democratic and Judicial Controls in the EU' in Sergio Carrera, Juan Santos Vara and Tineke Strik (eds), *Constitutionalising the External Dimensions of EU Migration Policies in Times of Crisis – Legality, Rule of Law and Fundamental Rights Reconsidered* (Cheltenham, Edgar Elgar Publishing, 2019) 21. See more generally: Eisele n 1095 at 135–153.

[1104] A prominent example of the informalisation of migration cooperation between the EU and third states is the 2005 Global Approach to Migration (GAM) which sought to tackle the root causes of migratory movements. See for a discussion on informal arrangements within the EU legal order and the CJEU's approach to such informal arrangements: Casolari n 1096 at 216–218, 220.

[1105] Casolari n 1096 at 220; Santos Vara n 1103 at 21.

[1106] In 2011, the GAM was renamed by the EU to include the reference to 'mobility' thus entailing it was titled the 'Global Approach to Migration and Mobility'. See: Communication from the Commission to the European Parliament, the Council, the European Economic and Social Committee and the Committee of the Regions – the Global Approach to Migration and Mobility [2011] COM(2011) 743 final.

migratory surges,[1107] the Migration Partnership Framework (*hereafter* MPF) of 2016[1108] was adopted, which was implemented in parallel to the GAM (eventually GAMM). The MPF differed somewhat from the GAM in that it was an informal means of cooperation in the particular field of readmission, as opposed to migratory management in the GAMM generally.[1109] Despite the apparent difference in objectives however, both informal instruments ultimately sought to strengthen ties with third countries in an attempt to facilitate migration management.[1110] The MPF sought to achieve accelerated and effective results in the realm of readmission through more informal methods, which the GAM could not achieve in light of its focus on *formal* readmission agreements.[1111] In addition to the GAM and the MPF, there are a number of additional informal EU arrangements to facilitate migratory movement management, including but not limited to, the Joint Way Forward on Migration Issues with Afghanistan,[1112] the Standard Operating Procedures with Bangladesh,[1113] and modes of cooperation that are interchangeably referred to as mobility partnerships, common agendas on migration and mobility, compacts and (infamous) statements.[1114] The 2015 European Agenda on Migration solidified the focus on the need for an externalised approach to EU migration management and the need to work with third countries to achieve to achieve the latter.[1115] Specifically, the European Commission reiterated that readmission agreements and policy were integral to the implementation of an effective migration policy.[1116]

[1107] Tineke Strik, 'Migration Deals and Responsibility Sharing: Can the Two Go Together?' in Sergio Carrera, Juan Santos Vara and Tineke Strik (eds), *Constitutionalising the External Dimensions of EU Migration Policies in Times of Crisis – Legality, Rule of Law and Fundamental Rights Reconsidered* (Cheltenham, Edgar Elgar Publishing, 2019) 61.

[1108] Communication from the Commission to the European Parliament, the European Council, the Council and the European Investment Bank on establishing a new Partnership Framework with third countries under the European Agenda on Migration [2016] COM(2016) 385 final.

[1109] Santos Vara n 1103 at 26.

[1110] ibid 25–26.

[1111] ibid 27–28.

[1112] EEAS, 'Joint Way Forward on Migration Issues Between Afghanistan and the EU' (*EEAS*, 2016) eeas.europa.eu/sites/eeas/files/eu_afghanistan_joint_way_forward_on_migration_issues.pdf. See in particular the focus on readmission and returns at pages 3–5. Notably this informal arrangement is characterized as being operational in nature, and not construed to 'create legal rights or obligations under international law' (p. 1 §3). Jean-Pierre Cassarino and Mariagiulia Giuffré, 'Finding Its Place in Africa: Why Has the EU Opted for Flexible Arrangements on Readmission?' *(Migration Research Hub Policy Brief No 01/2017*, 1 December 2017) www.nottingham.ac.uk/hrlc/documents/pb-1-finding-its-place-in-africa.pdf 4. See also: Casolari n 1096 at 222. For an additional discussion: ECRE, 'Joint Statement: Afghanistan is Not Safe: the Joint Way Forward Means Two Steps Back' (*ECRE*, 15 September 2020) www.ecre.org/joint-statement-afghanistan-is-not-safe-the-joint-way-forward-means-two-steps-back/.

[1113] European Commission, 'Decision on the signature of the EU-Bangladesh Standard Operating Procedures for the Identification and Return of Persons without an Authorisation to Stay – Annex 1: EU-Bangladesh Standard Operating Procedures for the Identification and Return of Persons without an Authorisation to Stay' [2017] COM(2017) 6137 final arts.unimelb.edu.au/__data/assets/pdf_file/0009/3409830/Bangladesh-1.pdf.

[1114] Van Elsuwege and Vankova n 897 at 167; Casolari n 1096 at 220; Santos Vara n 1103 at 21, 28.

[1115] European Commission, 'Communication from the Commission to the European Parliament, the Council, the European Economic and Social Committee and the Committee of the Regions – A European Agenda on Migration – COM(2015)240' (*European Commission*, 13 May 2015) ec.europa.eu/home-affairs/sites/homeaffairs/files/what-we-do/policies/european-agenda-migration/background-information/docs/communication_on_the_european_agenda_on_migration_en.pdf 5, 8; Casolari n 1096 at 220; Strik n 1098 at 62.

[1116] Communication from the Commission to the European Parliament and the Council on a more effective return policy in the European Union – a renewed action plan [2017] COM(2017) 200 final, 13; Eisele n 1095 at 144.

Informal modes of cooperation ensure flexibility between the partners on readmission, but such forms of cooperation similarly allow for political sensitivities to be taken into regard. Conversely, formal arrangements may be less capable of exhibiting and ensuring such flexibility, due to the technicalities and complexities inherent to the conclusion of internationally binding agreements.[1117] The complexities of formal arrangements between the EU and third states is evidenced for example, by the excessive duration for the negotiations of the EU-Albania agreement, which prompted bilateral negotiations between Italy and Albania in order to accelerate readmission practices.[1118] Bearing these hurdles in mind, informal cooperation is increasingly relied upon, as evidenced, by the executive powers that have been accorded to deployed statutory staff of Frontex. According to these 'executive powers' Frontex agents have been granted the authorization to cooperate with third countries (together with Member States) for the purpose of 'contributing to the prevention and fight against illegal immigration and the return of returnees',[1119] without any clarification as to how such (informal) cooperation may be conducted.

The expediency of informal cooperation comes at the expense of a number of significant concerns attached to informalisation. The lack of an overarching legal framework regulating responsibility stemming from unlawful readmission and return, generates profound issues on access to an effective legal remedy for the individuals being returned to either their state of origin or a third state.[1120] In an informal context of diffused responsibility (through cooperation of Member States, third states, agencies such as Frontex and possibly, international organizations), determinations of attribution and causation will be difficult to establish. On the first point, Santos Vara goes as far as claiming that the informality of arrangements is not just the result of the political sensitivities that cannot duly be considered in an EU formalised readmission agreement, but the use of such informal arrangements is also precisely 'to avoid the Court of Justice's jurisdiction to review and interpret the agreements adopted in this area'.[1121] So rather than being 'policy ghosts in search of EU normative identity' as he puts it,[1122] he argues that these arrangements are policy ghosts seeking to avoid EU normative review. In addition, the lack of (democratic) oversight in both the conclusion and implementation of such arrangements may generate problems of legality regardless of whether an adjudicatory body asserts adjudicatory jurisdiction over such informal arrangements.[1123] Finally, the obscurity as to the legal status and legal effects

[1117] Majcher n 1099 at 624–625. Santos Vara n 1103 at 23.

[1118] The Albanian Parliament recently approved an EU Commission endorsed five-year agreement with Italy to detain TCNs rescued or intercepted at sea. See n 96. Mariagiullia Giuffré, *The Readmission of Asylum Seekers under International Law* (London, Bloomsbury, 2020) 9/52; Gatti n 1002 at 144–147; Van Elsuwege and Vankova n 897 at 167; Eisele n 1095 at 141.

[1119] Article 77 EBCG Regulation.

[1120] Majcher n 1099 at 640–645; Hülya Kaya, *The EU-Turkey Statement on Refugees: Assessing Its Impact on Fundamental Rights* (Cheltenham, Edward Elgar Publishing, 2020) 69–70; Santos Vara n 1103 at 33–36.

[1121] Santos Vara n 1103 at 33.

[1122] ibid 22.

[1123] ibid 29–33; Eisele n 1095 at 145–146.

such arrangements may or may not have, again present issues in terms of the legal reviewability of such arrangements, possibly to the detriment of effective human rights protection.[1124]

One of the consequences of the informalisation of readmission agreements is that there is neither explicit inclusion of human rights safeguard clauses, nor is there *post facto* human rights compliance review.[1125] Fahey coins this as the 'hyper-legalisation and de-legalisation' of EU external migration law, which depicts 'the growing mass of law and law-related instruments often with tangible and/or meaningful legal effects which surrounds EU external migration law … inextricably linked to de-legalisation through judicial review'[1126] precisely because of the absence of the latter. Yet, Article 51 CFR *in juncto* Article 21 TEU require Member States and the EU, its institutions, bodies, offices and agencies, to uphold human rights even in an informal setting (see above). However, this obligation holds little value if informal readmission arrangements and the implementation thereof are shielded from (judicial) scrutiny.[1127]

Whatever the nature of the readmission arrangements – formal or informal – such arrangements have the effect of transferring the responsibility for TCNs that have or have not been subject to an accelerated *prima facie* status-determination procedure, to the hands of external third country partners.[1128] This entails that likewise in this fourth limb of IBM, there is profound diffusion of responsibility in case of unlawful human rights conduct: the (legitimate or not) return of an individual, is the direct consequence of a number of actors working together. Such diffusion, yet again, works to the detriment of determinations of responsibility for unlawful human rights conduct stemming therefrom.

1. LEGAL FRAMEWORK AND COMPETENCES

The first steps concerning the EU's readmission policy were adopted in 1994 and 1995 with the adoption of a template bilateral readmissions agreement and guiding principles for the drafting of readmission agreements between EU Member States and third countries, respectively.[1129] These recommendations by the Council of Justice and Home Affairs, sought to facilitate standardized approaches to readmission, despite the fact that divergence in the bilateral readmission agreements were bound to occur on account of political idiosyncrasies that characterise the relations between

[1124] Santos Vara argues on this point rightfully notes that there is a difference between whether an arrangement internationally and whether an informal arrangement on EU level, can generate legal effects. See for a discussion on the matter concerning both the legal status and effects of informal arrangements and the implications this had for the CJEU to interpret such informal arrangements in light of general principles of EU law: Santos Vara n 1103 at 33–34. See also: Kaya n 1120 at 69–70. Strik n 1107 at 63.

[1125] Strik n 1098 at 59–60; Casolari n 1096 at 226. See also: Majcher n 1099 at 640–645; Kaya, n 1120 at 69–70.

[1126] Fahey n 83 at 132.

[1127] For an overview of such informal '*non-entrée*' measures, see Kaya n 1120 at 64.

[1128] Strik n 1107 at 59.

[1129] Steve Peers and Nicola Rogers, 'EC Readmission Agreements' in Steve Peers and Nicola Rogers (eds), *EU Immigration and Asylum Law: Text and Commentary* (Leiden, Brill, 2006) 886.

individual Member States with third country counterparts.[1130] With the Treaty of Amsterdam, the EU was accorded the powers to adopt measures in the field of irregular migration generally, including 'repatriation of illegal residents',[1131] but it was only following the Treaty of Lisbon that the EU was conferred the competence to conclude international agreements with third countries concerning readmission.[1132] Incrementally, return and readmission was concretized, as evidenced by the 2009 Stockholm Programme on an Open and Secure Europe and as reiterated in the 2015 Agenda on Migration, with readmission agreements considered as the building blocks of EU migration management.[1133]

2. TRACING HUMAN RIGHTS IMPLICATIONS

Within the context of readmission, the informal working arrangements between a number of actors that may or may not include the EU as a formal partner is particularly worrisome through the lens of responsibility for human rights harms stemming from such arrangements. Specifically, the 2019 EBCG Regulation allows for deployed statutory Frontex staff to work alongside and with third country officials to facilitate readmission and return (see above).[1134] It is unclear whether this may or may not result in readmissions arrangements and how this affects the availability of legal recourse and remedies for TCNs, again in part due to the obscurity that taints such informal working arrangements. This is aggravated by the fact, that the arrangements may differ in content (despite any overarching similarities), precisely because of the different political context in which they are concluded and in light of the differing incentives that are used to coax third countries in readmitting their own nationals, as well as other TCNs.[1135]

For the purpose of the present analysis the focus will be on the controversial and much-debated, informal EU-Turkey Statement[1136] from 2016, which epitomizes the informalisation of readmission and return within the EU, and has functioned as a precedent-setting blue-print since.[1137]

[1130] ibid.

[1131] Article 63(3)(b) Treaty of Amsterdam.

[1132] Article 79(3) TFEU. See also: Van Elsuwege and Vankova n 897 at 166; Eisele n 1095 at 137.

[1133] The European Council Stockholm Programme – An Open and Secure Europe Serving and Protecting Citizens [2010] OJ C 115/1, 31, 35–37. See also: Giuffré n 1118 at 13/52.

[1134] Article 77 EBCG Regulation.

[1135] Whereas the EU-Tunisia agreement was introduced as a press release and encompasses a wider range of reciprocated (soft-law) engagements (n 96), the agreement between Albania and Italy is a formal agreement on migration management specifically, which was formally approved by the Albanian Constitutional Court and the Albanian legislator. Pierre Emmanuel Ngendakumana, 'Albania MPs Approve Deal with Italy to House Migrants' (*Politico*, 22 February 2024) www.politico.eu/article/albania-approves-migration-deal-with-italy/.

[1136] Although formally concluded agreements involving the EU as a treaty party may be amenable to judicial review before the CJEU, the high thresholds for and obstacles inherent to an application for damages resurface here too.

[1137] Analogously to the EU-Turkey Statement, the EU-Tunisia arrangement was posted as a press release on the European Commission website, lacking any further legal qualifications. Memorandum of Understanding on a strategic and global partnership between the European Union and Tunisia (European Commission, 16 July 2023) ec.europa.eu/commission/presscorner/detail/en/ip_23_3887.

The responsibility question that arises in the context of such informal readmission agreements is the extent to which the EU can incur responsibility for contributing to (quasi-)automated returns of TCNs to Turkey, without any *(prima facie)* individualized assessments of claims for international protection. This is particularly relevant now that the General Court,[1138] the CJEU[1139] and the ECtHR[1140] have all implicitly and/or explicitly confirmed that the Turkey Statement is not an EU act, and instead an act of the EU Member States. As such, the practice of informal readmission agreements concluded by the Member States with third countries appear to have been condoned, with the support (and authorization?) of EU entities. In other words, although the Courts have refuted the qualification of the EU-Turkey Statement as a formal EU act, the EU's role in the execution of such informal agreements arises on account of not only its acquiescence thereto, but also its authorization of the Statement and similar arrangements that have been adopted since. As evidenced by the multi-layered judicial review that has already occurred by the General Court, the CJEU and the ECtHR of the compliance of the EU-Turkey statement with the *non-refoulement* principle, it is clear that access to *effective* legal review contesting EU involvement therein for an individual applicant subjected to such arrangements is extremely limited, precisely because of its joint nature. Indeed, Member States in implementing the EU-Turkey Statement remain fully responsible for their human rights obligations stemming from international, regional and domestic law (see above). However, in keeping with the overarching research question, it must be determined whether the EU can incur (shared) responsibility for unlawful human rights consequences stemming from the EU-Turkey Statement which it condones and arguably, authorizes and/or directs. In addressing this question, the practice must first be deconstructed in light of the responsibility framework, to highlight precisely where the obstacles to EU responsibility arise and are most acute. Only then can suggestions be made on how to move forward.

a. The EU-Turkey Statement Contextualized

i. The Statement in Context

The controversy of the EU-Turkey Statement of 18 March 2016 provides an interesting angle to determine how EU responsibility may be established for its (arguably implicit) authorization and facilitation thereof.

At the time of the proclamation of the infamous Statement, the predominant migratory routes towards Europe were the Eastern Mediterranean Route, the Western Balkan

[1138] CJEU (General Court) Order of 28 February 2017, *NF v European Council*, T-192/16, ECLI:EU:T:2017:128.

[1139] CJEU Order of 12 September 2018, *NF v European Council*, Joined Cases C-208/17P to C-210/17P, ECLI:EU:C:2018:705.

[1140] ECtHR Judgment of 25 January 2018, *JR and others v Greece*, App no. 22696/16, §7, 39. The ECtHR appears to implicitly endorse the EU-Turkey Statement as having been concluded between the Member States and Turkey, as opposed to between the EU and Turkey. See for a discussion of the case: Annick Pijnenburg, '*JR and others v Greece*: What Does the Court (Not) Say about the EU-Turkey Statement?' (*Strasbourg Observers*, 21 February 2018) strasbourgobservers.com/2018/02/21/jr-and-others-v-greece-what-does-the-court-not-say-about-the-eu-turkey-statement/.

Route and the Central Mediterranean Route.[1141] In deterring irregular migration and externalising external border management, the EU in cooperation with the Member States, opted to address the increasingly popular Central Mediterranean Route in particular, by proactively collaborating with Turkey.[1142] This route provides for irregular entry via Turkey to Greece, Cyprus and Bulgaria. Precisely due to the fact that Turkey typically acts as a transit country, the EU enhanced its cooperation with Turkey in an attempt to bring a halt to the use of this route.[1143]

Enhanced cooperation with Turkey concerning border management dates back to 2014 when a readmission agreement was concluded pursuant to Article 79(3) TFEU.[1144] This facilitated further cooperation with Turkey, which translated into the Joint Action Plan presented in October 2015,[1145] as well as a communication on 7 March 2016.[1146,1147] Both of the latter acts however, merely conveyed the intention of parties within the scope of irregular migration and readmission. Conversely, the Joint Statement of 18 March 2016, which encompasses not only intentions but following a textual interpretation, reciprocal rights and obligations, as demonstrated by paragraphs 1,[1148] 2,[1149] 3,[1150] 6,[1151] and 9[1152] thereof.

The most contentious aspects of the Statement concern the provisions on the return of *all* irregular TCNs to Turkey from Greece.[1153] While readmission agreements generally may be in complete conformity with (international) human rights law as long as certain conditions are met, it is questionable whether *this* particular arrangement also adheres to the same relevant standards, and the *non-refoulement* principle in particular.

ii. Recalling the Law

Article 51 CFR and Article 21 TEU require (formal *and* informal) EU measures to comply with human rights law, including the *non-refoulement* principle.

[1141] European Commission, 'Questions and Answers: Smuggling of Migrants in Europe and the EU Response – Fact Sheet' (*European Commission*, 13 January 2015) ec.europa.eu/commission/presscorner/api/files/document/print/en/memo_15_3261/MEMO_15_3261_EN.pdf.

[1142] European Council, 'Press Release: EU-Turkey Statement, 18 March 2016' (*European Council – Council of the European Union*, 18 March 2016) www.consilium.europa.eu/en/press/press-releases/2016/03/18-eu-turkey-statement/.

[1143] ibid.

[1144] Steve Peers and Emanuela Roman, 'The EU, Turkey and the Refugee Crisis: What could possibly go wrong?' (*EU Law Analysis*, 5 February 2016) eulawanalysis.blogspot.be/2016/02/the-eu-turkey-and-refugee-crisis-what.html.

[1145] European Commission, 'EU-Turkey Joint Action Plan – Fact Sheet' (*European Commission*, 15 October 2015) ec.europa.eu/commission/presscorner/detail/en/MEMO_15_5860.

[1146] European Council, 'Press Release – Statement of the EU Heads of State or Government' (*European Council – Council of the European Union*, 7 March 2016) www.consilium.europa.eu/en/press/press-releases/2016/03/08/eu-turkey-meeting-statement/.

[1147] Mauro Gatti, 'The EU-Turkey Statement: A Treaty That Violates Democracy' (*EJIL:Talk!*, 18 April 2016) www.ejiltalk.org/the-eu-turkey-statement-a-treaty-that-violates-democracy-part-1-of-2/.

[1148] Regarding the return of TCNs to Turkey.

[1149] Regarding resettlement of Syrians back to Europe.

[1150] Regarding Turkey's obligation to prevent irregular travel.

[1151] Regarding the EU's disbursement of 3 billion euros under the Facility for Refugees in Turkey and additional funding.

[1152] Regarding the joint EU-Turkey endeavour to improve humanitarian conditions in Syria.

[1153] See EU-Turkey Statement §1.

As with all human rights, the question invariably arises as to the tolerated exceptions to the rule. Whereas the Refugee Convention and the EU Asylum Procedures Directive arguably permit for a limited number of 'exceptions' to the *non-refoulement* principle, the ECtHR and (by virtue of Article 52(3) CFR) the CFR, proclaim its absolute and non-derogable nature.[1154] This means that the *non-refoulement* principle may be triggered irrespective of the status of the individual concerned or their past activities[1155] and additionally demands individualised assessments when international protection is requested. However, to be triggered, the *non-refoulement* principle presupposes a significant and individualised risk of ill-treatment upon return. Conversely, when it can be (pre-emptively) established that such a significant and individualised risk does not exist, the *non-refoulement* principle will not be triggered.

According to Article 33 and Articles 36–38 Asylum Procedures Directive, requests for international protection will be considered inadmissible and may result in the (semi-)automatic return of an individual to a 'safe third country', a first country of asylum, a safe country of origin or a European safe third country (see above). The qualification of a 'safe third country' in particular, is considered a 'disconnection' technique, following which the *non-refoulement* principle is considered not to apply.[1156] In other words, the *non-refoulement* principle is prevented from being applied in cases of return to purportedly 'safe third countries', as in these countries no risk of ill-treatment capable of meeting the required severity threshold of *non-refoulement* exists. The rationale behind designations of (Member States and) third states as being safe, is that where equivalent (not necessarily identical) protection is provided (procedurally and substantively) there can be no risk of ill treatment reaching the severity threshold required for *non-refoulement* to be triggered.

The ECtHR has repeatedly confirmed that safe third country designations are not a priori irreconcilable with the *non-refoulement* principle.[1157] Yet, a safe third country designation does not absolve the expelling (Member) State from any and all positive obligations under the *non-refoulement* principle, precisely on account of its absolute nature.[1158] In this respect the Strasbourg Court makes the distinction between positive obligations that arise in cases concerning expulsion to the *country of origin*, which necessarily require an assessment on the merits, and expulsions to a (safe) *third country*.[1159] As concerns expulsions to the latter, the Strasbourg Court

[1154] See for example (and cases cited therein): 'The prohibition in question is absolute, for no derogation from it is permissible even in the event of a public emergency threatening the life of the nation or in the most difficult circumstances, such as the fight against terrorism and organised crime, irrespective of the conduct of the person concerned'. ECtHR (Grand Chamber) Judgment of 15 December 2016, *Khlaifia and others v Italy*, App. No. 16483/12, §158.

[1155] FRA Handbook n 803 at 63.

[1156] González Vega n 1096 at 78.

[1157] ECtHR Judgment of 23 July 2020, *MK and others v Poland*, App nos 40503/17, 42902/17 and 43643/17, §172; ECtHR (Grand Chamber) Judgment of 21 November 2019, *Ilias and Ahmed v Hungary*, App no 47287/15, §132–133.

[1158] ECtHR Judgment of 27 October 2020, *MA v Belgium*, App no 19656/18, §77; ECtHR Judgment of 23 July 2020, *MK and others v Poland*, App nos 40503/17, 42902/17 and 43643/17, §166.

[1159] ECtHR Judgment of 23 July 2020, *MK and others v Poland*, App nos 40503/17, 42902/17 and 43643/17, §171–172; ECtHR (Grand Chamber) Judgment of 21 November 2019, *Ilias and Ahmed v Hungary*, App no 47287/15, §128–133.

recognizes that safe third country designations (such as envisaged by Article 33 and Articles 36–38 Asylum Procedures Directive) may give rise to inadmissibility decisions in requests for international protection and the return of the individual to that safe third country.[1160] However, the ECtHR has also consistently reaffirmed that the expelling (Member) States remain bound by a procedural obligations following such designations. Where a (Member) State recognizes a third country as being safe, and thus does not assess the merits of a request for international protection by declaring it inadmissible, it remains bound by a two-tiered procedural positive obligation.

To expel an individual to a safe third country, the expelling State must firstly assess *ex officio*, whether the individual will have access to an adequate international protection proceedings, which would eliminate the risk of direct or indirect *refoulement* upon return to the third country.[1161] This was reaffirmed in *MK and others v Poland*, where the ECtHR held that expelling States must 'examine thoroughly the question of whether or not there is a real risk of the asylum-seeker being denied access, in the receiving third country, to an adequate asylum procedure, protecting him or her against refoulement. If it is established that the existing guarantees in this regard are insufficient, Article 3 implies a duty that the asylum-seeker should not be removed to the third country concerned'.[1162] Adequacy is determined on a case-by-case basis and presupposes accessibility and reliability.[1163] This requires a rigorous examination of the international protection proceedings in the country of return generally, and if necessitated, of the individual circumstances of the individual concerned. The fact that a (safe) third country adheres to the ECHR standards according to the letter of the law, will not suffice in discharging this procedural positive obligation.[1164] The expelling State must investigate and demonstrate that the accessibility and reliability of an adequate international protection proceeding translates into practice as well. When investigating the adequacy of the international protection procedure in the country of return, the expelling (Member) State must likewise ensure that the reception conditions throughout the international protection procedure do not fall below a particular gravity threshold at risk of otherwise triggering *non-refoulement*.[1165]

Secondly, expulsions to purportedly safe third countries can only be effectuated when internal mechanisms have been developed to ensure that individual applicants may (legally) contest the safe third country designation and subsequent return decision.[1166] As has been repeatedly confirmed both within an inter-Member State context, as well as beyond the EU Member States – safe third country designations

[1160] ECtHR (Grand Chamber) Judgment of 21 November 2019, *Ilias and Ahmed v Hungary*, App no 47287/15, §132–133.

[1161] ECtHR Judgment of 23 July 2020, *MK and others v Poland*, App nos 40503/17, 42902/17 and 43643/17, §172; ECtHR (Grand Chamber) Judgment of 21 November 2019, *Ilias and Ahmed v Hungary*, App no 47287/15, §130–133.

[1162] ECtHR Judgment of 23 July 2020, *MK and others v Poland*, App nos 40503/17, 42902/17 and 43643/17, §173.

[1163] See (and sources cited therein): ECtHR (Grand Chamber) Judgment of 21 November 2019, *Ilias and Ahmed v Hungary*, App no 47287/15, §131, 139, 140–141.

[1164] ECtHR (Grand Chamber) Judgment of 21 November 2019, *Ilias and Ahmed v Hungary*, App no 47287/15, §141.

[1165] ibid §131.

[1166] ibid §151–164; ECtHR Judgment of 10 May 2016, *Babajanov v Turkey*, App no 49867/08, §43; ECtHR Judgment of 23 June 2011, *Diallo v the Czech Republic*, App no 20493/07, §76–85. See for a discussion:

constitute *rebuttable* presumptions of equivalent (procedural and substantive) protection in the country of return.[1167] Where manifest deficiencies have surfaced in the country of return, individual TCNs must be provided an effective mechanism to contest returns thereto.[1168]

Where does that leave the TCN invoking *non-refoulement*, when faced with (semi-)automated returns on the basis of (in)formal readmission or return arrangements to purported safe third countries?

iii. Human Rights Harms

References to human rights obligations within formal or informal readmission agreements and declarations regarding safe third countries do not provide insight into the effective compliance with human rights standards, particularly when legal remedies are limited.[1169] What the aforementioned Strasbourg case law unveils, is that signatory States may indeed be held legally responsible for not respecting their procedural positive obligations under the *non-refoulement* principle when effectuating returns to safe third countries. What this strand of case law does not elaborate upon, however, is whether the EU can incur legal responsibility for contributing to such (semi-) automated returns. In keeping with the Strasbourg stance adopted in *Bosphorus* (see above) and in keeping with the adopted approach in *Opinion 2/13* (see above), it is steadfast practice that insofar the Member States retain any discretion in effectuating their obligations under EU law, they remain independently responsible for safeguarding fundamental rights of individual TCNs *in casu*. Yet, through the adoption of readmission and return arrangements of a formal and informal nature, and the condoning and lauding of such agreements, the EU facilitates automated returns and is increasingly placing Member States in a position of tension arising from their obligations under the recently developed case law by the ECtHR concerning expulsions and the obligation to effectuate efficient returns under EU law. In other words, while the EU's adopted approach to readmission and return does not directly result in (illegitimate) returns of individuals, it appears to authorize, if not direct, such returns, which in turn, places Member States in a state of competing legal obligations: on the one hand, Member States remain bound by their human rights obligations under human rights law, while on the other hand, in line with the duty of sincere cooperation, they are under an obligation to adopt an approach that coincides with that of the EU, and subsequent EU-mandated guidelines.

Directorate of the Jurisconsult, 'Articles 2, 3, 8 and 13 – The Concept of a "Safe Third Country" in the Case-Law of the Court' (*Council of Europe*, 9 February 2018) www.asgi.it/wp-content/uploads/2020/01/Research_report_safe_third_country_ENG.pdf.

[1167] ECtHR Judgment of 23 July 2020, *MK and others v Poland*, App nos 40503/17, 42902/17 and 43643/17, §173.

[1168] ECtHR (Grand Chamber) Judgment of 21 November 2019, *Ilias and Ahmed v Hungary*, App no 47287/15, §141.

[1169] Kees Groenendijk, 'Insights from Agreements on Migration Between the EU and Turkey' in Sergio Carrera, Juan Santos Vara and Tineke Strik (eds), *Constitutionalising the External Dimensions of EU Migration Policies in Times of Crisis – Legality, Rule of Law and Fundamental Rights Reconsidered* (Cheltenham, Edgar Elgar Publishing, 2019) 201–219.

The EU-Turkey Statement provides an emblematic example of the tension that arises from this (potentially) dichotomous situation. The terminology of the Statement as such, does not violate international human rights law and pursues respect for the *non-refoulement* principle. Nevertheless, the discretion accorded to Greece by the EU, through its qualification of Turkey as a safe country third country[1170] in a generalised manner, has seemingly resulted in violations of the *non-refoulement* principle, even if there is no adjudicatory mechanism (other than the domestic Greek Asylum Appeals Committees) willing or capable of making this assessment.[1171] In this regard, it is notable that while the European Commission praises the impact of and the continued need for the EU-Turkey Statement,[1172] NGOs underscore the forcible deportation of Syrians back to Syria, despite assurances to the contrary and academics continue to express doubt as to the qualification of Turkey as a safe third country.[1173] Leaving aside any definitive determinations on the overall legality and the nature of the EU-Turkey Statement as such, there are significant indicators of systemic deficiencies with respect to the reception conditions of (Syrian) TCNs being returned to Turkey from the EU and the required adequate access to international protection proceedings in Turkey.[1174] In terms of reception conditions, indiscriminate violence instigated by Turkish border guards vis-à-vis (Syrian) TCNs returned to Turkey has been repeatedly documented.[1175] Moreover, the reception of (Syrian) irregular TCNs has been noted as being deplorable resulting in deaths,[1176] the documented sexual abuse of

[1170] Maarten Den Heijer and Thomas Spijkerboer, 'Is the EU-Turkey Refugee and Migration Deal a Treaty?' (*EU Law Analysis*, 7 April 2016) eulawanalysis.blogspot.be/2016/04/is-eu-turkey-refugee-and-migration-deal.html.

[1171] Human Rights Watch, 'EU/Greece: First Turkey Deportations Riddled with Abuse' (*Human Rights Watch*, 16 April 2016) www.hrw.org/news/2016/04/19/eu/greece-first-turkey-deportations-riddled-abuse 9; Amnesty International, 'Turkey: Illegal Mass Returns of Syrian Refugees Expose Fatal Flaw in the EU-Turkey Deal' (*Amnesty International*, 1 April 2016) www.amnesty.org/en/latest/news/2016/04/turkey-illegal-mass-returns-of-syrian-refugees-expose-fatal-flaws-in-eu-turkey-deal/ 5; UN High Commissioner for Refugees, 'Legal Considerations on the Return of Asylum-Seekers and Refugees from Greece to Turkey as Part of the EU-Turkey Cooperation in Tackling the Migration Crisis Under the Safe Third Country and First Country of Asylum Concept' (*UNHCR*, 23 March 2016) www.refworld.org/docid/56f3ee3f4.html 8.

[1172] European Commission, 'Report from the Commission to the European Parliament, the European Council, and the Council – Seventh Report on the Progress Made in the Implementation of the EU-Turkey Statement' [2017] COM(2017) 470 final; European Commission, 'Report from the Commission to the European Parliament, the European Council, and the Council – Fifth Report on the Progress Made in the Implementation of the EU-Turkey Statement' [2017] COM(2017) 204 final.

[1173] European Council on Refugees and Exiles, 'EU-Turkey Deal 5 Years on: Fundamentals Remain Unchanged' (*ECRE*, 19 March 2021) www.ecre.org/editorial-eu-turkey-deal-5-years-on-fundamentals-remain-unchanged/; Human Rights Watch, 'Joint Letter to HRVP Borrell on EU-Turkey Relations' (*Human Rights Watch*, 18 March 2021) www.hrw.org/news/2021/03/18/joint-letter-hrvp-borrell-eu-turkey-relations.

[1174] Andrea Ott, 'EU-Turkey Cooperation in Migration Matters: a Game Changer in a Multi-Layered Relationship?' in Francesca Ippolito and Federico Casolari (eds), *Bilateral Relations in the Mediterranean* (Cheltenham, Edward Elgar Publishing, 2020) 200; European Council on Refugees and Exiles, 'EU-Turkey Deal 5 Years on: Fundamentals Remain Unchanged' (*ECRE*, 19 March 2021) www.ecre.org/editorial-eu-turkey-deal-5-years-on-fundamentals-remain-unchanged/; Human Rights Watch, 'Joint Letter to HRVP Borrell on EU-Turkey Relations' (*Human Rights Watch*, 18 March 2021) www.hrw.org/news/2021/03/18/joint-letter-hrvp-borrell-eu-turkey-relations.

[1175] Human Rights Watch, 'Turkey: Border Guards Kill and Injure Asylum Seekers. Border Lockdown Puts Syrian Lives at Risk', (*Human Rights Watch*, 10 May 2016) www.hrw.org/news/2016/05/10/turkey-border-guards-kill-and-injure-asylum-seekers.

[1176] Zia Weise 'Turkish refugee camp hailed as success by Merkel hit by child sex abuse scandal' (*The Telegraph*, 12 May 2016) www.telegraph.co.uk/news/2016/05/12/turkish-refugee-camp-hailed-as-success-by-merkel-hit-by-child-se/.

over 30 children, and ongoing physical and mental violence to which Syrian TCNs are subjected.[1177] Regarding access to adequate international protection proceedings, Carrera, den Hertog and Stefan observe that a significant backlog prevents effective access thereto, in addition to the limitations *ratione personae* with respect to who may enjoy refugee status in Turkey.[1178] Finally, in keeping with the ECtHR in *Ilias and Ahmed*, the mere fact that Turkey is a signatory to the ECHR does not confirm whether access to adequate international protection proceedings is established in practice.[1179] In any event, the objective of the present analysis is not to establish the systemic nature of violations of *non-refoulement* following the EU-Turkey Statement as these concerns have been raised from the very onset of the Statement.[1180] Conversely, the objective of this analysis, is to establish whether the EU as a complicit actor in the EU-Turkey Statement, through condoning, assisting and facilitating its implementation can be held responsible in cases of such *de facto* violations, or whether instead, systemic obstacles prevent EU responsibility.[1181]

Bearing in mind the positive obligation under the *non-refoulement* principle, for duty-bearers to investigate *ex officio* – mindful of readily available reports – the reception conditions in a country of return, as well as the availability of *adequate* international protection proceedings,[1182] it may be questioned whether this obligation was sufficiently respected by Member States and the EU alike, when implementing and contributing to the EU-Turkey Statement. Whereas the Strasbourg case law

[1177] Amnesty International, 'EU-Turkey deal: Greek decision highlights fundamental flaws' (*Amnesty International*, 20 May 2016) www.amnesty.org/en/latest/news/2016/05/eu-turkey-deal-greek-decision-highlights-fundamental-flaws/.

[1178] Sergio Carrera, Leonhard den Hertog and Marco Stefan, 'The EU-Turkey deal: reversing 'Lisbonisation' in EU Migration and Asylum Policies' in Sergio Carrera, Juan Santos Vara and Tineke Strik (eds), *Constitutionalising the External Dimensions of EU Migration Policies in Times of Crisis – Legality, Rule of Law and Fundamental Rights Reconsidered* (Cheltenham, Edgar Elgar Publishing, 2019) 166.

[1179] ECtHR (Grand Chamber) Judgment of 21 November 2019, *Ilias and Ahmed v Hungary*, App no 47287/15, §141. In this respect it is notable to recall that violations of Article 3 ECHR have already been established vis-à-vis Turkey on account of not sufficiently abiding by the procedural positive obligation under Article 3 ECRH by transferring TCNs back to Iran. In then assessing whether Turkey constitutes a safe third country and in discharging the procedural positive obligations under the *non-refoulement* principle as a Member State, it would have to be ensured that the international protection proceedings *in Turkey*, at this point provide for sufficient safeguards and procedural protection against indirect and direct *refoulement*. ECtHR Judgment of 10 May 2016, *Babajanov v Turkey*, App no 49867/08.

[1180] See more recently: Casolari n 1096 at 220–222; Carrera, den Hertog and Stefan n 1178 at 155–174; Mauro Gatti and Andrea Ott, 'The EU-Turkey Statement: Legal Nature and Compatibility with EU Institutional Law' in Sergio Carrera, Juan Santos Vara and Tineke Strik (eds), *Constitutionalising the External Dimensions of EU Migration Policies in Times of Crisis – Legality, Rule of Law and Fundamental Rights Reconsidered* (Cheltenham, Edgar Elgar Publishing, 2019) 175–200; Groenendijk n 1169 at 201–219.

[1181] See Mitsilegas who raises concerns whether current practice such as informal readmission agreements with supposed safe third countries aren't shielding the EU and Member States alike from any legal responsibility: 'As evidenced by the CJEU ruling on the (non) applicability of EU law on the EU-Turkey Statement, there is a worrying trend towards shielding EU and Member States cooperation with third states from European rule of law and human rights accountability mechanisms'. Valsamis Mitsilegas, 'Extraterritorial Immigration Control, Preventive Justice and the Rule of Law' in Sergio Carrera, Juan Santos Vara and Tineke Strik (eds), *Constitutionalising the External Dimensions of EU Migration Policies in Times of Crisis – Legality, Rule of Law and Fundamental Rights Reconsidered* (Cheltenham, Edgar Elgar Publishing, 2019) 306.

[1182] Reference is made to the more general term 'duty-bearers', as these positive obligations have been developed vis-à-vis (Member) States and it is not certain whether such obligations can or should also be borne by the EU for example. See (and sources cited therein): ECtHR Judgment of 27 October 2020, *MA v Belgium*, App no 19656/18, §79, 81–82.

indicates that Member States may indeed be held liable for returns to (un)safe third countries when such positive obligations have not been respected, the question in the present analysis concerns whether the *EU* can be held responsible for its complicity in effectuating this EU-Turkey Statement.

b. An Initial Appraisal: NF, NG, and NM v European Council

The Statement sparked much controversy and resulted in abundant academic debate regarding its legality, the legal nature and the unlawful consequences stemming from the Statement.[1183] On the one hand, an international law perspective holds that the terminology employed in the Statement suggests that it constitutes an enforceable legal agreement between Turkey and the EU.[1184] On the other hand, it was held by the CJEU that the Statement amounted to no more than the product of an informal meeting between Member State representatives that took place *prior* to the European Council meeting, and thus did not constitute a legally binding agreement between the EU and Turkey – irrespective of the adopted terminology.

The General Court[1185] and the CJEU on appeal,[1186] did not engage in a substantive merit-based analysis of the Statement on account of lacking jurisdiction, indicating their implicit consent to the qualification of the Statement as a political agreement (if not, an international agreement between the Member States and Turkey). In other words, in both proceedings, the Court was reluctant to acknowledge the Statement as a measure having been adopted by the European Council, which in any event, would not be possible on account of Article 15 TEU.[1187] This stance appears to be corroborated by the EU institutions more generally, as well as the Member States, regardless of the potential qualification of the Statement under international law.[1188] The ECtHR interestingly (and despite consternation following the implementation and consequences of the Statement (see above)), likewise, did not raise any concerns on its legal qualification in *JR and Others v Greece*, which concerned its implementation

[1183] Ott n 1174 at 185–214; Casolari n 1096 at 220–222; Carrera, den Hertog and Stefan n 1178 at 155–174; Gatti and Ott n 1180 at 175–200; Groenendijk n 1169 at 201–219; Gloria Fernández Arribas, 'The EU-Turkey Statement, the Treaty-Making Process and Competent Organs. Is the Statement an International Agreement?' (2017) 2 *European Papers* 1,1–8; Enzo Cannizzaro, 'Disintegration Through Law?' (2016) 1 *European Papers* 1, 3–6; Olivier Corten, 'Accord politique ou juridique: Quelle est la nature du 'machin' conclu entre l'UE et la Turquie en matière d'asile' (*EU Migration Law Blog*, 10 June 2016) eumigrationlawblog.eu/accord-politique-ou-juridique-quelle-est-la-nature-du-machin-conclu-entre-lue-et-la-turquie-en-matiere-dasile/; Den Heijer and Spijkerboer n 1170; Steve Peers, 'The Draft EU/Turkey Deal on Migration and Refugees: Is It Legal?' (*EU Law Analysis*, 16 March 2016) eulawanalysis.blogspot.com/2016/03/the-draft-euturkey-deal-on-migration.html.

[1184] See for example: Den Heijer and Spijkerboer n 1170.

[1185] CJEU (General Court) Order of 28 February 2017, *NF v European Council*, T-192/16, ECLI:EU:T:2017:128, §46–75.

[1186] CJEU Order of 12 September 2018, *NF v European Council*, Joined Cases C-208/17P to C-210/17P, ECLI:EU:C:2018:705, §23–30.

[1187] Article 15(1) TEU: 'The European Council shall provide the Union with the necessary impetus for its development and shall define the general political directions and priorities thereof. It shall not exercise legislative functions'. See for a recent discussion: Ott n 1174 at 204–212.

[1188] CJEU (General Court) Order of 28 February 2017, *NF v European Council*, T-192/16, ECLI:EU:T:2017:128, §27–30.

only days after it had been publicized.[1189] In any event, the current study does not permit an in-depth analysis on the (implicit) legal qualification of the EU-Turkey Statement, as even its qualification as an *informal* readmission arrangement *with EU support* raises significant concerns due to EU involvement therein and the precedent this may set for future informal EU (mandated) readmission agreements.

The legal mechanisms available and relied upon under the ECtHR and CJEU framework, did not yield a successful outcome for the Applicants thus far. Indeed, it may be contended that this is because the conditions of detention in Vial Hotspot complained of by the Applicants in *JR and Others*, effectively did not reach the minimum threshold required under Article 3 and 5 ECHR. Similarly, there may be merit to the argument by the General Court in *NF v European Council* that the Statement was no more than a political accord between Heads of State and Turkey and is thus not a formal act of the EU capable of being annulled. However, it can also be held – as hinted at by Fink – that a successful procedure against unlawful human rights conduct in the implementation of EU IBM, very much depends on the type of procedure that is relied upon, as well as what actors the review procedures are directed at.[1190] In this regard, the question could be raised whether alternative routes of judicial review (such as recourse to an action for damage under EU law), with a greater focus on the *contents* and *consequences* of the Statement, which is not contingent on the legal qualification of the Statement as such, could have yielded a different outcome.

The EU has explicitly condoned (authorized, supported and/or assisted) the implementation of the EU-Turkey statement, allowing for expedited and (semi-)automatic returns to Turkey without individualized assessments of TCN international protection requests. This authorization is part evidenced by the European Commission's acknowledgement of Turkey as a 'safe third country',[1191] but likewise by the promise of the expedited visa liberalization roadmap by the EU concerning Turkey, the expedited EU disbursement of 3 billion euros under the Facility for Refugees in Turkey, along with an additional mobilization of 3 billion euros.[1192] The Seventh Report on the Implementation of the EU-Turkey Statement foresees additional disbursement of funds to ensure the implementation of the Statement, and endeavours to facilitate and upgrade the Customs Union with Turkey.[1193] Bearing in mind the (legal) effects and the adopted approach by the EU, Casolari summarizes the EU-Turkey Statement succinctly by holding that the Statement embodies 'the trappings of an international agreement proper, one the EU has concluded informally, that is, bypassing the procedure that under article 218 TFEU it is required to follow in exercising

[1189] ECtHR Judgment of 25 January 2018, *JR and others v Greece*, App no. 22696/16, §7, 39. The ECtHR appears to implicitly endorse the EU-Turkey Statement as having been concluded between the Member States and Turkey, as opposed to between the EU and Turkey. See for a discussion of the implications of the case on the EU-Turkey Statement: Pijnenburg n 1140.

[1190] Fink n 27 at 237.

[1191] European Commission, 'Communication from the Commission to the European Parliament, the European Council and the Council – Second Report on the progress made in the implementation of the EU-Turkey Statement' [2016] COM (2016) 349 final, 5. See also: Strik n 1098 at 68.

[1192] See for example: Point 5 and 6 EU-Turkey Statement.

[1193] European Commission, 'Report from the Commission to the European Parliament, the European Council, and the Council – Seventh Report on the Progress Made in the Implementation of the EU-Turkey Statement' [2017] COM(2017) 470 final, 11–13.

its treaty-making power'.[1194] This is all the more relevant, as immediately following the publication of the EU-Turkey Statement, Greece indeed adopted legislation to expedite international protection proceedings for TCNs,[1195] which is indicative of the dynamic at play between the EU's adopted stance on the EU-Turkey Statement and the subsequent conduct by the EU Member States.

Despite the support provided by the EU institutions in the implementation of the Statement and the subsequent legislative reform in Greece, the Greek Asylum Appeals Committees prevented the automated implementation of the EU-Turkey statement in 390 out of 393 cases at the time of the conducted study by Gkliati. These prevented transfers were justified on account of the fact that the transfers would violate the *non-refoulement* principle.[1196] Additional research shows that out of 20,953 Syrians arriving upon Greek territory in the first two years following the publication of the EU-Turkey Statement, only 2,383 have been returned to Turkey on the basis of the EU-Turkey Statement.[1197]

Bearing this in mind, and notwithstanding the annulment proceedings brought against the EU-Turkey Statement (which were dismissed solely on account of the legal qualification of the Statement), the question remains whether the EU could be held responsible for its complicity in the ensuing unlawful automated returns to Turkey irrespective of its legal qualification, focusing instead on the human rights harms stemming therefrom. This question arises not only because of the explicit acknowledgment and support of the Statement by the European institutions at the time, thereby providing Member States (*in casu* Greece) with the necessary assurances to cooperate 'bilaterally' with Turkey, but likewise for the absence of intervention and prevention of automated transfers, which arguably can be construed as a violation of the EU's positive obligation to prevent (the obligation to protect and fulfil) the principle of *non-refoulement*.

3. RESPONSIBILITY IN PRACTICE

At this point, the analysis of responsibility may appear repetitive. This repetition underscores that the EU's Human Rights Responsibility Regime evinces serious risks of *systemic* issues in establishing EU responsibility. Yet careful to avoid self-crafted confirmation bias, it is crucial to underline that (in)formal readmission agreements

[1194] Casolari n 1096 at 221.

[1195] Law on the organisation and operation of the Asylum Service, the Appeals Authority, the Reception and Identification Service, the establishment of the General Secretariat for Reception, the transposition into Greek legislation of the provisions of Directive 2013/32/EC [2016] Law No. 4375. See for a discussion: Carrera, den Hertog and Stefan n 1178 at 164.

[1196] See on the matter: Mariana Gkliati, 'The Application of the EU-Turkey Agreement: A Critical Analysis of the Decisions of the Greek Appeals Committees' (2017) 10 *European Journal of Legal Studies* 1, 80, 99, 122. In this study, Gkliati discusses 8 cases dealt with by the Greek Appeals Committees on the return of TCN protection seekers to Turkey, flowing from the EU-Turkey statement. Out of 393 decisions at the time of the study, 390 were overturned and return was prevented inter alia because of potential violations of the *non-refoulement* principle and potential violations of the Refugee Convention.

[1197] Strik notes that despite the assurances of the legitimacy of the Statement by the EU, the implementation thereof is problematic. Strik n 1107 at 68.

such as the EU-Turkey Statement differ somewhat from the previous two examples concerning EU operational conduct, when applying the responsibility mechanisms. *In casu*, arguably, the EU has done no more than acquiesce to (and arguably support) the use of bilateral arrangements (coincidentally with the agreement of all Member States *and* with repeated reference to the EU's involvement in the text of the Statement) between Greece and Turkey. As such, the focus of responsibility for unlawful human rights conduct is not on the active (operational) involvement of the EU. Instead, the focus here is on the *omission* to intervene and complicity in unlawful human rights conduct through support in the implementation of the Statement. At the same time, readmission policy and practice *are* again reminiscent of operational EU conduct as aforementioned, in the sense that it requires the involvement of a number of actors, namely, third countries (of origin or of return), the EU and its institutions, Member States and as of recent, Frontex to the extent that its deployed statutory staff have been accorded executive powers. The multiplicity of involved actors again diffuses responsibility across different actors, the dynamic of which will differ depending on every specific (in)formal readmission agreement. This inevitably complicates and frustrates determinations of whether the EU can or cannot be held responsible for unlawful human rights complicity pursuant to informal readmission and return arrangements.

a. The EU *Lex Specialis* Applied

i. Independent Responsibility

– Causal Conduct Attributable to the EU

Recalling the high threshold on the one hand for the causality condition to be met, and the ambiguity on the other hand, on how to determine attribution, it is unlikely that an Applicant will be able to meet the first condition for independent responsibility under an action for damages. Recalling that for causality to be established, the conduct must be the direct and immediate cause of the damage, entailing that there is *no intervening* act breaking the chain of causality, it is clear that this cannot be established vis-à-vis the EU in respect of the EU-Turkey Statement. Irrespective of the approach adopted to assess its nature (a binding agreement or not), the Statement requires implementation by Member States. Accordingly, the damage (potential *non-refoulement* violations) stems from the conduct of the Member State (Greece) implementing the Statement, which is responsible for the physical return of the TCNs to Turkey. Hence, an intervening act does occur between the 'adoption' of the Statement and the ensuing damage.

Applying the test of causation, however, does presuppose that the adoption of the Statement was effectively an act attributable to the EU. The CJEU already clarified that the act was effectively one stemming from the Member States, as opposed to an act attributable to the EU. The outcome in *NF, NG and NM v European Council* thus may very well function as a precedent and an example for how informal cooperation with third states should be organised to escape legal scrutiny by the CJEU. This, of course, does not necessarily affect the ability of Applicants to address individual Member States for the (unlawfulness of the) implementation of such readmission agreements, but in terms of answering the overarching question of EU responsibility, the first condition(s) for independent responsibility will likely not be met.

– Sufficiently Serious Breach of EU Law

The question that arises here is reminiscent of the 'chicken and egg' dilemma. If the conduct (namely, the conclusion of the readmission arrangements) cannot be attributed to the EU, can it be considered an unlawful act or omission by the EU, which is a prerequisite for a successful application for damage? On the other hand, if there is no clearly identifiable human rights obligation which renders the EU's commitment to *non-refoulement* actionable, can such unlawful conduct ever be attributed to the EU?

Either way, even if causation and attribution could be met, the human rights obligations stemming from *non-refoulement* do not yet appear sufficiently adapted to be transposable to the EU. Particularly in the case of 'safe third country' qualifications and associated (informal) readmission agreements, the legality of 'safe third country' determinations by Member States is not even established. While States mostly agree that a 'safe third country' designation entails that the state of return should provide for *effective* protection, there is no concurrence on what effective protection entails *in practice* – must states of return provide for the same level of protection as the Refugee Convention? As the ECtHR?[1198] And most importantly, what is the role of the EU in facilitating safe third country determinations, which currently remain the prerogative of domestic authorities? Where specific human rights obligations are not clear for States, it becomes even more convoluted for IOs. Do recommendations by the European Commission to consider Turkey as a 'safe third country' *in casu*, give rise to responsibility for complicity in enacting unlawful human rights conduct pursuant to the Statement? Do attempts at expediting visa liberalisation roadmaps and the disbursements function as a form of complicity in potentially illegitimate returns to third countries? Again, according to the letter of the law, the purported adherence to human rights appears in complete conformity with the CFR: the Statement references human rights, and in the Seventh Report on the Implementation of the EU-Turkey Statement, the European Commission recalls that any further accession negotiations with Turkey continue to require adherence to inter alia, the rule of law and fundamental rights.[1199] Nevertheless, (semi-)automated returns of (Syrian) TCNs are being effectuated.[1200]

Despite these human rights concerns implicating the EU, and absent precedent-setting decisions by the CJEU on shared responsibility of the EU for unlawful human

[1198] Strik n 1107 at 65–66.

[1199] European Commission, 'Report from the Commission to the European Parliament, the European Council, and the Council – Seventh Report on the Progress Made in the Implementation of the EU-Turkey Statement' [2017] COM(2017) 470 final, 12.

[1200] See inter alia: Deutsche Welle, 'Turkey: Nearly 100,000 Unregistered Syrians Removed from Istanbul' (*Deutsche Welle*, 4 January 2020) www.dw.com/en/turkey-nearly-100000-unregistered-syrians-removed-from-istanbul/a-51888092; Amnesty International, 'Turkey: Syrians Illegally Deported into War Ahead of Anticipated "Safe Zone"' (*Amnesty International*, 25 October 2019) www.amnesty.org/en/latest/news/2019/10/turkey-syrians-illegally-deported-into-war-ahead-of-anticipated-safe-zone/; Human Rights Watch, 'Turkey: Syrians Being Deported to Danger' (*Human Rights Watch*, 24 October 2019) www.hrw.org/news/2019/10/24/turkey-syrians-being-deported-danger.

rights conduct – to date it remains legally uncertain by what precise positive and negative obligations the EU would be bound in discharging the requirement to respect (fulfil and protect) the *non-refoulement* principle in facilitating or objecting to informal readmission and return arrangements. The positive and negative obligations as they have been conceptualised under EU law and under the ECHR, have consistently considered the (Member) States as duty bearers, including in the context of safe third country designations – seemingly blind to the involvement of actors such as the EU, capable of influencing Member State conduct in this regard.

As access to the CJEU has already been significantly limited for informal readmission arrangements on jurisdictional grounds for annulment proceedings, it seems unlikely that the CJEU would reverse its stance on the matter in a proceeding for damages. In the hypothesis that the CJEU would adopt a different approach, however, it would still remain legally uncertain whether the EU was effectively bound by concrete (positive and/or negative) obligations, which it violated in a manner that is sufficiently serious. Again, the EU, its institutions, bodies, offices and agencies can only be held responsible insofar conduct resulted in a violation of an EU norm by which they were bound at the time of the unlawful conduct. Without any certainty in this respect, it seems unlikely that under the *lex specialis* the EU will be held independently responsible (in an exculpatory manner) for any unlawful returns of individuals to Turkey stemming from the EU-Turkey Statement.

– Interim Conclusions on the *Lex Specialis* for Independent Responsibility

From the outset, it is clear that informal nature of readmission agreements generally, and the political qualification of the EU-Turkey Statement specifically, have resulted in a much-lamented absence of legal review before the CJEU. In the annulment proceedings concerning the EU-Turkey Statement, the CJEU appears to have conflated jurisdiction with attribution, noting that because of the fact that the Statement cannot be considered an EU act, it cannot rule on the validity thereof. While this strict(er) test may be understandable given the proceeding at stake, it raises the question of how the CJEU would approach the notion of jurisdiction and attribution – two separate concepts – in an application for damages. Previous practice has demonstrated that determinations of attribution (as far as EU law is concerned) are contingent on the substantive area of EU law that is at stake. In keeping with the approach adopted by the ECtHR in *Bosphorus*, *ND and NT v Spain*, and *MK and others v Poland* (all cases where the Member States argued they were implementing EU law to refute attribution), as well as the approach adopted by the Draft Accession Agreement and *Opinion 2/13*, and finally the orders by the General Court and the CJEU concerning the EU-Turkey Statement, it appears highly unlikely that the CJEU would backtrack in a proceeding for damages and find that the EU-Turkey Statement is attributable to the European Council (or the EU generally). Likewise, the test of causation and the identification of unlawful human rights conduct that is sufficiently serious exhibit the same structural issues as previously discussed in the other phases of IBM. Mindful of the foregoing, does shared responsibility under the EU *lex specialis* regime provide any potential for responsibility vis-à-vis the EU?

ii. Shared Responsibility

Recalling the variety of manners in which international adjudicatory mechanisms on the one hand, and the CJEU on the other hand, have approached shared responsibility for substantive areas of EU law and mindful of the general reluctance within the realm of (shared competences in) IBM of the EU to accredit conduct exclusively or predominantly to the EU, again, the question of shared responsibility remains a guessing game. In the particular case of the EU-Turkey Statement, it is not clear whether the normative control exercised by the CJEU over the conduct of the Member States, the absence of intervention by the Union in tolerating the implementation of the Statement and the assurances by the EU institutions are sufficient to establish complicity – a notion under EU law of which the content remains shrouded by ambiguity in any event (see Chapter 6, 7, and 8). As such, again the determinations of responsibility for (mere) complicity can only be the result of *post facto* judicial control, without an *ex ante* normative reference frame against which the conduct or absence thereof by the EU, can be tested.

b. The *Lex Generalis* Applied

i. Independent Responsibility

– Attribution

As the model of attribution under Article 7 ARIO is predominantly directed at situations of operational conduct, the implementation of the EU-Turkey Statement via the Member States and the apportionment of attribution, is not determined by reference thereto. Instead, Article 6 ARIO may be relied upon in the determination of responsibility. Yet it becomes clear very quickly that the ground for attribution under Article 6 ARIO for independent responsibility too, will not be helpful in determining whether any responsibility can be incurred by the EU. From the outset, under the strict application of the normative control test for attribution, Member States do not qualify as organs or agents that are structurally embedded in the architecture of the organisation (see above). Under the broader conceptualisation of the normative control test for attribution of Article 6 ARIO, it must be recalled that the Member States would first have to be conceived as *de facto* organs or agents. Disregarding briefly the renunciation by the General Court and the CJEU of the Statement being an act of the European Council, the characterization as a *de facto* organ or agent requires that the Member States were under a level of normative control depriving them of any effective leeway to disregard its provisions for Article 6 ARIO to trigger attribution to the EU. Hoffmeister underscores that the functional classification of the Member States as organs or agents of the EU requires that EU law governs the substantive legality of the act, and that judicial review is available by the organization over the act (see above). *In casu*, assuming the EU-Turkey Statement was indeed an international agreement between the EU and Turkey, Member States could not have been considered to be deprived of any leeway to apply its provisions. This is evidenced, *inter alia* by the mere fact that the Greek Asylum Appeals Committees disregarded the Statement in its entirety.

Furthermore, doctrine suggests that Article 6 ARIO additionally encompasses the competence model, which may be broadly or strictly construed. Again, disregarding the decision in *NF, NG and NM v European Council*, Article 6 ARIO would still not necessarily provide for responsibility on behalf of the EU *in casu*. Return and readmission as aforementioned, remains a shared competence. Although it can be argued that the EU contributed to the Statement, the Statement was not adopted according to the legislative procedure it should have followed for it to be considered as an EU legal act. Instead, it falls within the trend of the informalisation of EU external migration policy. Bearing this in mind, it is hard to construe an argument whereby Member States would have been prevented from concurrently concluding agreements on return and readmission. Despite the legal effects that may thus stem from the non-legal Statement, no argument can be construed where the EU was *exclusively* competent to conclude informal agreements such as the Statement, warranting the attribution thereof (in an exculpatory) manner to the EU as opposed to the Member States in line with Article 6 ARIO. However, an argument could be construed that the EU-Turkey Statement was attributable to both the EU *and* the Member States, albeit in a relational dynamic, as briefly addressed under shared responsibility.

– Internationally Wrongful Act

At this point, the argument is clear. Absent any *ex ante* legislative guidance, it is unclear whether the EU could even be held to account for any potentially unlawful conduct it has committed and/or contributed to. Article 10 ARIO holds that international responsibility will only arise when there is a breach of an international obligation. The prohibition of *non-refoulement* from a rights-holder perspective does not convey much more than the negative obligation to refrain from engaging in returns of individuals to a country of return where they run the risk of being subjected to a significant threshold of harm.

In casu, this has not occurred. In the most extreme internationalist view, the EU concluded an internationally binding agreement with Turkey, which allows for administrative simplification in readmission procedures executed by Member States, while *prima facie* requiring full compliance with the *non-refoulement* principle. Conversely, from an EU vantage point, the EU has simply not intervened in and condoned the execution of expedited returns of individuals with accelerated (or no) status determination proceedings. What is clear, however, is that regardless of how the conduct is perceived, the EU did and continues to actively facilitate a situation where the *essence* of the *non-refoulement* principle is at risk, without any concrete indicators on how to correctly pinpoint the violation of a concrete obligation.

At best, again, the argument can be construed that the EU failed to intervene and facilitated even, potential violations of the *non-refoulement* principle, by disregarding the more abstract obligation to protect and fulfil its safeguards. In other words, the EU failed to prevent potential violations. However, this would have to be determined in an *ex post facto* review, without any predefined legal guidance imposing a positive due diligence obligation upon the EU as such. Accordingly, it cannot be stated neither under EU law, nor international law, that the EU has concretely violated an obligation to act or refrain from acting, by which it was bound for the purpose of establishing independent responsibility.

ii. Shared Responsibility

The conditions for independent responsibility pose a number of obstacles to any determinations of responsibility vis-à-vis the EU for its contribution (from either an international 'active' perspective or an EU 'passive' perspective) in the enactment and implementation of the EU-Turkey Statement. In light of the executive federalist structure of the EU, the concrete implementation of the EU-Turkey Statements, and similar forms of cooperation that may follow, will have to be largely implemented by the Member States. As such, there is always a given dynamic between the Member States and the EU. The ARIO provisions on shared responsibility may thus provide for a better basis to address apportionment of responsibility.

Departing from the idea that the EU-Turkey Statement is *not* an international agreement, the fact remains that no measures were adopted by the EU to bring a halt to its execution, or (with the exception of the European Ombudsman decision on the topic[1201]) to ensure compliance in the execution thereof, with the *non-refoulement* principle and human rights more generally. Moreover, no effective legal review on an EU level occurred with respect to the substantive *de facto* compliance of the EU-Turkey Statement with human rights and this despite the widespread consternation concerning its human rights impact and the concrete suggestions made by the European Ombudsman on the topic.[1202]

The tacit consent on the implementation of the EU-Turkey Statement, the reassurances by the European Commission that Turkey qualifies as a safe third country and the lack of initiatives to halt or monitor more closely its implementation, may be considered to fall within the category of aid and assistance as per Article 14 ARIO. It could not fall within the ambit of direction and control according to Article 15 ARIO, as this requires that the conduct of the organization exceeds mere oversight and influence and would have to exceed incitement to act unlawfully. Pre-supposing that the Statement is somehow attributable to the EU, given the discretion that the Statement provides for its application, it appears that it would not exceed incitement. Similarly, given the non-legal nature of the agreement, it cannot be considered as a coercive act (Article 16 ARIO) that left the Member States with no choice but to comply therewith. The mere fact that the Greek Asylum Appeals Committees refused an automated application of the Statement, suggests that such discretion was in fact

[1201] The European Ombudsman decision called upon the European Commission to include more concrete measures aimed at mitigating risks of human rights violations in the enactment of the EU-Turkey Statement. Emily O'Reilly, 'Decision of the European Ombudsman in the Joint Inquiry into Complaints 506-509-674-784-927-1381/2016/MHZ against the European Commission Concerning a Human Rights Impact Assessment in the Context of the EU-Turkey Agreement' (*European Ombudsman*, 18 January 2017) www.ombudsman.europa.eu/en/decision/en/75160.

[1202] Emily O'Reilly, 'Decision of the European Ombudsman in the Joint Inquiry into Complaints 506-509-674-784-927-1381/2016/MHZ against the European Commission Concerning a Human Rights Impact Assessment in the Context of the EU-Turkey Agreement' (*European Ombudsman*, 18 January 2017) www.ombudsman.europa.eu/en/decision/en/75160.

retained by the Member States, striking out the possibility of invoking coercion. Similarly, circumvention cannot be invoked as the act does not bind a Member State to adopt a certain type of action (Article 17 ARIO). Hence, only Article 14 ARIO provides a potential basis for shared responsibility of the EU, for its contribution to, or omission to prevent, the implementation of the EU-Turkey Statement.

For aid and assistance by an IO to generate responsibility for the latter, three conditions must be met: the organization must have been aware of the unlawful conduct it was facilitating (1), must have had the intent of facilitating the unlawful conduct (2) and the conduct would have been wrongful if it had been committed by the IO alone (3).

Disregarding the condition of 'knowing intent', the opposability criterion poses the recurring issue that has resurfaced throughout the entirety of the analysis – without *ex ante* determinations of what concrete obligations the EU is or is not bound by under the CFR and international human rights law generally, determinations of unlawful conduct are determined at the sole discretion of the judge presented with such questions. That said, there is room to argue that even the EU, limited by its functional speciality, would likewise be bound by the negative obligation to refrain from taking measures that would result in the return and readmission of individuals in violation of the *non-refoulement* principle. On the surface, it could thus be argued that these conditions could be met. But much would depend however, on the burden and standard of proof required, which in turn would depend on the chosen forum or Court before which the international responsibility for shared responsibility of the EU is brought. Not only would the applicant have to overcome the theoretical obstacles of demonstrating 'knowing intent' and demonstrating that the opposability requirement is met, but the Applicant would also have to find the appropriate forum and meet the standard and burden of proof, for an application of Article 14 ARIO to be successful.

The latter presupposes that the chosen forum would be amenable to the application of the ARIO. As has been repeatedly demonstrated however, where the responsibility of the EU is concerned, different adjudicatory mechanisms have applied a wide array of techniques, none of which have concerned a simplistic application of shared responsibility as conceptualized under Article 14 ARIO. Instead, much has depended upon the substantive area of EU law at stake, the willingness of the EU to acknowledge conduct as its own and procedural mechanisms to settle claims of international responsibility. Finally, all of the foregoing presupposes the existence of a forum *other than the CJEU* before which the responsibility of the EU may be invoked and be declared admissible, without immunity from enforcement preventing an effective remedy. Domestic courts may enjoy jurisdiction in accordance with Article 274 TFEU which holds that 'Save where jurisdiction is conferred on the Court of Justice of the European Union by the Treaties, disputes to which the Union is a party shall not on that ground be excluded from the jurisdiction of the courts or tribunals of the Member States'. However, the CJEU enjoys *exclusive* jurisdiction in terms of actions for damages against the EU in accordance with Article 268, 340 and 344 TFEU. Hence domestic courts could not provide an alternative form of legal recourse against the EU for its complicity in the EU-Turkey Statement. Similarly, absent any consent on jurisdiction by alterative international adjudicatory mechanisms, no other forum appears available for the Applicant to turn that would allow the application of Article 14 ARIO.

iii. Interim Conclusions on Responsibility for Control Measures at the EU External Border

Conclusively, neither the *lex specialis* regime nor the *lex generalis* regime provide for an adequate form of legal review of the complicity of the EU in the enactment of the EU-Turkey Statement. The question invariably rises as to whether this is not just the result of the fact that there simply should not be any responsibility of the EU? Indeed, there is merit to the argument that analogously to the *Lotus* principle under international law, conduct which is not prohibited, cannot generate responsibility. However, *in casu* the EU has conducted itself in a manner that disregards the *essence* of the *non-refoulement* principle, no matter the vantage point that is adopted (international agreement or not). The politicized nature of informalized readmission cooperation does not detract from the fact that the essence of the *non-refoulement* principle must be respected.[1203] This last point is echoed (indirectly) in *ND and NT v Spain*, where the Strasbourg Court recalls that the difficulties associated to managing irregular migration and the obligations to secure the EU external border according to EU law, may not result in an artificial reduction of human rights protection under the Convention and render those rights meaningless.[1204]

[1203] ECtHR (Grand Chamber) Judgment of 15 December 2016, *Khlaifia and others v Italy*, App no 16483/12, §241; Emily O'Reilly, 'Decision of the European Ombudsman in the Joint Inquiry into Complaints 506-509-674-784-927-1381/2016/MHZ against the European Commission Concerning a Human Rights Impact Assessment in the Context of the EU-Turkey Agreement' (*European Ombudsman*, 18 January 2017) www.ombudsman.europa.eu/en/decision/en/75160 9.

[1204] ECtHR (Grand Chamber) Judgment of 13 February 2020, *ND and NT v Spain* App nos 8675/15 and 8679/15 §109–110.

Part IV

Relational Human Rights Responsibility

10

Incongruence Clusters and EU Responsibility

THE TOPIC OF the responsibility of international organisations for unlawful human rights conduct is not novel. Similarly, the question of EU responsibility for unlawful human rights conduct is not novel. Scholarship on the matter has predominantly taken a bottom-up approach to these questions, focusing on particular case studies, in an attempt to understand the difficulties in holding the EU or international organisations such as the UN responsible. And to claim that no studies concerning the responsibility of international organisations (and the EU) for unlawful conduct have been conducted from a top-down approach would be fallacious. Yet, such top-down assessments have generally remained of a more abstract nature, not focusing specifically on the application thereof in practice. On account of the either/or approach adopted in doctrine and the inevitable case-specific analysis of responsibility of the EU by the CJEU, one of the larger unanswered questions in the law of international responsibilities, concerns the (systemic) deficiencies that lay at the heart of such responsibility mechanisms. Klabbers synopsises this responsibility question perfectly by stating that this 'raises the obvious question: does international institutional law lack any form of mechanism to prevent them [international organisations] from doing such things? The answer is both yes and no: yes, such mechanisms exist; no, they are not terribly effective'.[1205] The present research not only confirms this generalised statement but has demonstrated that this ineffectiveness taints both the *lex generalis*, but also the EU *lex specialis* when assessed in theory and in practice. More than that, this research lays bare the *specific* and *general* transversal deficiencies which result in a responsibility regime when applied to unlawful human rights conduct, that cannot meet the requirements of an IO based on the rule of law. Applying the *lex generalis* and the *lex specialis* responsibility rules to legislative and operational EU conduct in IBM, reveals normative incongruencies and liability incongruencies in the EU's Human Rights Responsibility Regime.

[1205] Jan Klabbers, 'Contending approaches to international organizations' in Jan Klabbers and Åsa Wallendahl (eds), *Research Handbook on the Law of International Organizations* (Cheltenham, Edward Elgar Publishing, 2011) 5.

1. NORMATIVE INCONGRUENCE

a. Juxtaposing Member States and the EU as Public Actors

'Normative incongruence' refers to the Charter-based human rights obligations by which the EU Member States and EU entities are legally bound, and how these commitments translate to actionable or justiciable obligations. From the onset it is crucial to underscore that for a human rights violation to be established, a distinction must be made between the abstract commitment to respect, fulfil and protect the fundamental rights in the Charter, and the concrete obligations – positive, negative, procedural and substantive – that such commitments give rise to. The right to life (Art. 2 CFR) as such, does not reveal much about how EU entities can and should respect, protect and fulfil this right. It hints at a negative interdiction whereby these actors must refrain from arbitrarily taking life. It does not, however, explain how this interdiction applies to questions of euthanasia, self-defence, abortion, and so forth. Different still, it does not explain what positive obligations this brings about for EU entities. In other words, are the EU Member States bound by an obligation to *take action* (rather than refrain from arbitrarily taking life) to ensure that there is a procedural and legal framework in place to regulate and remedy violations of the right to life? And different again, the abstract reference to the right to life in the text of Art 2 CFR does not prescribe whether certain (preventive) actions must be taken by State or EU actors in substantively safeguarding life. Much like the free movement provisions in the TFEU are further elaborated upon in secondary law, such further clarification is also necessary to grasp and articulate the scope of negative obligation (to refrain and respect) and positive obligations (to protect and fulfil) as they apply within the EU's legal framework. And it is precisely at this point that a crucial distinction between how the Charter applies to the Member States and how it applies to the EU institutions, bodies, offices and agencies emerges. For human rights found in the Charter that correspond to rights in the ECHR this contouring exercise has largely been done for Member States by the ECtHR, the case law of which informs the EU's human rights regime through Article 52(3) CFR. This is much less the case for how the Charter applies to the EU's institutions, bodies, offices and agencies which gives rise to the three risks associated to CJEU self-referentialism (Chapter 3).

Although it is clear that the EU's institutions, bodies, offices and agencies are bound by the same theoretical humans rights commitments as enumerated in the Charter as are the Member States, it remains largely undetermined what the concretised obligations are by which the EU is bound, and how these obligations vary – if at all – depending on the different type of human right at stake. This claim inevitably raises a number of questions: Why are the concretised obligations not the same for Member States and the EU? Shouldn't they be? Wouldn't it be unfair to impose different negative and positive obligations on the EU, as opposed to Member States? Wouldn't such differentiation subordinate the important role that the EU plays in the protection of human rights? While some may argue that these differences should exist, some may argue that only the negative obligations of fundamental rights should apply to the EU.

Whereas some positive and negative obligations may be identical for Member States and the EU due to the nature of the right, it is hard to compellingly argue that they should and can all be the same, given the different nature of the public actors at stake. Despite sharing some state-like qualities, the EU is not a state. It also does not possess over the same apparatus as does a State. Hence, can the same positive duty of care for example through the mobilisation of a police force for violent protests or preventative measures for anticipated environmental disasters, as it exists under the right to life be imposed on the EU, in the same manner as it applies to Member States? Probably not. Nevertheless, the competences enjoyed by the EU do provide it with a significant ability to impact the enjoyment of the right to life of individuals. Should there thus not be a concomitant articulation of the negative and positive obligations binding upon the EU to (1) contribute to the safeguarding of the essence of the right to life for individuals within the EU's jurisdiction and (2) ensure that the EU does not place Member States in a situation that facilitates threats to the right to life through Member State conduct? Simply put, should there not be at the very least be a different iteration of negative and positive obligations under the right to life, tailored to and enforceable vis-à-vis the EU as a public actor?

The same reasoning applies for other human rights, including the *non-refoulement* principle in the present analysis. In fact, notable advancements have been made in this field. Increasingly, we see iterations of concretised human rights obligations binding the EU, its institutions, bodies, offices and agencies articulated in secondary legislation. The 2019 EBCG Regulation for example, provides some examples, including the due diligence (positive) obligation resting with the Executive Director to take remedial action should a Frontex coordinated operation run afoul of fundamental rights. It is such explicit positive and negative obligations that provide individuals with the necessary tools and legal hooks to enforce their human rights within a courtroom.

Despite these initial developments vis-à-vis Frontex, the current human rights landscape is tainted by normative incongruence. While ample debate has been devoted to the *sui generis* nature of the EU, this has not translated in a clear understanding of how this impacts the EU's ability to comply with the to-date state-centric positive and negative human rights obligations. In other words, the current EU human rights landscape is normatively incongruent, showcasing significant disharmony between the objectives of the Charter on the one hand, and its enforceability on the other hand. This is partially on account of insufficient recognition that States, and the EU are different types of actors by nature and by consequence cannot respect, protect and fulfil human rights in the same manner. And sympathetic to the 'common but differentiated responsibilities approach' in other areas of (international environmental) law, such differences should be considered in developing the negative and positive obligations by which the EU is bound in complying with its fundamental rights obligations.

b. Implications of the State-IO Distinction

The business and human rights approach to human rights responsibility does not impose identical concretised human rights obligations on private corporations, instead adopting a nuanced and tailored approach to developing negative and positive human rights obligations. A similar approach may be advisable for the EU. And while I am sympathetic to the objection that it may be undesirable and untenable to articulate all the different negative, positive, procedural and substantive obligations as they apply to the EU and its institutions, bodies, offices and agencies, such objections may be overstated on three points.

First, it is currently overwhelmingly the CJEU's burden to determine how Charter rights may be enforced vis-à-vis the EU. However, this is largely done without the deliberative, political consensus-driven and experimentalist developments that drove the development of human rights obligations as they apply to States. This is difficult to reconcile with the underlying principles of the rule of law and access to an effective remedy enjoyed by individuals under EU jurisdiction, as legal certainty, the principle of effectiveness and legitimate expectations may be compromised when there is no predefined legal guidance informing how fundamental rights apply to the EU.

Second, spelling out concrete negative, positive, procedural and substantive obligations as they apply to the EU does not require the level of detail as one may presume. On the one hand, negative obligations may be inspired by international law concepts such as 'aid and assistance', 'direction and control', or 'coercion', which may complement or replace – depending on the type of human rights at stake – the negative obligations as they exist for States. On the other hand, the positive obligations need not all be result-based obligations in the same manner as they apply to States and may instead be comprised of means-based obligations of progressive realisation and non-regression, or reflecting duties of care, in addition to procedural, result-based obligations which may apply transversally across different human rights (complementing the right to an effective remedy enshrined in Article 47 CFR).

Finally, a common objection to the question of EU human rights responsibility and the clarification of concretised obligations is that the EU simply lacks the conferred power to regulate human rights in a general and holistic, horizontal or cross-sectional manner. This too is a flawed objection. It is realistic to adopt a sectoral approach – within specific subdomains of EU law – to concretised human rights standards in the EU. Much like concepts of 'national security and public order' resurface and are transplanted as exceptions to general rules in various domains of EU law, it is possible to construct a basic template of how EU human rights responsibility within specific domain of EU law and have that template replicated in other domains of EU law. In fact, a similar approach is found in the Trade and Sustainable Development chapters of EU trade agreements: while the idiosyncrasies of such chapters differ and are tailored slightly according to the EU's trade partner, the basic template is replicated.[1206] A similar approach concretizing EU human rights responsibility through secondary legislation is not unthinkable.

2. LIABILITY INCONGRUENCE

In addition to normative incongruence, whereby the current (EU and international) human rights landscape does not meaningfully recognise the nature of the EU as a *sui generis* legal actor, liability incongruence concerning both the 'traditional' conditions

[1206] Joyce De Coninck and Peter Van Elsuwege, 'Human Rights Respectful Trade' (2024) *Berkeley Journal of International Law* (forthcoming) papers.ssrn.com/sol3/papers.cfm?abstract_id=4576034.

for (independent) responsibility, as well as the conditions for shared responsibility also detrimentally affect the individual's access to an effective remedy against EU entities complicit in human rights harms stemming from IBM policy.

Even if abstract human rights commitments are translated to justiciable positive and negative obligations vis-à-vis the EU, the more difficult question arises as to how responsibility should be established and how such responsibility should be divided when a single human rights harm occurs as a result of (indivisible) cooperation between the EU and Member States. It is hard to think of a scenario in which the EU operates entirely on its own, with no Member State intervention whatsoever. The question then becomes how human rights responsibility should be apportioned, and who should bear the burden of reparations in scenarios where unlawful human rights conduct is not exclusively attributable to either the EU or the Member State(s).

The EU's general liability mechanism, as embedded in the action for damages, requires that a number of conditions must be met for liability and an ensuing obligation of reparations to arise. Specifically, in *Bergaderm* the CJEU affirms that responsibility will arise when there is EU unlawful conduct that is sufficiently serious (1), giving rise to damage (2) in a causal manner (3) that is unfettered by intervening acts that could break the chain of causation. Occasionally, the Court recognises a fourth condition of attribution (4). Yet, these conditions that make up the legal framework for EU liability are not adapted to deal with the aforementioned facts.

The requirement of a sufficiently serious breach of EU law presupposes clarity of the rule that applies to the EU. This requirement disregards that where human rights are concerned, the jury is out as to how – if at all – these concretised human rights obligations that apply to Member States may be transplanted to the EU entities.

The test of causation does not tolerate intervening acts, as this is considered to break the chain of causation. But particularly in settings of operational cooperation between the EU and the Member States and transnational cooperative governance more generally, it is difficult to construe a situation in which there is simply no intervening act by a Member State or third party. In other words, more likely than not, the chain of causation *will* be broken, and EU responsibility will not be an available avenue for aggrieved applicants.

Finally, the occasional reference to attribution under EU law misses its mark on two points. Firstly, attribution is more frequently than not conflated with the concept of causation, as was recently shown in the *WS and others v Frontex* ruling by the EU's General Court. Yet, these two concepts operate at different levels of the responsibility question. Attribution attaches a particular line of conduct to a particular actor, whereas in a next step, causation attaches the unlawful conduct to the damage. A systematic approach to and clarification of the concept of attribution in joint responsibility questions would be much welcomed. Secondly, the haphazard references to attribution also negate the fact that there are a number of (different) attribution tests used by the Court and the EU's institutions alike, with no real coherence or motivation for its varied use. This same issue resurfaces under international law.

Given the multiplicity of legal fora at stake due to the different implicated actors (domestic or regional regimes for states, the CJEU for EU entities) it is entirely plausible – as has happened – that a domestic court will apply the effective control test to assess Member State human rights responsibility, while the EU's courts may apply the strict competence test of attribution for the harm caused by both together. In both cases, the unlawful conduct (e.g., return of individuals to Libya) would not be attributable to the EU Member States or EU entities, leaving individual victims without any meaningful recourse against these actors.

Unlike international law, the current EU (human rights) responsibility regime does not explicitly foresee joint responsibility in its constituent instruments, leaving it instead to the CJEU and legislator to further develop the idea of joint responsibility. In a limited number of cases, the CJEU has acknowledged that joint responsibility between the EU and its Member States may be possible, albeit without providing much clarity on the notions of attribution, the determination of what constitutes unlawful conduct and the requirement of causation. At best, the conclusion can be drawn that in theory, responsibility will not be exculpatory – meaning that in theory, Member State responsibility does not *ipso facto* absolve the involved EU actor from responsibility. Additionally, the primary burden of responsibility and ensuing reparations is typically placed with the Member State, entailing a domestic court will be tasked with ruling upon state responsibility first, to avoid applicants being '... excessively compensated for the same damage by the different assessment of two different courts applying different rules of law'.[1207]

Nevertheless, no consistent approach to joint liability can be inferred from CJEU case law thus far. Crucially, the limited case law that does consider joint liability, does not (yet) develop and clarify the conditions for EU joint responsibility to arise, much less explains how such responsibility would be operationalised in practice. Not surprisingly, these questions that plague the understanding and application of joint responsibility generally also resurface when cooperation between Member States and the EU give rise to a single human rights harm. In other words, the current approach to joint responsibility under EU liability generally appears equally insufficient in allocating responsibility between the EU and its Members for human rights harms they jointly give rise to.

The proliferation of attribution tests, lacking clarity on the scope of applicable negative and positive human rights obligations applicable to EU entities, the absence of a clear legal framework on shared responsibility and a test of causation that does not reflect the reality of operational conduct by the EU suggests that the liability rules as they apply to the EU and inspired by both international and EU law are inadequate in ensuring that EU entities can be held to account in practice. Said inadequacy appears at least in part to stem from the fact that the approach to human rights responsibility for Member States developed independently from EU responsibility. In fact, these two regimes of human rights responsibility appear blind to each other inasmuch as absolution of one actor does not *ipso facto* bring about the responsibility of the other – quite the contrary. As it stands, the implications of joint responsibility under EU law currently depend on the findings of the relevant domestic court as well as the EU's courts, both which are governed by different bodies of law – domestic and

[1207] CJEU Judgment of 14 July 1967, *Firma E Kampffmeyer and others v Commission of the EEC*, C-5, 7 and 13-24/66, ECLI:EU:C:1967:13.

EU law respectively. This means that there is currently no joint forum that synchronously and holistically considers the role of the complicit actors in a particular harm, while safeguarding the right to an effective remedy.

Liability incongruence thus points to international and EU responsibility rules and adjudicatory mechanisms not considering the outcome for the individual victim, focusing instead on exculpating the EU's own wrongdoing.

11

EU Relational Human Rights Responsibility?

BUILDING UPON THE foregoing analysis of the challenges inherent in defining EU human rights responsibility, this chapter introduces 'Relational Human Rights Responsibility' as an alternative model for delineating the EU's role in upholding human rights. The concept of 'Relational Human Rights Responsibility' suggests a departure from traditional and dominant models of *independent* responsibility under international and EU law, to better accommodate the power dynamics in EU transnational cooperative governance and avoid disproportionately placing the human rights responsibility burden with one complicit actor in a manner that exonerates other complicit actors. More importantly, this model prioritises the right to an effective remedy of the individual and seeks to eradicate the jurisdictional and legal protection blackholes, all the while avoiding the cited risk of 'overcompensation' of the individual.

1. INTEGRATED BORDER MANAGEMENT OR THE EU'S HUMAN RIGHTS RESPONSIBILITY REGIME?

While drafting this book, I was frequently asked whether the responsibility gap I encountered was due not so much to the legal framework governing the EU's human rights responsibilities, but to the design of the EU's Integrated Border Management (IBM) system, that is, the fact that border management is a field integrating both EU and Member State authorities along with private actors, into hybrid modes of governance within, at, and beyond the EU's external border. Many colleagues in the field of border management have pointed out the various transformations of the EU's IBM and how these transformations are designed exactly to avoid the applicability of human rights safeguards. In fact, while drafting and re-drafting the introductory chapter, a valued colleague replied in her comments to me, that she could not believe that I was not hammering down on the intentionality behind the human rights-eviscerating legal design of IBM. And while in principle I agree that the IBM transformations are increasingly pitted against human rights of third-country nationals, the argument I have been advancing here, has a slightly different focus. In this book I examined whether the issues that give rise to the EU's responsibility gap predate the development of the EU's IBM. This is not to say that the legal design of IBM isn't problematic as such. It very much is. However, with this book I sought to investigate whether the origins of the flawed design of IBM are not at least partially the result of the flaws inherent to the human rights responsibility framework more generally. Naturally, a critical reader might ask whether I can show any compelling causality between the EU's responsibility gap in IBM and the underlying EU's human rights responsibility regime. This would be a hard thing to prove, and I wonder whether it is necessary to show causality. That is because I am not claiming that the underlying responsibility regime is the sole reason for the EU's human rights responsibility gap in IBM, any less than I am trying to show that it's the main driver behind the gap. Critiques directed at international law and European law more generally, are so often focused on its lacking enforceability, as well as its distributive and othering effects. Less attention goes to critically appraising the very architecture of the human rights responsibility framework and the conditions that exist to hold complicit duty-bearers to account. But if the objective is to design IBM in a manner that is compliant with human rights, it seems a justifiable endeavour to at least diagnose and try to remedy potential drivers of this human rights responsibility gap also beyond the sole confines of IBM.

Turning to the very architecture of the human rights responsibility framework, intentionality is simply not the point. Through this lens, it becomes a hard sell to contend that, when drafting the ARIO, Giorgio Gaja set out to develop a set of (soft law) rules that were specifically intended to allow IOs to escape culpability for (internationally) wrongful conduct. Inspired by Soave's work,[1208] it is an equally hard sell to claim that the judicial infrastructure behind the CJEU along with its judges in deliberating matters of EU responsibility in the absence of prescriptive legally defined guidelines on EU (shared) responsibility, are specifically concerned with the erosion of rights of third-country nationals. Nor do I think that the myriad of different actors (eg, different Directorate Generals, different European Parliamentary aides and officials) involved in the EU legislative process and its enforcement, are all working towards the exclusion of third-country nationals from human rights. To ignore that nuance, is to do more injustice in a field that is already rife with injustice, to individuals working tirelessly towards a human rights responsibility framework that better maps onto the hybrid forms of governance that shape the EU's IBM. At the same time, I do concede that the very loopholes, inconsistencies, and legal lacuna which characterise the EU's human rights responsibility framework and that of IOs more generally, form an excellent breeding ground for the design of a border management system that instrumentalises these very drawbacks to construct a regime that in its very architecture pursues an anti-human rights agenda in its effects. In other words, the complicated interplay of actors and rules across different regimes, results in a complex web of political and judicial decision-making, following which rules are drafted that are subsequently abusively enacted.

With that in mind, migration is here to stay – particularly in light of the now widely accepted anthropogenic climate change catastrophes reverberating around the globe. And if the EU (considered briefly as a monolithic *sui generis* organization) is

[1208] Tommaso Soave, *The Everyday Makers of International Law – From Great Halls to Back Rooms* (Cambridge University Press, 2022).

serious about being '*founded on the values of respect for human dignity, freedom, democracy, equality, the rule of law and respect for human rights, including the rights of persons belonging to minorities*',[1209] then the need to diagnose, ameliorate and align the EU's human rights regime with current-day realities is imperative.

2. A RELATIONAL REGIME OF RESPONSIBILITY

With this caveat in mind, the analysis in this book reveals two significant and largely under-scrutinised obstacles to obtaining access to an effective remedy in the EU's human rights responsibility regime, particularly in light of the hybrid modes of governance that IBM exemplifies: firstly, the rules governing attribution and relatedly, causation, under both international law and EU law, and secondly, the manner in which human rights commitments of IOs (and the EU specifically) are translated into actionable and justiciable concretised obligations. The book sought to explain that liability incongruence entails that despite the availability of liability rules, these rules are too embryonic, not aligned across different regimes and actors, and too incoherent to truly meet their objective. Relatedly, normative incongruence suggests that despite the availability of sources of human rights commitments for the EU and IOs generally, these commitments have not yet sufficiently translated into justiciable human rights obligations that may be relied upon by individuals in challenging independent and shared (EU) conduct in court.

Redesigning IBM will not necessarily resolve the EU's responsibility gap in that area if the EU's human rights responsibility regime is not reconsidered at a more fundamental level. But how may this be done? One potential alternative route to human rights responsibility could be to 'relationalise' responsibility. What does this mean? As with many things that are the object of scholarly scrutiny, there appears to have been a proliferation of scholarship on relationality, albeit without this giving rise to an overarching relationality theory, instead resulting in frequently competing and at times contradictory ways of thinking about relationality.[1210] These different understandings of relationality nevertheless appear to share two common themes: firstly, decentring the focus on and prioritisation of independent actors, and secondly, focusing instead 'on the theoretical and analytical significance of connections, ties, transactions, and others kinds of relations'.[1211] Taking stock of contemporary approaches to relationality in international relations, Kavalski posits that relationality entails recognizing 'the interdependence of international actors but also their mutual implication in each other's interactions and roles as well as the overwhelming embeddedness of these relations in the world'.[1212] These elemental commonalities suggest foregrounding the relations of actors in the international arena rather than prioritising individual actors. Applied to the question of (human rights) responsibility

[1209] Article 2 TFEU.
[1210] Emilian Kavalski, 'Relational theories in international relations' in *Oxford Research Encyclopedia of International Studies* (Oxford University Press 2023).
[1211] ibid 2.
[1212] ibid 16.

in situations of hybrid, transnational forms of governance, this is reminiscent of *shared* responsibility under international law. Nollkaemper holds that: '*If cooperative conduct in transnational law enforcement cannot be reduced to conduct of individual participating actors, responsibility needs to connect to the relationship between the individual actors. Individualising responsibility may miss the point.*'[1213] Without explicitly mentioning relationality theory, Nollkaemper appears to point to one of its main tenets: decentring of the individualistic roles of actors, and instead focusing on their interaction with each other, albeit within the realm of the law of responsibility at large. In other words, relationality theories in international relations appear to capture and map well onto the basic rationale undergirding shared responsibility as developed by Nollkaemper and colleagues, in that unlawful conduct stemming from evolving hybrid forms of cooperative governance – comprised of any iteration of public and private actors – can no longer be reduced to individual, singular contributions to unlawful conduct.

The proposed turn to relationality – that is to say, foregrounding the relations between different public actors engaged in unlawful human rights conduct to establish responsibility – rather than focusing on establishing individual human rights violations of the different complicit actors, may be warranted for two reasons. The first and most evident reason relates to the increased recourse to hybrid modes of governance, as exemplified by the EU's governance of its external borders. The EU necessarily cooperates (to varying degrees), with its Member States, but it also increasingly cooperates with (transnational) private actors, and third countries. This comes as no surprise in light of competence division and the supranationalism that characterises the EU's legal framework, and the increasing role of private actors at the international level more generally. Such interdependence and interaction between these actors necessarily obfuscates the (causal) degree to which the different various actors may contribute to unlawful conduct, warranting a different approach to human rights responsibility that is not contingent on being able to establish the individual violations of each of the complicit actors. But the call for relationality is not limited to just this 'actor interwovenness'.

A second call for relational human rights responsibility is prompted by what this book has described as normative incongruence. Under the traditional human rights regime and specifically, the manner in which human rights *obligations* have been developed, certain forms of conduct by certain actors to human rights harms will not be considered violative of human rights obligations, despite contributing to human rights harms. Conduct considered lawful under traditional human rights law is being leveraged through interactions with other actors, resulting in situations where the combined effect of their actions is violative of overarching human rights *commitments*. Although each actor's individual contributions may not inherently breach human rights *obligations*, their collective conduct does. When such conduct is judged from an independent and individualistic perspective, in a siloed manner that does not consider the (also potentially) lawful conduct of contributing actors as

[1213] André Nollkaemper, 'Shared responsibility for human rights violations: a relational account' in Thomas Gammeltoft-Hansen and Jens Vedsted-Hansen (eds.) *Human Rights and the Dark Side of Globalisation – Transnational law enforcement and migration control* (Routledge 2017) 31.

well as the effect of their cooperation, the adjudication of such conduct may result in a finding that there is no responsibility. Consider, for example, the use of aerial and satellite surveillance of the Mediterranean, where location data are obtained by private actors, transferred to EU entities and Member States, and this same data is subsequently transferred to third parties who effectuate a push- or pullback. Under what has traditionally been understood as being the positive and negative obligations flowing from the *non-refoulement* principle, no concretised obligation has actually been violated by the EU as a duty-bearing entity. In fact, from a strictly positivist reading of the law, it is not even certain that a due diligence obligation would have been violated by contributing States. Transfers of data simply do not amount to a violation of the traditional obligations inherent to the *non-refoulement* principle, because there is no immediate exercise of effective control. Yet, the outcome gives rise to a human rights harm, as the individuals pushed and pulled back are subjected to a return without having been provided the opportunity to lodge an application for international protection. When the return is subsequently effectuated to places that are widely acknowledged as being unsafe, the violative nature of the composite conduct becomes all the more egregious. Or consider the outsourcing and externalisation techniques of contemporary IBM more generally: as such, outsourcing cannot be considered *per se* violative of international law or EU law. At the same time, the outsourcing allows states to eschew their human rights obligations, and results in a set of outcomes that works at the expense of third-country nationals, ultimately showcasing the 'othering' effect of EU law and policy in IBM. Lawyers, scholars and policymakers alike, have come up with creative and compelling ways to argue that such techniques remain violative of human rights standards in a manner that fits under the traditional human rights framework, focusing on due diligence obligations, the decentring of territorial jurisdiction, and so forth. In response, Member States and the EU have become equally creative in finding ways to circumvent human rights safeguards. Think for example of the transit legislation enacted by Hungary where it was argued that EU human rights safeguards did not apply in the same manner to artificially constructed transit zones,[1214] or the argument advanced by Spain in *ND and NT v Spain*, where it was argued that the zone of the Melilla fence could not be considered as constituting Spanish territory and therefor territorial jurisdiction could not be triggered.[1215] Consider for example the recurring response by Frontex to any and all allegations of wrongdoing, whereby its representatives insist that Frontex does no more than simply assist the Member States in the implementation of IBM or the enhanced recourse to informal 'arrangements' with third states to manage migratory flows, not to mention the obscure recourse to 'Team Europe'[1216] as of late. Some of these creative responses are successfully contested in court, while

[1214] CJEU Judgment of 14 May 2020, *FMS and Others v Országos Idegenrendészeti Főigazgatóság Dél-alföldi Regionális Igazgatóság and Országos Idegenrendészeti Főigazgatóság*, Joined Cases C-924/19 PPU and C-925/19 PPU, ECLI:EU:C:2020:367.

[1215] ECtHR (Grand Chamber) Judgment of 13 February 2020, *N.D. and N.T. v. Spain*, App nos 8675/15 and 8679/15, §110–111.

[1216] European Commission, 'Team Europe Initiatives' (European Commission, 2024) https://international-partnerships.ec.europa.eu/policies/team-europe-initiatives_nl.

others are not. But this legalistic back-and-forth exemplifies one of the elemental points of this book: trying to pin down who did what, and subsequently trying to fit that into a paradigm that was never intended to govern these modes of hybrid governance where complicit actors act in dubious but not necessarily illegal manners under the letter of the law, seems increasingly counterproductive. Shouldn't the focus instead be on the relation between those actors and the cumulative effects such relations give rise to?

As aforementioned, relational human rights responsibility seen through this lens bears resemblance to and takes as a starting point, shared responsibility as developed in the Guiding Principles on Shared Responsibility in International law.[1217] Under the shared responsibility framework, contributing actors may very well incur responsibility for their share in unlawful outcomes on the basis of the previously discussed forms of aid and assistance, direction and control and so forth. I can imagine a critical reader thinking, 'ok, but this already exists – where is the novelty?'. But based on the foregoing analysis, shared responsibility would have to be further developed to meet the objective of relational responsibility: attribution – currently ambiguously treated under the existing soft law rules on shared responsibility – would have to feature and be disentangled from independent and shared responsibility, and 'contributory human rights obligations' would have to be articulated in a prescriptive manner through legislative developments. This call for relational human rights responsibility is not all that radical, as hints of it have already emerged in the business and human rights field, and just recently the CJEU has recognized that establishing attribution is problematised in composite conduct (albeit pertaining to data protection specifically).[1218]

Within the realm of business and human rights on an international and a European plane, obligations of private companies are inextricably connected to the human rights obligations of states. This is evidenced for example in Article 2 of the latest draft of the proposed treaty on Business and Human Rights currently under negotiation, where it is held that the purpose of the treaty is to '*clarify and facilitate effective implementation of the obligation of States to respect, protect, fulfil and promote human rights in the context of business activities*' as well as to '*To clarify and ensure respect and fulfilment of the human rights responsibilities of business enterprises*'.[1219] While with the latter provision it is clear that there is continued focus on the individualistic obligations of enterprises, the former provision underscores the relational nature of the anticipated obligations of states in governing their relations with (transnational) enterprises and other private actors. Similarly, the EU's trade toolbox as well as EU legislative measures such as the EU Regulation on Conflict Minerals and the recent Corporate Sustainability Due Diligence Directive

[1217] Nollkaemper, d'Aspremont, Ahlborn, Boutin, Nedeski and Plakokefalos n 26.

[1218] CJEU (Grand Chamber) Judgment of 5 March 2024, *Marián Kočner v Europol*, C-755/21 P, ECLI:EU:C:2024:202.

[1219] Office of the High Commissioner for Human Rights, 'Legally Binding Instrument to Regulate, in International Human Rights Law, the Activities of Transnational Corporations and Other Business Enterprises (9th updated draft) '(OHCHR, 2023) https://www.ohchr.org/sites/default/files/documents/hrbodies/hrcouncil/igwg-transcorp/session9/igwg-9th-updated-draft-lbi-clean.pdf.

specifically, impose binding human rights obligations on private corporations.[1220] This same trend of concretising human rights *obligations* for non-state actors is also slowly emerging for EU entities. For example, first steps have been taken in this direction in Article 46 EBCG Regulation whereby the Executive Director of Frontex is under an obligation to act in case of credible threats to human rights throughout a Frontex mandated operation. Beyond the IBM domain this trend is evinced by the 'joint and several liability' mechanism in the Europol Regulation. In the *Kočner* judgment concerning cooperation between Europol – an EU agency – and EU Member States, the CJEU held that, where it is difficult to attribute unlawful data processing to one or the other, a system of joint and several liability applies.[1221] This signals that the EU legislator and the CJEU appear to have recognised the complex relational nature of such cooperation, which complicates or even undermines access to an effective remedy for individual applicants.

Threading these final observations into the two overarching, systemic issues that were identified throughout this work – that of the convoluted dynamic between attribution and causation and the transposition of human rights commitments to human rights obligations – four observations emerge which inform a rudimentary sketch of what relational human rights responsibility could look like.

Firstly, in situations of hybrid governance, involving different iterations of public and private cooperation which give rise to indissociable contributions to a single outcome, it may be preferable to move towards a system of joint and several liability. This would place individuals in a situation in which they no longer have to attribute specific unlawful conduct to each of the complicit actors, before different courts and according to different rules. This would also eliminate the mis-alignment issues stemming from exculpatory attribution rules for independent conduct of IOs and potential forms of shared responsibility concerning the same fact pattern. It relieves the burden on the individual to strategically decide on the more appropriate venue to lodge a claim. Moreover, in cases involving EU entities, this would entail that the duration of proceedings become less lengthy as the CJEU will no longer be inclined to await the outcome of the domestic procedure before adjudicating on EU responsibility for the same fact pattern, if the preceding domestic procedure is not successful. However, joint and several liability does bring about a number of risks and questions. Should it be the EU legislator that sets the parameters of joint and several liability for human rights harms in specific domains of EU law, and how does this impact the manner in which the conditions of independent responsibility have been established by the CJEU in *Bergaderm*? What implications does a joint and several liability regime have for the determinations of reparations? If for example, a damages claim is lodged before the CJEU against an EU entity, does this impact the scope of reparations compared to claims against a Member State before a domestic court in light of

[1220] Regulation (EU) 2017/821 of the European Parliament and of the Council of 17 May 2017 laying down supply chain due diligence obligations for Union importers of tin, tantalum and tungsten, their ores, and gold originating from conflict-affected and high-risk areas) (Conflict Minerals Regulation); Proposal for a Directive of the European Parliament and of the Council on Corporate Sustainability Due Diligence and amending Directive (EU) 2019/1937 (CSDDD).

[1221] CJEU (Grand Chamber) Judgment of 5 March 2024, *Marián Kočner v Europol*, C-755/21 P, ECLI:EU:C:2024:202.

the fact that the two actors are different in nature? Finally, joint and several liability mechanisms as a way to solve attribution questions do not necessarily result in joint – or shared – responsibility. Attribution is only one of the cumulative conditions to establish responsibility. Solving the question of attribution does not solve how obligations of EU entities are articulated and defined.

This last point prompts the second observation: there is a need to reconceptualise how human rights obligations are understood as they apply to the EU and IOs generally. In designing relational human rights responsibility, it appears crucial to reconsider human rights violations as solely occurring when a *primary* norm has been violated. Currently, when ascertaining whether human rights violations have occurred, the focus is overwhelmingly, if not exclusively, on whether a state has violated its primary norm obligations. Mindful of modes of hybrid governance, it is necessary to further refine how and when contributory conduct – in addition to primary norm obligations and meaning to also consider obligations such as to refrain from aiding and assisting wrongful conduct – may give rise to a human rights violation. And on that note, current developments are missing some specificity. The business and human rights approach is more developed than its counterpart for IOs and envisages concrete obligations such as due diligence, certification, impact assessments and review mechanisms both independently and in relation to States. Conversely, the provisions in the EU's CFR are almost entirely copy-pasted from state-centric human rights instruments, with only limited consideration of the functional difference that distinguishes the EU from its Members States. Concretely, what are the implications of the EU being bound by the right to asylum in Article 18 CFR? What are the positive and negative duties that the EU has in meeting this commitment?

An EU relational human rights regime would complement the negative and positive obligations that have been developed for states with 'common but differentiated' obligations for the EU. The recurring objection here is of course that it is inconceivable to identify and enumerate all negative and positive human rights obligations *ex ante*, particularly in light of the dynamic nature of competence division and powers between the various actors engaged in transnational cooperative governance. A caveat is necessary in response to this objection. Spelling out human rights obligations to ensure that the abstract commitment to human rights protection of all parties is respected, does not mean that all concretised human rights obligations need be defined in a static and overly detailed manner. In fact, doing this would surely entail that public actors construct new ways of bypassing such ossified and entrenched obligations. Instead, this relational approach proposes to work with (closed-finite) procedural obligations, and (open) standard-setting substantive human rights obligations.

Threaded into EU legislation, this could entail an explicitly defined negative substantive obligation (means-based) of the EU not to aid and assist human rights violations of any kind through its border management measures abroad. Aid and assistance could then be pre-emptively defined as including (but not limited to) the provision of financial assistance without verification of a human rights compliant manner of using the funds, the absence of due diligence, and the absence of annual human rights impact assessments to monitor the legitimacy of the funding. The concomitant positive procedural obligation (result-based) could be to impose an internal complaint mechanism, which would require halting funding and/or aborting missions that violate human rights. This is reminiscent of the Frontex internal complaint mechanism and the duty on behalf of the Frontex Executive Director to abort Frontex missions on those grounds.[1222] However, this approach is not yet streamlined into the EU's human rights regime more generally and has only developed in such detail *vis-à-vis* Frontex. Without institutional connections between the EU's judiciary and such internal mechanisms however, internal procedures can continue to be conducted in a manner that ultimately obstructs access to an effective remedy rather than facilitating it.

Such obligations for the EU would differ from the highly concretised human rights obligations of states, but they would nevertheless contribute to ensuring the observance of human rights commitments through explicit legislative human rights responsibility – much like different organs contribute differentially to the overall health of the body. Modulating human rights obligations in this manner may also solve many questions regarding (exculpatory) attribution, as acknowledging the common but differentiated human rights obligations of different actors means no longer trying to attribute the so-called *primary norm violation* to one or the other entity. Instead, different types of obligations would be attributed to different actors. In turn, it is far more likely that individual victims will have effective access to an effective remedy *vis-à-vis* all EU Member States and EU entities, for different contributions to a single human rights harm.

With these observations in mind, a third observation emerges, one which is less directly related to relational human rights responsibility as such. As we have seen with the liability mechanisms for IOs generally and for the EU specifically, the effectiveness of these mechanisms is intimately tied to clearly articulated rules on causation and on the burden, standard and method of proof. The absence of clear standards on both counts is inimical to procedural fairness in establishing responsibility for cooperative conduct where acts and omissions are diffused across different public and private actors.

Finally, in light of the envisaged accession of the EU to the ECHR, relational human rights responsibility would entail taking an effects-based approach to ascertaining which actors (Member States, EU entities or both) bear responsibility for human rights harms. Where clear human rights harms have arisen, accession would ideally ensure a remedy, particularly in situations where convoluted conduct between multiple actors forms the basis for such harms and complicates attribution to one or the other. Without an effects-based approach in mind throughout the negotiations and in a new accession agreement, there is a risk that the question of responsibility will continue to be determined by different courts, across different legal regimes and according to different rules, notwithstanding the envisaged institutional connection. And it is precisely this issue – different courts, ruling on the conditions of responsibility across different regimes and according to different rules for single human right harms that arise out of convoluted, cooperative conduct – that risks creating and exacerbating the EU's human rights responsibility gap.

[1222] Article 46 EBCG Regulation.

Index

www.ingramcontent.com/pod-product-compliance
Ingram Content Group UK Ltd.
Pitfield, Milton Keynes, MK11 3LW, UK
UKHW020844290926
15470UKWH00004B/1551

9 781509 977352